Australasian Language Technology Association Workshop (ALTA 2016)

Caulfield, Australia
5 – 7 December 2016

Editor:

Trevor Cohn

ISBN: 978-1-5108-3316-6

Australasian Language Technology Association Workshop 2016

Proceedings of the Workshop

Editor:

Trevor Cohn

5–7 December 2016
Monash University
Caulfield, Australia

Australasian Language Technology Association Workshop 2016

(ALTA 2016)

http://alta2016.alta.asn.au

Online Proceedings:

http://alta2016.alta.asn.au/proceedings

Gold Sponsor:

Silver Sponsors:

Bronze Sponsors:

Volume 14, 2016

ISSN: 1834-7037

ALTA 2016 Workshop Committees

Workshop Co-Chairs

- Gholamreza Haffari (Monash University)
- Andrew Mackinlay (IBM Research)

Workshop Programme Chair

- Trevor Cohn (University of Melbourne)

Programme Committee

- Oliver Adams, University of Melbourne
- Timothy Baldwin, University of Melbourne
- Julian Brooke, University of Melbourne
- Alicia Burga, Universitat Pompeu Fabra - UPF
- Mark Dras, Macquarie University
- Long Duong, University of Melbourne
- Dominique Estival, Western Sydney University
- Ben Hachey, University of Sydney / Hugo.ai
- Graeme Hirst, University of Toronto
- Vu Hoang, University of Melbourne
- Nitin Indurkhya, University of New South Wales
- Sarvnaz Karimi, CSIRO
- Alistair Knott, University of Otago
- François Lareau, Université de Montréal
- Shervin Malmasi, Macquarie University
- Nitika Mathur, University of Melbourne
- Meladel Mistica, Intel
- Diego Mollá, Macquarie University
- Anthony Nguyen, CSIRO
- Joel Nothman, University of Sydney
- Scott Nowson, Accenture
- Bahadorreza Ofoghi, University of Melbourne
- Nagesh Panyam-Chandrasekarasastry, University of Melbourne
- Cécile Paris, CSIRO
- Lizhen Qu, Data61
- Will Radford, Hugo.ai
- Andrea Schalley, Griffith University
- Rolf Schwitter, Macquarie University
- Ehsan Shareghi, Monash University
- Hanna Suominen, Australian National University
- Karin Verspoor, University of Melbourne
- Ming Zhou, Microsoft Research Asia
- Ingrid Zukerman, Monash University

Preface

This volume contains the papers accepted for presentation at the Australasian Language Technology Association Workshop (ALTA) 2016, held at Monash University in Caulfield, Australia on 5–6 December 2016.

The goals of the workshop are to:
- bring together the Language Technology (LT) community in the Australasian region and encourage interactions and collaboration;
- foster interaction between academic and industrial researchers, to encourage dissemination of research results;
- provide a forum for students and young researchers to present their research;
- facilitate the discussion of new and ongoing research and projects;
- increase visibility of LT research in Australasia and overseas and encourage interactions with the wider international LT community.

This year's ALTA Workshop presents 20 peer-reviewed papers, including 13 long papers and 7 short papers. We received a total of 28 submissions for long and short papers. Each paper was reviewed by three members of the program committee, using a double-blind protocol. Great care was taken to avoid all conflicts of interest.

ALTA 2016 includes a presentations track, following on from 2015 when it was first introduced. This aims to encourage broader participation and facilitate local socialisation of international results, including work in progress and work submitted or published elsewhere. Presentations were lightly reviewed by the ALTA chairs to gauge overall quality of work and whether it would be of interest to the ALTA community. In total 11 of 12 submissions where selected for presentation. Offering both archival and presentation tracks allows us to grow the standard of work at ALTA, to better showcase the excellent research being done locally.

ALTA 2016 continues the tradition of including a shared task, this year addressing cross-KB coreference. Participation is summarised in an overview paper by organisers Andrew Chisholm, Ben Hachey, and Diego Mollá. Participants were invited to submit a system description paper, which are included in this volume without review.

We would like to thank, in no particular order: all of the authors who submitted papers; the programme committee for the time and effort the put into maintaining the high standards of our reviewing process; the chairs Gholamreza Haffari and Andrew Mackinlay for coordinating all the logistics that go into running the workshop, from arranging the space, catering, budgets, sponsorship and more; the shared task organisers Andrew Chisholm, Ben Hachey, and Diego Mollá; our keynote speakers Mark Steedman, Hercules Dalianis and Steven Bird for agreeing to share their perspectives on the state of the field; and the tutorial presenters Wray Buntine, Simon Gog and Matthias Petri for their efforts towards the two tutorial sessions. We would like to acknowledge the constant support and advice of the ALTA Executive Committee.

Finally, we gratefully recognise our sponsors: Capital Markets CRC, Google, CSIRO/Data61, Voicebox and Monash University. Importantly, their generous support enabled us to offer travel subsidies to all students presenting at ALTA, and helped to subsidise conference catering costs and student paper awards.

Trevor Cohn
ALTA Programme Chair

ALTA 2016 Programme

* Denotes shared session with ADCS.

Monday, 5 December 2016

*Tutorial Session 1 (Monash Caulfield, B214)	
09:00–10:15	Tutorial 1: Wray Buntine *Simpler Non-parametric Bayesian Models*
10:15–10:45	Morning tea
10:45–12:15	Tutorial 1 (continued)
12:15–13:30	Lunch
*Tutorial Session 2 (Monash Caulfield, B214)	
13:30–15:15	Tutorial 2: Simon Gog and Matthias Petri *Succinct Data Structures for Text and Information Retrieval*
15:15–15:45	Afternoon tea
15:45–16:45	Tutorial 2 (continued)

Tuesday, 6 December 2016

Session 1: Opening & Invited talk (Monash Caulfield Campus, B214)

9:00–9:15	Opening
9:15–10:15	Invited talk: Mark Steedman *On Distributional Semantics*

10:15–10:45	Morning tea

Session 2: Translation (Monash Caulfield Campus, B214)

10:45–11:10	Presentation: Kyo Kageura, Martin Thomas, Anthony Hartley, Masao Utiyama, Atsushi Fujita, Kikuko Tanabe and Chiho Toyoshima *Supporting Collaborative Translator Training: Online Platform, Scaffolding and NLP*
11:10–11:25	Presentation: Nitika Mathur, Trevor Cohn and Timothy Baldwin *Improving Human Evaluation of Machine Translation*
11:25–11:40	Paper: Cong Duy Vu Hoang, Reza Haffari and Trevor Cohn *Improving Neural Translation Models with Linguistic Factors*
11:40–11:55	Presentation: Daniel Beck, Lucia Specia and Trevor Cohn *Exploring Prediction Uncertainty in Machine Translation Quality Estimation*
11:55–12:00	CLEF eHealth 2017 Shared tasks

12:00–13:15	Lunch

Session 3a: Invited talk (Monash Caulfield Campus, B214)

13:15–13:55	*Invited talk: Hercules Dalianis
13:55–14:00	Break

Session 3b: Health (Monash Caulfield Campus, B214)

14:00–14:15	Presentation: Raghavendra Chalapathy, Ehsan Zare Borzeshi and Massimo Piccardi *An Investigation of Recurrent Neural Architectures for Drug Name Recognition*
14:15–14:30	Paper: Hamed Hassanzadeh, Anthony Nguyen and Bevan Koopman *Evaluation of Medical Concept Annotation Systems on Clinical Records*
14:30–14:45	Paper: Mahnoosh Kholghi, Lance De Vine, Laurianne Sitbon, Guido Zuccon and Anthony Nguyen *The Benefits of Word Embeddings Features for Active Learning in Clinical Information Extraction*
14:45–15:00	Presentation: Rebecka Weegar and Hercules Dalianis *Mining Norwegian pathology reports: A research proposal*
15:00–15:15	Paper: Pin Huang, Andrew MacKinlay and Antonio Jimeno *Syndromic Surveillance using Generic Medical Entities on Twitter*
15:15–15:30	Paper: Yufei Wang, Stephen Wan and Cecile Paris *The Role of Features and Context on Suicide Ideation Detection*

15:30–16:00	Afternoon tea

Session 4: Relation & Information extraction (Monash Caulfield Campus, B214)

16:00–16:15	Presentation: Dat Quoc Nguyen and Mark Johnson *Modeling topics and knowledge bases with embeddings*
16:15–16:30	Paper: Zhuang Li, Lizhen Qu, Qiongkai Xu and Mark Johnson *Unsupervised Pre-training With Seq2Seq Reconstruction Loss for Deep Relation Extraction Models*
16:30–16:45	Presentation: Hanieh Poostchi, Ehsan Zare Borzeshi and Massimo Piccardi *PersoNER: Persian Named-Entity Recognition*
16:45–17:00	Paper: Nagesh C. Panyam, Karin Verspoor, Trevor Cohn and Rao Kotagiri *ASM Kernel: Graph Kernel using Approximate Subgraph Matching for Relation Extraction*
17:00–17:15	Paper: Gitansh Khirbat, Jianzhong Qi and Rui Zhang *N-ary Biographical Relation Extraction using Shortest Path Dependencies*

Wednesday, 7 December 2016

Session 5: Invited talk & Shared task (Monash Caulfield Campus, B214)

9:00–9:45	Invited talk: Steven Bird *Getting started with an Australian language*
9:45–10:15	Shared Task

10:15–10:45	Morning tea

Session 6: Short-papers & posters (Monash Caulfield Campus, B214)

10:45–11:10	Short-paper lightning talks

Aditya Joshi, Vaibhav Tripathi, Pushpak Bhattacharyya, Mark Carman, Meghna Singh, Jaya Saraswati and Rajita Shukla
How Challenging is Sarcasm versus Irony Classification?: A Study With a Dataset from English Literature
Ming Liu, Gholamreza Haffari and Wray Buntine
Learning cascaded latent variable models for biomedical text classification
Bo Han, Antonio Jimeno Yepes, Andrew MacKinlay and Lianhua Chi
Temporal Modelling of Geospatial Words in Twitter
Antonio Jimeno Yepes and Andrew MacKinlay
NER for Medical Entities in Twitter using Sequence to Sequence Neural Networks
Dat Quoc Nguyen, Mark Dras and Mark Johnson
An empirical study for Vietnamese dependency parsing
Will Radford, Ben Hachey, Bo Han and Andy Chisholm
:telephone::person::sailboat::whale::okhand: ; or âĂIJCall me IshmaelâĂİ âĂŞ How do you translate emoji?
Xavier Holt, Will Radford and Ben Hachey
Presenting a New Dataset for the Timeline Generation Problem

11:10–12:00	Poster Session

12:00–13:15	Lunch
13:15–13:35	Business Meeting

Session 7: Applications (Monash Caulfield Campus, B214)

13:35–13:50	Paper: Hafsah Aamer, Bahadorreza Ofoghi and Karin Verspoor *Syndromic Surveillance through Measuring Lexical Shift in Emergency Department Chief Complaint Texts*
13:50–14:05	Paper: Rui Wang, Wei Liu and Chris McDonald *Featureless Domain-Specific Term Extraction with Minimal Labelled Data*
14:05–14:30	Presentation: Ehsan Shareghi *Unbounded and Scalable Smoothing for Language Modeling*
14:30–14:45	Paper: Shunichi Ishihara *An Effect of Background Population Sample Size on the Performance of a Likelihood Ratio-based Forensic Text Comparison System: A Monte Carlo Simulation with Gaussian Mixture Model*
14:45–15:00	Presentation: Oliver Adams, Shourya Roy and Raghu Krishnapuram *Distributed Vector Representations for Unsupervised Automatic Short Answer Grading*
15:00–15:15	Paper: Andrei Shcherbakov, Ekaterina Vylomova and Nick Thieberger *Phonotactic Modeling of Extremely Low Resource Languages*
15:15–15:30	Presentation: Oliver Adams, Adam Makarucha, Graham Neubig, Steven Bird and Trevor Cohn *Cross-Lingual Word Embeddings for Low-Resource Language Modeling*

15:30–16:20	Afternoon tea

Session 8: Closing (Monash Caulfield Campus, B214)

16:20–16:30	Awards for best paper and best presentation
16:30–16:45	ALTA Closing

Contents

Invited talks   1

Tutorials   4

Long papers   6

Improving Neural Translation Models with Linguistic Factors
   Cong Duy Vu Hoang, Reza Haffari and Trevor Cohn   7

Evaluation of Medical Concept Annotation Systems on Clinical Records
   Hamed Hassanzadeh, Anthony Nguyen and Bevan Koopman   15

The Benefits of Word Embeddings Features for Active Learning in Clinical Information Extraction
   Mahnoosh Kholghi, Lance De Vine, Laurianne Sitbon, Guido Zuccon and Anthony Nguyen
                                                                                                 25

Syndromic Surveillance using Generic Medical Entities on Twitter
   Pin Huang, Andrew MacKinlay and Antonio Jimeno Yepes   35

*Syndromic Surveillance through Measuring Lexical Shift in Emergency Department Chief Complaint
   Texts*
   Hafsah Aamer, Bahadorreza Ofoghi and Karin Verspoor   45

Unsupervised Pre-training With Seq2Seq Reconstruction Loss for Deep Relation Extraction Models
   Zhuang Li, Lizhen Qu, Qiongkai Xu and Mark Johnson   54

ASM Kernel: Graph Kernel using Approximate Subgraph Matching for Relation Extraction
   Nagesh C Panyam, Karin Verspoor, Trevor Cohn and Rao Kotagiri   65

N-ary Biographical Relation Extraction using Shortest Path Dependencies
   Gitansh Khirbat, Jianzhong Qi and Rui Zhang   74

Phonotactic Modeling of Extremely Low Resource Languages
   Andrei Shcherbakov, Ekaterina Vylomova and Nick Thieberger   84

The Role of Features and Context on Suicide Ideation Detection
   Yufei Wang, Stephen Wan and Cecile Paris   94

Featureless Domain-Specific Term Extraction with Minimal Labelled Data
   Rui Wang, Wei Liu and Chris McDonald   103

*An Effect of Background Population Sample Size on the Performance of a Likelihood Ratio-based
   Forensic Text Comparison System: A Monte Carlo Simulation with Gaussian Mixture Model*

Shunichi Ishihara   113

Short papers   122

How Challenging is Sarcasm versus Irony Classification?: A Study With a Dataset from English Literature
Aditya Joshi, Vaibhav Tripathi, Pushpak Bhattacharyya, Mark Carman, Meghna Singh, Jaya Saraswati and Rajita Shukla   123

Learning cascaded latent variable models for biomedical text classification
Ming Liu, Gholamreza Haffari and Wray Buntine   128

Temporal Modelling of Geospatial Words in Twitter
Bo Han, Antonio Jimeno Yepes, Andrew MacKinlay and Lianhua Chi   133

NER for Medical Entities in Twitter using Sequence to Sequence Neural Networks
Antonio Jimeno Yepes and Andrew MacKinlay   138

An empirical study for Vietnamese dependency parsing
Dat Quoc Nguyen, Mark Dras and Mark Johnson   143

:telephone::person::sailboat::whale::okhand: ; or âĂIJCall me IshmaelâĂİ âĂŞ How do you translate emoji?
Will Radford, Ben Hachey, Bo Han and Andy Chisholm   150

Presenting a New Dataset for the Timeline Generation Problem
Xavier Holt, Will Radford and Ben Hachey   155

ALTA Shared Task papers   160

Overview of the 2016 ALTA Shared Task: Cross-KB Coreference
Andrew Chisholm, Ben Hachey and Diego Mollá   161

Disambiguating Entities Referred by Web Endpoints using Tree Ensembles
Gitansh Khirbat, Jianzhong Qi and Rui Zhang   165

Filter and Match Approach to Pair-wise Web URI Linking
S. Shivashankar, Yitong Li and Afshin Rahimi   170

Pairwise FastText Classifier for Entity Disambiguation
Cheng Yu, Bing Chu, Rohit Ram, James Aichinger, Lizhen Qu and Hanna Suominen   175

Invited talks

Mark Steedman (University of Edinburgh)

On Distributional Semantics

The central problem in open domain-question answering from text is the problem of entailment. Given enough text, the answer is almost certain to be there, but is likely to be expressed in a different form from the one the question suggest—either in a paraphrase, or in a sentence that entails or implies the answer.

We cannot afford to bridge this gap by open-ended theorem-proving search. Instead we need a semantics for natural language that directly supports common-sense inference, such as that *arriving somewhere* implies subsequently *being there*, and *invading* a country implies *attacking* it. We would like this semantics to be compatible with traditional logical operator semantics including quantification, negation and tense, so that *not being there* implies *not having arrived*, and *not attacking* implies *not invading*.

There have been many attempts to build such a semantics of content words by hand, from the generative semantics of the '60s to WordNet and other resources of the present. The '60s saw attempts based on generative semantics, while more recently, they have engendered WordNet and other computational resources. However, such systems have remained incomplete and language-specific in comparison to the vastness of human common-sense reasoning. One consequence has been renewed interest in the idea of treating the semantics as "hidden", to be discovered through machine learning, an idea that has its origins in the "semantic differential" of Osgood, Suci, and Tannenbaum in the '50s.

There are two distinct modern approaches to the problem of data-driven or "distributional" semantics. The first, which I will call "collocational", is the direct descendant of the semantic differential. In its most basic form, the meaning of a word is taken to be a vector in a space whose dimensions are defined by the lexicon of the language, and whose magnitude is defined by counts of those lexical items within a fixed window over the string (although in practice the dimensionality is reduced and the relation to frequency less direct). Crucially, semantic composition is defined in terms of linear algebraic operations, notably vector addition.

A second "denotational" approach defines the meaning of a word in terms of the entities that it is predicated over and the ensembles of predications over entities of the same types, obtained by machine-reading with wide coverage parsers. (Names or designators in text are generally used as a proxy for the entities themselves.) Semantic composition can then be defined as an applicative system using logical opertors such as quantifiers and negation, as in traditional formal semantics.

The talk reviews recent work in both collocation- and denotation- based distributional semantics, and asks for each what dimensions of meaning are actually being represented. It argues that the two approaches are largely orthogonal on these dimensions. Collocational representations are good for representing ambiguity, with linear algebraic composition most effective at disambiguation and representing distributional similarity. Denotational representations represent something more like a traditional compositional semantics, but one in which the primitive relations correspond to those of a hidden language of logical form representing paraphrase and common-sense entailment directly.

To make this point, the talk discusses recent work in which collocational distributional representations such as embeddings have been used as proxies for semantic features in models such as LSTM, to guide disambiguation during parsing, while a lexicalized denotation-based distributional semantics is used to support inference of entailment. I will show that this hybrid approach can be applied with a number of parsing models, including transition-based and supertagging, to support entailment-based QA with denotation-based distributional representations. I will discuss work at Edinburgh and elsewhere in which the semantics of paraphrases is represented by a single cluster identifier, and where common-sense inference (derived from a learned entailment graph) is built into the lexicon and projected by syntactic derivation, rather than delegated to a later stage of inference. The method can be applied cross-linguistically, in support of machine translation. Ongoing work extends the method to extract multi-word items, light-verb constructions, and an aspect-based semantics for temporal/causal entailment, and to the creation and interrogation of Knowledge Graphs and Semantic Nets via natural language.

Hercules Dalianis (Stockholm University)

HEALTH BANK — A Workbench for Data Science Applications in Healthcare

Healthcare has many challenges in form of monitoring and predicting adverse events as healthcare associated infections or adverse drug events. All this can happen while treating a patient at the hospital for her disease. The research question is: When and how many adverse events have occurred, how can one predict them? Nowadays all information is contained in the electronic patient records and are written both in structured form and in unstructured free text. This talk will describe the data used for our research in HEALTH BANK - Swedish Health Record Research Bank containing over 2 million patient records from 2007-2014. Topics are detection of symptoms, diseases, body parts and drugs from Swedish electronic patient record text, including deciding on the certainty of a symptom or disease and detecting adverse (drug) events. Future research are detecting early symptoms of cancer and de-identification of electronic patient records for secondary use.

Steven Bird (University of Melbourne, University of California Berkeley)

Getting started with an Australian language

At least a dozen Australian indigenous languages are still being learnt by children as their first language. These children have limited access to western-style education and often gain only limited proficiency in English. The languages are effectively unwritten, as there are no naturally occurring contexts where people would need to write the language. The same situation is repeated around the world, where remote communities do not write their language and do not acquire the national language, and government and NGO employees who work with these communities must learn to speak an unwritten language without the help of written resources. In this presentation I will report on early experiences working with Kunwinjku, a polysynthetic language spoken by 1,200 people in western Arnhem Land, leading to several open research questions in the area of tools for adult learners of unwritten languages.

Tutorials

Simpler Non-parametric Bayesian Models

Wray Buntine (Monash University)

Many interesting non-parametric models are now used for modelling discrete, structured data as we find in language, document and graph analysis. These non-parametric Bayesian models are often based on a variety of different process models such as the Gamma process, the Beta process, the Pitman-Yor process, etc. This tutorial will give an introduction to these models and connect to modern Bayesian non-parametric theory, though doing so in a less former manner.

The basic process models can all be understood in terms of Poisson point processes (PPs) which can be viewed as an extension of standard prior distributions. When using PPs, one can easily model infinite lists, where new entries are unfurled and put to use only as data requires it. The Beta process in this interpretation is just an extension of the Beta prior for Bernoulli models that allows an infinite list of such Bernoullis. Modern Bayesian non-parametric theory provides general solutions for reasoning with these kinds of models, including the hierarchical case, though the results are not well known in the machine learning community. For instance, a hierarchical Pitman-Yor process is acting like an analogue to the Dirichlet distribution where instead of normalising gamma variables we normalise positive alpha-stable variables.

With the basic process models introduced, we will then look at some of the standard variants and Bayesian reasoning with them: hierarchical probability models for trees and n-gram language models, infinite feature vector models such as the Indian buffet process, infinite stochastic block models and various models for matrix and tensor factorisation. Some of these results are unpublished or not readily accessible to neophytes.

Succinct Data Structures for Text and Information Retrieval

Simon Gog (Karslruhe Institute of Technology) and Matthias Petri (University of Melbourne)

The current growth and availability of massive amounts of data gathered and processed by applications such as Web search engines or translation services has had a profound impact on the algorithmic requirements of many fundamental data processing tools. At the same time, this has provided ample motivation for a great deal of new theoretical and practical research on resource efficient algorithms and data structures.

Over the last decades the research field of the so-called succinct and compressed data structures has emerged to tackle these challenges. These new kind of data structures provide the same operations as their classical counterparts within a comparable time complexity but requiring substantially less space. These solutions usually resort to a careful combination of ideas from data compression and data structures.

The tutorial will introduce this field of research by presenting the most important succinct data structures to represent set of integers, set of points, trees, graphs and strings together with applications to Information Retrieval and Natural Language Processing problems. The introduction of the succinct data structures will be sustained with a practical session with programming handouts to solve. This will allow the attendees to directly experiment with implementations of these solutions on real datasets and understand the potential benefits to their own projects.

Long papers

Improving Neural Translation Models with Linguistic Factors

Cong Duy Vu Hoang
University of Melbourne
Melbourne, VIC, Australia
vhoang2@student.unimelb.edu.au

Gholamreza Haffari
Monash University
Clayton, VIC, Australia
gholamreza.haffari@monash.edu

Trevor Cohn
University of Melbourne
Melbourne, VIC, Australia
t.cohn@unimelb.edu.au

Abstract

This paper presents an extension of neural machine translation (NMT) model to incorporate additional word-level linguistic factors. Adding such linguistic factors may be of great benefits to learning of NMT models, potentially reducing language ambiguity or alleviating data sparseness problem (Koehn and Hoang, 2007). We explore different linguistic annotations at the word level, including: lemmatization, word clusters, Part-of-Speech tags, and labeled dependency relations. We then propose different neural attention architectures to integrate these additional factors into the NMT framework. Evaluating on translating between English and German in two directions with a low resource setting in the domain of TED talks, we obtain promising results in terms of both perplexity reductions and improved BLEU scores over baseline methods.

1 Introduction

Neural Machine Translation (NMT) (Devlin et al., 2014; Bahdanau et al., 2015) is a new paradigm in machine translation (MT) powered by recent advances in sequence to sequence learning frameworks (Graves, 2013; Sutskever et al., 2014). NMT has already made remarkable results and improvements over conventional SMT (Luong et al., 2015).

The core idea of NMT is the encoder-decoder framework where an *encoder* encodes the source sequence into a vector representation, and then a *decoder* generates the target sequence sequentially via a recurrent neural network (RNN). The use of a RNN provides the ability to memorize longer range dependencies that are impossible with standard n-gram modeling - a core component of the traditional Statistical Machine Translation (SMT) framework (Koehn et al., 2003; Lopez, 2008; Koehn, 2010). Unlike the traditional SMT, NMT offers unique mechanisms to learn translation equivalence without extensive feature engineering efforts.

Though promising, NMT still lacks of the ability of modeling deeper semantic and syntactic aspects of the language. Koehn and Hoang (2007) presented a *factored* translation model to address this issue for the traditional SMT framework (Koehn et al., 2007), where the model incorporates various linguistic annotations for the surface level words. Particularly for low-resource conditions, these extra annotations can lead to better translation of OOVs (or low-count words) and resolve ambiguities, hence increase the generalization capabilities of the model.

In machine translation with a low-resource setting, resolving data sparseness and semantic ambiguity problems can help improve its performance. In this paper, we investigate utilizing extra syntactic and semantic linguistic factors in the context of the NMT framework. Linguistic factors can include bundles of features, e.g., stems, roots, lemmas, morphological classes, data-driven clusters, syntactic analyses (part-of-speeches, constituency parsing, dependency parsing). Adding such extra factors may be of great benefits to NMT models, potentially reducing language ambiguity and alleviating data sparseness further. In this paper, we explore four word-level factor annotations, including: lemmatization, word clusters, Part-of-Speech tags, and relation labels in dependency parse trees (see Figure 1 for an example). We then propose different neural attention architec-

Cong Duy Vu Hoang, Reza Haffari and Trevor Cohn. 2016. Improving Neural Translation Models with Linguistic Factors. In *Proceedings of Australasian Language Technology Association Workshop*, pages 7–14.

they	've	expanded	and	enriched	our	lives	.
they	've	expand	and	enrich	our	life	.
011011	0100110	010111110	0111101	010111100	11100	1011	000
PRP	VBP	VBN	CC	VBN	PRP$	NNS	/
nsubj	aux	ROOT	cc	conj	nmod	dobj	none
1	1	0	0	0	1	0	-1

(text — lemma — word cluster — part-of-speech — labelled dependency)

Figure 1: An example of linguistic factor annotations for a source sentence in English.

tures to integrate these additional factors into the NMT framework. Evaluating on translating between English and German in two directions with a low resource setting in the TED talks data, we obtain perplexity reductions and improved BLEU score over the baseline.

2 Incorporating Linguistic Factors

In this work, we investigate the feasibility of factored model idea (Koehn and Hoang, 2007) into attentional neural translation model (Bahdanau et al., 2015). As an initial work, we aim to find how the neural model can benefit from incorporating the additional linguistic factors in source language. Our work is an extension of (Bahdanau et al., 2015) with the integration of additional linguistic factors. A fully factored neural translation model for both source and target sides is considered as our future work. The following section will discuss our extensions of (Bahdanau et al., 2015) in §2.1. Assume that we have L layers of linguistic factor annotations. The training data then consists of N training parallel sentences $\{((\{\boldsymbol{x}^{(n,\ell)}\}_{\ell=0}^{L}, \boldsymbol{y}^{(n)})\}_{n=1}^{N}$ where the word sequence of the nth sentence-pair is denoted in the layer zero $\boldsymbol{x}^{(n,0)}$, its length is denoted by $|\boldsymbol{x}^{(n)}|$, its L layers of annotations are denoted by $\{\boldsymbol{x}^{(n,\ell)}\}_{\ell=1}^{L}$, and the target sentence is denoted by $\boldsymbol{y}^{(n)}$. In what follows, we review and extend the attentional encoder-decoder neural machine translation for this setting, and explore various neural attention mechanisms operating on the multiple layers of linguistic factors over the source sentence.

2.1 Multi-Factor Encoder-Decoder

Encoder. First, to encode the source-side information, we first run each layer of linguistic annotations through bidirectional RNNs (biRNN) for dynamically representing the sequence embeddings, i.e.,

$$h_j^\ell = \text{biRNN}_{enc}^{\ell,\psi}\left(\boldsymbol{x}_j^\ell, \left[\overrightarrow{\boldsymbol{h}}^\ell_{j-1}; \overleftarrow{\boldsymbol{h}}^\ell_{j+1}\right]^T\right); \quad (1)$$

where $\boldsymbol{x}_j^\ell \in \mathbb{R}^{H^\ell}$ is the word embedding at position j in sequence layer ℓ, and $\overrightarrow{\boldsymbol{h}}^\ell_j$ and $\overleftarrow{\boldsymbol{h}}^\ell_j$ are the RNN[1] hidden states. This encoding scheme captures not only the position specific information, but also the information coming from the left and right contexts.

Decoder. Next, a *decoder* operated by another RNN is used to predict the target $\boldsymbol{y}$ sequentially, from left to right:

$$\boldsymbol{g}_i = \text{RNN}_{dec}^\phi\left(\boldsymbol{c}_i, y_{i-1}, \boldsymbol{g}_{i-1}\right)$$
$$y_i \sim \text{softmax}\left(\boldsymbol{W}_o \cdot \text{MLP}\left(\boldsymbol{c}_i, y_{i-1}, \boldsymbol{g}_i\right) + \boldsymbol{b}_o\right);$$

where MLP is a single hidden layer neural network with tanh activation. The model parameters include ϕ the weight matrix $W_o \in \mathbb{R}^{V_y \times H}$ and the bias $\boldsymbol{b}_o \in \mathbb{R}^{V_y}$, with V_y and H denoting the target vocabulary size and hidden dimension size, respectively.

Note that the state of the decoder $\boldsymbol{g}_i$ is conditioned on its previous state $\boldsymbol{g}_{i-1}$, the previously generated target word y_{i-1}, and the source side *context* $\boldsymbol{c}_i$ summarizing the areas of the source sentence needs to be *attended* to. Finally, the model is trained end-to-end by minimizing the cross-entropy loss over the target sequence and stochastic gradient descent (SGD) is used for optimizing the model parameters .

In what follows, we explore various attention mechanisms for our case where the input sentence is annotated with multiple linguistic factors, and show how the source context $\boldsymbol{c}_i$ is constructed.

2.2 Multi-Factor Attention Architectures

In this paper, we explore various attention mechanisms of integrating linguistic factors as briefly summarized in Figure 2, including Global Attention, Local Attention, and hybrid Global-Local Attention.

Global Attention. Our first approach has one shared attention vector for all the annotation layers, forcing each layer to attend to the same positions. This essentially means stacking the representations of all the input embeddings $\boldsymbol{x}^\ell$ into one vector, i.e., $\boldsymbol{x}_j^g = \left[\boldsymbol{x}_j^0, \ldots, \boldsymbol{x}_j^L\right]^T$. This stacked

---

[1] Generally, an RNN can be employed as Long-Short Term Memory (LSTM) (Hochreiter and Schmidhuber, 1997) or Gated Recurrent Unit (GRU) (Cho et al., 2014). Since the RNN recurrent structure is not our focus, we ignored its formulation in this paper.

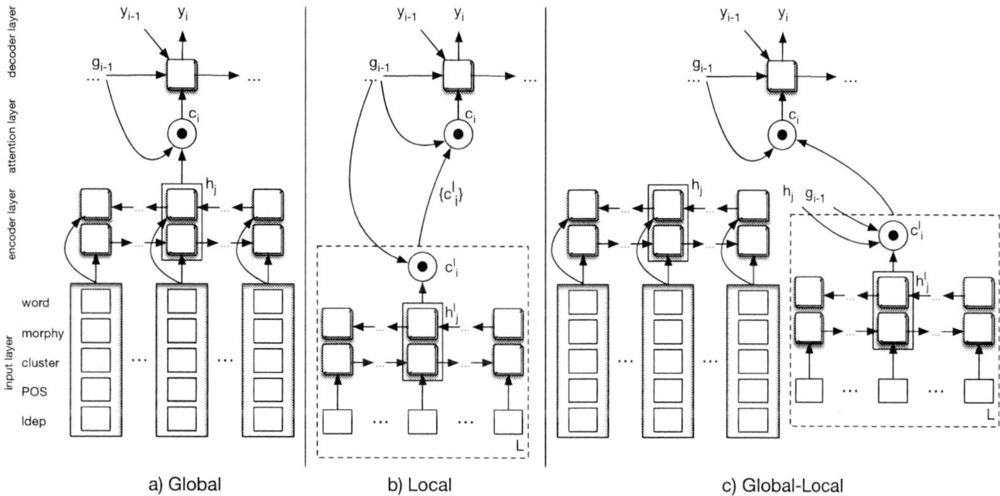

Figure 2: Proposed attention architectures of integrating linguistic factors for the NMT framework.

representation is used in place of only word embedding x_j to encode the input position (eqn 1) to h_j^g. It is then used to construct the source context for the decoder, using $c_i = \sum_{j=1}^{|x|} \alpha_{ij} h_j^g$ with

$$\alpha_i = \text{softmax}(e_i) \quad ; \quad e_{ij} = \text{MLP}\left(g_{i-1}, h_j^g\right)$$

$$h_j^g = \text{biRNN}_{enc}^\theta \left(x_j^g, \left[\overrightarrow{h^g}_{j-1}; \overleftarrow{h^g}_{j+1}\right]^T\right),$$

where scalar e_{ij} denotes the unnormalized alignment probability between the source word annotation j and target word i, which is produced by single hidden layer neural network with $\tanh$ activation.

Local Attention. The model may benefit from different attentions learned for different layers. Thus, the second idea is to have multiple attentions for linguistic layers independently, and compute layer-specific context vectors $\{c_i^\ell\}_{\ell=0}^L$ and stack them up:

$$c_i = \left[c_i^0, \ldots, c_i^L\right]^T \quad ; \quad c_i^\ell = \sum_{j=1}^{T_x} \alpha_{ij}^\ell h_j^\ell$$

$$\alpha_i^\ell = \text{softmax}(e_i^\ell) \quad ; \quad e_{ij}^\ell = \text{MLP}\left(g_{i-1}; h_j^\ell\right)$$

where e_{ij}^ℓ denotes the alignment score between the annotation at layer ℓ and the target word. The MLP for each layer has a different parameterization.

Global-Local Attention. Finally, we consider a hybrid global-local attention mechanism which makes use of the *global* hidden representation h^g across all of the layers in generating the *local* attentions, formulated as:

$$e_{ij}^\ell = \text{MLP}\left(g_{i-1}, h_j^g\right).$$

In contrast to the local attention the attention for layer ℓ depends on the global encoding, h^g, rather than the local encoding for that layer, h^l.

In training, we *encourage* the model to have similar attentions across the layers by adding a penalty term to the cross-entropy training objective,

$$\sum_{n=1}^N \sum_{i=1}^{|y^{(n)}|} \sum_{\ell=0}^L \left\| \bar{\alpha}_i^{(n)} - \alpha_i^{(n),\ell} \right\|_2^2$$

where $\alpha_i^{(n),\ell}$ is the attention to the layer ℓ when generating the target word i, and we define $\bar{\alpha}_i^{(n)} := \frac{1}{L+1} \sum_{\ell=0}^L \alpha_i^{(n),\ell}$ as the average attention across all layers. Essentially, our regularizer penalizes parameters which induce layer-specific attentions deviating from the average attention.

3 Experiments

Data. We conducted our experiments on TED Talks datasets (Cettolo et al., 2012) and translate between English (en) ↔ German (de). For training, we used about 200K parallel sentences, and used tst2010 for tuning model parameters (phrase-based SMT) and early stopping (NMT). We evaluated on the official test sets tst2013 and tst2014,

dataset	# tokens (K)		# types (K)		# sents	# docs
en↔de						
train	4384.68	4161.58	19.42	26.22	198968	1597
tune-tst2010	35.13	33.42	3.29	3.87	1565	16
test1-tst2013	22.86	21.64	2.67	3.08	993	15
test2-tst2014	27.40	26.44	3.21	3.66	1305	16

Table 1: Statistics of the training & evaluation sets from IWSLT'14,15 MT track (including en↔de) showing in each cell the count for the source language (left) and target language (right). "#types" refers to filtered vocabulary with word frequency cut-off 5.

configuration	tst2013	tst2014	#param (M)
en→de			
Vanilla Attentional Model	8.20	10.98	47.80
w/ *glo*+all-factors	**7.84**	**10.35**	50.88
w/ *loc*+all-factors	8.02	10.80	52.06
w/ *glo-loc*+all-factors (w/o regularization penalty)	**7.81**	**10.28**	57.52
w/ *glo-loc*+all-factors (w/ regularization penalty)	**7.48**♠	**10.15**♠	57.52
de→en			
Vanilla Attentional Model	8.76	11.81	44.46
w/ *glo*+all-factors	**8.50**	**11.26**	47.58
w/ *loc*+all-factors	**8.50**	**11.48**	48.76
w/ *glo-loc*+all-factors (w/ regularization penalty)	**8.29**♠	**10.95**♠	54.22

Table 2: Perplexity scores for attentional model variants evaluated on en↔de translations, and "#param" refers to no. of model parameters (in millions). **bold**: "statistically significantly better than vanilla attentional model", ♠: best performance.

following Cettolo et al. (2014). We chose a word frequency cut-off of ≥ 5 for limiting the vocabulary when training neural models, resulting in 19K and 26K word types for English and German, respectively. All details of data statistics can be found in Table 1.

As linguistic factors, we annotated the source sentences with lemmas,[2] word clusters,[3] and POS tags. We also annotated with the labelled dependency, i.e. by taking the dependency label between each word and its head (together with its direction, i.e. left or right)[4] in the dependency parse tree. Also note that the POS tags and dependency parse trees were extracted from parsing results produced by Stanford Parser[5] and ParZu.[6]

Set-up and Baselines. We used the *cnn* library[7] for our implementation. All neural models were configured with 512 input embedding and hidden layer dimensions, and 384 alignment dimension, with 1 and 2 hidden layers in the source and target, respectively. We employed LSTM recurrent structure (Hochreiter and Schmidhuber, 1997) for both source and target RNN sequences. For the phrase-based SMT baseline, we used the Moses toolkit (Koehn et al., 2007) with its standard configuration. To encode the linguistic factors, we used 128, 64, 64, 64 embedding dimensions for each of lemma, word cluster, Part-of-Speech (POS), and labelled dependency sequences, respectively. For training our neural models, the best perplexity scores on tuning sets were used for early stopping of training, which was usually between 5-8 epochs. For decoding, we used a simple greedy algorithm with length normalization. For evaluation of translations, we applied bootstrapping resampling (Koehn, 2004) to measure the statistical significance ($p < 0.05$) of BLEU score differences between translation outputs of proposed models compared to the baselines.

Results and Analysis. We report our experimental results based on standard perplexity and BLEU (Papineni et al., 2002) scores, as shown in Tables 2 and 3, respectively. Table 2 shows that the attentional model with our extensions is noticeably better than the vanilla NMT in terms of perplexity. Among the three attention architectures,

---

[2]NLTK, `http://www.nltk.org/`

[3]Brown clustering, `https://github.com/percyliang/brown-cluster`

[4]The direction is encoded effectively as 3-bit vector.

[5]`http://nlp.stanford.edu/software/lex-parser.shtml` (en)

[6]`https://github.com/rsennrich/ParZu` (de)

[7]`https://github.com/clab/cnn/tree/master/cnn`

configuration	tst2013	tst2014
en→de		
Moses baseline	21.31	19.16
Vanilla Attentional Model	25.03	20.96
w/ *glo*+all-factors	**25.43**	**22.15**♠
w/ *loc*+all-factors	25.04	21.24
w/ *glo-loc*+all-factors (w/o regularization penalty)	25.06	21.29
w/ *glo-loc*+all-factors (w/ regularization penalty)	**25.92**♠	**21.84**
de→en		
Moses baseline	29.96	25.13
Vanilla Attentional Model	29.85	24.84
w/ *glo*+all-factors	29.63	**25.30**♠
w/ *loc*+all-factors	29.32	24.40
w/ *glo-loc*+all-factors (w/ regularization penalty)	**30.45**♠	24.72

Table 3: BLEU scores for attentional model variants evaluated on en↔de translations.

the *glo-loc* attention outperformed others, giving significant improvement compared to the vanilla model. The use of the *loc* attention did not give much improvement. We suspect that the learned model itself has difficulties deciding which factors to attend to. The drawback of the *glo* attention is that it enforces only one attention mechanism for all of the layers. This may cause the loss of individual effects that potentially exist in each of layers. The *glo-loc* attention aims at taking advantage of *glo* attention and solving the limitation of *loc* attention with the penalty term, hence giving better performance.

Table 3 shows the BLEU score results. Compared to Moses baseline, the vanilla attentional model is superior for en→de and comparable for de→en translation tasks. It is noticeable that the attentional model is capable of working remarkably well, despite the relatively small amounts of parallel data. However, table 3 shows the inconsistency, compared to the respective perplexity scores in Table 2. For en→de, both *glo* and *glo-loc* attention architectures worked competitively well, giving significantly better BLEU scores than the vanilla attentional model. Compared to *glo*, the *glo-loc* attention is superior in tst2013, but slightly detrimental in tst2014 although (its respective perplexity scores are better). These results show that reductions in perplexity scores do not guarantee improved BLEU scores, which is particularly true for de→en translation.

For the analysis, we further investigate the improvement of the translation quality versus sentence complexity. This would show the extent to which the extra linguistic layers have been helpful in resolving ambiguities of source sentences in translation. We formalize sentence complexity by taking either its length or the depth of its parse tree into consideration. Figure 3 and 4 plot the BLEU score versus these two measures of complexity in two evaluation sets. As seen, the extra linguistic layers has helped the translation quality of more complex sentences compared to the vanilla attentional model.

4 Related Work

Recent advances in deep learning research facilitate innovative ideas in machine translation. The attentional encoder-decoder framework pioneered by Bahdanau et al. (2015) is the core, opening a new trend in neural machine translation. Luong et al. (2015) followed the work of (Bahdanau et al., 2015) by experimenting various options on the generation of soft alignments with global and local attention mechanisms. Inspired by remarkable characteristics of state-of-the-art SMT models, Cohn et al. (2016) incorporated structural alignment biases inspired from conventional statistical alignment models (e.g. IBM models 1, 2) to encourage more linguistic structures in the alignment process. Similar in spirit to this, Feng et al. (2016) made use of additional RNN structure for the attention mechanism, hence likely capturing long range dependencies between the attention vectors. Tu et al. (2016) further proposed a so-called coverage vector to trace the attention history for flexibly adjusting future attentions.

Though having been developed for almost 2 years, the NMT models are currently competitive with state-of-the-art SMT models. However, NMT models are still lacking of capabilities to modelling shallow language characteristics, e.g. the additional annotation at word level of linguistic factors. Such kinds of factors can provide extra

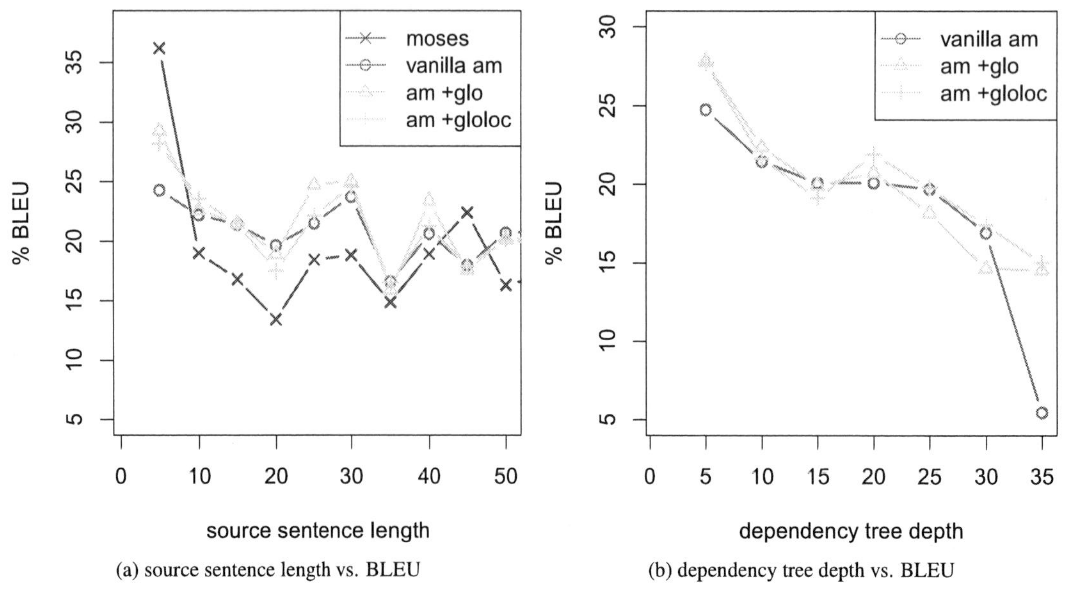

(a) source sentence length vs. BLEU

(b) dependency tree depth vs. BLEU

Figure 3: Analysis based on the evaluation set tst2013 in en→de translation.

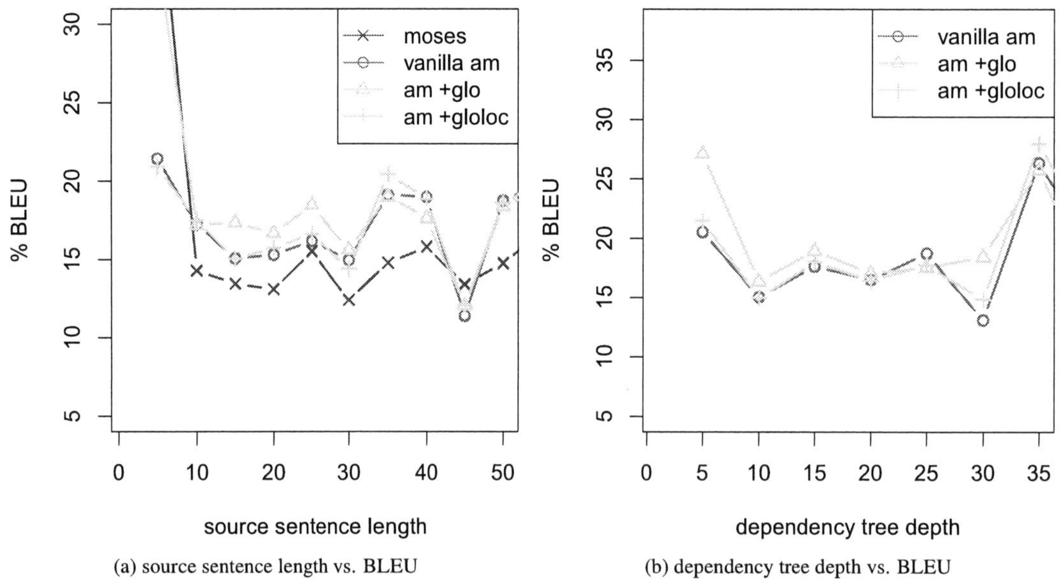

(a) source sentence length vs. BLEU

(b) dependency tree depth vs. BLEU

Figure 4: Analysis based on the evaluation set tst2014 in en→de translation.

dimensions for data sparseness problem as shown in earlier works in SMT models, e.g., (Zhang and Sumita, 2007; Rishøj and Søgaard, 2011; Wuebker et al., 2013). The most closely related work to ours is the factored translation model for SMT framework proposed by Koehn and Hoang (2007). This model evaluated the effects of various linguistic factors (including lemma, POS, morphology) which are annotated for both source and target sides. Our work explored the same manner

in the context of NMT framework though only considering source side. However, we further explored the annotation with labelled dependency which potentially inject syntactic information into neural model. Concurrent to our work, Sennrich and Haddow (2016) proposed similar idea for the NMT framework, however, their work has only explored the so-called global attention whereas we proposed more attention mechanisms with local and hybrid global-local attentions. Also, our experiments were conducted in a low-resourced setting in a different domain with TED talk data.

5 Conclusion & Future Work

In this paper, we have presented a novel attentional encoder-decoder for translation capable of integrating linguistic factors in the source language. Four linguistic factors were evaluated, including lemmatization, word clustering, part-of-speech tagging, and labeled dependencies. We proposed several neural attention mechanisms operating over the factors. Our experimental results on two language pairs show that the neural translation model with integrated linguistic factors can be improved, in terms of both perplexity and BLEU scores.

As our future work, we aim to explore whether the attentional neural translation model can benefit from linguistic factors, operating over the *target* language. This work can be considered as the first work towards fully-factored neural translation model.

References

Dzmitry Bahdanau, Kyunghyun Cho, and Yoshua Bengio. 2015. Neural Machine Translation by Jointly Learning to Align and Translate. In *Proc. of 3rd International Conference on Learning Representations (ICLR2015)*.

Mauro Cettolo, Christian Girardi, and Marcello Federico. 2012. WIT^3: Web Inventory of Transcribed and Translated Talks. In *Proceedings of the 16th Conference of the European Association for Machine Translation (EAMT)*, pages 261–268, Trento, Italy, May.

M. Cettolo, J. Niehues, S. Stuker, L. Bentivogli, and M. Federico. 2014. Report on the 11th IWSLT Evaluation Campaign. In *Proc. of The International Workshop on Spoken Language Translation (IWSLT)*.

Kyunghyun Cho, Bart van Merrienboer, Caglar Gulcehre, Dzmitry Bahdanau, Fethi Bougares, Holger Schwenk, and Yoshua Bengio. 2014. Learning Phrase Representations using RNN Encoder–Decoder for Statistical Machine Translation. In *Proceedings of the 2014 Conference on Empirical Methods in Natural Language Processing (EMNLP)*, pages 1724–1734, Doha, Qatar, October. Association for Computational Linguistics.

T. Cohn, C. D. V. Hoang, E. Vymolova, K. Yao, C. Dyer, and G. Haffari. 2016. Incorporating Structural Alignment Biases into an Attentional Neural Translation Model. In *Proceedings of the 2016 Conference of the North American Chapter of the Association for Computational Linguistics: Human Language Technologies*, San Diego, California, June. Association for Computational Linguistics.

Jacob Devlin, Rabih Zbib, Zhongqiang Huang, Thomas Lamar, Richard Schwartz, and John Makhoul. 2014. Fast and Robust Neural Network Joint Models for Statistical Machine Translation. In *Proceedings of the 52nd Annual Meeting of the Association for Computational Linguistics (Volume 1: Long Papers)*, pages 1370–1380, Baltimore, Maryland, June. Association for Computational Linguistics.

S. Feng, S. Liu, M. Li, and M. Zhou. 2016. Implicit Distortion and Fertility Models for Attention-based Encoder-Decoder NMT Model. *ArXiv e-prints*, January.

A. Graves. 2013. Generating Sequences With Recurrent Neural Networks. *ArXiv e-prints*, August.

Sepp Hochreiter and Jurgen Schmidhuber. 1997. Long Short-Term Memory. *Neural Comput.*, 9(8):1735–1780, November.

Philipp Koehn and Hieu Hoang. 2007. Factored Translation Models. In *Proceedings of the 2007 Joint Conference on Empirical Methods in Natural Language Processing and Computational Natural Language Learning (EMNLP-CoNLL)*, pages 868–876, Prague, Czech Republic, June. Association for Computational Linguistics.

Philipp Koehn, Franz Josef Och, and Daniel Marcu. 2003. Statistical Phrase-based Translation. In *Proceedings of the 2003 Conference of the North American Chapter of the Association for Computational Linguistics on Human Language Technology - Volume 1*, NAACL '03, pages 48–54, Stroudsburg, PA, USA. Association for Computational Linguistics.

Philipp Koehn, Hieu Hoang, Alexandra Birch, Chris Callison-Burch, Marcello Federico, Nicola Bertoldi, Brooke Cowan, Wade Shen, Christine Moran, Richard Zens, Chris Dyer, Ondřej Bojar, Alexandra Constantin, and Evan Herbst. 2007. Moses: Open Source Toolkit for Statistical Machine Translation. In *Proceedings of the 45th Annual Meeting of the ACL on Interactive Poster and Demonstration Sessions*, ACL '07, pages 177–180, Stroudsburg, PA, USA. Association for Computational Linguistics.

Philipp Koehn. 2004. Statistical Significance Tests for Machine Translation Evaluation. In Dekang Lin and Dekai Wu, editors, *Proceedings of Conference on Empirical Methods on Natural Language Processing (EMNLP)*, pages 388–395, Barcelona, Spain, July. Association for Computational Linguistics.

Philipp Koehn. 2010. *Statistical Machine Translation*. Cambridge University Press, New York, NY, USA, 1st edition.

Adam Lopez. 2008. Statistical Machine Translation. *ACM Comput. Surv.*, 40(3):8:1–8:49, August.

Thang Luong, Hieu Pham, and Christopher D. Manning. 2015. Effective Approaches to Attention-based Neural Machine Translation. In *Proceedings of the 2015 Conference on Empirical Methods in Natural Language Processing*, pages 1412–1421, Lisbon, Portugal, September. Association for Computational Linguistics.

Kishore Papineni, Salim Roukos, Todd Ward, and Wei-Jing Zhu. 2002. BLEU: A Method for Automatic Evaluation of Machine Translation. In *Proceedings of the 40th Annual Meeting on Association for Computational Linguistics*, ACL '02, pages 311–318, Stroudsburg, PA, USA. Association for Computational Linguistics.

Christian Rishøj and Anders Søgaard. 2011. Factored Translation with Unsupervised Word Clusters. In *Proceedings of the Sixth Workshop on Statistical Machine Translation*, WMT '11, pages 447–451, Stroudsburg, PA, USA. Association for Computational Linguistics.

Rico Sennrich and Barry Haddow. 2016. Linguistic input features improve neural machine translation. In *Proc. of the First Conference on Machine Translation (WMT16)*.

Ilya Sutskever, Oriol Vinyals, and Quoc V Le. 2014. Sequence to Sequence Learning with Neural Networks. In Z. Ghahramani, M. Welling, C. Cortes, N. D. Lawrence, and K. Q. Weinberger, editors, *Advances in Neural Information Processing Systems 27*, pages 3104–3112. Curran Associates, Inc.

Z. Tu, Z. Lu, Y. Liu, X. Liu, and H. Li. 2016. Coverage-based Neural Machine Translation. In *Proceedings of the 4th International Conference on Learning Representations (ICLR 2016 Workshop Track)*, ICLR '16 Workshop Track.

Joern Wuebker, Stephan Peitz, Felix Rietig, and Hermann Ney. 2013. Improving Statistical Machine Translation with Word Class Models. In *Proceedings of the 2013 Conference on Empirical Methods in Natural Language Processing*, pages 1377–1381, Seattle, Washington, USA, October. Association for Computational Linguistics.

Ruiqiang Zhang and Eiichiro Sumita. 2007. Boosting Statistical Machine Translation by Lemmatization and Linear Interpolation. In *Proceedings of the 45th Annual Meeting of the ACL on Interactive Poster and Demonstration Sessions*, ACL '07, pages 181–184, Stroudsburg, PA, USA. Association for Computational Linguistics.

Evaluation of Medical Concept Annotation Systems
on Clinical Records

Hamed Hassanzadeh   **Anthony Nguyen**   **Bevan Koopman**

The Australian e-Health Research Centre, CSIRO, Brisbane, QLD, Australia

`{hamed.hassanzadeh, anthony.nguyen, bevan.koopman}@csiro.au`

Abstract

Large volumes of electronic health records, including free-text documents, are extensively generated within various sectors of healthcare. Medical concept annotation systems are designed to enrich these documents with key concepts in the domain using reference terminologies. Although there is a wide range of annotation systems, there is a lack of comparative analysis that enables thorough understanding of the effectiveness of both the concept extraction and concept recognition components of these systems, especially within the clinical domain. This paper analyses and evaluates four annotation systems (i.e., MetaMap, NCBO annotator, Ontoserver, and QuickUMLS) for the task of extracting medical concepts from clinical free-text documents. Empirical findings have shown that each annotator exhibits various levels of strengths in terms of overall precision or recall. The concept recognition component of each system, however, was found to be highly sensitive to the quality of the text spans output by the concept extraction component of the annotation system. The effects of these components on each other are quantified in such way as to provide evidence for an informed choice of an annotation system as well as avenues for future research.

1 Introduction

With the advent of electronic health records, large volumes of mostly free-text clinical documents — discharge summaries, radiology reports, pathology reports, and patients progress notes — are now present in the health ecosystem. While these documents contain much valuable information, it can only be exploited if effective computational methods of dealing with clinical free-text are devised. The goal here is to automatically extract clinical concepts from unstructured clinical documents, thus providing a structured representation that enables fast and effective access and analysis.

To facilitate the extraction of clinical concepts from free-text, many automatic systems (known as medical concept annotators) have been developed. These systems analyse natural language and annotate specific spans of text to concepts defined in some external medical terminology/thesaurus. This workflow can be considered as a two-step process of extracting candidate spans of concepts within a given document (known as "concept extraction") and then assigning appropriate concept identifiers to each candidate span based on the defined concepts in the domain ontologies (known as "concept recognition"). Such systems are widely used in a variety of e-health settings and are critical for activities such as clinical information analysis and reporting (Zuccon et al., 2013), derivation of phenotypic descriptions (Groza et al., 2013b; Collier et al., 2014) and medical information retrieval (Zuccon et al., 2012; Koopman, 2014).

Although there are a wide range of available annotation systems, there is a lack of comparative analysis that provides enough evidence for an informed decision in choosing the most suitable system. Many of these system are developed for a specific domain (e.g., medical journal article abstracts) and may not be suited to dealing with clinical text. Deployment of these systems can often only be done in a black-box fashion: without an underlying understanding of the individual components of a system and its effectiveness.

This paper aims to analyse and evaluate four annotation systems on the task of extracting medical concepts from clinical free-text documents. Specifically, we investigate the following research

Hamed Hassanzadeh, Anthony Nguyen and Bevan Koopman. 2016. Evaluation of Medical Concept Annotation Systems on Clinical Records. In *Proceedings of Australasian Language Technology Association Workshop*, pages 15–24.

questions:

1. How well do common medical concept annotation systems perform on clinical free-text?

2. What is the impact of the core components of an annotation system (i.e., concept extraction and concept recognition) on their overall performance?

The analysis of the performances of the annotation systems show that different components of the annotation systems exhibit different levels of strengths in terms of overall precision or recall. When evaluating the performance of the individual concept extraction and concept recognition components of the systems, it was found that the concept recognition performance was highly dependent on a high performing concept extraction component. This leads to a set of insights over annotation systems from both application and development perspectives.

2 Related Work

Due to the advances in electronic health records and the availability of large volumes of clinical text documents, significant interest has been directed towards automating their processing and analyses. Several workshops and shared tasks have been designed in recent years to attract researchers to the domain and challenge different ideas and methodologies for such tasks. The ShARe/CLEF eHealth shared task in 2013 is one of them that focuses on the application of Natural Language Processing (NLP), Machine Learning (ML), and Information Retrieval (IR) for leveraging health care data[1]. Task 1 in the CLEF ShARed Task focuses on the concept recognition problem, more specifically, on identifying disorder concepts from clinical documents. It comprises two subtasks: *(i) Task 1a* a concept extraction task that evaluates the systems according to their ability to extract correct spans of text for disorder concepts; and *(ii) Task 1b* a concept recognition task that is about assigning the correct class of concept (i.e., a Concept Unique Identifier or CUI) to each text span using the Unified Medical Language System (UMLS) terminology (Suominen et al., 2013; Keith and others, 1998). Note that, only a subset of UMLS concepts were used for this annotation

task (i.e., only those UMLS concepts that were associated to particular disorder-related concepts in the Systematized Nomenclature of Medicine - Clinical Terms (SNOMED CT ontology)) A data set was provided to the participants in order to develop and test their automatic systems (more information about the data set is described in Section 3.3). A similar task was offered in the following year in SemEval 2014 Task 7 (Pradhan et al., 2014), which applied the same data set as the ShARe/CLEF task as a follow-up on the concept recognition task. In this paper, we also apply the ShARe/CLEF data set as it provides manually annotated concepts that can be used to evaluate concept annotation systems. However, different to the systems that were specifically designed for the task and tailored to the data set, we investigate the performance of off-the-shelf annotation systems for annotating this data set with medical concepts.

Mirhosseini et al. (Mirhosseini et al., 2014) also applied a subset of the same data set (i.e., the train set of ShARe/CLEF data) to compare medical annotation systems (e.g. MetaMap (Aronson, 2001; Aronson and Lang, 2010), Ontoserver (McBride et al., 2012)), and a number of standard IR techniques for the concept recognition component of the shared task (i.e. Task 1b). They considered the concept recognition task as an Information Retrieval technique and used queries with the spans of text associated with the concepts in the gold standard. The responses of annotation systems were then evaluated using standard IR evaluation measures, such as Reciprocal Ranker and Success@K. They converted all the UMLS concepts IDs in the ShARe/CLEF data to one or more corresponding SNOMED CT IDs and performed the evaluation on this new version of the data. In this paper, we investigate an extended number of annotation systems and use the original dataset and evaluation metrics for evaluating the end-to-end effectiveness of the annotation systems (as opposed to only the concept recognition component of the systems).

Funk et al. (Funk et al., 2014) compared three annotation systems (i.e., MetaMap, NCBO Annotator (Jonquet et al., 2009a), and ConceptMapper (Tanenblatt et al., 2010)) by focusing on tuning their configurable parameters according to particular ontologies on full-text articles in the biomedical domain. They evaluated the systems un-

---

der different settings according to eight ontologies. They found that the systems did not achieve the best performance with their default parameters and changes in these parameters had a significant effect on effectiveness. The ConceptMapper system was found to be the best performing system across the majority of the ontologies. Different to our study, is their use of mainly genetic-related ontologies as opposed to the clinical SNOMED CT ontology, and their use of published articles (which are written in more formal language) compared to narrative clinical documents (which are often in the form of unstructured, ungrammatical, and often fragmented free-text).

Groza et al. (Groza et al., 2013c) compared four open medical concept recognition systems (i.e., cTAKES (Savova et al., 2010), NCBO Annotator (Jonquet et al., 2009a), BeCAS (Nunes et al., 2013) and MetaMap) with their default settings. These comparisons are performed over one semi-gold and one silver standard data sets comprising of clinical trials and published abstracts. Their silver and semi-gold standard corpora were (semi-)automatically generated using different combinations of the output of their studied annotation systems. Like Groza et al. (Groza et al., 2013c), we study a range of medical concept recognition systems but with a focus on clinical records and associated gold standard that has been curated by domain experts.

3 Methodology

3.1 Annotation Systems

Automatic annotation systems commonly comprise of two distinct components: *(i) Concept Extraction*, and *(ii) Concept Recognition*. The concept extraction component of the systems is responsible for the extraction of candidate text spans from the input document that potentially refer to medical concepts, such as, disorders as in the ShARe/CLEF data. The concept recognition component then aims to assign a domain concept (using one or more base terminologies) that is semantically related to the candidate span of text.

In this paper, we evaluated medical concept annotation systems from both the concept extraction and concept recognition perspectives. The investigated systems in this study include two of the most popular medical concept annotators (i.e., MetaMap and NCBO annotators) and two of the more recent systems (i.e., QuickUMLS and On-

toserver). Brief descriptions of the systems are provided in the following:

MetaMap is an annotation program that is developed by the National Library of Medicine (NLM) to annotate a given text with appropriate concepts (i.e., UMLS Metathesaurus). MetaMap has a range of configurable parameters and options to tune its different NLP and retrieval components and its output (Aronson, 2001; Aronson and Lang, 2010). The MetaMap service usually requires considerable time in order to process the input text and annotate concepts (Shah et al., 2009; Soldaini and Goharian, 2016).

NCBO Annotator is an annotation service that covers a wide range of ontologies (i.e., more than 500 ontologies) (Jonquet et al., 2009a). Its workflow consists of a syntactic concept extraction step that employs concept names and synonyms and a semantic expansion step that tries to enrich the extracted concepts with the semantic features from ontologies. NCBO provides a set of configurable options that can be customised according to different settings and applications (Jonquet et al., 2009b).

QuickUMLS is a concept recognition approach that employs an approximate dictionary matching technique (Soldaini and Goharian, 2016). Given a text, it tries to find highly similar concepts (using the concept's string) to the given text. Instead of calculating similarities between all the concepts in the dictionary and the given text, it applies CP-Merge to reduce computation costs (Okazaki and Tsujii, 2010). CPMerge is an algorithm for approximate dictionary matching. It finds a subset of concepts that have a number of features in common with the given input.

Ontoserver is a terminology server that provides an Information Retrieval solution to medical concept annotation [2]. It employs SNOMED CT as the base terminology but also supports the Australian Medicines Terminology (AMT) and Logical Observation Identifiers Names and Codes (LOINC). It exploits a purposely-tuned retrieval function and linguistic capabilities such as spell checking, restrictions and inferences on the source ontology (McBride et al., 2012). Unlike the above systems, Ontoserver currently only supports the concept recognition phase of an annotation system. As a result, Ontoserver is currently unable to use as input the whole document and perform the

---

[2] http://ontoserver.csiro.au:8080/

concept extraction to generate suitable text spans for concept recognition.

Table 1 shows an overview of main components of the above-mentioned annotation systems. It can be observed that the annotation systems support the UMLS terminology to annotate input documents, with the exception that Ontoserver is based on the SNOMED CT ontology. MetaMap and NCBO annotators are mainly designed to annotate biomedical literature while Ontoserver is targeted towards searching for specific clinical terminology and QuickUMLS is a generic annotator. All of the annotation systems provide APIs to access and deploy their respective medical concept annotation systems.

3.2 Concept Extraction

Concept extraction refers to the identification of appropriate spans of text that can represent a domain concept. Most annotation systems have built-in concept extraction modules. However, to control for the concept extraction component of these systems, three different concept extraction approaches, one manual and two computational approaches, were investigated to generate candidate text spans to evaluate the concept recognition component of the annotation systems.

3.2.1 Gold Standard

In order to assess the systems concept recognition performance, the exact gold standard spans of text were submitted to the systems. The gold standard text spans were generated by human experts, and hence, they can be used as a benchmark to assess the effectiveness of automatic concept extraction approaches.

3.2.2 Noun Phrase Parser

From a lexical perspective, the disorder-related terminologies are mainly in the form of subjects or objects of sentences rather than predicates or actions (e.g., the post-verb component in the following sentence: "The patient was admitted with headache and dysarthria."). It is considered that the noun phrases of sentences in clinical documents are the dominant sources of medical concepts, especially for disorder concepts. Hence, a parser is employed to extract noun phrases from documents and form the input for concept annotation systems. One issue associated with this approach is that the clinical documents are commonly ungrammatical. As a result, an English noun phrase parser algorithm used as a black-box will face issues around the parsing of improper sentences, and hence, likely to produce noisy noun phrase text spans.

3.2.3 CRF Concept Extractor

A Conditional Random Field classifier (CRF) (Lafferty et al., 2001) can be used to automatically extract the boundary of candidate text chunks. CRF is a probabilistic undirected graphical model that has shown promising results in sequence labelling and text classification problems, especially in medical domain (Hassanzadeh et al., 2014; Kholghi et al., 2016; Groza et al., 2013a; de Bruijn et al., 2011; Hassanzadeh and Keyvanpour, 2013). The CRF model was trained over the training set of the ShARe/CLEF task corpus using the following features: words and their lemmas, Part of Speech (POS) tags, orthographic information (e.g., flagging if words contain initial capital letter, numerics, punctuations, etc.), character n-grams (i.e, 2 to 4-grams), and sequential features by including previous and next words (and their POS tags) in the feature vector of a given word and flagging if the word is the first/last word of a sentence. All-punctuation tokens (such as "||||" used as a separator) and determiner tokens (including numerical values) are removed in a preprocessing step. Although punctuations and determiners are not considered as independent tokens, they still participate in the feature vector of their adjacent words (i.e., a word that has such tokens in its preceding or following keeps this information in its feature vector).

3.3 Data

The ShARe/CLEF corpus was employed to evaluate the performance of the annotation systems (Suominen et al., 2013). This corpus contains de-identified clinical reports of diverse types, such as discharge summaries, electrocardiogram reports, and echocardiogram and radiology reports. In each document, those spans of text that correspond to disorder concepts were manually annotated by experts. These annotations were based on the UMLS Concept Unique Identifiers (CUIs) (Keith and others, 1998). Disorder concepts were considered to be concepts that are subcategories of the Disorder semantic group in the SNOMED CT ontology. Each span of text, which can refer to non-adjacent tokens in the documents, is annotated with a single CUI. Spans of text in the

Table 1: Annotation Services Specifications.

	Supported Terminology	Domain	Software Infrastructure
Metamap	UMLS	Biomedical literature	Prolog
NCBO	UMLS/NCBO	Biomedical literature	Java
Ontoserver	SNOMED CT/AMT/LOINC*	Clinical terminology use within health sector	Java
QuickUMLS	UMLS*	Generic	Python & C++

* Can be extended to employ other terminologies.

Table 2: The ShARe CLEF disorder concept recognition corpus statistics.

	Train Set	Test Set
No. Documents	199	99
All disorder	5,874	5,351
CUI-less disorder	1,661(28%)	1,750 (33%)
Non-CUI-less disorder	4,213 (72%)	3,601 (67%)
Disjoint disorder	660 (11%)	439 (8%)
Non-disorder tokens	59,835	56,610

corpus where annotators annotated them as disorders but no UMLS concept have been found for them were annotated with a "CUI-less" label. The ShARe CELF corpus comprises separate train and test sets that consist of 199 and 99 clinical documents, respectively. Detailed statistics of this corpus are shown in Table 2. *Disjoint* concepts refer to concepts where their spans cover discontinuous tokens. Recognising such concepts is more challenging than the regular concepts as the recogniser should be able to foresee possible tokens that can be assigned to a concept as a whole.

3.4 Evaluation Measures

The annotation systems were evaluated based on standard Information Extraction measures, namely, Precision, Recall, and F1-Score:

Precision (P): TP / (TP + FP);

Recall (R): TP / (TP + FN);

F1-Score (F1): (2 * Recall * Precision) / (Recall + Precision); i.e, Harmonic mean of Precision and Recall.

where true positive (TP) indicates that a system identified a disorder in the same span as that identified by the expert assessors, false positive (FP) refers to the identification of an incorrect span, and false negative (FN) indicates that a system failed to identify a disorder-span that was identified by the expert assessors.

For the evaluation of the concept extraction component, The "exact span" and "overlapping span" evaluation settings refer to the case where

the automatically identified span is identical to the gold standard span boundaries, and that the identified span overlaps with the gold standard span boundaries, respectively.

3.5 Experimental Setup

The ShARe/CLEF data set only contains disorder concepts. Hence, the annotation systems were guided to look for disorder concepts only. Due to the annotation guideline of ShARe/CLEF data set (Suominen et al., 2013), a concept is in the disorder semantic group if it belonged to one of the following UMLS semantic types: Congenital Abnormality, Acquired Abnormality, Injury or Poisoning, Pathologic Function, Disease or Syndrome, Mental or Behavioral Dysfunction, Cell or Molecular Dysfunction, Experimental Model of Disease, Anatomical Abnormality, Neoplastic Process, and Signs and Symptoms. Occurrences of *"CUI-less"* spans and concepts in the gold standard were removed from the data set as we cannot expect the annotation systems to find appropriate concepts for disorder text spans if appropriate concepts cannot be found by a human expert.

Table 3 shows the settings of the annotation systems. These parameters can be used to reproduce the results that are reported in this paper. It can be observed that MetaMap, NCBO, and QuickUMLS systems were restricted to the above-mentioned UMLS semantic types. Since Ontoserver does not provide options for such restriction, we filter the output of this system to only those semantic types in a post-processing step. In addition, Ontoserver's annotations are based on SNOMED CT concept IDs. Since the annotations in the data set are UMLS concept IDs, the resulting SNOMED CT IDs were mapped to UMLS concept IDs using NLM's Metathesaurus mapping table [3].

The Stanford CoreNLP toolkit was applied to extract noun phrases from the clinical docu-

---

[3] Version 2015AB: `https://www.ncbi.nlm.nih.gov/books/NBK9685`

Table 3: Annotation System Settings.

	System Parameters
Metamap	-J acab,comd,anab,cgab,dsyn,emod,inpo,mobd,neop,patf,sosy, -R SNOMEDCT_US, -q
NCBO	include=prefLabel,cui, ontologies=SNOMEDCT, exclude_numbers=true,
	longest_only=true, semantic_types=T020,T049,T190,T019,T047,T050,T037,T048,T191,T046,T184
Ontoserver	findConceptsByTermPrefixes, versionedId=http://snomed.info/sct/32506021000036107/version/20160731
QuickUMLS	threshold=0.7, window=5, similarity_name=jaccard,
	accepted_semtypes='T020','T049','T190','T019','T047','T050','T037','T048','T191','T046','T184'

ments (Manning et al., 2014). In this approach, the resulting parse tree generated from each document was processed to extract the noun phrases (NPs) from the associated subtrees of clauses of sentences.

The MALLET implementation of CRF was used in this paper to train a concept recogniser model (McCallum, 2002). The text spans of disorder concepts from the ShARe/CLEF training data set was used to train the CRF model. The data was converted into BIO format (Begin/Inside/Outside of spans) in order to have an appropriate formulation of concepts with multiple tokens.

4 Results

Table 4 presents the performance of the annotation systems. The first column of results shows system results when the whole document was used as input. The results here would reflect the end-to-end annotation system for both their built-in concept extraction and concept recognition components of the system. MetaMap achieved the highest results with 0.5948 F1-score followed by Quick-UMLS and then NCBO. Despite NCBO having the lowest F1-score of the three systems, its precision was considerably higher than MetaMap and QuickUMLS. Ontoserver currently only supports the annotation of short phrases and does not have a built-in concept extraction module to support annotations at a document level.

To further investigate the effectiveness of an annotation system's concept recognition component, the input to the annotation systems were controlled by providing each system the same spans of text. The second column of results in Table 4 shows the results when spans from the gold standard dataset were used as input into the annotators. The remaining columns show the performance of the annotation systems when input spans were generated by the noun phrase parser and the CRF model were used as input.

As expected, system performance on the gold standard chunks achieved the highest results compared to other concept extraction techniques. This simulated the upper bounds of these annotation systems as the human expert generated spans of text were used as input to the systems. The best performing concept recognition system in this setting was Ontoserver with 0.7426 F1-score. Quick-UMLS and MetaMap achieved comparable results of 0.7409 and 0.7321 F1-score respectively. Noteworthy was Ontoserver's ability to achieve a very high precision of 0.9058, while QuickUMLS achieved the best recall (i.e., 6893).

For the input spans generated by the noun phrase parser and the CRF model, a similar pattern could be observed in the performance of the systems: MetaMap and QuickUMLS achieved higher F1-scores while NCBO and Ontoserver showed similar performance. Again, Ontoserver achieved the highest precision, particularly when applied to the span generated by the noun phrase parser (precision = 0.6305).

Concept extraction techniques generated candidate spans of text to input into the concept recognition component of the systems. The results suggest that the concept extraction technique greatly impacted the performance of the concept recognition component. To further investigate this impact, Table 5 shows the evaluation of the two concept extraction approaches against the gold standard text spans. For some application, it may be sufficient to identify overlapping rather than exact spans. Therefore, two evaluation scenarios (i.e., *Exact* and *Overlapping*, as described in Section 3.4) were employed to report the results. The results show that the concept extraction approaches studied follow a naive methodology and were far from optimal. The results for both noun phrase generation approaches, however, show that if the text span evaluation criteria were relaxed to overlapping spans then a significant improvement can be achieved in both precision and recall results.

Table 4: Concept recognition results. For whole documents as input, MetaMap and QuickUMLS achieved higher overall F1 scores, while NCBO showed higher precision. Over the various noun phrases, systems showed much superior results on the gold standard input spans with Ontoserver, in general, achieving the highest precision and QuickUMLS achieving the highest recall.

| | Document input (built-in concept extractor) | | | Span input (via concept extraction) | | | | | | | | |
| | | | | Gold standard | | | Noun phrase parser | | | CRF | | |
	P	**R**	**F1**	**P**	**R**	**F1**	**P**	**R**	**F1**	**P**	**R**	**F1**
MetaMap	0.5650	0.6278	0.5948	0.8076	0.6695	0.7321	0.5027	0.4903	0.4964	0.3702	0.0401	0.0723
NCBO	0.6364	0.3742	0.4712	0.7679	0.3758	0.5047	0.5789	0.2982	0.3936	0.3767	0.0226	0.0426
Ontoserver	-	-	-	0.9058	0.6292	0.7426	0.6305	0.3335	0.4363	0.3322	0.0267	0.0495
QuickUMLS	0.5140	0.6197	0.5619	0.8008	0.6893	0.7409	0.4622	0.5075	0.4838	0.3518	0.0406	0.0729

Table 5: Performance of concept extraction approaches in identifying the gold standard text spans. "Exact Spans" and "Overlapping Spans" refer to the case where the automatically identified span is identical to the gold standard span boundary, and that the identified span overlaps with the gold standard span boundaries, respectively. Results show that concept extraction performance is very poor but significant improvements can be achieved when the text span evaluation criteria was relaxed to overlapping spans.

	Precision	**Recall**	**F1**
	Exact Spans		
Noun phrase parser	0.0686	0.4986	0.1206
CRF	0.0517	0.0443	0.0477
	Overlapping Spans		
Noun phrase parser	0.1262	0.9334	0.2224
CRF	0.1884	0.1608	0.1735

To assist in the analysis of the concept extraction and concept recognition components of the systems, Table 6 was included to show the number of input text spans and the number of concept annotations output by each of the annotation systems. It can be observed that the noun phrase parser generates a large number of candidate spans (i.e., all noun phrases in a document), which leads to higher recall in both exact and overlapping text span scenarios (0.4986 and 0.9334, respectively) but low precision (0.0686 and 0.1262). On the other hand, the CRF model generated fewer candidates and achieved poorer results, especially in the exact text span scenario.

5 Discussion

Annotation systems perform two primary steps: concept extraction and concept recognition. While most previous evaluations considered the end-to-end process (Jonquet et al., 2009a; Aronson and Lang, 2010; Groza et al., 2013c; Nunes et al., 2013; Mirhosseini et al., 2014), this papers attempts to consider the impact of these two components separately. The findings are that the concept extraction component significantly impacts the concept recognition phase. One reason for this was that the various concept extraction methods (noun phrase parser, CRF and the built-in methods within each annotator) all produced widely varying spans of text. There was a large difference in the performance between using the gold standard span, which represent an upper bound, and the spans produced by concept extraction methods. The built-in concept extraction methods all performed better than the naive noun phrase parsing and CRF methodology. Therefore we, conjecture that the noun phrase parser and CRF start to show promise when the text span evaluation criteria was relaxed to overlapping spans. Despite this, there was less variation in different concept recognition methods for the same spans of text. The lesson here is that efforts to improve annotation systems are best directed toward improving concept extraction.

The concept recognition results show that some methods were optimal in terms of precision (e.g., Ontoserver), while others were optimal in terms of recall (e.g., QuickUMLS). There are different use cases for concept annotation systems — some precision focused (e.g, accurate coding of diagnoses according to medical classification systems for reimbursement purposes where incorrect codes could lead to substantial penalties (Pestian et al., 2007)) and some recall focused (e.g. searching pa-

Table 6: Number of output annotations by the systems over the test set. NCBO's built-in concept extractor found far less concepts compared to MetaMap and QuickUMLS. In addition, Noun phrase parser generated a large number of candidate input spans while the CRF model generated fewer candidates.

	Built-in concept extractor	Gold Standard	Noun phrase parser	CRF
# Input spans	-	3,610	26,113	3,074
MetaMap	4,599	3,456	4,036	445
NCBO	2,246	1,874	1,963	231
Ontoserver	-	2,499	1,900	289
QuickUMLS	4,331	3,103	3,944	415

tient records for rare diseases where clinicians are concerned with trying to get as high recall as possible, and will tolerate lower precision results). To facilitate these different use cases it would be advantageous to configure the annotation system to optimise for either precision or recall. This may involve adapting the system to use different concept extraction or concept recognition methods. In general, it would be advantageous, both from a system design and system evaluation perspective, to decouple the concept extraction and concept recognition component of such systems.

5.1 Future Work

The medical concept annotation systems studied were observed to comprise of concept extraction and concept recognition components with different levels of strengths (e.g., NCBO's concept extraction module showed less success than its concept recognition module – resulting in low recall but considerable precision). Investigating the effectiveness of the integration of these components across annotation systems should see gains in the overall performances. For example, using the QuickUMLS concept extractor (as it resulted in the best recall) as inputs to the Ontoserver concept recogniser (as it showed the highest precision). Furthermore, an ensemble of these systems working together may also show promising results (Kang et al., 2012). For example, a voting system can be designed to enrich the final annotations with the best outcomes of different systems.

A thorough investigation into the effectiveness and efficiency of annotation systems including evaluations of systems for recognising concepts beyond disorders is also warranted. Comparison of other dimensions, such as execution time, robustness in terms of domain (e.g., radiology, pathology, emergency) and type of input clinical document (e.g., discharge letter vs progress notes),

and larger datasets (e.g., i2b2 (Uzuner et al., 2011) or CADEC (Karimi et al., 2015) corpora), and more detailed comparison of concept extraction and recognition components (e.g., effect of overlapping spans on concept recognition) will all be the subject of ongoing work.

6 Conclusion

This paper investigated and evaluated four annotation systems (i.e., MetaMap, NCBO, Ontoserver, and QuickUMLS). The focus was on evaluating and assessing the performances of annotation systems on annotating clinical free-text documents. Concept extraction and concept recognition, which are two main components of a concept annotation system, were independently evaluated in order to provide an in-depth comparison of their performances. The experimental results showed that each annotator exhibited varied performance and that the text spans output by the concept extraction component of an annotation system significantly impacts on the performance of the concept recognition and overall end-to-end performance of the system.

References

Alan R Aronson and François-Michel Lang. 2010. An overview of metamap: historical perspective and recent advances. *Journal of the American Medical Informatics Association*, 17(3):229–236.

Alan R Aronson. 2001. Effective mapping of biomedical text to the umls metathesaurus: the metamap program. In *Proceedings of the AMIA Symposium*, page 17. American Medical Informatics Association.

Nigel Collier, Anika Oellrich, and Tudor Groza. 2014. Concept selection for phenotypes and disease-related annota-tions using support vector machines. In *Proc. PhenoDay and Bio-Ontologies at ISMB 2014*.

Berry de Bruijn, Colin Cherry, Svetlana Kiritchenko, Joel Martin, and Xiaodan Zhu. 2011. Machine-learned solutions for three stages of clinical information extraction: the state of the art at i2b2 2010. *Journal of the American Medical Informatics Association*, 18(5):557–562.

Christopher Funk, William Baumgartner, Benjamin Garcia, Christophe Roeder, Michael Bada, K Bretonnel Cohen, Lawrence E Hunter, and Karin Verspoor. 2014. Large-scale biomedical concept recognition: an evaluation of current automatic annotators and their parameters. *BMC bioinformatics*, 15(1):1.

Tudor Groza, Hamed Hassanzadeh, and Jane Hunter. 2013a. Recognizing scientific artifacts in biomedical literature. *Biomedical informatics insights*, 6:15.

Tudor Groza, Jane Hunter, and Andreas Zankl. 2013b. Mining skeletal phenotype descriptions from scientific literature. *PloS one*, 8(2).

Tudor Groza, Anika Oellrich, and Nigel Collier. 2013c. Using silver and semi-gold standard corpora to compare open named entity recognisers. In *Bioinformatics and Biomedicine (BIBM), 2013 IEEE International Conference on*, pages 481–485. IEEE.

Hamed Hassanzadeh and Mohammadreza Keyvanpour. 2013. A two-phase hybrid of semi-supervised and active learning approach for sequence labeling. *Intelligent Data Analysis*, 17(2):251–270.

Hamed Hassanzadeh, Tudor Groza, and Jane Hunter. 2014. Identifying scientific artefacts in biomedical literature: The evidence based medicine use case. *Journal of biomedical informatics*, 49:159–170.

Clement Jonquet, Nigam Shah, and Mark Musen. 2009a. The open biomedical annotator. In *AMIA summit on translational bioinformatics*, pages 56–60.

Clement Jonquet, Nigam Shah, Cherie Youn, Chris Callendar, Margaret-Anne Storey, and M Musen. 2009b. Ncbo annotator: semantic annotation of biomedical data. In *International Semantic Web Conference, Poster and Demo session*, volume 110.

Ning Kang, Zubair Afzal, Bharat Singh, Erik M Van Mulligen, and Jan A Kors. 2012. Using an ensemble system to improve concept extraction from clinical records. *Journal of biomedical informatics*, 45(3):423–428.

Sarvnaz Karimi, Alejandro Metke-Jimenez, Madonna Kemp, and Chen Wang. 2015. Cadec: A corpus of adverse drug event annotations. *Journal of biomedical informatics*, 55:73–81.

E Keith et al. 1998. The unified medical language system: Toward a collaborative approach for solving terminological problems. *JAMIA*, 5:12–16.

Mahnoosh Kholghi, Laurianne Sitbon, Guido Zuccon, and Anthony Nguyen. 2016. Active learning: a step towards automating medical concept extraction. *Journal of the American Medical Informatics Association*, 23(2):289–296.

Bevan Koopman. 2014. *Semantic Search as Inference: Applications in Health Informatics*. Ph.D. thesis, Queensland University of Technology, Brisbane, Australia.

John Lafferty, Andrew McCallum, and Fernando Pereira. 2001. Conditional random fields: Probabilistic models for segmenting and labeling sequence data. In *Proceedings of the eighteenth international conference on machine learning, ICML*, volume 1, pages 282–289.

Christopher D Manning, Mihai Surdeanu, John Bauer, Jenny Rose Finkel, Steven Bethard, and David McClosky. 2014. The stanford corenlp natural language processing toolkit. In *ACL (System Demonstrations)*, pages 55–60.

Simon McBride, Michael Lawley, Hugo Leroux, and Simon Gibson. 2012. Using australian medicines terminology (amt) and snomed ct-au to better support clinical research. In *Studies in Health Technology and Informatics*, pages 144–149.

Andrew Kachites McCallum. 2002. Mallet: A machine learning for language toolkit. http://mallet.cs.umass.edu.

Shahin Mirhosseini, Guido Zuccon, Bevan Koopman, Anthony Nguyen, and Michael Lawley. 2014. Medical free-text to concept mapping as an information retrieval problem. In *Proceedings of the 2014 Australasian Document Computing Symposium*, page 93. ACM.

Tiago Nunes, David Campos, Sérgio Matos, and José Luís Oliveira. 2013. Becas: biomedical concept recognition services and visualization. *Bioinformatics*, 29(15):1915–1916.

Naoaki Okazaki and Jun'ichi Tsujii. 2010. Simple and efficient algorithm for approximate dictionary matching. In *Proceedings of the 23rd International Conference on Computational Linguistics*, pages 851–859. Association for Computational Linguistics.

John P Pestian, Christopher Brew, Paweł Matykiewicz, Dj J Hovermale, Neil Johnson, K Bretonnel Cohen, and Włodzisław Duch. 2007. A shared task involving multi-label classification of clinical free text. In *Proceedings of the Workshop on BioNLP 2007: Biological, Translational, and Clinical Language Processing*, pages 97–104. Association for Computational Linguistics.

Sameer Pradhan, Noémie Elhadad, Wendy Chapman, Suresh Manandhar, and Guergana Savova. 2014. Semeval-2014 task 7: Analysis of clinical text. *Proceedings of the 8th International Workshop on Semantic Evaluation (SemEval 2014)*, pages 54–62.

Guergana K Savova, James J Masanz, Philip V Ogren, Jiaping Zheng, Sunghwan Sohn, Karin C Kipper-Schuler, and Christopher G Chute. 2010. Mayo clinical text analysis and knowledge extraction system (ctakes): architecture, component evaluation and applications. *Journal of the American Medical Informatics Association*, 17(5):507–513.

Nigam H Shah, Nipun Bhatia, Clement Jonquet, Daniel Rubin, Annie P Chiang, and Mark A Musen. 2009. Comparison of concept recognizers for building the open biomedical annotator. *BMC bioinformatics*, 10(Suppl 9):S14.

Luca Soldaini and Nazli Goharian. 2016. Quickumls: a fast, unsupervised approach for medical concept extraction. In *MedIR Workshop, SIGIR*.

Hanna Suominen, Sanna Salanterä, Sumithra Velupillai, Wendy W Chapman, Guergana Savova, Noemie Elhadad, Sameer Pradhan, Brett R South, Danielle L Mowery, Gareth JF Jones, et al. 2013. Overview of the share/clef ehealth evaluation lab 2013. In *International Conference of the Cross-Language Evaluation Forum for European Languages*, pages 212–231. Springer.

Michael A Tanenblatt, Anni Coden, and Igor L Sominsky. 2010. The conceptmapper approach to named entity recognition. In *Proceedings of Seventh International Conference on Language Resources and Evaluation (LREC?10)*.

Özlem Uzuner, Brett R South, Shuying Shen, and Scott L DuVall. 2011. 2010 i2b2/va challenge on concepts, assertions, and relations in clinical text. *Journal of the American Medical Informatics Association*, 18(5):552–556.

Guido Zuccon, Bevan Koopman, Anthony Nguyen, Deanne Vickers, and Luke Butt. 2012. Exploiting Medical Hierarchies for Concept-based Information Retrieval. In *Proceedings of the Seventeenth Australasian Document Computing Symposium*, Dunedin, New Zealand, December.

Guido Zuccon, Amol S Wagholikar, Anthony N Nguyen, Luke Butt, Kevin Chu, Shane Martin, and Jaimi Greenslade. 2013. Automatic classification of free-text radiology reports to identify limb fractures using machine learning and the snomed ct ontology. *AMIA Summits on Translational Science Proceedings*, 2013:300.

The Benefits of Word Embeddings Features for Active Learning in Clinical Information Extraction

Mahnoosh Kholghi, Lance De Vine, Laurianne Sitbon, Guido Zuccon
Queensland University of Technology
{m1.kholghi, l.devine, laurianne.sitbon, g.zuccon}@qut.edu.au
Anthony Nguyen
The Australian e-Health Research Centre, CSIRO
anthony.nguyen@csiro.au

Abstract

This study investigates the use of unsupervised word embeddings and sequence features for sample representation in an active learning framework built to extract clinical concepts from clinical free text. The objective is to further reduce the manual annotation effort while achieving higher effectiveness compared to a set of baseline features. Unsupervised features are derived from skip-gram word embeddings and a sequence representation approach. The comparative performance of unsupervised features and baseline hand-crafted features in an active learning framework are investigated using a wide range of selection criteria including least confidence, information diversity, information density and diversity, and domain knowledge informativeness. Two clinical datasets are used for evaluation: the i2b2/VA 2010 NLP challenge and the ShARe/CLEF 2013 eHealth Evaluation Lab. Our results demonstrate significant improvements in terms of effectiveness as well as annotation effort savings across both datasets. Using unsupervised features along with baseline features for sample representation lead to further savings of up to 9% and 10% of the token and concept annotation rates, respectively.

1 Introduction

Active learning (AL) has recently received considerable attention in clinical information extraction, as it promises to automatically annotate clinical free text with less manual annotation effort than supervised learning approaches, while achieving the same effectiveness (Boström & Dalianis, 2012; Chen et al., 2015; Chen et al., 2012; Figueroa et al., 2012; Kholghi et al., 2015, 2016; Ohno-Machado et al., 2013). Active learning is particularly important in the clinical domain because of the costs incurred in preparing high quality annotated data as required by supervised machine learning approaches for a wide range of data analysis applications such as retrieving, reasoning, and reporting. Active learning is a human-in-the-loop process in which at each iteration, a set of informative instances is automatically selected by a *query strategy* (Settles, 2012) and annotated in order to re-train or update the supervised model (see Figure 1). The query strategy, as a key component of the AL process, plays an important role in the performance of AL approaches.

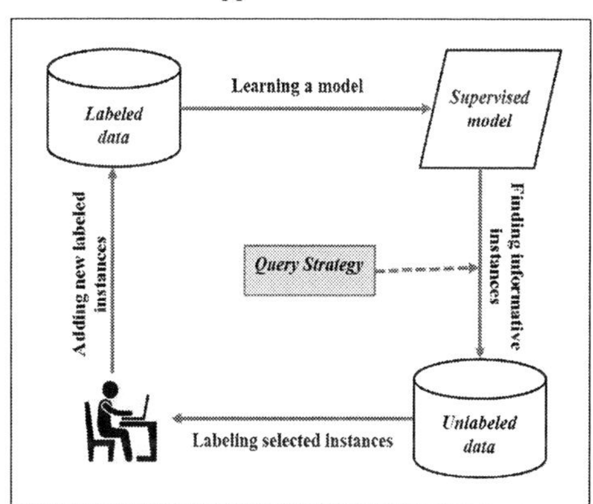

Figure 1. Active learning process.

The learning models at each iteration are typically built using supervised learning algorithms. The associated output of the learning model (i.e. the posterior probability) is usually leveraged in identifying and selecting the next set of informative instances. Hence, it is important to build ac-

Mahnoosh Kholghi, Lance De Vine, Laurianne Sitbon, Guido Zuccon and Anthony Nguyen. 2016. The Benefits of Word Embeddings Features for Active Learning in Clinical Information Extraction. In *Proceedings of Australasian Language Technology Association Workshop*, pages 25–34.

curate statistical models early in the process, and at each iteration. Previous studies have highlighted that the feature set, which is used to represent data instances, is an important factor that affects the stability, robustness, and effectiveness of the learning models built across the AL iterations (Kholghi et al., 2014).

In previous studies of AL for clinical information extraction, a set of common hand-crafted features, such as orthographical and morphological features, was used to build supervised models across AL iterations and suggested that more effective models would lead to reduced annotation rates in addition to improved effectiveness (Kholghi, et al., 2014, 2015, 2016). On the other hand, the application of unsupervised features, such as clustering-based representations, distributional word representations, and skip-gram word embeddings has been shown to improve fully supervised clinical information extraction systems (De Vine et al., 2015; Jonnalagadda et al., 2012; Nikfarjam et al., 2015; Tang, Wu, et al., 2013). We can therefore hypothesize that their use within an active learning framework may result in further reduction of manual annotation effort; however, no previous study has formally evaluated this in the clinical information extraction context.

In this paper, we investigate the effects of an improved sample representation using word embeddings and sequence features on an active learning framework built for clinical concept extraction. Concept extraction is a significant primary step in extracting meaningful information from clinical free text. It is a type of sequence labeling task in which sequences of terms that express meaningful concepts within a clinical setting, such as medication name, frequency, and dosage, are identified. We examine a wide range of hand-crafted and automatically generated unsupervised features to improve supervised and AL-based concept extraction systems. Our contributions are as follow:

(1) We validate the impact of word embeddings and sequence features on improving the clinical concept extraction systems, as previously studied by De Vine, et al. (2015), by using an additional dataset (ShARe/CLEF 2013 dataset) for evaluation. We generate unsupervised features using a different corpus and then investigate the combinations of features that lead to the most significant improvements on supervised models across the datasets.

(2) We demonstrate that selected combinations of unsupervised features lead to more effective models across the AL batches and also less annotation effort compared to common hand-crafted features. We do this across a selected set of query strategies.

2   Related Work

The two primary areas that relate to this work are: (i) the use of unsupervised sample representations in clinical information extraction, and (ii) active learning approaches for clinical information extraction.

2.1   Unsupervised Sample Representations in Clinical Information Extraction

The recent development of shared datasets, such as i2b2 challenges (Uzuner et al., 2010; Uzuner et al., 2011) and the ShARe/CLEF eHealth Evaluation Lab (Suominen et al., 2013) has stimulated research into new approaches to improve the current clinical information extraction systems. Unsupervised approaches to extract new features for representing data instances have proven to be key to more effective clinical information extraction systems (De Bruijn et al., 2011; De Vine, et al., 2015; Jonnalagadda, et al., 2012; Tang, Cao, et al., 2013).

Three main categories of unsupervised word representation approaches have been used in clinical information extraction systems: (1) clustering-based representations using Brown clustering (Brown et al., 1992), (2) distributional word representation using random indexing (Kanerva et al., 2000), and (3) word embeddings from neural language models, such as skip-gram word embeddings (Mikolov et al., 2013).

De Bruijn, et al. (2011) extracted clustering-based word representation features using Brown clustering and used them along with a set of hand-crafted features in developing their systems for the i2b2/VA 2010 NLP challenge. Their system achieved the highest effectiveness amongst systems in the challenge. In the same challenge, Jonnalagadda, et al. (2012) significantly improved the effectiveness of their system by adding distributional semantic features (using random indexing) to their feature set. Tang, et al. (2013) compared different word representation features extracted from Brown clustering and random indexing and found that they are complementary and when combined with common basic features the effectiveness of clinical

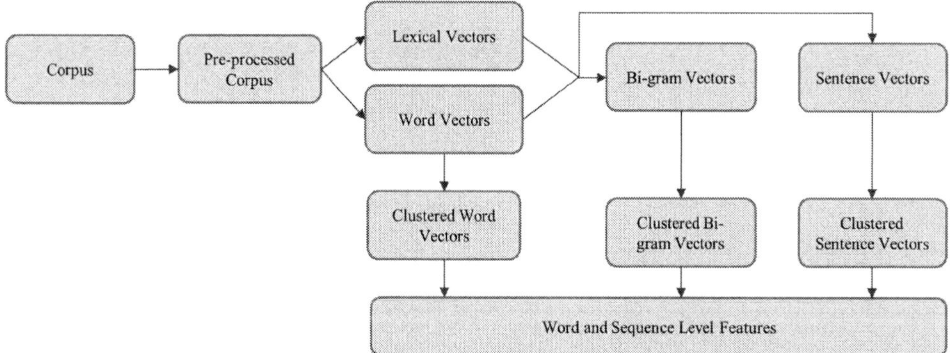

Figure 2. Word and sequence level feature generation process.

information extraction systems increased. De Vine, et al. (2015) developed a novel approach to generate sequence level features by concatenating the accumulated and normalized word and lexical vectors of each token in a phrase or sentence. Their results demonstrated that unsupervised features generated using word embeddings and sequence level representations led to supervised models of significantly higher effectiveness compared to those built with baseline hand-crafted features.

2.2 Active Learning in Clinical Information extraction

Active learning aims to significantly reduce the high costs of manual annotation required to build a high quality annotated data for training phase of supervised approaches.

Kholghi, et al. (2016) developed an active learning based framework to investigate the effect of AL in reducing the burden of manual annotation for clinical information extraction systems. In their framework, they apply state-of-the-art AL query strategies for sequence labelling tasks (i.e., Least Confidence (LC) and information density) to the extraction of clinical concepts. They found that AL achieves the same effectiveness as supervised learning while saving up to 77% of the total number of sequence that require manual annotation. Chen, et al. (2015) proposed new AL query strategies under groupings of uncertainty-based and diversity-based approaches. They conducted a comprehensive empirical evaluation of existing and their proposed AL approaches on the clinical concept extraction task and found that uncertainty sampling-based approaches, such as LC, resulted in a significant reduction of annotation effort compared to diversity-based approaches. Kholghi, et

al. (2015) also conducted a comprehensive empirical comparison of a wide range of AL query strategies and found that the least confidence, which is an informativeness based selection criterion, is a better choice for clinical data in terms of effectiveness and annotation effort reduction. They also developed a new query strategy, called Domain Knowledge Informativeness (DKI), which makes use of external clinical resources. They showed that DKI led to a further 14% of token and concept annotation rates compared to LC.

3 Methodology

3.1 Unsupervised Sample Representation

We follow the same approach as described by De Vine, et al. (2015) to generate the unsupervised features. Figure 2 depicts our pipeline for generating the unsupervised features; these will be used to augment the supervised hand-crafted features of our classifier.

The pre-processing step includes lower-casing, substitution of matching regular expressions, and removing punctuations on the training corpus. We then generate word embeddings from the pre-processed corpus using the Skip-gram model (Mikolov, et al., 2013). We also generate lower dimensional "lexical" vectors from the pre-processed corpus, which encode character n-grams (i.e., uni-grams, bi-grams, tri-grams, tetra-grams, and skip-grams). These vectors are used to capture lexicographic patterns. A lexical vector is generated for each token by accumulating and normalizing all the n-gram vectors comprising the token.

We then use the word embeddings and the lexical vectors to construct representations for both bi-grams and sentences. First, all the lexical

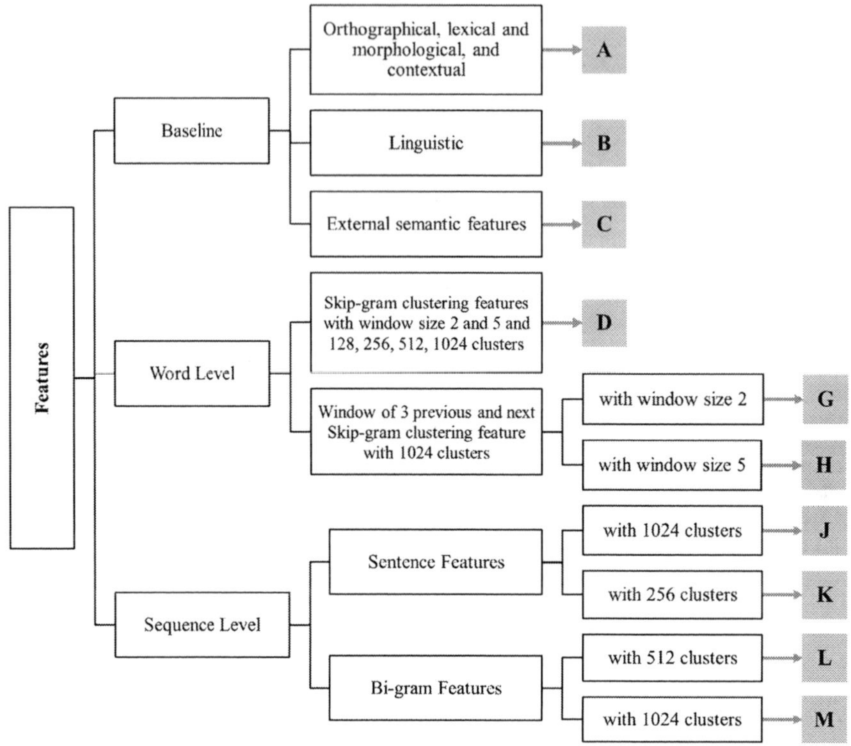

Figure 3. Description of the features used in this study.

vectors associated with the tokens within a bi-gram or sentence are accumulated and normalized. The word embeddings for those tokens are also accumulated and normalized. Then, the resulting lexical and word vectors are concatenated and normalized to form a sequence representation for the corresponding bi-gram or sentence.

We further cluster the word vectors, bi-gram vectors and sentence vectors to generate feature identifiers which are then used in our classifier.

3.2   Active Learning Query Strategies

A key element of the AL process (Figure 1) is the query strategy, which, at each iteration, selects the instances that contain the most useful information (i.e., informative samples) for the learning model. We now outline the state-of-the-art AL query strategies for clinical concept extraction (Chen, et al., 2015; Kholghi, et al., 2015).

Least Confidence (LC) (Culotta & McCallum, 2005) is an uncertainty-based approach in which the model's confidence (certainty) in predicting the label of a sample is the criterion to measure the informativeness of that sample. The model's confidence is estimated based on the posterior probability of the model. The less the posterior probability, the less confident the model is about the sample's label. The samples for which the model's uncertainty is the highest are the most informative for the AL model.

Information Diversity (IDiv) (Kholghi, et al., 2015) is based on the idea that in addition to an informativeness measure, the similarity between samples can be useful to inform the model. IDiv selects samples that are informative and diverse (i.e., those that are less similar to the labeled set).

Information Density and Diversity (IDD) (Kholghi, et al., 2015) is similar to IDiv with the difference that, to avoid choosing outliers, it also considers the similarity between the samples in the unlabeled set.

Domain Knowledge Informativeness (DKI) (Kholghi, et al., 2015) leverages the domain knowledge extracted from an external resource such as SNOMED CT, in addition to an informativeness measure, to better inform the model. The domain knowledge in DKI is estimated based on the longest span of a concept that each

28

token belongs to, according to a pre-defined set of semantic types in the external resource.

4 Experimental Setup

4.1 Feature Groups

Figure 3 shows a short description of all the features used in this study. The baseline feature groups (A, B, C) include orthographical (regular expression patterns), lexical and morphological (suffixes/prefixes and character n-grams), contextual (window of k words), linguistic (POS tags (Toutanova et al., 2003)), and external semantic features (UMLS and SNOMED CT semantic groups as described in (Kholghi, et al., 2015)).

As the previous work demonstrated, learning word embeddings and sequence features from a clinical corpus with an adequate amount of data, and a good coverage of the target data, results in higher effectiveness compared to a general or relatively small clinical corpus (De Vine, et al., 2015). In this study, we use a clinical corpus composed of the concatenation of the i2b2/VA 2010 train set (Uzuner, et al., 2011), the Med-Track collection (Voorhees & Tong, 2011), and the ShARe/CLEF 2013 train set (Suominen, et al., 2013) to generate word embeddings.

4.2 Supervised and Active Learning Settings

In this study, we use an incremental, pool-based, active learning framework (Kholghi, et al., 2014, 2016). We build models across AL batches using tuned linear chain Conditional Random Fields (CRFs) (Kholghi, et al., 2014; Lafferty et al., 2001) with different feature groups. The implementation of CRFs for both supervised and active learning is based on the MALLET toolkit (McCallum, 2002). In this study, Random Sampling (RS) is used as a baseline for the AL framework. RS randomly selects samples at each iteration. All active learning and random sampling baseline setups including the initial labeled set and batch size (i.e., both less than 1% of the size of the train set) are based on previous findings (Kholghi, et al., 2015, 2016).

4.3 Datasets

We use the annotated train sets developed for the concept extraction task in the i2b2/VA 2010 NLP challenge (Uzuner, et al., 2011) and ShARe/CLEF 2013 eHealth Evaluation Lab (Task 1) (Pradhan et al., 2013) to build learning models across AL batches using different feature groups.

Table 1. Number of documents (#doc) and sequences (#seq) in the train and test sets of the two considered datasets.

	Train Set		Test Set	
	#doc	#seq	#doc	#seq
i2b2/VA 2010	349	30,673	477	45,025
ShARe/CLEF 2013	200	10,171	100	9,273

The corresponding test set of each dataset is used to evaluate the effect of feature groups on the performance of models built across AL batches (see Table 1). The i2b2/VA 2010 task comprises the extraction of clinical problems, tests and treatments from clinical reports, while the ShARe/CLEF 2013 eHealth Evaluation Lab (task 1) requires to identify mentions of disorders.

4.4 Evaluation measures

In our evaluation, the learning model effectiveness is measured by Precision, Recall and F1-measure. The evaluation measures are computed on the test set using MALLET's multi-segmentation evaluator (McCallum, 2002). To demonstrate statistically significant improvements on F1- measures, we perform a 5*2 cross validated paired t-test (Dieterich, 1998).

The performance of the AL framework is evaluated using Annotation Rate (AR), which measures the number of Sequences (SAR), Tokens (TAR), and Concepts (CAR) required by the AL framework to reach the target supervised effectiveness. The lower the annotation rate, the better the AL framework is considered to be.

$$AR = \frac{\# \; labeled \; annotation \; units \; used \; by \; AL}{\# \; total \; labeled \; annotation \; units \; in \; train \; set}$$

5 Results

5.1 Target Supervised Performance

Table 2 presents the effectiveness of the supervised CRFs models, which employ all the labeled instances in the train sets of the considered datasets, using the different combinations of features described in Figure 3. The highest effectiveness obtained in each feature group is highlighted in bold.

Table 2 shows that the inclusion of the unsupervised word and sequence level features improves the effectiveness of the supervised model compared to the best baseline feature set ABC. The models' effectiveness built using feature groups ABCD, ABCDGH, ABCDGHK, and ABCDGHJKM are selected for subsequent

Table 2. Supervised target performance for all sets of features. Statistically significant improvements (p<0.05) for F1 when compared with ABC are indicated by *.

	Features	i2b2/VA 2010			ShARe/CLEF 2013		
		Precision	Recall	F1 measure	Precision	Recall	F1 measure
Baseline	Word	0.6571	0.6011	0.6279	0.2225	0.4317	0.2936
	A	0.8404	0.8031	0.8213	0.7858	0.6461	0.7091
	B	0.6167	0.6006	0.6085	0.5157	0.4027	0.4523
	C	0.7691	0.6726	0.7192	0.7022	0.5118	0.5921
	BC	0.7269	0.712	0.7194	0.7163	0.518	0.6012
	AB	0.8368	0.8038	0.82	0.7832	0.6472	0.7087
	AC	0.8378	0.8059	0.8216	0.8035	0.6808	0.7371
	ABC	0.8409	0.8066	**0.8234**	0.8095	0.6804	**0.7394**
Word Level	D	0.7773	0.7393	0.7578	0.6815	0.5581	0.6137
	GH	0.8056	0.7547	0.7793	0.7225	0.5625	0.6325
	ABCD	0.8424	0.8127	0.8273	0.8042	0.6916	0.7436
	ABCDGH	0.8502	0.8124	**0.8309***	0.8092	0.6898	**0.7448***
Sequence Level	J	0.6551	0.6242	0.6393	0.6564	0.4054	0.5012
	K	0.6852	0.6433	0.6636	0.6305	0.4189	0.5033
	ABCDGHJ	0.8488	0.8126	0.8303*	0.7992	0.6916	0.7415
	ABCDGHK	0.8495	0.8132	**0.8309***	0.8111	0.69	**0.7457***
	ABCDGHJK	0.8449	0.8116	0.8279	0.8093	0.6889	0.7443
	L	0.7361	0.6169	0.6713	0.7015	0.3854	0.4975
	M	0.7531	0.6358	0.6895	0.672	0.3924	0.4955
	ABCDGHJKL	0.8458	0.8086	0.8268	0.8068	0.6881	0.7427
	ABCDGHJKM	0.8488	0.8113	**0.8296***	0.8105	0.69	**0.7454***
	ABCDGHJKLM	0.8447	0.8062	0.825	0.8117	0.6873	0.7444

active learning experiments as target supervised effectiveness, because they result in considerable improvements in the supervised models' effectiveness across both datasets.

5.2 Active Learning Performance

We now consider the performance of the active learning framework in terms of annotation rates.

It is important to note that in these experiments, the models built across AL batches, using selected feature sets, are required to reach the target supervised effectiveness achieved using the corresponding feature set (F1-measures in Table 2).

Table 3 presents SAR, TAR and CAR for different AL query strategies and for the Random Sampling baseline. The most effective feature sets, compared to the baseline feature set ABC (highlighted in gray), for the models built across AL batches using different query strategies are highlighted in bold.

Word and sequence representations result in less annotation effort across all query strategies in both datasets compared to the hand-crafted feature set. We observe 9% and 10% reduction in token (TAR) and concept (CAR) annotation rates for the IDiv query strategy (highlighted in orange) when using ABCDGH feature set com-

pared to the baseline ABC feature set in ShARe/CLEF 2013 dataset. The same feature set (ABCDGH) results in 4% and 6% less TAR and CAR in i2b2/VA 2010 dataset (highlighted in green) compared to the baseline ABC feature set when using LC as the query strategy.

Generally, the addition of word level features (D, G, and H) gives the best results. Also, on occasions, the addition of sequence level features (J, K, and M) gives further improvements, although not consistently. The previous study also showed that the addition of sequence level features results in less remarkable improvement on supervised models' effectiveness compared to word level features (De Vine, et al., 2015).

6 Discussion

The results from our empirical evaluation confirm the previous findings suggesting that the use of unsupervised features significantly improves clinical information extraction systems in a supervised learning setting (De Vine, et al., 2015). Here we have further studied the use of these features within an active learning framework.

Our results highlight that the use of unsupervised word and sequence level features not only increases the effectiveness of the models built

Table 3. Annotation rates for all active learning query strategies and the baseline RS using different sample representations (feature groups). Results for the baseline feature set (ABC) are highlighted in gray.

Query Strategy	Features	i2b2/VA 2010			ShARe/CLEF 2013		
		SAR	TAR	CAR	SAR	TAR	CAR
RS	ABC	90%	90%	90%	97%	97%	98%
	ABCD	88%	88%	88%	83%	84%	83%
	ABCDGH	82%	82%	82%	88%	88%	87%
	ABCDGHK	88%	88%	88%	91%	91%	91%
	ABCDGHJKM	87%	87%	87%	76%	76%	76%
LC	ABC	24%	43%	55%	24%	38%	63%
	ABCD	22%	40%	50%	19%	31%	55%
	ABCDGH	20%	39%	49%	20%	33%	58%
	ABCDGHK	20%	39%	49%	22%	35%	61%
	ABCDGHJKM	22%	41%	52%	20%	33%	57%
IDiv	ABC	23%	41%	52%	24%	38%	64%
	ABCD	20%	37%	48%	20%	31%	55%
	ABCDGH	20%	39%	50%	18%	29%	54%
	ABCDGHK	22%	42%	52%	20%	31%	57%
	ABCDGHJKM	22%	41%	52%	20%	31%	56%
IDD	ABC	22%	41%	52%	25%	41%	66%
	ABCD	22%	41%	51%	23%	38%	62%
	ABCDGH	20%	39%	49%	20%	33%	57%
	ABCDGHK	22%	40%	51%	21%	35%	59%
	ABCDGHJKM	20%	39%	49%	22%	36%	61%
DKI	ABC	22%	27%	37%	20%	31%	57%
	ABCD	19%	25%	36%	17%	27%	52%
	ABCDGH	18%	24%	35%	18%	29%	54%
	ABCDGHK	18%	24%	35%	20%	30%	55%
	ABCDGHJKM	19%	25%	36%	19%	28%	53%

across AL batches, but also leads to lower manual annotation efforts in the active learning framework compared to the baseline feature set ABC (no unsupervised features). We can assume that the reason is that the better the sample representation, the stronger the updated model is in terms of effectiveness at each iteration of active learning. This means that AL query strategies use a better updated model at each iteration and therefore choose a better set of informative instances. Hence, by using these data representations, AL requires a smaller number of sequences, tokens, and concepts to reach the target supervised effectiveness. This, in turn, translates into lower annotation rates. However, not all combinations of different features always lead to lower annotation rates in the AL framework (Kholghi, et al., 2014).

We thus next study the trade-off between effectiveness (F1 measure from Table 2) and annotation rate (CAR from Table 3) to better understand the performance of five selected feature groups (ABC, ABCD, ABCDGH, and ABCDGHK). Figure 4 demonstrates the concept annotation rate (CAR) values (horizontal axis) for the best performing query strategy, in each dataset, when reaching: (1) the corresponding target supervised effectiveness for each feature set showed by ■, and (2) a fixed effectiveness for all feature sets showed by ◆. These values are depicted against the effectiveness when training on the full train set (vertical axis) for each feature set (F1 measure from Table 2). We are presenting these for LC and IDiv for i2b2/VA 2010 and ShARe/CLEF datasets, respectively as they achieved the lowest concept annotation rates as discussed in section 5.2. The fixed effectiveness for all feature sets is determined as follow: F1 measure = 0.80 for i2b2/VA 2010 and F1 measure = 0.70 for ShARe/CLEF 2013. The aim of this analysis is to verify whether improvements in terms of supervised effectiveness when using different feature sets (F1 measure from Table 2) necessarily scale into improvements in CAR (i.e., lower annotation effort) and whether the same behavior is observed in terms of annotation effort reduction when a fixed F1 measure value is considered for all feature groups. It is

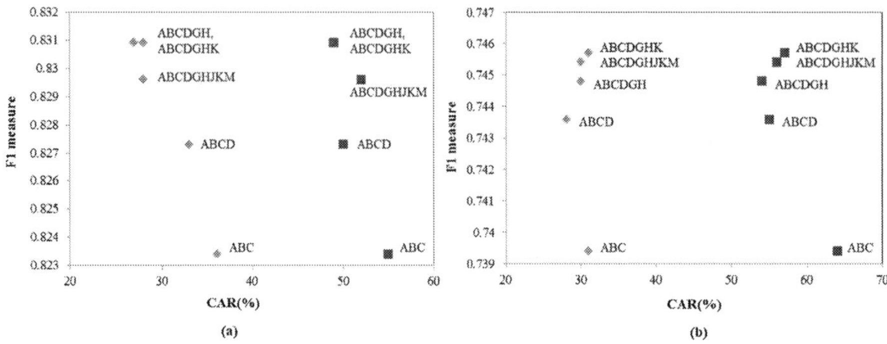

Figure 4. Analysis of concept annotation rates (CAR) (horizontal axis) at (1) target supervised effectiveness for each feature set (■), and (2) a fixed effectiveness for all feature sets (◆) with respect to the corresponding F1 measure for each feature set from Table 2 (vertical axis). (a) i2b2/VA 2010; (b) ShARe/CLEF 2013.

important to note that the higher the F1 measure and the lower the CAR, the better the feature set. Hence, those points towards the left upper corner of both plots in Figure 4 perform better both in terms of effectiveness and annotation rate. Points marked with the same symbol should be compared to each other.

In terms of target supervised effectiveness (■), Figure 4 shows that feature groups ABCDGH and ABCDGHK outperform the other feature groups in i2b2/VA 2010 dataset, both in terms of effectiveness (F1 measure) and annotation rate (CAR). While ABCDGH achieves the best CAR (i.e., the lowest) in ShARe/CLEF 2013 dataset, it is not the best performing feature group in terms of supervised effectiveness. The highest F1 measure was achieved by feature group ABCDGHK in this dataset. The same pattern is observed when considering a fixed F1 measure value (◆). Hence, the feature set that leads to a supervised model with the highest effectiveness (F1 measure) does not always lead to an AL model with the lowest annotation rate. These results demonstrate that improving supervised models built across the AL batches does not necessarily guarantee a reduction in annotation rates.

Interestingly, the updated model has no role in selecting the next batch of instances when using the Random Sampling baseline, as this randomly selects instances at each iteration. Yet, a better feature set (e.g., ABCDGHJKM) helps RS to reduce the annotation rate. If we compare the updated models at the same batch of RS using different data representations, for instance ABC vs. ABCDGHJKM, we observe that by even adding random instances to the labeled set, more information is injected into the updated model

using the feature set ABCDGHJKM compared to ABC. This suggests that RS with unsupervised features has a reduced rate of annotation errors compared to using the ABC feature set.

These results can be summarized into the following observations:

- A better sample representation using unsupervised features leads to higher effectiveness and less manual annotation effort not only in an AL framework, but also in a Random Sampling approach.
- Although there is a relationship between high effectiveness and low annotation effort, not all combinations of features conducive to the highest effectiveness necessarily lead to the lowest annotation effort.
- The combination of word level features (D, G, and H) with the baseline handcrafted features, i.e., ABCDGH, generally performs better than the other feature combinations across all AL query strategies and datasets, both in terms of effectiveness and annotation rates.

7 Conclusion

This paper presented an analysis of different data representations using a wide range of feature sets and investigated their impact on active learning performance in terms of both model effectiveness and annotation effort reduction. We believe this is the first study analyzing the effect of unsupervised sample representation using word embeddings and sequence level features on an active learning framework built for clinical information extraction.

The empirical results highlighted the benefits of unsupervised features in achieving higher effectiveness and lower manual annotation effort in our AL framework. Word and sequence level features significantly increase the effectiveness of the models built across AL batches. In addition, compared to the baseline feature set, they reduce the manual annotation effort by using a small number of sequences, tokens, and concepts to reach the target supervised performance. Hence, it can be concluded that the manual annotation of clinical free text for information extraction applications can be accelerated using an improved sample representation in an active learning framework. While this could seem intuitive, we have also shown that improvements demonstrated in a fully supervised framework do not necessarily translate into improvements in an active learning framework.

Reference

Boström, H., & Dalianis, H. (2012). De-identifying health records by means of active learning. *Recall (micro), 97*(97.55), 90-97.

Brown, P. F., deSouza, P. V., Mercer, R. L., Pietra, V. J. D., & Lai, J. C. (1992). Class-based n-gram models of natural language. *Comput. Linguist., 18*(4), 467-479.

Chen, Y., Lasko, T. A., Mei, Q., Denny, J. C., & Xu, H. (2015). A study of active learning methods for named entity recognition in clinical text. *Journal of Biomedical Informatics, 58*, 11-18.

Chen, Y., Mani, S., & Xu, H. (2012). Applying active learning to assertion classification of concepts in clinical text. *Journal of Biomedical Informatics, 45*(2), 265-272.

Culotta, A., & McCallum, A. (2005). Reducing labeling effort for structured prediction tasks. *Proceedings of the Twentieth National Conference on Artificial Intelligence (AAAI)* (pp. 746–751): AAAI Press.

De Bruijn, B., Cherry, C., Kiritchenko, S., Martin, J., & Zhu, X. (2011). Machine-learned solutions for three stages of clinical information extraction: the state of the art at i2b2 2010. *Journal of the American Medical Informatics Association, 18*(5), 557-562.

De Vine, L., Kholghi, M., Zuccon, G., Sitbon, L., & Nguyen, A. (2015). Analysis of word embeddings and sequence features for clinical information extraction. *Proceedings of Australasian Language Technology Association Workshop* (pp. 21-30).

Dietterich, T. G. (1998). Approximate statistical tests for comparing supervised classification learning algorithms. *Neural computation, 10*(7), 1895-1923.

Figueroa, R. L., Zeng-Treitler, Q., Ngo, L. H., Goryachev, S., & Wiechmann, E. P. (2012). Active learning for clinical text classification: is it better than random sampling? *Journal of the American Medical Informatics Association, 19*(5), 809-816.

Jonnalagadda, S., Cohen, T., Wu, S., & Gonzalez, G. (2012). Enhancing clinical concept extraction with distributional semantics. *Journal of Biomedical Informatics, 45*(1), 129-140.

Kanerva, P., Kristofersson, J., & Holst, A. (2000). Random indexing of text samples for latent semantic analysis. *Proceedings of the 22nd annual conference of the cognitive science society* (Vol. 1036).

Kholghi, M., Sitbon, L., Zuccon, G., & Nguyen, A. (2014). Factors influencing robustness and effectiveness of conditional random fields in active learning frameworks. *Proceedings of the 12th Australasian Data Mining Conference (AusDM 2014)* (Vol. 158): Conferences in Research and Practice in Information Technology, Australian Computer Society Inc.

Kholghi, M., Sitbon, L., Zuccon, G., & Nguyen, A. (2015). External knowledge and query strategies in active learning: a study in clinical information extraction. *Proceedings of the 24th ACM International on Conference on Information and Knowledge Management* (pp. 143-152). ACM.

Kholghi, M., Sitbon, L., Zuccon, G., & Nguyen, A. (2016). Active learning: a step towards automating medical concept extraction. *Journal of the American Medical Informatics Association, 23*(2), 289-296.

Lafferty, J. D., McCallum, A., & Pereira, F. C. N. (2001). Conditional Random Fields: Probabilistic Models for Segmenting and Labeling Sequence Data. *Proceedings of the Eighteenth International Conference on Machine Learning (ICML)* (pp. 282-289). San Francisco, CA, USA: Morgan Kaufmann Publishers Inc.

McCallum, A. K. (2002). MALLET: A Machine Learning for Language Toolkit. Retrieved from http://mallet.cs.umass.edu

Mikolov, T., Chen, K., Corrado, G., & Dean, J. (2013). Efficient estimation of word representations in vector space. *arXiv preprint arXiv:1301.3781.*

Nikfarjam, A., Sarker, A., O'Connor, K., Ginn, R., & Gonzalez, G. (2015). Pharmacovigilance from social media: mining adverse drug reaction mentions using sequence labeling with word embedding cluster features. *Journal of the American Medical Informatics Association, 22*(3), 671-681.

Ohno-Machado, L., Nadkarni, P., & Johnson, K. (2013). Natural language processing: algorithms and tools to extract computable information from EHRs and from the biomedical literature. *Journal of the American Medical Informatics Association, 20*(5), 805.

Pradhan, S., Elhadad, N., South, B., Martinez, D., Christensen, L., Vogel, A., Suominen, H., Chapman, W., & Savova, G. (2013). Task 1: ShARe/CLEF ehealth evaluation lab 2013. *CLEF 2013 Evaluation Labs and Workshops: Working Notes*: CLEF.

Settles, B. (2012). *Active learning* (Vol. 6): Morgan & Claypool Publishers.

Suominen, H., Salanterä, S., Velupillai, S., Chapman, W., Savova, G., Elhadad, N., Pradhan, S., South, B., Mowery, D., Jones, G. F., Leveling, J., Kelly, L., Goeuriot, L., Martinez, D., & Zuccon, G. (2013). Overview of the ShARe/CLEF eHealth Evaluation Lab 2013. In P. Forner, H. Müller, R. Paredes, P. Rosso & B. Stein (Eds.), *Information Access Evaluation. Multilinguality, Multimodality, and Visualization* (Vol. 8138, pp. 212-231): Springer Berlin Heidelberg.

Tang, B., Cao, H., Wu, Y., Jiang, M., & Xu, H. (2013). Recognizing clinical entities in hospital discharge summaries using structural support vector machines with word representation features. *BMC Medical Informatics and Decision Making, 13*(1), 1-10.

Tang, B., Wu, Y., Jiang, M., Denny, J. C., & Xu, H. (2013). Recognizing and Encoding Discorder Concepts in Clinical Text using Machine Learning and Vector Space Model. *Workshop of ShARe/CLEF eHealth Evaluation Lab 2013*.

Toutanova, K., Klein, D., Manning, C. D., & Singer, Y. (2003). Feature-rich part-of-speech tagging with a cyclic dependency network. *Proceedings of the 2003 Conference of the North American Chapter of the Association for Computational Linguistics on Human Language Technology* (Vol. 1, pp. 173-180): Association for Computational Linguistics.

Uzuner, Ö., Solti, I., & Cadag, E. (2010). Extracting medication information from clinical text. *Journal of the American Medical Informatics Association, 17*(5), 514-518.

Uzuner, Ö., South, B. R., Shen, S., & DuVall, S. L. (2011). 2010 i2b2/VA challenge on concepts, assertions, and relations in clinical text. *Journal of the American Medical Informatics Association, 18*(5), 552-556.

Voorhees, E. M., & Tong, R. (2011). Overview of the TREC 2011 medical records track. *Proceedings of Text REtrieval Conference (TREC)* (Vol. 4).

Syndromic Surveillance using Generic Medical Entities on Twitter

Pin Huang$^\diamond$, Andrew MacKinlay$^{\diamond\spadesuit}$ and Antonio Jimeno Yepes$^\diamond$
$^\diamond$ IBM Research – Australia, Melbourne, VIC, Australia
$^\spadesuit$ Dept of Computing and Information Systems, University of Melbourne, Australia
`pinhuang@outlook.com`, {`admackin,antonio.jimeno`}`@au1.ibm.com`

Abstract

Public health surveillance is challenging due to difficulties accessing medical data in real-time. We present a novel, effective and computationally inexpensive method for syndromic surveillance using Twitter data. The proposed method uses a regression model on a database previously built using named entity recognition to identify mentions of symptoms, disorders and pharmacological substances over GNIP Decahose Twitter data. The result of our method is compared to the reported weekly flu and Lyme disease rates from the US Center of Disease Control and Prevention (CDC) website. Our method predicts the 2014 CDC reported flu prevalence with 94.9% Spearman correlation using 2012 and 2013 CDC flu statistics as training data, and the CDC Lyme disease rate for July to December 2014 with 89.6% Spearman correlation. It also predicts the prevalences for the same diseases and time periods using the Twitter data from the previous week with 93.31% and 86.9% Spearman correlations respectively.

1 Introduction

Real-time public health surveillance for tasks such as syndromic surveillance is challenging due to difficulties accessing medical data. Twitter is a social media platform in which people share their views, opinions and their lives. Data from Twitter is accessible in real-time and it could potentially be used for syndromic surveillance. Even if only a small portion of the tweets contains potentially information about the health of Twitter users (Jimeno-Yepes et al., 2015a), there is still a large volume of data that could be useful for public health surveillance.

Several approaches to predict flu prevalences from Twitter data already exist. These approaches either rely on topic modelling (e.g. Latent Dirichlet Allocation (LDA) (Blei et al., 2003)) (Paul and Dredze, 2012; Paul and Dredze, 2011) or rely on regression models on keyword frequency (Culotta, 2010a; Culotta, 2010b).

The topic modelling approach for flu prevalence prediction requires manually labelling a large number of tweets (e.g. 5,128 tweets) that are used to train a Support Vector Machine (SVM) (Joachims, 1999) classifier applied on 11.7 million messages. The predictions on the tweets are applied on a LDA based topic model to over millions of tweets (Paul and Dredze, 2012; Paul and Dredze, 2011). Regression approaches (Culotta, 2010a; Culotta, 2010b) require prior knowledge to develop a keyword list {*flu,cough,sore throat,headache*} that could identify tweets relevant to flu.

In this paper, we propose an effective and computationally efficient alternative for disease prevalence prediction based on an already existing database developed by (Jimeno-Yepes et al., 2015b). Our approach to predict disease prevalence does not require manual labelling of Twitter posts to determine whether the posts are related to a particular disease or not. Our training dataset uses aggregated weekly term frequencies, so it is less computationally expensive to train compared to other approaches trained on millions of tweets. In addition, compared with regression approaches (Culotta, 2010a; Culotta, 2010b), no prior knowledge was used to manually develop a list of keywords indicative of a disease. Overall, we used our method to effectively predict the prevalence of flu and Lyme disease one week ahead of reported CDC data.

Pin Huang, Andrew MacKinlay and Antonio Jimeno Yepes. 2016. Syndromic Surveillance using Generic Medical Entities on Twitter. In *Proceedings of Australasian Language Technology Association Workshop*, pages 35–44.

2 Modelling weekly syndromic rate

2.1 Dataset Introduction

The Twitter data for years 2012, 2013 and 2014 was obtained from the GNIP Decahose,[1] which provides a random 10% selection of available tweets. From here, only English tweets were considered and retweets were removed.

Each tweet was annotated with three types of medical named entities: disorders, symptoms and pharmacological substances (PharmSub) (Jimeno-Yepes et al., 2015b). These entity types are defined using the UMLS (Unified Medical Language System) semantic types (Bodenreider, 2004). Recognition of entities was performed using a trained conditional random field annotator. Statistics on the annotated entities by this classifier for the first half year of 2014 is available from (Jimeno-Yepes et al., 2015a). Annotation of pharmacological substances is complemented by using a dictionary based annotator using terms from the UMLS.

Since just a small portion of tweets contain declared location information, posts containing medical entities were automatically geolocated using the method presented in (Han et al., 2012). This geolocation has been used to select tweets from the USA, since our reference is US CDC.

Based on the annotated tweets in USA, Twitter terms' counts are aggregated into a weekly basis; then the terms' counts are normalized by the weekly total number of the tweets. For three years data, the sample size of the dataset used for the prevalence prediction is 156, because only about 52 weeks per year.

The weekly terms' frequencies data set is then mapped to the weekly CDC's data. Three years' data are available for the flu prevalence prediction. While year 2013 and 2014's CDC data is available for Lyme Disease prevalence prediction, therefore, the dataset for Lyme disease is with 104 sample size.

2.2 Overall Architecture

The proposed methodology is a predictive model which aims to achieve the following goals:

- Predict reported CDC flu and Lyme disease trend using weekly term frequencies to predict syndromic weekly rates.

- Predict reported CDC flu and Lyme disease trend one week in advance using weekly term frequencies to predict the following week syndromic rates.

The overall architecture of the proposed methodology is shown in Figure 1. The first step is data preprocessing, followed by feature engineering and support vector machines (SVM) (Gunn and others, 1998) regression modelling.This regression model is trained to combine the engineered features from our Twitter database to perform syndromic prediction.

A major challenge of the first step is mapping Twitter terms with similar meanings from our database to a unique term. A mapping algorithm is proposed to map synonyms into a unique term.

After the synonyms mapping, a series of feature engineering methods are applied to engineer a final set of the most important features. Finally, prediction is made by using a trained SVM regression model on the final set of features.

Twitter Term	Concept	Entity Type
adrenal disease	adrenal disease	Disease
adrenal disorder	adrenal disease	Disease
adrenal gland disease	adrenal disease	Disease
adrenal gland disorder	adrenal disease	Disease
acne treatment	acne treatment	PharmSub
treatment acne	acne treatment	PharmSub
abdomen pain	abdominal pain	Symptom
abdominal pain	abdominal pain	Symptom
abdominal pains	abdominal pain	Symptom
gut pain	abdominal pain	Symptom

Table 1: A sample of Concept Mapping

EntityType	Found in UMLS	Not Found in UMLS
Disease	9162	19454
PharmSub	15891	23556
Symptom	2604	53142

Table 2: Unique Twitter entities found in UMLS

2.3 Twitter entity synonyms mapping

Terms in medical entities from our Twitter dataset may have the same meaning but different surface form, e.g. *vomit* and *throw up*. Treating these synonyms as different input features to a regression model may result in a performance bias. Aggregating weekly term counts for synonyms maximize the probability that each input feature is not highly correlated to each other.

Therefore, we propose a synonym mapping algorithm that uses the UMLS to map Twitter medical entity synonyms to a unique term. Table 2

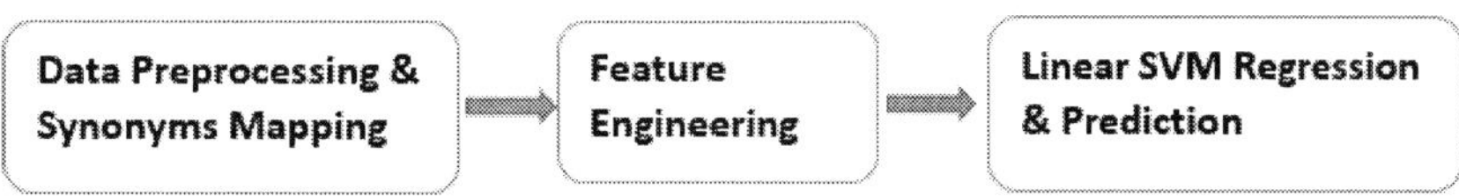

Figure 1: Overall Architecture

shows the statistics of how many Twitter entities could be found or not in UMLS. The unique term is considered to be a concept term for synonyms. In UMLS, medical terms with the same meanings are associated with one concept ID. Twitter terms are mapped to the UMLS medical terms in order to find concept IDs for the Twitter synonyms. A C sharp program is developed to automate this task. Details of the algorithm is explained as below.

As already mentioned, Twitter terms are annotated with three types of medical entities: symptoms, disorders and pharmacological substances. So based on the medical entity associated with each Twitter medical term, these terms are segmented into three groups: Symptom Terms, Disorder Terms and Pharmacological Substance Terms. In UMLS, each concept ID is associated to a TUI (Type Unique Identifier), indicating the semantic type of the concept ID. Three types of TUI are used for the synonyms mapping: symptom, disorder and pharmacological substances. Each group of the Twitter medical terms mentioned above are mapped to three types of concept IDs in UMLS respectively.

If a Twitter medical term can be found in the UMLS dataset and it is mapped to only one UMLS concept ID, the concept ID will be used as reference for the term. If the Twitter term cannot be found in UMLS, the term will be the reference concept for itself.

An advantage of mapping three types of Twitter terms separately is that when a term is associated with more than one UMLS concept ID, the medical entity type associated to the term may help to determine the most suitable UMLS concept ID that is from the same type. For example, a concept ID in UMLS is associated with two semantic types: symptom and disorder; a Twitter term annotated with the disorder entity is mapped to this concept ID. The medical entity type of the Twitter term helps the algorithm to determine the most suitable concept ID for the term is the UMLS concept ID associated with the disorder semantic type. But it could still be possible that a term is mapped

to more than one UMLS concept IDs. In this case, each UMLS concept ID is related one or more than one Twitter terms. The most appropriate concept ID for the Twitter term is the UMLS concept ID associated with a largest number of Twitter terms.

After determining the most suitable concept ID for each term, the algorithm continues to identify the best concept label for each concept ID. Using concept label instead of the ID helps us have a better understanding of the model outcomes.

A UMLS concept ID may be associated to more than one Twitter medical terms. The best label for a concept ID is a Twitter term that appears the most in the Twitter database. Table 1 shows a sample of the concept mapping.

2.4 Feature Engineering

After mapping synonyms to unique terms, the dataset contained 112,690 unique terms. A series of feature engineering steps are conducted to improve the computational efficiency and the predictive performance of our methodology. With the feature engineering, a set of the most important features is selected and mathematically reduced using Partial Least Square and Recursive Feature Elimination with SVM. These engineered features are the input features for the final regression model that is trained to predict weekly disease rates.

The architecture of the feature engineering is shown in Figure 2. We use a nested cross-validation strategy. The outer division is two-fold or three-fold, into a training dataset and a separate validation set. We then apply 10-fold CV to the training set of each outer fold.

Non frequent and irrelevant features are first removed. Partial Least Square (PLS) regression (Abdi, 2003) is then applied to reduce the number of dimensions. Different number of PLS components are computed from PLS. A dimension reduction technique of selecting the optimal number of PLS components is proposed in later subsection. With the optimal number of components selected from PLS, each feature's 'Variable Importance of Project (VIP)' (Wold and others, 1995) is

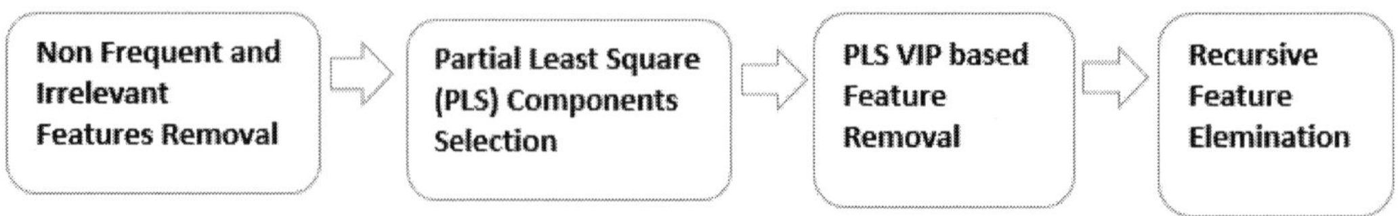

Figure 2: Feature Engineering Workflow.

Algorithm 1 Pseudocode of Selecting The Optimal Number of PLS Components

---

```
1: N = Maximum Number of Components resulted from PLS
2: MC = Maximum Validation Correlation
3: BN = Selected Optimal Number of Components
4: for n = 1, n = n+1, n <= N do
5:      Let Validation Correlation be the correlation for the outer
        validation dataset
6:      Validation Correlation = Cor(Predicted Result,CDC Rates of
        validation set)
7:    if MC < Validation Correlation then
8:        MC = Validation Correlation
9:        BN = n
10:    end if
11: end for
12: Return MC, BN
```

---

calculated. Wold and others (1995) suggest that features with very low VIP are unimportant and can be removed. A PLS VIP based feature removal technique is proposed to further remove non important features. Recursive Feature Elimination using Support Vector Machines (SVM) (Guyon et al., 2002; Gunn and others, 1998) is then used to retrieve the final set of the most important features.

2.4.1 Non Frequent and Irrelevant Features Removal

Non frequent unique terms tend to have zero variance in the dataset, which do not significantly impact the prediction outcome. Therefore, unique terms were removed if they appeared in less than 30 tweets in our dataset. This threshold was selected based on the examination of a histogram to determine the cutoff point to exclude the "long tail" of terms while still retaining important terms likely to be useful for our modelling process. Applying this cutoff the number of unique concept terms is reduced from 112,690 to 8,525. However, the number of the features is still far more than the number of samples in the reference CDC dataset (8,525 features vs 52 weeks per year each year in our study). Recent studies have shown that

PLS is able to deal with datasets with more features than the sample size (Li and Zeng, 2009), therefore PLS is our first preferred algorithm to train the dataset. It has been shown that PLSs predictive performance will be improved if the irrelevant features are removed beforehand (Li et al., 2007). Our approach to determine irrelevant features is different to Li et al. (2007). In this paper, the PLS's predictive performance is considered to the correlation between the predictive CDC weekly rates and the actual CDC weekly rates. We apply Pearson correlation to determine irrelevant features. Pearson correlation measures linear relationship between two sets of variables. For each input feature, the correlation between the feature's weekly frequency and the CDC's weekly rates is calculated in the training set. If the correlation is less than 0.1, it is assumed that the linear relationship between the feature and the CDC rates is very weak, so the feature is regarded as irrelevant and removed. The remaining set of relevant features are used as input features for the next step.

2.4.2 PLS Components Selection

With a set of relevant features obtained from previous step, the PLS algorithm is applied to the train-

Algorithm 2 Pseudocode of VIP Based Feature Removal

```
1: T = {T₁,..Tᵢ,...Tₙ} as the collection of VIP Threshold
2: T₁ =0.02, Tₙ=1
3: MaxValCor = Maximum Validation Correlation among each Tᵢ in T
4: BestVIPThreshold = VIP threshold associated with MaxValCor
5: for  Tᵢ = 0.02, Tᵢ = Tᵢ+ 0.02, Tᵢ <=1 do
6:     Remove features with VIP < Tᵢ
7:     Run PLS on the dataset, and let MC be the 'Maximum Validation
   Correlation among PLS Components'
8:     MC = result of running Pseudocode of Selecting The Number of
   PLS Components
9:     if MaxValCor < MC  then
10:         MaxValCor = MC
11:         BestVIPThreshold = Tᵢ
12:     end if
13: end for
```

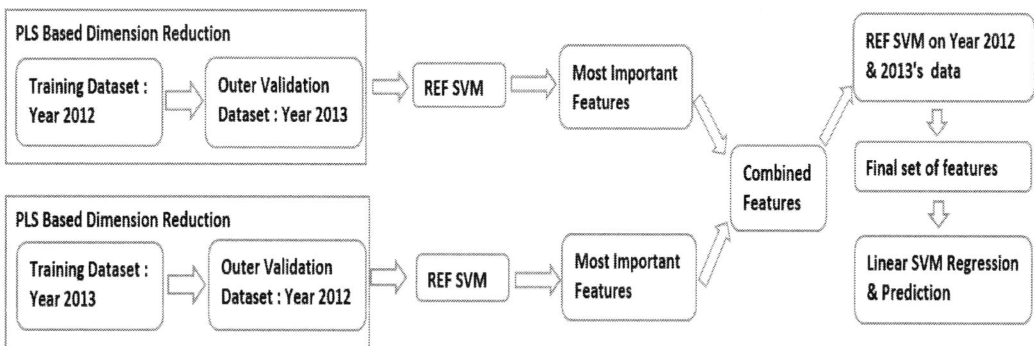

Figure 3: Flu Trend Prediction Experiment Work Flow

ing dataset with a 10-fold cross validation (Results of this are not shown in the paper). Different number of components are created by applying PLS. In order to select the optimal number of components from PLS, the "outer" validation set (from the outer CV and separate to training) is used to validate the predictive performance of applying different number of PLS components. The term 'outer validation set' is used in the later sections to refer to the validation set that is separate to the training set. The optimal number of PLS components is selected based on the maximum correlation among all components on the validation set.

Algorithm 1 shows pseudocode of a selection process to determine the optimal number of PLS components with the best predictive performance on the validation set. A loop of calculating the correlation for the validation set by using all number of PLS components is used in Algorithm 1.

2.4.3 PLS VIP based Feature Removal

With the selected number of PLS components, each input feature's VIP is calculated. Features' VIP values are only valid for the selected set of PLS components; they would be different if a different set of PLS components was selected. Each feature's VIP value is related to the feature's weights for each latent component and the variance explained by each latent component. Formula for the j_{th} feature's VIP calculation is shown below (Wold and others, 1995; Mehmood et al., 2011), where N is the number of features, m is the number of PLS latent components, w_{mj} is the PLS weight of the j_{th} feature for the m_{th} latent component, P_m is the percentage of the response factor (in our experiment, it is CDC weekly disease rate) explained by the m_{th} latent component:

$$VIP_j = \sqrt{\frac{N}{\sum_{m=1}^{M} \cdot P_m} \sum_{m=1}^{M} w_{mj}^2 \cdot P_m}$$

Features' VIP values are used to determine whether the feature should be removed or not. If a feature's VIP is less than a particular threshold, this feature is removed before applying PLS again to train the dataset.

We set the VIP threshold using the following methodology: Values from 0.02 to 1 are considered. We use 1 as the maximum possible, as heuristically anything greater indicates that the feature is important (Cassotti and Grisoni, 2012). The optimal VIP threshold is determined by running a loop, in which different VIP threshold values ranging from 0.02 to 1 are all used to remove features. Let $T = T_1,..T_i,...T_n$ be a collection of VIP thresholds, n is the number of thresholds, T_i is the i_{t_h} threshold in T. For each T_i ($1 \leq i \leq n$) in T, features with VIP less than T_i are removed, then PLS is used to train on the rest of features, which results in different number of PLS components. The optimal number of PLS components is selected if it has the maximum value of correlation for the outer validation dataset. This outer validation set is the same dataset used in previous step. These components are the representation for the best result produced by removing features with VIP lower than T_i. The optimal VIP threshold in T is the one that yields the maximum correlation for the outer validation dataset. Pseudocode for VIP Based Feature Removal is shown in Algorithm 2. Any features with VIP less than the selected optimal VIP threshold are not included for the next step.

2.4.4 Recursive Feature Elimination (RFE)

In terms of the computational cost, if hundreds of features resulted from the previous step are input features for RFE, it might take too much time for RFE to present results. Therefore, if the number of features is greater than 200, features with VIP less than 0.2 are removed before applying RFE. The reduced number of features are then used as input features for linear SVM based RFE (Guyon et al., 2002; Gunn and others, 1998). Five times ten fold cross validation is used for RFE with SVM. Features selected from RFE with SVM is the final set of features, which are the input feature for the next step.

2.5 Linear SVM Regression and Prediction

After feature engineering, an SVM regression model with a linear kernel function (Gunn and others, 1998) is trained on the most important features

selected from previous RFE. The final prediction is made using this SVM regression model.

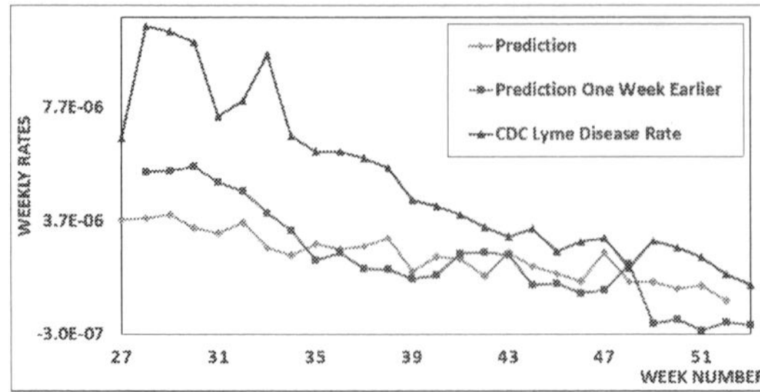

Figure 5: Second Half Year of 2014 predicted weekly Lyme Disease rates versus US CDC

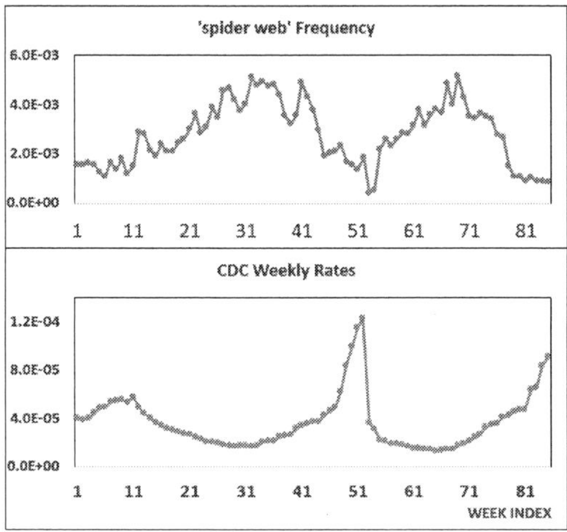

Figure 6: Weekly frequency of *spider web* versus US CDC weekly flu rate

3 Experimental Results

In this section, we show results for flu prevalence prediction for the year 2014, as well as Lyme disease prevalence prediction for the second half year of 2014, based both on the current week's data as well as using posts from a week in advance to evaluate the possibility of getting a signal earlier. Data from 2012 and 2013 is used as the training set, year 2014's weekly data is used to predict the weekly flu rates of the year 2014. For Lyme disease prediction, only 18 months of data (from 2013 to the first half of 2014) is available as the training set for Lyme disease prevalence prediction.

Two fold cross validation is used for feature tuning for flu prevalence. Figure 3 shows details of

	Stage	Training Set	Validation / Test Set	Features For PLS	VIP Feature Removal	VIP > 0.2	RFE SVM
Flu, current	1st	2012	2013	5353	412	103	61
	2nd	2013	2012	5353	992	154	74
	Final	2012, 2013	2014	–	–	–	22
Flu, one week in advance	1st	2012	2013	5060	141	–	141
	2nd	2013	2012	5060	78	–	77
	Final	2012, 2013	2014	–	–	–	21
Lyme Disease, current	1st	2013 H1, 2013 H2	2014 H1	6139	693	103	22
	2nd	2013 H1, 2014 H1	2013 H2	6139	65	–	35
	3rd	2013 H2, 2014 H1	2013 H1	6139	627	105	24
	Final	2013, 2014 H1	2014 H2	–	–	–	41
Lyme Disease, one week in advance	1st	2013 H1, 2013 H2	2014 H1	6076	63	–	21
	2nd	2013 H1, 2014 H1	2013 H2	6076	61	–	36
	3rd	2013 H2, 2014 H1	2013 H1	6076	167	–	67
	Final	2013, 2014 H1	2014 H2	6076	–	–	54

Table 3: Number of Input Features After Each Dimension Reduction

	Testing Period	Pearson Correlation	Spearman Correlation	R^2	RMSE
Flu, current	2014	92.4%	94.9%	85.3%	1.51E-05
	2014 H1	96.3%	96.6%	92.7%	1.06E-05
	2014 H2	94.8%	92.3%	89.8%	1.90E-05
Flu, one week in advance	2014	91.3%	93.3%	83.3%	1.55E-05
	2014 H1	91.6%	94.6%	84.0%	1.41E-05
	2014 H2	96.0%	92.3%	92.1%	1.69E-05
Lyme Disease, current	2014 H2	86.6%	89.6%	75%	3.41E-06
Lyme Disease, one week in advance	2014 H2	90.32%	86.9%	81.6%	3.02E-06

Table 4: Flu and Lyme Disease trend prediction results

the flu trend prediction experiment. When data from 2012 is used for training, data from 2013 is used as an outer validation set, and vice versa. After PLS based dimension reduction, RFE with SVM is applied to obtain the most important features from each fold. Another round of RFE with SVM is applied to train on the year 2012 and 2013's data with all unique input features selected from the previous step. This results in a final input feature set, and then a regression based SVM with linear kernel function is trained using 2012 and 2013 data. Finally, prediction of weekly flu rates of the year 2014 is made from the trained SVM.

For Lyme disease, we have only two years of CDC data (2013 and 2014) which overlap with our dataset of NER-tagged tweets. We set aside 2013 and the first 6 months of 2014 as for training and feature tuning, keeping the final six months for testing. We use three-fold cross-validation for feature tuning. With each fold, six months of data is used as an outer validation set, with the remainder used as a training set. Similar to the flu trend experiment procedure shown in Figure 3, important features selected from each cross-validation

round are all included for another round of feature reduction by using RFE with SVM. With the final feature set determined by RFE with SVM, an SVM with a linear kernel function is then trained on the training set to make the final prediction for the Lyme disease trend for the second half of 2014.

3.1 Results of Flu and Lyme Disease Trend Prediction and Detection

Table 3 shows number of features being reduced after each step of dimension reduction. After VIP based feature removal, if the number of features exceeds 200, only features with VIP greater than 0.2 are selected. Otherwise, these features are the input features for the next step.

Experimental results for flu and Lyme disease trend prediction are presented in Table 4. Both Pearson and Spearman correlations are included. Pearson correlation measures the linear relationship between two sets of variables, while Spearman correlation measures correlation between two set of ranked variables, which is used to check whether one variable increases, the other increases or not. Therefore, Spearman correlation is used in this paper as an alternative measurement to ex-

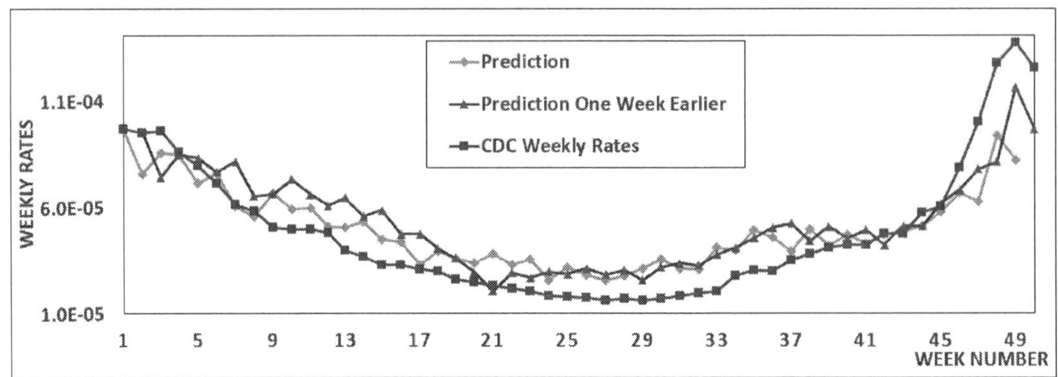

Figure 4: Year 2014 predicted weekly flu rates versus the US CDC weekly flu rates.

Flu, Current	'stomach flu' 'pneumonia' 'bronchitis' 'coughing' 'sick' 'cough medicine' 'cold sore' 'cough syrup' 'sickness' 'cold' 'red nose' 'fever' 'sinus infection' 'ear infection' 'body ache' 'blush' 'spider web' 'throat hurt' 'aching' 'strep throat' 'alcide' 'gelato'
Flu, In Advance	'stomach flu' 'pneumonia' 'bronchitis' 'coughing' 'sick' 'cough medicine' 'red nose' 'cough syrup' 'cold sore' 'cold' 'sickness' 'sinus infection' 'aloe' 'ear infection' 'fever' 'spider web' 'sleepy' 'aching' 'body ache' 'sore' 'seeing double'
Lyme Disease, Current	'coughing' 'bronchitis' 'pneumonia' 'runny nose' 'stuffy nose' 'cold' 'stomach flu' 'sick' 'throat hurt' 'sinus infection'
Lyme Disease, In Advance	'cold' 'coughing' 'pneumonia' 'bronchitis' 'runny nose' 'stuffy nose' 'sick' 'stress' 'aloe' 'stomach flu' 'sinus infection' 'caffeine' 'shaking' 'snoring' 'fart' 'concussion' 'throw up' 'migraine' 'dizzy' 'sore throat'

Table 5: Important Features for Flu and Lyme Disease Trend Prediction

amine similarities among downward or upward movements of the predicted trend and the CDC trend.

When making flu prevalence predictions for the first half, second half and the whole year of 2014, Spearman correlations are 96.6%, 92.3% and 94.9% respectively. The first half year's Spearman correlation is higher than the second half year. When the proposed methodology is used to predict flu trend one week earlier, the first half year's Spearman correlation (with 94.6%) is higher than the second half (with 92.3%). This means the final set of the most important features selected tends to represent more for the first half year's flu prevalence than the second half of year 2014. The Spearman correlation for predicting flu trend one week before CDC for the year 2014 is 93.5%, which indicates that the proposed methodology has some advance predictive power ahead of the CDC data, which is inherently less timely due to delays in collection. Figure 4 illustrates predicted flu prevalence against current CDC data as well as one week before.

For Lyme disease, as shown in Table 4, the Pearson correlation between the predicted prevalence and CDC weekly rates is 86.6%, while the Spearman correlation is higher, as 89.6%. A few weeks at the end of the year are predicted with negative rates, contributing to a relatively low Pearson correlation; without considering the last five weeks, the Pearson correlation increases to 93.3%. The relatively high Spearman correlation for Lyme disease has indicated that the upward or downward trends are well predicted. The Spearman correlation of detecting Lyme disease trend one week before CDC is 86.9%, which is lower than for the current week but still shows that a useful signal is being predicted. Predicted Lyme disease prevalence and CDC-reported Lyme disease weekly rates are shown in Figure 5.

The most important features selected by the proposed methodology for flu and Lyme disease trend predictions are presented in Table 5. Most of the features for flu prevalence prediction are reasonable, such as *coughing*, *cold* and *fever*, which are flu symptoms. However, *spider web* has been ranked as one of the features for flu prediction which appears in our database because *spider web* appears as a pharmacological substance in the UMLS. The weekly term frequency for *spider web* is highly negatively correlated to CDC weekly flu rates as shown in Figure 6, due to many spider webs being observed in the Northern hemisphere in September, close to the low point of the flu season. *Gelato* is also detected as relevant for a similar reason, due to an coincidental (negative) correlation with the flu season. *Gelato* has been wrongly annotated by our system as a pharmacological substance since in the UMLS it refers *gelato sodium fluoride* instead of *ice cream*.

Table 5 shows the most important features for Lyme disease prevalence prediction. Many features selected are very similar to flu symptoms, in line with many symptoms of Lyme disease matching those of flu;[2] in addition, *dizzy* matches a Lyme disease symptom. However, overall the term list for Lyme disease is less convincing than for flu, with more symptoms of Lyme disease missed and more terms included with no immediately obvious relationship to the disease. It seems that the relative rarity of Lyme disease is leading to noisier signal in tweets about its symptoms.

4 Discussion

The proposed methodology is an effective approach to predict prevalences for influenza and Lyme disease based on social media posts. It predicts flu prevalences for 2014 with Pearson correlations range from 92.4% to 96.3%. Similar results have been reported with other existing approaches for flu prevalence prediction: Paul and Dredze (2012) and Paul and Dredze (2011) predicted flu rate from August 2009 to May 2010 with Pearson correlations of 95.8% and 93.4% respectively; Culotta (2010a) made predictions for flu rate from September 2009 to May 2010 with 95% Pearson correlation. However, our method has some advantages over these, as they require labour-intensive manual labelling of tweets and significant computational resources to train their system using millions of data samples, in contrast with the method proposed here, where the only computationally-intensive step is a one-off step (reusable for other diseases and other kinds of analytics) of applying an NER tagger to a large Twitter corpus. In addition, Culotta (2010a) presented a method that requires prior knowledge to manually identify flu-related key words. Here, a manually pre-built keyword list is not required as the most important features related to flu are au-

tomatically selected based on the data. We also show that our method can predict disease prevalence with some reliability in a small time window ahead of the reported CDC figures, which has potential utility for real-time disease monitoring and alerts.

Our method is somewhat generalisable, with roughly the same approach achieving good correlations against CDC data for Lyme disease. An existing approach to track Lyme disease (Seifter et al., 2010) requires knowledge to select key words from Google trends, but there is no evaluation provided. To our knowledge there is relatively little other work on Lyme disease surveillance so this application is somewhat novel. However, accuracy for Lyme disease was weaker than for flu, in terms of raw correlations as well as basic plausibility checks on the most important indicative terms – canonical indicators such as the erythema migrans rash did not make the list. An important factor is probably the lower overall prevalence of the disease (an average of 1500 reported to the CDC per week in our test set versus 15,000 for flu), there are fewer instances of Twitter users experiencing the disease and the relevant symptoms, which they could then tweet about.

This hints a limitation of the method we have developed. Terms showing a natural seasonal fluctuation but are not indicative of disease (such as *gelato*) happen to coincide with a disease may accidentally come out as important terms in the analysis. One way to mitigate this would be to improve the accuracy of the named entity tagging in the source data.

Future extensions may also be generalisable to other regions with a high number of English-language tweets.

5 Conclusion

We have presented an effective methodology which produce predictions for flu and Lyme disease prevalences with strong or moderate correlations with current CDC figures for the whole of the US, and those of a week later and we expect the approach to be somewhat generalisable across diseases and regions.

References

Hervé Abdi. 2003. Partial least square regression (pls regression). *Encyclopedia for research methods for the social sciences*, pages 792–795.

---

[2]http://www.cdc.gov/lyme/signs_symptoms/

David M Blei, Andrew Y Ng, and Michael I Jordan. 2003. Latent dirichlet allocation. *Journal of machine Learning research*, 3(Jan):993–1022.

Olivier Bodenreider. 2004. The unified medical language system (umls): integrating biomedical terminology. *Nucleic acids research*, 32(suppl 1):D267–D270.

Matteo Cassotti and Francesca Grisoni. 2012. Variable selection methods: an introduction.

Aron Culotta. 2010a. Detecting influenza outbreaks by analyzing twitter messages. *arXiv preprint arXiv:1007.4748*.

Aron Culotta. 2010b. Towards detecting influenza epidemics by analyzing twitter messages. In *Proceedings of the first workshop on social media analytics*, pages 115–122. ACM.

Steve R Gunn et al. 1998. Support vector machines for classification and regression. *ISIS technical report*, 14.

Isabelle Guyon, Jason Weston, Stephen Barnhill, and Vladimir Vapnik. 2002. Gene selection for cancer classification using support vector machines. *Machine learning*, 46(1-3):389–422.

Bo Han, Timothy Baldwin, and Paul Cook. 2012. Geolocation prediction in social media data by finding location indicative words. *Proceedings of COLING 2012: Technical Papers*, pages 1045–1062.

Antonio Jimeno-Yepes, Andrew MacKinlay, and Bo Han. 2015a. Investigating public health surveillance using twitter. *ACL-IJCNLP 2015*, page 164.

Antonio Jimeno-Yepes, Andrew MacKinlay, Bo Han, and Qiang Chen. 2015b. Identifying diseases, drugs, and symptoms in twitter. *Studies in health technology and informatics*, 216:643–647.

Thorsten Joachims. 1999. Svmlight: Support vector machine. *SVM-Light Support Vector Machine http://svmlight. joachims. org/, University of Dortmund*, 19(4).

Guo-Zheng Li and Xue-Qiang Zeng. 2009. Feature selection for partial least square based dimension reduction. In *Foundations of Computational Intelligence Volume 5*, pages 3–37. Springer.

Guo-Zheng Li, Xue-Qiang Zeng, Jack Y Yang, and Mary Qu Yang. 2007. Partial least squares based dimension reduction with gene selection for tumor classification. In *2007 IEEE 7th International Symposium on BioInformatics and BioEngineering*, pages 1439–1444. IEEE.

Tahir Mehmood, Harald Martens, Solve Sæbø, Jonas Warringer, and Lars Snipen. 2011. A partial least squares based algorithm for parsimonious variable selection. *Algorithms for Molecular Biology*, 6(1):1.

Michael J Paul and Mark Dredze. 2011. You are what you tweet: Analyzing twitter for public health. *ICWSM*, 20:265–272.

Michael J Paul and Mark Dredze. 2012. A model for mining public health topics from twitter. *Health*, 11:16–6.

Ari Seifter, Alison Schwarzwalder, Kate Geis, and John Aucott. 2010. The utility of google trends for epidemiological research: Lyme disease as an example. *Geospatial health*, 4(2):135–137.

S Wold et al. 1995. Pls for multivariate linear modeling. *Chemometric methods in molecular design*, 2:195.

Syndromic Surveillance through Measuring Lexical Shift in Emergency Department Chief Complaint Texts

Hafsah Aamer, Bahadorreza Ofoghi, Karin Verspoor
Department of Computing and Information Systems
The University of Melbourne
Parkville Victoria 3010, Australia
`haamer@student.unimelb.edu.au`
`bahadorreza.ofoghi@unimelb.edu.au`
`karin.verspoor@dunimelb.edu.au`

Abstract

Syndromic Surveillance has been performed using machine learning and other statistical methods to detect disease outbreaks. These methods are largely dependent on the availability of historical data to train the machine learning-based surveillance system. However, relevant training data may differ from region to region due to geographical and seasonal trends, meaning that the syndromic surveillance designed for one area may not be effective for another. We proposed and analyse a semi-supervised method for syndromic surveillance from emergency department chief complaint textual notes that avoids the need for large training data. Our new method is based on identification of lexical shifts in the language of Chief Complaints of patients, as recorded by triage nurses, that we believe can be used to monitor disease distributions and possible outbreaks over time. The results we obtained demonstrate that effective lexical syndromic surveillance can be approached when distinctive lexical items are available to describe specific syndromes.

1   Introduction

The increase in new emerging pathogenic diseases like SAARS, Ebola, and the Zika virus requires an ongoing effective syndromic surveillance system. A syndromic surveillance system keeps track of the frequency of patients experiencing specific syndromes over time. Any abnormality in the normal trend of syndromes with respect to time may imply a proximal disease outbreak.

There are many data sources that can be used to perform syndromic surveillance, such as data from hospital emergency departments. Chief complaints provide us with one such rich data source to perform syndromic surveillance. A chief complaint is the set of signs and symptoms that the triage nurse registers upon a patient's arrival at the emergency department of a hospital. The symptoms are usually described in a terse, ungrammatical, and abbreviated language. Once the chief complaint is registered at the initial assessment, the patient sees the doctor and receives a detailed check up. This may include sending the patient's specimen for testing in the laboratory especially when dealing with a potentially dangerous infectious disease. The results from the laboratory tests may take days before the end result is available and by then, there is a large risk of spreading the disease to other people who may come in contact with the infected person.

Chief complaints are readily available in a digital format and can therefore be easily processed using natural language processing algorithms. In the past, various work has been done to perform syndromic surveillance using supervised machine learning and statistical algorithms (Tsui et al., 2003; Espino et al., 2007; Chapman et al., 2005; Bradley et al., 2005). The major drawback of machine learning methods is the requirement of historical data that can be used to train the system, and a sensitivity to the characteristics of specific text types (Baldwin et al., 2013). In the case of syndromic surveillance, there is evidence of a need for localized training data; as Ofoghi and Verspoor (2015) found, a machine learning classifier trained on an American data set may not be effective on an Australian data set. The authors found that the American off-the-shelf syndromic classifier (CoCo) achieved a lower F-score on the Australian data set compared with another classifier (SyCo) that was trained with the Australian data set. Moreover, there may be a lack of resources to collect ongoing data for chief complaints, especially in remote areas. Therefore, there is a need for a surveillance system that can work without the

Hafsah Aamer, Bahadorreza Ofoghi and Karin Verspoor. 2016. Syndromic Surveillance through Measuring Lexical Shift in Emergency Department Chief Complaint Texts. In *Proceedings of Australasian Language Technology Association Workshop*, pages 45–53.

availability of historical data for a long period of time.

In this work, rather than using machine learning algorithms to classify the new chief complaint of a patient into pre-defined syndromic groups, we explored the lexical content of chief complaints over time, specifically the changes in the distribution of terms, that may indicate an impending event. We hypothesise that when the probability distribution of terms in chief complaints of consecutive time-frames exhibits a large divergence, then there has been a measurable change in the trend of syndromes, which can be used for detecting an outbreak. The Jensen-Shannon Divergence (JSD) (Lin, 1991), also known as information radius, between consecutive time-frames over a chief complaint corpus was used in combination with CUSUM (Cumulative Sum) algorithms (Fricker Jr et al., 2008) to detect any aberrancy in the data. We also experiment with the text segmentation algorithm Link Set Median (LSM) (Hoey, 1991) to find segmentations in the chief complaints texts, as a proxy for lexical shift.

The remainder of this paper is organized as follows. We first describe the *SynSurv* data set used for our experiments. Then, the three different types of time-frames necessary to perform our lexical analyses will be introduced. This is followed by the discussion of how we modeled chief complaints for textual analysis using statistical methods. Finally, we discuss the utilization of abnormality detection algorithms and the results obtained in our experiments.

2   The SynSurv Data Set

The Syndromic Surveillance (SynSurv) data we used for our analyses was collected from two of the main hospitals in Melbourne, Australia; the Royal Melbourne Hospital and the Alfred Hospital. The data was collected on behalf of the Victorian Department of Health, initially to enable monitoring during the 2006 Commonwealth Games held in Melbourne. The data contains 314,630 chief complaints labeled with a syndromic group as well as with disease codes in the ICD-10 and SNOMED terminologies. The original SynSurv data set contained data with respect to eight syndromes *Flu-Like Illness*, *Diarrhea*, *Septic Shock*, *Acute Flaccid Paralysis*, *Acute Respiratory*, *Radiation Injury*, *Fever with CNS*, and *Rash with Fever*. Due to the sparsity of data for many of the syn-

dromes in the data, we chose the top three with the highest numbers of positive cases in the SynSurv data, i.e., *Flu-Like Illness*, *Diarrhea*, and *Acute Respiratory*.

Chief complaints differ from the majority of other free text that can be found in textual documents or social media posts in that they contain medical acronyms, abbreviations, as well as numeric values representing body temperature, blood pressure, and the like. They are notes entered by the triage nurses lacking well-defined linguistic structure. Therefore, some preprocessing was carried out on the set of chief complaints.

We approached the chief complaint preprocessing task first by lowercasing, lemmatization using Stanford Lemmatizer, and removing stop words and the already assigned ICD-10 and SNOMED disease codes from the end of the chief complaint strings. These are the disease codes assigned to each chief complaint upon a patient's discharge. We removed these codes to retain the chief complaint texts in their original format. We also removed all the non-alphanumeric symbols except "/", which plays a meaningful role in the medical domains. For instance, blood pressure is recorded as two numbers, as 120/80, the first number representing systolic blood pressure and the second number representing diastolic blood pressure. If we remove "/", this numeric reading becomes "12080" or "120 80" which results in a loss of information; neither choice may define a good feature to represent a chief complaint with a specific syndrome. In addition, the same symbol "/" is used for shorthand notations while making notes, for example, the chief complaint texts heavily contained "o/a" meaning "overall pale". Other notations included: "r/a", "p/s", "c/o", and "r/t". We also observed that the use of such notation depended on the nurse's own preference; while there were many chief complaints with "o/a" there were also many occurrences of "o a" without the symbol "/" in between the characters. This meant we could not target all the notations consistently.

However, we did not remove any numeric values from the chief complaints because numeric values may be relevant for diagnosing a syndrome. For example, body temperature is one of the main recordings that a doctor (or a nurse) takes when a patient visits the emergency department to observe if there is a serious illness.

3 The Choice of Time-Frame

The number of patients that visit emergency departments varies between weekdays and weekends and also seasonally. To cater for such day-of-the-week and seasonal trends, we used different time-frames to accumulate chief complaints, some of which normalize the frequencies of chief complaints over longer (seven-day) periods. We experimented with the following three time-frames:

Intersecting seven-day windows

The chief complaints over seven days were accumulated as one time-frame window; then, this time-frame window was advanced by one day. The seven-day time-frame windows cater for the varying frequency of patients visiting over weekdays and weekends. The one-day shifting time-frame is popular for supervised syndromic surveillance as it allows for real-time syndromic surveillance at the end of each day (Hutwagner et al., 2003). Note that for lexical shift analysis with seven-day windows shifting by one day, there is a large vocabulary overlap for the six intersecting days; however, the variance would be significant enough to be captured by aberrancy detection algorithms that will be discussed later.

Disjoint seven-day windows

The chief complaints over seven days were accumulated as one time-frame corpus; then, the time-frame was advanced by seven days so the two consecutive windows were disjoint.

Disjoint one-day windows

In this case, all of the chief complaints in a day formed one time-frame corpus of chief complaints. The time shift was for one day and therefore, the chief complaints in the next day formed the next time-frame corpus. Although this time-frame does not normalize day-of-the-week variances, we incorporated this type in order to find some daily patterns in the SynSurv data set.

4 Textual Modeling of Chief Complaints

We examine the distribution of lexical items in chief complaints to find the differences in the terminology used in consecutive time-frames. For this, statistical methods were utilized, as will be discussed in the following sections. Such statistical methods have been previously used for corpus analysis and comparison (Verspoor et al., 2009; Rayson and Garside, 2000). We follow that prior work here, considering chief complaints in the consecutive time-frames as separate corpora to be compared with each other.

4.1 Jensen-Shannon Divergence

The Jensen-Shannon divergence, also known as Information Radius, is a symmetric measure that measures the similarity between two probability distributions P and Q over the same event space. The JSD between the two probability distributions P and Q is a symmetrized and smoothed version of the Kullback-Leibler Divergence (KLD) and is calculated using Equation 1.

$$JSD(P\|Q) = \frac{1}{2}D(P\|M) + \frac{1}{2}D(Q\|M) \quad (1)$$

where, $M = \frac{1}{2}(P+Q)$ and D represents the KLD distance between the two probability distributions; on a finite set χ is calculated using Equation 2.

$$D(P\|Q) = \sum_{x \in \chi} P(x) \log_n \frac{P(x)}{Q(x)} \quad (2)$$

When modeling the chief complaint corpora, the union set of the vocabularies of two corpora to be compared was constructed ($V = V_{c_1} \cup V_{c_2}$), where (c_1) and (c_2) were the chief complaint corpora belonging to the two consecutive time-frames. P and Q represent the probability of corpus terms. Since JSD inherently performs probability smoothing, to find the probability distribution of each term t_k over V_{c_i} for each corpus, the conditional probability of term t_k in each corpus was calculated using Equation 3, based on the raw term frequencies (tf) of the terms in c_i.

$$P(t_k|c_i) = \frac{tf(t_k, c_i)}{\sum_{t_x \in V_{c_i}} tf(t_x, c_i)} \quad (3)$$

4.2 Log-Likelihood for Term-Level Filtering

When two corpora are lexically compared with each other, especially in the case of overlapping time-frames, they may share a large number of terms. Therefore, calculating probability distributions over the entire union set of terms contained in the text of the two corpora may not be an effective method, as all the terms will have equal importance. In this case, there is a need for filtering out the terms that do not distinguish the two corpora well (i.e., terms that are common in both corpora).

The log-likelihood score of a term represents the relative frequency difference of that term in the two different corpora under comparison (Rayson and Garside, 2000). This measure is calculated based on the expected value for term $t_k \in V$ using the total frequency of all terms in the corpus and the actual frequency (or the sum of occurrences) of term t_k in the same corpus. Equation 4 shows how the log-likelihood score is calculated for $t_k \in V$ where N_{c_i} is the total frequency of all terms in corpus c_i, and O_{t_k,c_i} represents the observed frequency of term t_k in the same corpus c_i.

$$E_{t_k,c_i} = \frac{N_{c_i} \sum_i O_{t_k,c_i}}{\sum_i N_{c_i}} \qquad (4)$$

The expected frequency of term t_k in corpus c_i denoted by E_{t_k,c_i} is a frequency that is expected for t_k if the occurrences were evenly distributed across the two corpora (Verspoor et al., 2009). The log-likelihood of the term is therefore a measure that tells us how different the actual frequency of the term is from the expected frequency of the same term. For this, the log-likelihood is calculated using Equation 5.

$$LL = 2 \sum_i \left(O_{t_k,c_i} \ln\left(\frac{O_{t_k,c_i}}{E_{t_k,c_i}}\right) \right) \qquad (5)$$

An alternative to the log-likelihood measure for statistical analysis of textual corpora is Pearson's χ^2 statistic. This measure assumes a normal distribution of terms in the corpora and has been shown in (Dunning, 1993) to be less reliable especially in the case of small textual corpora with rare terms. Given the relatively small size of the chief complaint corpora for each time-frame, the log-likelihood analysis was preferred here.

Once the log-likelihood of each term was calculated, all of the terms with the log-likelihood below a set threshold were filtered out. The texts of the two corpora now contained only the most important terms that participated in the calculation of probability distributions using JSD.

To estimate the best log-likelihood threshold, we calculated the JSD between consecutive time-frames when filtering terms based on different log-likelihood thresholds ranging from 0 to 20. Since we were not comparing two distinct corpora (cf., (Rayson and Garside, 2000; Baldwin et al., 2013)) but consecutive time-frames over a single corpus, we calculated the JSD values between all of the consecutive time-frames and then

took the mean of all JSD values for each possible log-likelihood threshold value. It can be seen from Figure 1 that as the threshold increases, more terms are filtered out and eventually, hardly any terms remain and the divergence between consecutive time-frames approaches zero. A threshold this high is not ideal. We therefore applied the elbow method (Kodinariya and Makwana, 2013) to set the log-likelihood thresholds to 1.75, 3.0, and 1.25 for the one-day, disjoint seven-day, and intersecting seven-day time-frames when filtering out the non-important terms.

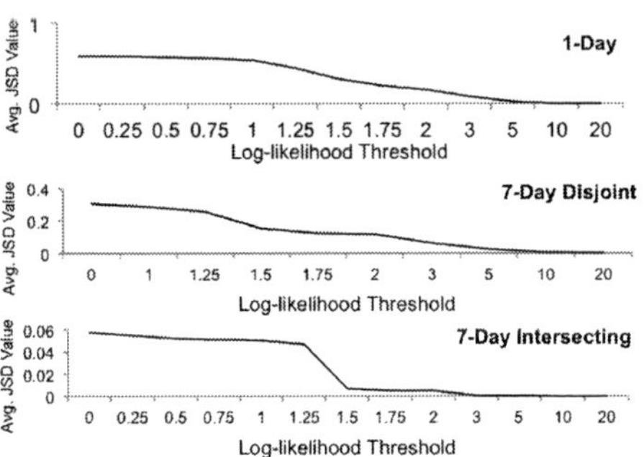

Figure 1: The analysis of the effect of different log-likelihood threshold values on the changes in the JSD distances between consecutive chief complaint corpora in the SynSurv data set

5 Lexical Shift Analysis with Link Set Median

In a separate set of experiments from the statistical JSD distance analysis of the SynSurv data set, we used the Link Set Median (LSM) algorithm (Hoey, 1991) to find segments in the set of chief complaints that suggest lexical shifts in the data set.

The LSM algorithm is based on the idea that a typical text has a cohesive format. Therefore, lexical overlaps can be used to measure the similarity between two sentences. If two sentences share similar terms, then the sentences may be on the same or similar topic. The LSM method identifies lexical repetitions across sentences within a corpus to find textual segments of similar topics. The algorithm has a technique to represent each sentence in the corpus based on its links with other sentences in the same corpus. The lexical link is a repetition between a pair of sentences in the corpus. The set of the links per sentence contains the number of times each sentence has lexical overlaps with any other sentence in the corpus. For instance, if sentence 1 shares two terms with sentence 2 and one term with sentence 4, then "2" is added twice in the link set of sentence 1 as $\{2,2,4\}$. After the link sets have been created for all sentences in the text, the median of the link sets are calculated. This median represents the lexical span of that sentence in the text. If the sentence has a median of "5" for instance, this means that the sentence has a lexical span from $i - 5$ to $i + 5$ where i equals the original position of the sentence. Once each sentence in the text has a corresponding median, an average median of the entire text is calculated. This average median is used as a threshold to find segment boundaries. If the median difference between two consecutive sentences is larger than the threshold, then a segment boundary is placed between two sentences.

In our experiments, we modeled a "sentence" as a set of chief complaints over a specific time-frame and assume a "segment" boundary to be indicative of a lexical shift. We applied the LSM algorithm on the SynSurv data set to understand whether the algorithm will place segment boundaries where the lexical contents of chief complaints deviate and whether such lexical shifts are tied with the changes in the frequencies of syndromic groups.

6 Aberrancy Detection

When using the JSD values to find changes in the term probability distributions in consecutive time-frames, there was a need for a method to detect abnormalities in the probability deviations over time. The Early Aberration Reporting System (EARS) C algorithms (Hutwagner et al., 2003) were designed to detect such changes in syndromic surveillance data. The CUSUM algorithms are based on a statistically detectable change in counts of relevant events over specified windows of time. The EARS implemented three CUSUM algorithms known as C1:mild, C2:medium, and C3:ultra for detecting large, sudden deviations of occurrences of specific events that significantly depart from the norm over time. These algorithms have been named after their level of sensitivity and represent an unsupervised monitoring approach that omits the requirement for long historical data for system training. Since syndromic surveillance systems require real-time analysis of chief complaints, the EARS CUSUM algorithms

are ideal. The algorithms have recently been used in another study to find possible disease outbreaks along with machine learning classification techniques (Aamer et al., 2016).

The C1 algorithm calculates the sample mean and the sample standard deviation over rolling windows of samples for $t - 7$ to $t - 1$ days, where t is the current day. C2 adds a two-day lag onto the calculation of the mean and the standard deviation, and C3 is calculated on the basis of the previous two C2 values, details to be found in (Hutwagner et al., 2003). In our work, we used the pre-set threshold values for the C algorithms, i.e., the threshold for C1=3, C2=3, and for C3=2.

Note that the LSM algorithm has an internal method to calculate a threshold based on which textual segment boundaries are identified. Therefore, when using the LSM algorithm, we did not apply the CUSUM algorithms.

7 Results and Discussion

We applied the JSD and log-likelihood filtering algorithms on the chief complaints in the SynSurv data set with the different time-frames described in section 3. Then, the aberrancy detection algorithms were utilized over the JSD measures of consecutive time-frames to retrospectively find any disease outbreaks in the data set. We separately applied the LSM method on the same data set to find likely aberrancies.

Table 1 shows the results obtained (i.e., the number of dates for which an aberrancy was detected) when the aberrancy detection algorithms were applied based on the JSD lexical distribution values, derived from the chief complaints in the SynSurv data set over the different time-frames. As can be seen in Table 1, the C2 and C3 algorithms with higher levels of sensitivity set off a large number of signals. Algorithms that are overly sensitive to fluctuations in disease frequencies are not ideal; they may alert health practitioners too frequently, resulting in alert fatigue and mistrust of the algorithm. On the other hand, algorithms that miss viable shifts corresponding to meaningful events are also not desirable. The C1 algorithm is the least sensitive of the three algorithms while still raising alerts; it appears to balance the two criteria most effectively.

Note that to apply the aberrancy detection algorithms on the resulting JSD values over the disjoint seven-day windows, there was a need for 7 to

Time-frame	Method	#Aberrancies with ADA		
		C1	C2	C3
1-day	JSD+LL	64 (2.4%)	67 (4.0%)	205 (13.2%)
7-day disjoint	JSD+LL	10 (4.6%)	14 (6.5%)	30 (13.8%)
7-day intersecting	JSD+LL	36 (2.4%)	61 (4.0%)	201 (13.3%)

Table 1: The number of aberrancy dates detected by different algorithms in the chief complaints over different time-frames. The total number of windows differed for each time-frame. The 1-day time-frame consisted of 1522 windows starting from July 2005 to August 2009, the 7-day intersecting time-frame had 1516 windows, and the 7-day disjoint time-frame had 217 windows. Note: ADA=Aberrancy detection algorithm, JSD=Jensen-Shannon Divergence, and LL=Log-likelihood.

11 weeks of baseline data which would mean a 7 to 11 week wait before any aberrancy can be detected. For this reason, in practice, it may not be useful to apply the C algorithms on the JSD values for disjoint seven-day time-frames.

Further analysis of the C1 algorithm, however, showed that the weeks for which C1 detected outbreaks were spread throughout the years in the data set, indicating that LSM is highly sensitive and produces too many noisy signals, which is not desirable. Since the texts of chief complaints are all in a single text corpus assigned to various syndromes, a single chief complaint may correspond to more than one syndrome. For example, due to the very similar set of syndromes that *Flu-Like Illness* and *Acute Respiratory* share, a single chief complaint may be labelled *Flu-Like Illness, Acute Respiratory*, and *No Diarrhea* at the same time. Therefore, a large lexical shift in the SynSurv data set may correspond to any of the syndromes (including the original set of syndromes introduced in section 2). As a result, there was a need for a more informed method to distinguish between the aberrancies related to each syndrome. For this, instead of using log-likelihood of terms, we collected all the chief complaints signaling the presence of a syndrome into one corpus and extracted the terms with the largest term frequency for each syndrome. Table 2 shows the top 10 terms for the three syndromic groups. We can see is a large intersection for *Flu-Like Illness* and *Acute Respiratory*.

We calculated JSD values over the SynSurv data set with the original chief complaint terms (no filtering) removing stop words only, as well as with the top 10 terms based on term frequencies for each syndromic group. Figure 2 shows the resulting diagrams for *Flu-Like Illness* and *Diarrhea* over the different time-frames. The results for *Acute Respiratory* were not shown since this syndromic group is most similar to *Flu-Like Illness*.

TF rank	Diarrhea	FLI	AR
1	pain	sob	sob
2	vomiting	hr	hr
3	abdo	cough	cough
4	diarrhea	pain	chest
5	hr	o/a	pain
6	nausea	chest	o/a
7	nil	nil	hx
8	o/a	hx	respiratory
9	gastrointestinal	throat	nil
10	hx	respiratory	phx

Table 2: The top TF ranked terms related to each syndrome in the SynSurv data set. Note: TF=Term frequency, FLI=Flu-Like Illness, and AR=Acute Respiratory. The terms include many medical abbreviations such as "sob" for shortage of breath, "hr" for heart rate, etc.

When comparing the effect of the different time-frames, as shown in Figure 2, the results with the one-day window time-frames seem much noisier than those of the two other types of time-frames. It is hardly possible to detect any aberrancies in the one-day time-frame output data whereas with the seven-day windows, both disjoint and intersecting, some clear trends of peaks can be detected around a few dates in the data set.

More importantly, the utilisation of the top terms significantly changed the outputs of the aberrancy detection as indicated by the different patterns in the diagrams in Figure 2 with the original versus top 10 terms. However, it is noticeable that the peaks form at very similar dates for both *Flu-Like Illness* and *Diarrhea* conditions, when the top 10 terms are retained in the analysis. We suspect this is largely due to the significant intersection between the list of top 10 terms for these two syndromic groups, as seen in Table 2. Indeed, there is a 50% overlap between the lists of top frequency terms including "pain, "hr", "o/a", "nil", and "hx". These overlapping terms are general;

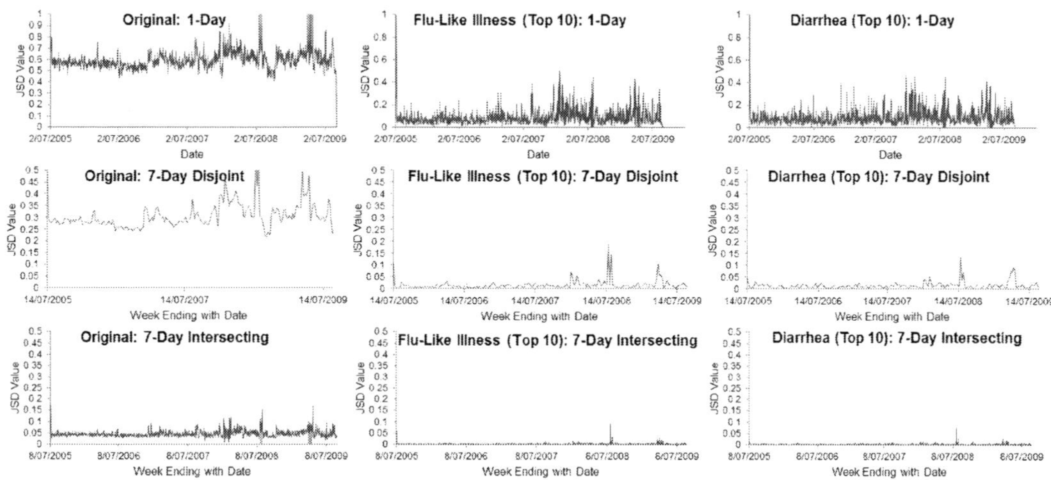

Figure 2: Variation of JSD values in the SynSurv data set with different time-frames when original and top 10 terms retained

they seem non-specific to any syndrome.

We then experimented with the top frequency terms that were not shared between the lists of the two syndromic groups. We took the top 3 terms from the two lists in Table 2 and calculated the JSD values over the disjoint one-day windows of chief complaints. The results are shown in Figure 3 in which the patterns of peaks are different with drastic increases of JSD values at different and separate dates. This suggests that if effective and descriptive sets of terms are found to represent each syndromic group (hence semi-supervised), the lexical shift as measured with deviating JSD values can be utilised as an indication of possible outbreaks of corresponding syndromes.

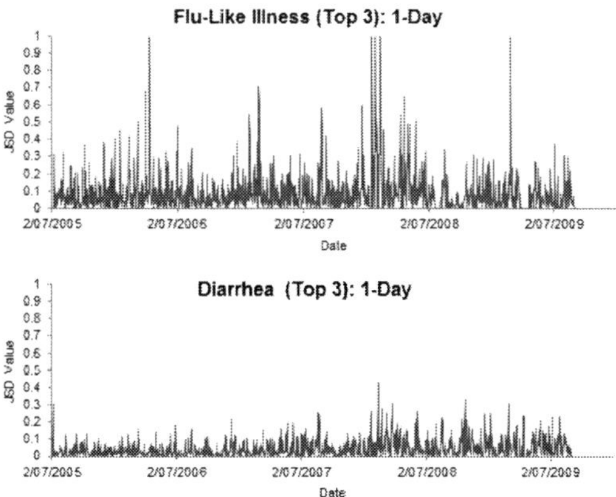

Figure 3: Variation of daily JSD values in the Syn-Surv data set when only top 3 terms retained

As a proof of concept to understand whether JSD is in fact sensitive to the raw frequencies of positive cases of syndromic groups, we cross-checked deviations of JSD values (over all terms) with reference to the actual positive cases of each syndrome in the SynSurv data set. The results are shown in Figure 4 where JSD is demonstrated to be sensitive especially to the cases where there are no positive labelled chief complaints for any of the syndromes. In such cases, as highlighted in the diagrams of Figure 4, JSD values deviate drastically, indicating a rapid change in the frequencies of syndromes of interest.

In the last round of experiments, we applied the LSM algorithm over the different time-frames of the SynSurv data set. The algorithm detected 77 segments with the disjoint seven-day time-frame, 178 with the one-day window, and 268 with the intersecting seven-day time-frame. When analysing the dates of segmentations, it was observed that although the dates were spread throughout the years, the segments by the disjoint seven-day and one-day time-frames were mostly in the years 2007, 2008, and 2009, similar to the times when the peaks were observed with JSD. However, the 268 segments found using the intersecting seven-day time-frame were distributed over the four years. This may be due to the large vocabulary over-laps where the windows intersect over six days of chief complaints. The intersecting seven-day time-frame, therefore, may not facilitate an effective process of outbreak detection using lexical

Time-frame	Method	# of Segments
1-day	LSM	178 (11.7%)
7-day disjoint	LSM	77 (35.5%)
7-day intersecting	LSM	268 (17.7%)

Table 3: The number of segments detected in the chief complaints over different time-frames. The total number of windows differed for each time-frame. The 1-day time-frame consisted of 1522 windows starting from July 2005 to August 2009, the 7-day intersecting time-frame had 1516 windows, and the 7-day disjoint time-frame had 217 windows. Note: LSM = LinkSetMedian

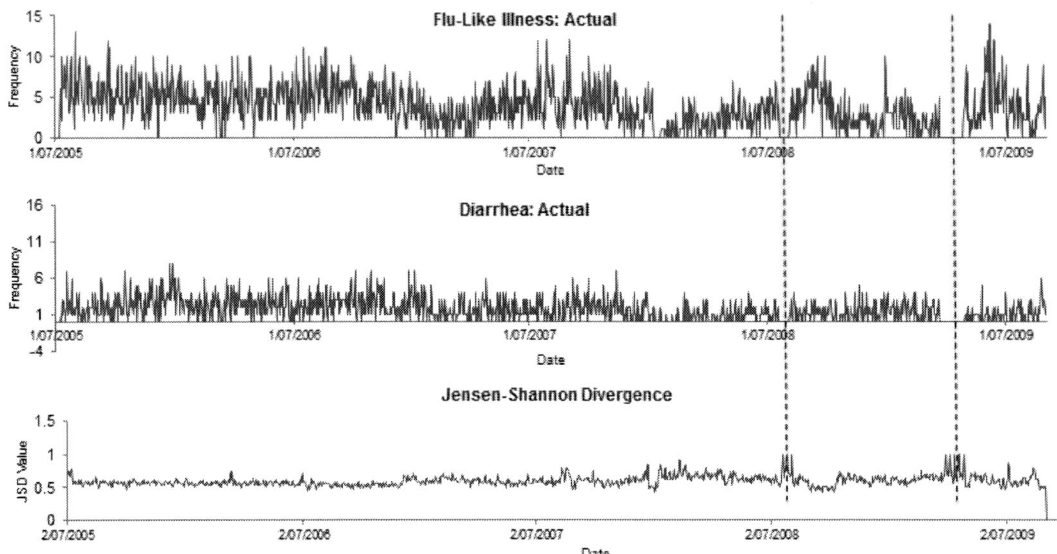

Figure 4: Analysing sensitivity of lexical shifts measured with JSD to actual deviations of the number of daily syndromic chief complaints. Vertical lines point to the dates when drastic disease frequency changes align with large JSD values.

shift analysis with LSM. Based on our results, the large number of deviations/outbreaks detected by the LSM algorithm (in its current form) seems to be an impediment in using the algorithm for syndromic surveillance.

8   Conclusion

We proposed a new semi-supervised method to perform syndromic surveillance over the SynSurv data set containing a large number of emergency department Chief Complaints in the Victoria State of Australia. This new method is based on locating significant lexical divergences in the texts of chief complaints accumulated over consecutive periods of time. We analysed the lexical shifts using Jensen-Shannon Divergence (JSD); a probability distribution divergence measure; and Link Set Median (LSM); a text segmentation algorithm; for the three syndromes *Flu-Like Illness*, *Acute Respi-*

ratory, and *Diarrhea*. The aim was to find whether lexical shifts are tied with possible disease outbreaks in the historical SynSurv data set. We evaluated the lexical shifts with three types of time-frames: i) one-day windows, ii) disjoint seven-day windows, and iii) intersecting seven-day windows advancing by one day.

We found that all three time-frames had some limitations: the disjoint seven-day time-frame when used in combination with the EARS C algorithms is not efficient, and inherently, it will result in longer periods of wait before a likely outbreak is signalled. The seven-day intersecting time-frame, on the other hand, resulted in noisy and frequent signals with the LSM algorithm, mostly as a result of large textual overlaps in consecutive overlapping time-frames. The one-day time-frame produced interesting results but suffers from the day-of-the-week effect.

Our results also demonstrate that if each syndromic group (i.e., disease) is represented with its corresponding distinguishable high-frequency terms, then the JSD measure provides evidence for lexical shifts that is aligned with drastic changes in the frequency of syndromic-labelled chief complaints. The need for distinguishable terms for each syndrome under consideration means that our methods are semi-supervised. Based on our experiments, therefore, the JSD method with syndrome-specific term sets analysed over the one-day time-frames resulted in the most promising outcomes.

In future work, we plan to expand the idea of using high frequency terms into the utilisation of related semantic representations, such as health-related synonyms. In addition, we are planning to analyse lexical shifts in chief complaints using other natural language processing techniques, such as textual novelty detection with Topic Tracking and Detection algorithms. TDT algorithms can track changes in text and find event-level shifts (or first stories) in a corpus. We would like to experiment with such unsupervised algorithms and find whether first story boundaries match drastic changes in the frequencies of chief complaints related to specific syndromic groups.

Acknowledgments

We acknowledge the Australian Defence Science and Technology Group (DST Group) for the support of our work on syndromic surveillance.

References

Hafsah Aamer, Bahadorreza Ofoghi, and Karin Verspoor. 2016. Syndromic surveillance on the victorian chief complaint data set using a hybrid statistical and machine learning technique. In K. Barbuto, L. Schaper, and K. Verspoor, editors, *Proceedings of the Health Data Analytics Conference*.

Timothy Baldwin, Paul Cook, Marco Lui, Andrew MacKinlay, and Li Wang. 2013. How noisy social media text, how diffrnt social media sources? In *Proceedings of the Sixth International Joint Conference on Natural Language Processing*, pages 356–364, Nagoya, Japan, October. Asian Federation of Natural Language Processing.

Colleen A. Bradley, H. Rolka, D. Walker, and J. Loonsk. 2005. BioSense: implementation of a national early event detection and situational awareness system. *MMWR Morb Mortal Wkly Rep*, 54(Suppl):11–19.

Wendy W. Chapman, Lee M. Christensen, Michael M. Wagner, Peter J. Haug, Oleg Ivanov, John N. Dowling, and Robert T. Olszewski. 2005. Classifying free-text triage chief complaints into syndromic categories with natural language processing. *Artificial intelligence in medicine*, 33(1):31–40.

Ted Dunning. 1993. Accurate methods for the statistics of surprise and coincidence. *Computational linguistics*, 19(1):61–74.

Jeremy U. Espino, John Dowling, John Levander, Peter Sutovsky, Michael M. Wagner, and Gregory F. Cooper. 2007. SyCo: A probabilistic machine learning method for classifying chief complaints into symptom and syndrome categories. *Advances in Disease Surveillance*, 2(5).

Ronald D. Fricker Jr, Benjamin L. Hegler, and David A. Dunfee. 2008. Comparing syndromic surveillance detection methods: EARS versus a CUSUM-based methodology. *Statistical Medicine*, 27(17):3407–29.

M. Hoey. 1991. *Patterns of lexis in text*. Oxford University Press.

Lori Hutwagner, William Thompson, G. Matthew Seeman, and Tracee Treadwell. 2003. The bioterrorism preparedness and response early aberration reporting system (ears). *Journal of Urban Health*, 80(1):i89–i96.

Trupti M. Kodinariya and Prashant R. Makwana. 2013. Review on determining number of cluster in k-means clustering. *International Journal of Advance Research in Computer Science and Management Studies*, 1(6):90–95.

Jianhua Lin. 1991. Divergence measures based on the Shannon entropy. *IEEE Transactions on Information theory*, 37(1):145–151.

Bahadorreza Ofoghi and Karin Verspoor. 2015. Assessing the performance of American chief complaint classifiers on Victorian syndromic surveillance data. In *Proceedings of Australia's Big Data in Biomedicine & Healthcare Conference*, Sydney, Australia.

P. Rayson and R. Garside. 2000. Comparing corpora using frequency profiling. In *Proceedings of the Workshop on Comparing Corpora, held in conjunction with ACL 2000*, pages 1–6.

Fu-Chiang Tsui, Jeremy U. Espino, Virginia M. Dato, Per H. Gesteland, Judith Hutman, and Michael M. Wagner. 2003. Technical description of RODS: a real-time public health surveillance system. *Journal of the American Medical Informatics Association*, 10(5):399–408.

Karin Verspoor, K. Bretonnel Cohen, and Lawrence Hunter. 2009. The textual characteristics of tradiational and Open Access scientific journals are similar. *BMC Bioinformatics*, page 10:183.

Unsupervised Pre-training With Sequence Reconstruction Loss for Deep Relation Extraction Models

Zhuang Li[1], Lizhen Qu[1,2], Qiongkai Xu[1,2], Mark Johnson[3]
[1] DATA61, Australia
[2] The Australian National University
[3] Macquarie University
lizhuang144@gmail.com,
{Lizhen.Qu,Qiongkai.Xu}@data61.csiro.au
mark.johnson@mq.edu.au

Abstract

Relation extraction models based on deep learning have been attracting a lot of attention recently. Little research is carried out to reduce their need of labeled training data. In this work, we propose an unsupervised pre-training method based on the sequence-to-sequence model for deep relation extraction models. The pre-trained models need only half or even less training data to achieve equivalent performance as the same models without pre-training.

1 Introduction

Relation extraction (RE) is the task of detecting and categorizing semantic relations between named entities mentioned in a text corpus. This is important for a wide variety of practical applications. For example, tourism planning bodies are interested in mining social media such as tweets to identifying which restaurants tourists eat in and which hotels those same tourists stay in.

RE has been intensively studied for several years (Chan and Roth, 2011; Chan and Roth, 2010). Recently, RE models based on deep neural networks (DNN) have achieved better performance than conventional RE models that rely on handcrafted features (Xu et al., 2015). However, these DNN models require a large amount of annotated training data, which is difficult and expensive to obtain. The data problem is not completely solved by relying on methods such as large external knowledge bases and distant supervision because i) models employing only large knowledge bases often still perform poorly on RE (Angeli et al., 2014); ii) the external knowledge bases are incomplete; and iii) many important applications lack the relevant domain specific knowledge bases. This paper asks the question: can we use unlabeled data to help training DNN RE

models? Although unsupervised pre-training is known to be effective for training deep neural networks, it remains unclear how to apply it to the recently proposed DNN RE models. The main advantage of deep models (compared to the shallow counterparts) is that they automatically learn distributed representations of the relevant components of the model (e.g., words, entities, relations, etc.). If we can encode rich syntactic-semantic patterns of relation expressions into the automatically learned, low-dimensional representations, and require these representations to be similar if they play a similar role using only unlabeled data, it should be possible for a DNN RE system to achieve a high level of generalization from only small amount of labeled data.

In a relational expression, the named entities and words around it provide useful context information. For example, in the sentence *"By 1982 the BL Cars Ltd division renamed itself Austin Rover Group shortly before the launch of the Maestro."* *renamed itself* is used much less often than an expression such as *was founded in* to indicate the relation *org:foundedIn*. Thus it is likely that *was founded in* will be found in the training set, even if *renamed itself* does not appear in the training set. Despite this, the co-occurrence of *1982* and *Austin Rover Group*, as well as keywords such as *by*, form a context that is similar to that of *Austin Rover Group was founded in 1982*. If such shared contextual information can require the similarity of the representations of these expressions, a classifier can easily infer that *renamed itself* is likely to indicate *org:foundedIn*. Inspired by observations such as these, we seek methods that exploit context information composed of words and named entities to learn representations of expressions, such that semantically similar expressions tend to have similar representations.

In this paper, we propose a pre-training method that generalizes well known sequence to sequence model (Dai and Le, 2015) for deep RE models. This approach formalizes unsupervised pre-training as minimizing reconstruction errors of input sequences. For a given DNN RE model, our approach first pre-trains it on a large, unlabeled, domain-general corpus, and then fine-tunes it on target corpora. Our experiments show that, especially when the size of the labeled training data is small, the deep relation extraction models pre-trained with our unsupervised pre-training method using half or even a quarter of the labeled data are able to achieve similar performance as the models without pre-training. Our unsupervised approach does not need domain-specific corpora for pre-training; in fact, they work well with 13,000 sentences randomly sampled from Wikipedia.

2   Related Work

Recent advance of relation extraction demonstrates the power of deep learning by showing that the deep models significantly outperform the conventional approaches (Jiang and Zhai, 2007; Chan and Roth, 2010; Chan and Roth, 2011) on the ACE relation extraction datasets. Except for the FCM model (Yu et al., 2015), at the core of almost all deep RE models are variants of convolutional neural networks (CNN) (Zeng et al., 2014; Nguyen and Grishman, 2015; Wang et al., 2016; Miwa and Bansal, 2016), recurrent neural networks (RNN) (Zhang et al., 2015; Socher et al., 2012; Ebrahimi and Dou, 2015; Lin et al., 2016), or both of them (Liu et al., 2015; Cai et al., 2016).

Several RE systems (Chen et al., 2006a; GuoDong et al., 2009; Li et al., 2010; LongHua and Qiaoming, 2008; Chen et al., 2006b; Kim and Lee, 2012) are built upon the semi-supervised learning algorithm *label propagation* to exploit the use of unlabeled data. This family of algorithms start with building a similarity graph between each pair of relation mentions, and propagate relation labels from labeled ones to unlabeled ones. However, deep RE models require substantial change in order to use these algorithms, while our methods just need to replace the training criterion during pre-training, which is easy-to-implement by using a standard deep learning toolkit. It is also too expensive to involve all unlabeled data in both training and prediction processes for each target dataset. In contrast, our pre-training algorithms are performed only once on a general corpus and the resulted models are fine-tuned only on target

corpora.

There is also ample of work exploring the idea of distant supervision for knowledge base completion (Riedel et al., 2013; Weston et al., 2013; Yang et al., 2014; Bordes et al., 2013) in order to avoid the use of manually labeled data. Although some of these models include a relation extraction component (Surdeanu et al., 2012; Angeli et al., 2014; Toutanova et al., 2015), the outputs of their systems are whether a relation holds between entities rather than entity mentions. In contrast, we aim to classify relation mentions no matter if a target relation exists in a knowledge base or not.

There have also been other efforts towards minimizing the use of labeled data. In (Sun, 2009), they proposed a bootstrapping approach to extract textual patterns for training a SVM-based relation extraction system. In (Chan and Roth, 2011), they show that supervised models equipped with syntactico-semantic features are capable of classifying relation mentions with a few labeled data. However, both work are customized for supervised models with handcrafted features and relations between nominals. In other lines of research, active learning (Fu and Grishman, 2013; Sun and Grishman, 2012) and domain adaptation (Nguyen and Grishman, 2014) pursued to select high quality training examples for training relation extraction models. Jiang (2009) leverages the knowledge of known relations to predict new relations in a weakly supervised setting. These approaches have different problem settings than ours, which focus on the use of unlabeled data.

Since 2006, various pre-training techniques are proposed to make the training of deep neural networks practical (Hinton and Salakhutdinov, 2006; Dahl et al., 2010; Bengio, 2009). They are not universally applicable for all problems and most of them focus on computer vision problems. To the best of our knowledge, we are the first to explore the use of pre-training for deep RE models.

3   Relation Extraction Models

Suppose we are given a relation mention, which is a pair of named entity mentions (m_h, m_t) together with its relation expression in a sentence S. Each mention m is disambiguated into an entity e. Let $x \in \mathcal{X}$ denote a relation mention, where $\mathcal{X}$ is the space of all relation mentions, RE models assign a binary relation $y \in \mathcal{Y}$ to x, where $\mathcal{Y}$ is a finite set

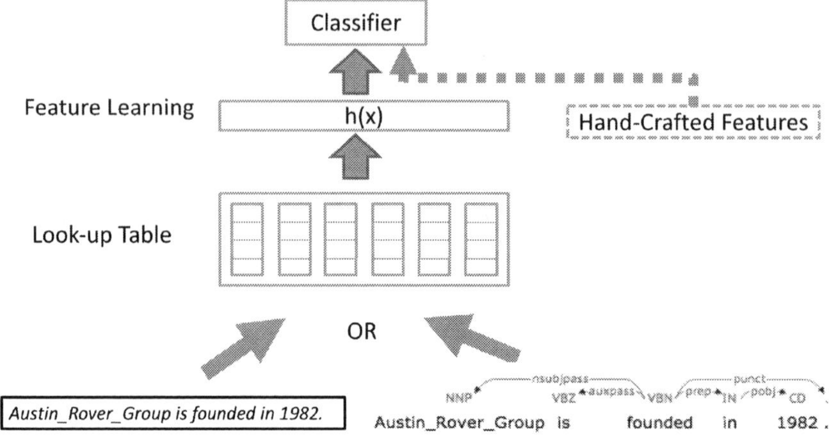

Figure 1: General Architecture for deep RE models.

of all possible relations. As a result, an RE model is a function $g : \mathcal{X} \to \mathcal{Y}$.

Given a training set $(x_1, y_1), ..., (x_n, y_n) \in \mathcal{X} \times \mathcal{Y}$, we can directly learn an RE model by minimizing a supervised loss function $L_s : \mathcal{X} \times \mathcal{Y} \to \mathbb{R}$. In absence of sufficient supervised training data, we resort to a two-stage approach. In the first stage, we pre-train RE models on a dataset annotated with named entity mentions and their corresponding entities by minimizing an unsupervised loss $L_u : \mathcal{X} \to \mathbb{R}$. In the second stage, we fine-tune the pre-trained models on the labeled dataset by applying the supervised loss L_s. In our experiments, L_s is the cross-entropy loss, as a result of applying multi-class logistic regression (LR) in the supervised setting.

The deep RE models proposed recently are variants of Long Short Term Memory (LSTM) (Graves and Schmidhuber, 2005) and Convolutional Neural Networks (CNN) (Krizhevsky et al., 2012). As representative examples we consider three recent RE models: i) bidirectional LSTM that takes words around entity mentions as input (Zhang et al., 2015), coined BiLSTM; ii) LSTM taking shortest paths in dependency trees as input, coined Dep-TreeLSTM; iii) CNN taking words sequences and position embeddings as input (dos Santos et al., 2015), coined PCNN.

All three RE models consist of four components. As illustrated in Figure 1, as input they take either word sequences between two entity mentions or the shortest dependency path between two entity mentions. A look up table maps each input word into its word embedding. Herein we denote the word embedding of a word i by $\mathbf{e}_i \in \mathbf{R}^M$, where M is the dimension of word embeddings. All word embeddings are initialized with the ones pre-trained on a large domain-general corpus (Qu et al., 2015). As suggested in (Qu et al., 2015), we do not update these word embeddings during training to avoid overfitting. In the next step, a feature learning component projects the embeddings into a hidden representation $\mathbf{h}$. If it is in a supervised setting, both $\mathbf{h}$ and handcrafted features are taken as the input of a multi-class LR classifier for categorizing target relations. In case of unsupervised pre-training, $\mathbf{h}$ is fed into a classifier for a designated unsupervised predictive task.

The RE models based on BiLSTM and TreeL-STM are extensions of LSTM. LSTM is a recurrent neural network capable of capturing long dependencies (Graves and Schmidhuber, 2005). At the t-th time step, the LSTM layer takes the form:

$$\mathbf{u}_t, \mathbf{c}_t = \text{LSTM}(\mathbf{x}_t, \mathbf{u}_{t-1}, \mathbf{c}_{t-1}) \qquad (1)$$

where $\mathbf{x}_t$ is the input to LSTM at time step t, and $\mathbf{u}_t$ and $\mathbf{c}_t$ are the hidden states and memory states of LSTM at time step t, respectively.

BiLSTM reads an input word sequence in both directions with two separate LSTM layers. As illustrated in Figure 2c, one LSTM reads the word sequence between two entity mentions in forwards direction, while the other with shared parameters reads the same sequence in the reverse direction. As a result, they generate two hidden representations $\overrightarrow{\mathbf{h}}$ and $\overleftarrow{\mathbf{h}}$, which are further concatenated to form the input vector $\mathbf{h}$ of the classifier.

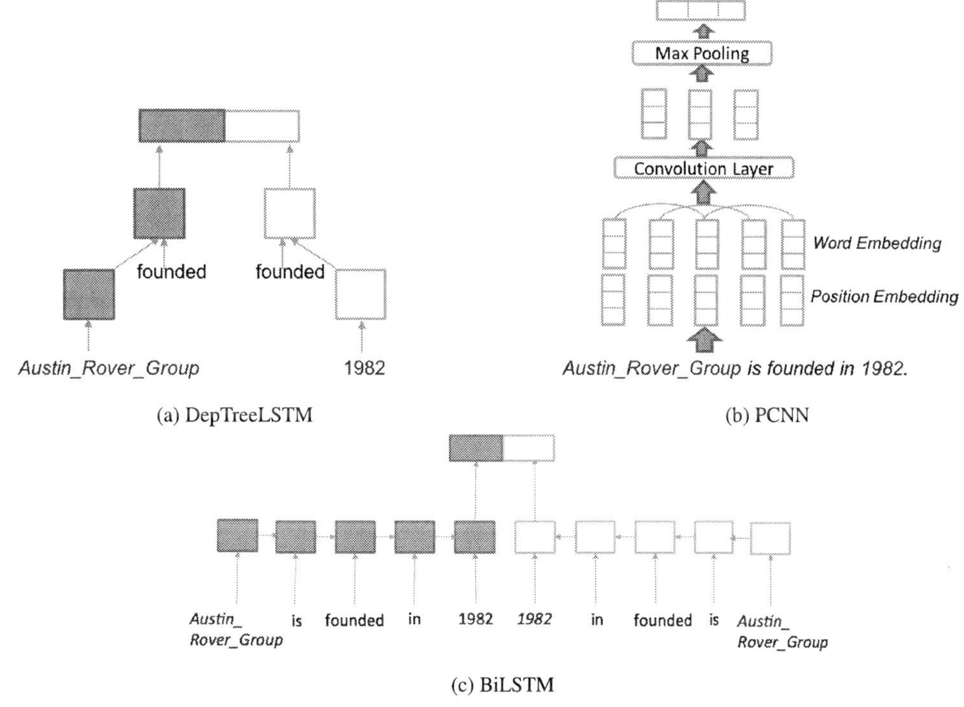

(a) DepTreeLSTM

(b) PCNN

(c) BiLSTM

Figure 2: Deep relation extraction models.

DepTreeLSTM takes as input the shortest path between two entity mention in a syntactic dependency tree. The shortest path consists of two subpaths, which starts from an entity mention and ends at their lowest common ancestor. Since both subpaths are word sequences, as shown in Figure 2a, the feature learning component is composed of two LSTM layers with shared parameters to read the two subpaths respectively. The resulted two representations are concatenated as the input of the classifier. This model can be viewed either as the model proposed in (Ebrahimi and Dou, 2015) by replacing the recursive neural networks with LSTM, or as simplifying the model proposed in (Xu et al., 2015) by removing the max-pooling layer. The max-pooling layer leads to degraded performance in our preliminary experiments.

PCNN implements the model in (dos Santos et al., 2015), which takes as input the word sequence between two entity mentions. It starts with mapping each input word to its word embedding. Each word embedding is further concatenated with its position embedding, which encodes relative distance of the word w.r.t. each entity mention. To cope with input word sequences of varying length, the embedding sequences smaller than the pre-

specified maximal length are padded with the embedding of the padding token. Then a convolutional layer and a max pooling layer are applied in sequel to generate the input h for the classifier.

For all three models, we augment them with the handcrafted features used in the top conventional RE systems that do not rely on deep learning techniques. They lead to improved results according to our preliminary experiments. In particular, we include lexical, collocation, and dependency features proposed in (Chan and Roth, 2010). The other features used in (Chan and Roth, 2010) are dropped because the relevant information is not available in our target datasets. In addition, we implemented the POS features and the base phrase chunk features introduced in (Chan and Roth, 2011).

4 Unsupervised Pre-training

Inspired by the semi-supervised sequence-to-sequence model (Dai and Le, 2015), our unsupervised pre-training methods tackle the learning of deep RE models in two steps. First, we learn entity embeddings by using a stepwise training strategy. Second, we train the feature learning components $h(x)$ of deep RE models by using *sequence recon-*

struction loss.

4.1 Learning Entity Embeddings

Entities often provide vital information for relation extraction (Chan and Roth, 2010). Qu et al. (2015) show that the extraction of entity mentions benefits significantly from distributional similarity, thus we learn entity embeddings by using the Skip-gram model (Mikolov et al., 2013). An entity mention such as *Austin Rover Group* often spans more than one word, while the Skip-gram model works on sequences of tokens. Therefore we retokenize text by mapping each entity mention into a single token, and replace them with the IDs of the referred entities.

The domain specific RE corpora are often small. The retokenization of documents further leads to a substantial number of infrequent entity tokens. We can only obtain embeddings of poor quality for these tokens if we train them from scratch (Collobert et al., 2011). To circumvent the problems, we employ a stepwise strategy. First, we initialize all word embeddings with the pre-trained ones on a large corpus (Qu et al., 2015). Second, we initialize each entity embedding by averaging the embeddings of all the words ever occurred in its mentions, following (Socher et al., 2013). Third, we update only entity embeddings by using the Skip-Gram model. This allows us to update them with an aggressive learning rate since we expect a large change of these embeddings. And we keep the pre-trained word embeddings intact to preserve the knowledge of distributional similarity learned from a large general corpus, as suggested in (Qu et al., 2015). After training with the Skip-gram model, we also do not update these entity embeddings while training with the deep RE models because updating these embeddings was not shown to be useful in our preliminary experiments.

4.2 Sequence Reconstruction Loss

Given pre-trained word and entity embeddings, the randomly initialized deep RE models still suffer from poor performance if the target training datasets are too small compared to their vast number of model parameters. Inspired by Autoencoders (Vincent et al., 2010), our key idea is to obtain high quality representations by reconstructing the corresponding inputs. During the process of reconstruction, if two expressions share similar context, we expect that they end up with having similar representations.

We draw inspiration from the semi-supervised sequence-to-sequence (seq2seq) model (Dai and Le, 2015) for pre-training deep RE models. Its underlying seq2seq (Sutskever et al., 2014) model consists of an LSTM encoder and an LSTM decoder. The encoder reads a sequence of words and map them into a hidden representation. Then the decoder takes the representation as input and predicts the most likely sequence of words. The training objective is to minimize the discrepancy between the predicted sequence and the input sequence.

All of the three deep RE models presented in Sec 3 take as input word sequences, and generate a hidden representation $\mathbf{h}$ for the classifier. Our key idea of generalizing the semi-supervised seq2seq model is to reuse the feature learning component $h(x)$ as the encoder and reconstruct the input sequence in each direction by using an LSTM decoder. The change of encoder is particularly interesting for *PCNN*, which adopts a different type of model than the decoder.

Given an entity mention pair, the input of both *PCNN* and *BiLSTM* is the word sequence between both mentions and the mentions themselves. *PCNN* applies CNN to read the input sequence in both forwards and backwards directions, and results in two hidden representations $\overrightarrow{\mathbf{h}}$ and $\overleftarrow{\mathbf{h}}$ respectively. Its LSTM decoder reads each representation and reconstructs the input sequence in the corresponding direction, respectively. In the same manner, *BiLSTM* applies the two LSTM layers to read and reconstruct input sequences in both directions. Although *DepTreeLSTM* takes input from dependency trees, it follows the same way as the other two models by reconstructing two word sequences in their respective reading direction. Herein, each sequence is read from the entity mention to their lowest common ancestor.

The LSTM decoder consists of an LSTM in the form of Equation (1) and a softmax classifier. At time step t, the LSTM layer reads the previous hidden state $\mathbf{u}_{t-1}$ and the predicted word x_{t-1} at time step $t-1$, followed by generating the current hidden state $\mathbf{u}_t$. The current hidden state $\mathbf{u}_t$ is fed into the softmax classifier to predict the word x_t, where the softmax classifier is defined as:

$$P(x = j|\mathbf{u}_t) = \frac{\exp(\mathbf{e}_j^{\mathrm{T}}\mathbf{u}_t)}{\sum_{k=1}^{|\mathcal{V}|} \exp(\mathbf{e}_k^{\mathrm{T}}\mathbf{u}_t)}$$

where $\mathcal{V}$ denotes the vocabulary. When $t = 1$, the LSTM initializes the initial state as $\mathbf{u}$ and $\mathbf{c}_0 = \mathbf{0}$.

For the sake of computational efficiency, we minimize the reconstruction loss by approximating the cross-entropy loss of the softmax function by using the negative sampling technique in (Mikolov et al., 2013). As a result, at the t-th time step during decoding, we minimize

$$-\log \sigma(\mathbf{e}_{x_t}^{\mathsf{T}} \mathbf{u}_t) - \sum_{j=1}^{k} \mathbb{E}_{x_j \sim P_n(x)} \log \sigma(-\mathbf{e}_{x_j}^{\mathsf{T}} \mathbf{u}_t)$$

where x_t is the corresponding word observed in the input sequence, σ denotes the sigmoid function, and $P_n(x)$ is the noise distribution for drawing k negative samples. In our experiments, we employ uniform distribution as the noise distribution. Then the loss function L_u is the sum of the above loss over all words in input sequences.

5 Experimental Setup

5.1 Datasets and Evaluation Protocol

We use the Stanford Relation Extraction corpus (`StanfordRE`) (Angeli et al., 2014) as the target corpus for evaluation. Each entity mention is associated with a canonical name. We map each canonical name to an entity ID in two ways. If the canonical name can be found in Freebase, we replace the mention with its Freebase machine ID. Otherwise we replace the mention with the ID based on its canonical name. In addition, we filter out the relation mentions with a annotator agreement lower than 80% as well as the ones labeled as *no relation*, because they are the source of label noise based on our manual inspection. This is beyond the scope of this work. As a result, we obtain 9150 relation mentions and 40 relations in total.

Among all relation mentions in the `StanfordRE` corpus, we hold out 20% relation mentions for testing, 10% for development, and the remaining for training. In order to test the impact of the volume of training data for fine-tuning, we split the training portion of the corpus into 10 partitions based on a log scale, and created 10 successively larger training sets $S_1, S_2, ..., S_{10}$ by merging these partitions from smallest to largest. As a result, S_{i+1} is twice the size of the S_i and S_{10} is the full training set.

For pre-training, we use the FIGER corpus, which is a sample of Wikipedia annotated with millions of entity mentions (Desmet and Hoste, 2014). Because each entity mention is also linked to a canonical name, we convert each mention to an entity ID in the same way as for `StanfordRE`.

To investigate the influence of size of pre-training corpora, we create three corpora for pre-training:

(i) `StanfordWiki`: to verify if the relation mentions from the FIGER corpus, whose entity mention pairs also occur in target corpora, are most relevant during pre-training, we collect all sentences, in which there are at least one entity pair occurring also in a sentence from the `StanfordRE` corpus. Then we merge them with the `StanfordRE` to build a corpus, which contains 133,793 relation mentions in total.

(ii) `WikiRandom`: we randomly sample five non-overlapped subsets from the FIGER corpus, each of them contains similar number of relation mentions as `StanfordWiki`.

(iii) `WikiWhole`: we collect all sentences in the whole FIGER corpus, which contain at least two entity mentions. As a result, we get 1,004,831 sentences and 3,886,998 relation mentions.

In this paper, we mainly present the pre-training results of all models on `WikiRandom`, because i) they are similar to those on `StanfordWiki` and `WikiWhole`; ii) random sentence samples are easy to acquire. For the experiments on `WikiRandom`, we perform one run on each of the five random samples, report averaged micro-F1 scores over all five runs as well as their standard deviations.

5.2 Baselines

We compared pre-trained deep RE models with their randomly initialized counterparts, which differ in their input features.

Handcrafted: an LR classifier with the same handcrafted features as the deep RE models.

Avg_embed: deep RE models with handcrafted features, pre-trained word embeddings, and entity embeddings generated by averaging the embeddings of the words occurred in mentions. The model parameters of the feature learning component and the LR classifier are randomly initialized.

Random_stepwise: deep RE models with handcrafted features, pre-trained word embeddings, and entity embeddings trained by our stepwise training strategy. Their model parameters are randomly initialized in the same way as *avg_embed*.

We compare both LSTM based RE models in two different settings of pre-training: i) the LSTM in the decoder does not share parameters with the

LSTM in the feature learning component; ii) both LSTM layers share parameters.

Given small training datasets, the performance of neural network models often depend on randomly initialized parameters, thus we perform five runs with different random initialization and report the averaged micro-F1 score.

5.3 Implementation Details

In our experiments, we reuse the 200-dimensional pre-trained word embeddings based on the Skipgram model from our prior work (Qu et al., 2015). The corresponding negative samples is 10 and the size of local context window is 5. During stepwise training, all entity embeddings are fine-tuned with a learning rate 0.001 for 50 epochs within a local context window of size 5, the number of negative samples is set to 10. For both LSTM variants, we implemented LSTM in the same way as in (Vinyals et al., 2014), the dimension of hidden units is fixed to 200. For $PCNN$, the dimension of each position embedding is 70, as in (dos Santos et al., 2015), the size of the context window is 3, and the output of the convolutional layer consists of 200 hidden units. During pre-training, the number of negative samples is set to 10. In both pre-training and fine-tuning, we adopt AdaGrad (Duchi et al., 2011) and L2 regularizer for optimization. We tune all hyperparameters on the development set. As a result, the initial learning rates ϵ of AdaGrad is 0.1 for both LSTM variants and 0.05 for $PCNN$ during pre-training, and it is fixed to 0.05 during supervised training. For all models, the hyperparameter of L2 regularization is fixed to $10E^{-6}$.

6 Results and Discussions

As illustrated in Figure 3, all deep RE models pre-trained with the best method outperform the baselines with a wide margin unless the full train set is used. And the performance of these pre-trained models has small variance across all five random training samples. Among all these models, pre-trained $DepTreeLSTM$ is the best performing model on StanfordRE on average. The pre-trained $BiLSTM$ achieves the largest improvement w.r.t. its randomly initialized counterpart with the entity embeddings computed by averaging word embeddings. It needs merely 800 sentences to achieve similar performance as the randomly initialized one trained on 3200 sentences.

Both LSTM based models show that it is better off not sharing the parameters of LSTM between encoders and decoders. Otherwise they achieve only similar performance as the best baselines. We also observe that the gap between both pre-trained LSTM variants and their competitors narrows as the size of the in-domain training data grows more than 1000 sentences. For them, pre-training is only useful when training data is small.

In contrast, the pre-trained $PCNN$ follows a different trend by achieving the highest improvement over the random initialized one when there are more than 3200 target relation mentions for training. Without pre-training, $PCNN$ performs even worse than the baseline with handcrafted features unless the full training set is used. We conjecture, the opposite trend is caused by the high variance introduced by max-pooling and the learning of position embeddings. This model is indeed more difficult to train than the other two models, because it obtains the highest variance among all three models when parameters are randomly initialized. Despite this, the pre-training provides significantly better initialization of model parameters and leads to small variance across all pre-training samples.

The stepwise training strategy is helpful for improving entity embeddings regardless the type of models, as shown in Figure 3. However, it is also not the main power booster during pre-training as the largest improvement is achieved always by unsupervised training losses. In case of $BiLSTM$, the improvement over the averaged word embeddings becomes clear when more than 800 training instances are used.

In order to gain a deeper understanding of the effect of pre-training, we compare the representations generated by the pre-trained models with the ones without pre-training. We compare them also at the begin and the end of fine-tuning respectively. In particular, we apply T-SNE (Maaten and Hinton, 2008) to visualize the expression representations generated by the feature learning component $h(x)$ of $PCNN$. As the Figure 4 illustrates, compare to the randomly initialized $PCNN$, at the begin of fine-tuning, we are more likely to find the representations closed to each other with the one pre-trained with the sequence reconstruction loss, if the corresponding expressions express the same relation. It is an evidence of our high-level intuition: our unsupervised pre-training losses are able to build similar representations for similar relation

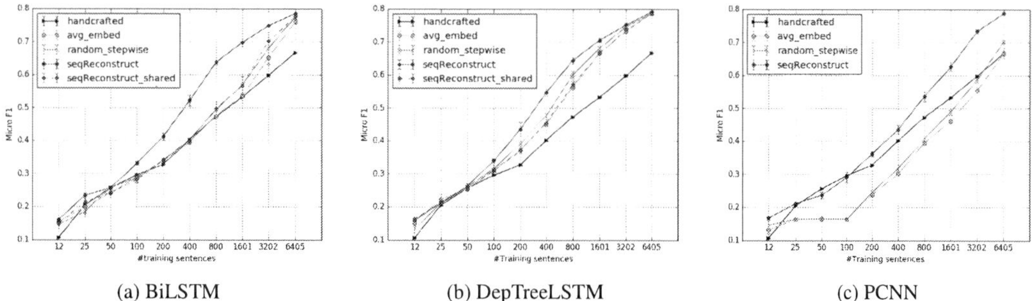

(a) BiLSTM   (b) DepTreeLSTM   (c) PCNN

Figure 3: Comparison between baselines, stepwise training of entity embeddings, and the pre-trained models. The error bars indicate standard deviation computed on all five experiments.

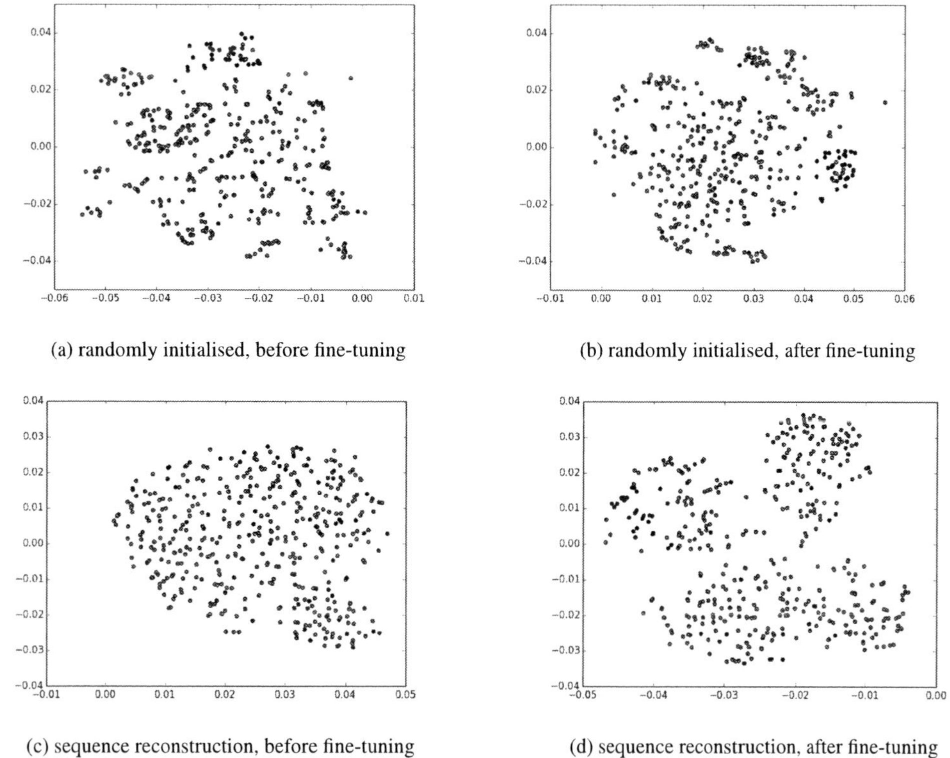

(a) randomly initialised, before fine-tuning   (b) randomly initialised, after fine-tuning

(c) sequence reconstruction, before fine-tuning   (d) sequence reconstruction, after fine-tuning

Figure 4: Visualization of the relation expressions of the top 5 most frequent relations sampled from the development set. The representations of these expressions are generated by using $h(x)$ of *PCNN* and further visualized by T-SNE. The top two figures are generated by randomly initialized *PCNN*, while the bottom ones are generated by *PCNN* pre-trained with *SeqReconstruct*. Different relations are marked with different colors.

expressions. After fine-tuning, the expressions of the same relation form more compact clusters by the pre-trained model than by the randomly initialized one. This explains the performance improvement achieved by the pre-trained *PCNN*.

The size and sampling strategies of unlabeled data have little influence on pre-training. Figure 5 shows that all models achieve similar results on random samples as on `WikiRandom`. Using the whole FIGER corpus leads to a marginal improvement up to 3% F1 score. This suggests that a few thousand randomly selected sentences are sufficient for achieving the pre-training effect with this sequence reconstruction loss.

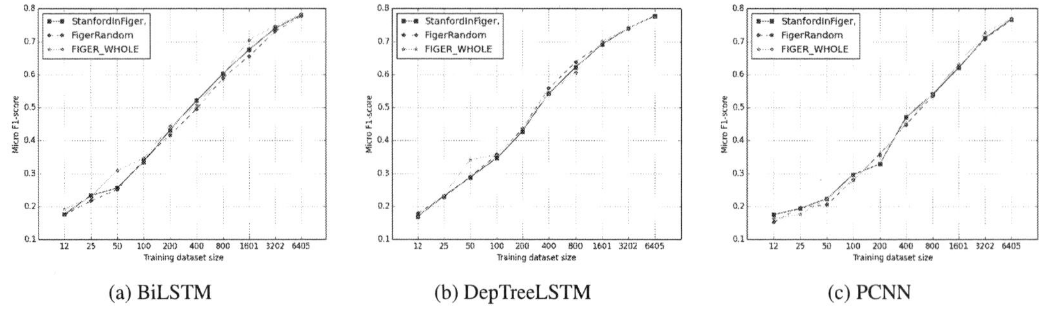

(a) BiLSTM   (b) DepTreeLSTM   (c) PCNN

Figure 5: Impact of the size of training data.

7 Conclusion

In the absence of large amount of manually labeled training data, we propose the sequence reconstruction loss as a generalization of semi-supervised seq2seq model for pre-training deep RE models. The pre-trained models achieve competitive performance as their counterparts without pre-training while employing merely half or even a quarter of the training data.

Acknowledgments

This research was supported by NICTA, funded by the Australian Government through the Department of Communications and the Australian Research Council through the ICT Centre of Excellence Program.

References

Gabor Angeli, Julie Tibshirani, Jean Wu, and Christopher D. Manning. 2014. Combining distant and partial supervision for relation extraction. In *Proceedings of the 2014 Conference on Empirical Methods in Natural Language Processing, October 25-29, Doha, Qatar*, pages 1556–1567.

Yoshua Bengio. 2009. Learning deep architectures for ai. *Foundations and trends® in Machine Learning*, 2(1):1–127.

Antoine Bordes, Nicolas Usunier, Alberto Garcia-Duran, Jason Weston, and Oksana Yakhnenko. 2013. Translating embeddings for modeling multi-relational data. In *Advances in Neural Information Processing Systems*, pages 2787–2795.

Rui Cai, Xiaodong Zhang, and Houfeng Wang. 2016. Bidirectional recurrent convolutional neural network for relation classification. In *Proceedings of the 54th Annual Meeting of the Association for Computational Linguistics, ACL 2016, August 7-12, 2016, Berlin, Germany, Volume 1: Long Papers*.

Yee Seng Chan and Dan Roth. 2010. Exploiting background knowledge for relation extraction. In *23rd International Conference on Computational Linguistics, Proceedings of the Conference, 23-27 August 2010, Beijing, China*, pages 152–160.

Yee Seng Chan and Dan Roth. 2011. Exploiting syntactico-semantic structures for relation extraction. In *Proceedings of the 49th Annual Meeting of the Association for Computational Linguistics*, pages 551–560. Association for Computational Linguistics.

Jinxiu Chen, Donghong Ji, Chew Lim Tan, and Zhengyu Niu. 2006a. Relation extraction using label propagation based semi-supervised learning. In *Proceedings of the 21st International Conference on Computational Linguistics and the 44th annual meeting of the Association for Computational Linguistics*, pages 129–136. Association for Computational Linguistics.

Jinxiu Chen, Donghong Ji, Chew Lim Tan, and Zhengyu Niu. 2006b. Semi-supervised relation extraction with label propagation. In *Proceedings of the Human Language Technology Conference of the NAACL, Companion Volume: Short Papers*, pages 25–28. Association for Computational Linguistics.

Ronan Collobert, Jason Weston, Léon Bottou, Michael Karlen, Koray Kavukcuoglu, and Pavel Kuksa. 2011. Natural language processing (almost) from scratch. *Journal of Machine Learning Research*, 12(Aug):2493–2537.

George Dahl, Abdel-rahman Mohamed, Geoffrey E Hinton, et al. 2010. Phone recognition with the mean-covariance restricted boltzmann machine. In *Advances in neural information processing systems*, pages 469–477.

Andrew M Dai and Quoc V Le. 2015. Semi-supervised sequence learning. In *Advances in Neural Information Processing Systems*, pages 3061–3069.

Bart Desmet and Véronique Hoste. 2014. Fine-grained dutch named entity recognition. *Language Resources and Evaluation*, 48(2):307–343.

Cícero Nogueira dos Santos, Bing Xiang, and Bowen Zhou. 2015. Classifying relations by ranking with convolutional neural networks. In *Proceedings of the 53rd Annual Meeting of the Association for Computational Linguistics and the 7th International Joint Conference on Natural Language Processing of the Asian Federation of Natural Language Processing, ACL 2015, July 26-31, 2015, Beijing, China*, pages 626–634.

John Duchi, Elad Hazan, and Yoram Singer. 2011. Adaptive subgradient methods for online learning and stochastic optimization. *Journal of Machine Learning Research*, 12(Jul):2121–2159.

Javid Ebrahimi and Dejing Dou. 2015. Chain based RNN for relation classification. In *NAACL HLT 2015, The 2015 Conference of the North American Chapter of the Association for Computational Linguistics: Human Language Technologies, Denver, Colorado, USA, May 31 - June 5, 2015*, pages 1244–1249.

Lisheng Fu and Ralph Grishman. 2013. An efficient active learning framework for new relation types. In *IJCNLP*, pages 692–698.

Alex Graves and Jürgen Schmidhuber. 2005. Framewise phoneme classification with bidirectional lstm and other neural network architectures. *Neural Networks*, 18(5):602–610.

Zhou GuoDong, Qian LongHua, and Zhu QiaoMing. 2009. Label propagation via bootstrapped support vectors for semantic relation extraction between named entities. *Computer Speech & Language*, 23(4):464–478.

Geoffrey E Hinton and Ruslan R Salakhutdinov. 2006. Reducing the dimensionality of data with neural networks. *Science*, 313(5786):504–507.

Jing Jiang and ChengXiang Zhai. 2007. A systematic exploration of the feature space for relation extraction. In *HLT-NAACL*, pages 113–120.

Jing Jiang. 2009. Multi-task transfer learning for weakly-supervised relation extraction. In *Proceedings of the Joint Conference of the 47th Annual Meeting of the ACL and the 4th International Joint Conference on Natural Language Processing of the AFNLP: Volume 2-Volume 2*, pages 1012–1020. Association for Computational Linguistics.

Seokhwan Kim and Gary Geunbae Lee. 2012. A graph-based cross-lingual projection approach for weakly supervised relation extraction. In *Proceedings of the 50th Annual Meeting of the Association for Computational Linguistics: Short Papers-Volume 2*, pages 48–53. Association for Computational Linguistics.

Alex Krizhevsky, Ilya Sutskever, and Geoffrey E Hinton. 2012. Imagenet classification with deep convolutional neural networks. In *Advances in neural information processing systems*, pages 1097–1105.

Haibo Li, Yutaka Matsuo, and Mitsuru Ishizuka. 2010. Semantic relation extraction based on semisupervised learning. In *Asia Information Retrieval Symposium*, pages 270–279. Springer.

Yankai Lin, Shiqi Shen, Zhiyuan Liu, Huanbo Luan, and Maosong Sun. 2016. Neural relation extraction with selective attention over instances. In *Proceedings of the 54th Annual Meeting of the Association for Computational Linguistics, ACL 2016, August 7-12, 2016, Berlin, Germany, Volume 1: Long Papers*.

Yang Liu, Furu Wei, Sujian Li, Heng Ji, Ming Zhou, and Houfeng Wang. 2015. A dependency-based neural network for relation classification. In *Proceedings of the 53rd Annual Meeting of the Association for Computational Linguistics and the 7th International Joint Conference on Natural Language Processing of the Asian Federation of Natural Language Processing, ACL 2015, July 26-31, 2015, Beijing, China, Volume 2: Short Papers*, pages 285–290.

ZHOU GuoDong LI JunHui QIAN LongHua and ZHU Qiaoming. 2008. Semi-supervised learning for relation extraction. In *Third International Joint Conference on Natural Language Processing*, page 32.

Laurens van der Maaten and Geoffrey Hinton. 2008. Visualizing data using t-sne. *Journal of Machine Learning Research*, 9(Nov):2579–2605.

Tomas Mikolov, Ilya Sutskever, Kai Chen, Greg S Corrado, and Jeff Dean. 2013. Distributed representations of words and phrases and their compositionality. In *Advances in neural information processing systems*, pages 3111–3119.

Makoto Miwa and Mohit Bansal. 2016. End-to-end relation extraction using lstms on sequences and tree structures. In *Proceedings of the 54th Annual Meeting of the Association for Computational Linguistics, ACL 2016, August 7-12, 2016, Berlin, Germany, Volume 1: Long Papers*.

Thien Huu Nguyen and Ralph Grishman. 2014. Employing word representations and regularization for domain adaptation of relation extraction. In *ACL (2)*, pages 68–74.

Thien Huu Nguyen and Ralph Grishman. 2015. Relation extraction: Perspective from convolutional neural networks. In *Proceedings of NAACL-HLT*, pages 39–48.

Lizhen Qu, Gabriela Ferraro, Liyuan Zhou, Weiwei Hou, Nathan Schneider, and Timothy Baldwin. 2015. Big data small data, in domain out-of-domain, known word unknown word: The impact of word representations on sequence labelling tasks. In *Proceedings of the 19th Conference on Computational Natural Language Learning (CoNLL 2015)*, pages 83–93.

Sebastian Riedel, Limin Yao, Andrew McCallum, and Benjamin M Marlin. 2013. Relation extraction with matrix factorization and universal schemas.

Richard Socher, Brody Huval, Christopher D. Manning, and Andrew Y. Ng. 2012. Semantic compositionality through recursive matrix-vector spaces. In *Proceedings of the 2012 Joint Conference on Empirical Methods in Natural Language Processing and Computational Natural Language Learning, EMNLP-CoNLL 2012, July 12-14, 2012, Jeju Island, Korea*, pages 1201–1211.

Richard Socher, Danqi Chen, Christopher D. Manning, and Andrew Y. Ng. 2013. Reasoning with neural tensor networks for knowledge base completion. In *Advances in Neural Information Processing Systems 26: 27th Annual Conference on Neural Information Processing Systems 2013. Proceedings of a meeting held December 5-8, 2013, Lake Tahoe, Nevada, United States.*, pages 926–934.

Ang Sun and Ralph Grishman. 2012. Active learning for relation type extension with local and global data views. In *Proceedings of the 21st ACM international conference on Information and knowledge management*, pages 1105–1112. ACM.

Ang Sun. 2009. A two-stage bootstrapping algorithm for relation extraction. In *Recent Advances in Natural Language Processing, RANLP 2009, 14-16 September, 2009, Borovets, Bulgaria*, pages 76–82.

Mihai Surdeanu, Julie Tibshirani, Ramesh Nallapati, and Christopher D Manning. 2012. Multi-instance multi-label learning for relation extraction. In *Proceedings of the 2012 Joint Conference on Empirical Methods in Natural Language Processing and Computational Natural Language Learning*, pages 455–465. Association for Computational Linguistics.

Ilya Sutskever, Oriol Vinyals, and Quoc V Le. 2014. Sequence to sequence learning with neural networks. In *Advances in neural information processing systems*, pages 3104–3112.

Kristina Toutanova, Danqi Chen, Patrick Pantel, Hoifung Poon, Pallavi Choudhury, and Michael Gamon. 2015. Representing text for joint embedding of text and knowledge bases. In *Proceedings of the 2015 Conference on Empirical Methods in Natural Language Processing, Lisbon, Portugal, September 17-21, 2015*, pages 1499–1509.

Pascal Vincent, Hugo Larochelle, Isabelle Lajoie, Yoshua Bengio, and Pierre-Antoine Manzagol. 2010. Stacked denoising autoencoders: Learning useful representations in a deep network with a local denoising criterion. *Journal of Machine Learning Research*, 11(Dec):3371–3408.

Oriol Vinyals, Alexander Toshev, Samy Bengio, and Dumitru Erhan. 2014. Show and tell: A neural image caption generator. *CoRR*, abs/1411.4555.

Linlin Wang, Zhu Cao, Gerard de Melo, and Zhiyuan Liu. 2016. Relation classification via multi-level attention cnns. In *Proceedings of the 54th Annual Meeting of the Association for Computational Linguistics, ACL 2016, August 7-12, 2016, Berlin, Germany, Volume 1: Long Papers*.

Jason Weston, Antoine Bordes, Oksana Yakhnenko, and Nicolas Usunier. 2013. Connecting language and knowledge bases with embedding models for relation extraction. *arXiv preprint arXiv:1307.7973*.

Yan Xu, Lili Mou, Ge Li, Yunchuan Chen, Hao Peng, and Zhi Jin. 2015. Classifying relations via long short term memory networks along shortest dependency paths. In *Proceedings of the 2015 Conference on Empirical Methods in Natural Language Processing, EMNLP 2015, Lisbon, Portugal, September 17-21, 2015*, pages 1785–1794.

Bishan Yang, Wen-tau Yih, Xiaodong He, Jianfeng Gao, and Li Deng. 2014. Embedding entities and relations for learning and inference in knowledge bases. *arXiv preprint arXiv:1412.6575*.

Mo Yu, Matthew R. Gormley, and Mark Dredze. 2015. Combining word embeddings and feature embeddings for fine-grained relation extraction. In *The Conference of the North American Chapter of the Association for Computational Linguistics: Human Language Technologies, Denver, Colorado, USA*, pages 1374–1379.

Daojian Zeng, Kang Liu, Siwei Lai, Guangyou Zhou, and Jun Zhao. 2014. Relation classification via convolutional deep neural network. In *COLING 2014, 25th International Conference on Computational Linguistics, Proceedings of the Conference: Technical Papers, August 23-29, 2014, Dublin, Ireland*, pages 2335–2344.

Shu Zhang, Dequan Zheng, Xinchen Hu, and Ming Yang. 2015. Bidirectional long short-term memory networks for relation classification. In *Proceedings of the 29th Pacific Asia Conference on Language, Information and Computation, PACLIC 29, Shanghai, China, October 30 - November 1, 2015*.

ASM Kernel: Graph Kernel using Approximate Subgraph Matching for Relation Extraction

Nagesh C. Panyam, Karin Verspoor, Trevor Cohn and Kotagiri Ramamohanarao
Department of Computing and Information Systems,
The University of Melbourne, Australia
npanyam@student.unimelb.edu.au
{karin.verspoor, t.cohn, kotagiri}@unimelb.edu.au

Abstract

Kernel methods have been widely studied in several natural language processing tasks such as relation extraction and sentence classification. In this work, we present a new graph kernel that is derived from a distance measure described in prior work as Approximate Subgraph Matching (ASM). The classical ASM distance, shown to be effective for event extraction, is not a valid kernel and was primarily designed to work with rule based systems. We modify this distance suitably to render it a valid kernel (ASM kernel) and enable its use in powerful learning algorithms such as Support Vector Machine (SVM).

We compare the ASM kernel with SVMs to the classical ASM with a rule based approach, for two relation extraction tasks and show an improved performance with the kernel based approach. Compared to other kernels such as the Subset tree kernel and the Partial tree kernel, ASM kernel outperforms in relation extraction tasks and is of comparable performance in a general sentence classification task. We describe the advantages of the ASM kernel such as its flexibility and ease of modification, which offers further directions for improvement.

1 Introduction

Many natural language processing tasks such as relation extraction or question classification are cast as supervised classification problems (Bunescu and Mooney, 2005), with the object to classify being an entity pair or a sentence. Traditional approaches have typically focussed on transforming the input into a feature vector which is then classified using learning algorithms such as decision trees or SVM. A primary limitation of this approach has been the manual effort required to construct a rich set of features that can yield a high performance classification. This effort is evident for the construction of features from the syntactic parse of the text, which is often represented as an ordered structure such as a tree or a graph. Linearizing a highly expressive structure such as a graph, by transforming it into a flat array of features is inherently harder. This problem of constructing explicit feature sets for complex objects is generally overcome by kernel methods for classification. Kernel methods allow for an implicit exploration of a vast high dimensional feature space and shift the focus from feature engineering to similarity score design. Importantly, such a kernel must be shown to be symmetric and positive semi-definite (Burges, 1998), to be valid for use with kernelized learning algorithms such as SVM. Deep learning based approches (Zeng et al., 2014; Xu et al., 2015) are other alternatives to eliminate the manual feature engineering efforts. However, in this work we are primarily focussed on kernel methods.

In NLP, kernel methods have been effectively used for relation extraction and sentence classification. Subset tree kernels (SSTK) and partial tree kernels (PTK) were developed to work with constituency parse trees and basic dependency parse trees. However, these kernels are not suitable for arbitrary graph structures such as the enhanced dependency parses (Manning et al., 2014). Secondly, tree kernels can only handle node labels and not edge labels. As a work around, these kernels require that the original dependency graphs be heuristically altered to translate edge labels into special nodes to create different syntactic representations such as the grammatical relation centered tree (Croce et al., 2011). These limitations were overcome with the Approximate Subgraph

Nagesh C Panyam, Karin Verspoor, Trevor Cohn and Rao Kotagiri. 2016. ASM Kernel: Graph Kernel using Approximate Subgraph Matching for Relation Extraction. In *Proceedings of Australasian Language Technology Association Workshop*, pages 65–73.

Matching (ASM) (Liu et al., 2013), that was designed to be a flexible distance measure to handle arbitrary graphs with edge labels and edge directions. However, the classic ASM is not a valid kernel and therefore cannot be used with powerful learning algorithms like SVM. It was therefore used in a rule-based setting, where it was shown to be effective for event extraction (Kim et al., 2011).

1.1 Contributions

In this work, our primary contribution is a new graph kernel (ASM kernel), derived from the classical approximate subgraph matching distance, that:

- is flexible, working directly with graphs with cycles and edge labels.
- is a valid kernel for use with powerful learning algorithms like SVM.
- outperforms classical ASM distance with rule based method for relation extraction.
- outperforms tree kernels for relation extraction and is of comparable performance for a sentence classification task.

2 Methods

In this section, we first describe the classical ASM distance measure that was originally proposed in (Liu et al., 2013). We then discuss the modifications we introduce to transform this distance measure into a symmetric, L_2 norm in a valid feature space. This step allows us to enumerate the underlying feature space and to elucidate the mapping from a graph to a vector in a high dimensional feature space. We then define the ASM kernel as a dot product in this high dimensional space of well defined features. Besides establishing the validity of the kernel, the feature map clarifies the semantics of the kernel and helps design of interpretable models.

2.1 Classic ASM distance

We describe the classic ASM distance in the context of a binary relation extraction task. Consider two sample sentences drawn from the training set and test set of such a task corpus, as illustrated in Figure 1. Entity annotations are given for the whole corpus, which are character spans referring to two entities in a sentence. In the illustrated example, the entities are chemicals (metoclopramide and pentobarbital) and diseases (dyskinesia and amnesia). The training data also contains relation

annotations, which are related entity pairs (metoclopramide, dyskinesia). We assume that the relation (causation) is implied by the training sentence and then to try to infer a similar relation or its absence in the test sentence.

Preprocessing The first step in the ASM event extraction system is to transform each sentence to a graph, whose nodes represent tokens in the sentence. Node labels are derived from the corresponding tokens properties, such as the word lemma or part of speech (POS) tag or a combination of both. The node labels for entities are usually designated as *Entity1* and *Entity2*. This process is referred to as *entity blinding* and is known to improve generalization (Thomas et al., 2011). Labelled edges are given by a dependency parser (Manning et al., 2014). A graph from a test sentence is referred to as a *main graph*. Given a training sentence and its corresponding graph, we extract the subgraph within it, that consists of only those nodes that represent the entities or belong to the shortest path[1] between the two entities. This is referred to as a *rule subgraph* (see Figure 1a).

Approximate Subgraph Isomorphism The main idea in ASM is that a test sentence is considered to be of same type or express the same relation as that of a training sentence, if we can find a subgraph isomorphism of rule graph (training sentence) in the main graph (test sentence). Exact subgraph isomorphism (boolean) is considered too strict and is expected to hurt generalization. Instead, ASM tries to compute a measure (a real number) of subgraph isomorphism. This measure is referred to as the *Approximate Subgraph Matching* distance. If the ASM distance between a rule graph and main graph is within a predefined *threshold*, then the test sentence is considered positive, or of the same relation type as the rule graph.

ASM distance We first compute an injective mapping M from rule graph to main graph. An injective matching scheme essentially maps each node of the subgraph to a node in the main graph, with identical labels. If no matching scheme can be found, then the ASM distance is set to a very large quantity (∞). Following the node matching, we do not demand a matching of edges between

---

[1] Throughout this paper, shortest path refers to the path with least number of edges in the undirected version of the graph.

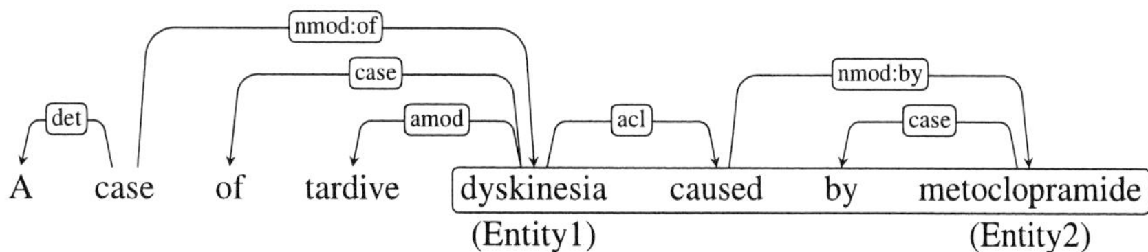

(a) Graph from a training sentence. The rule subgraph within is shown with a surrounding box.

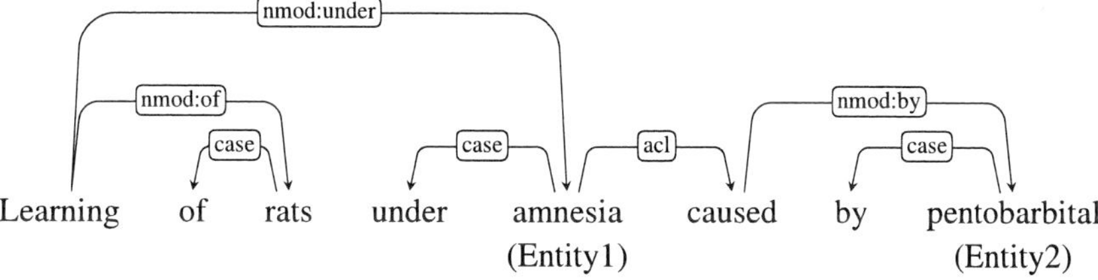

(b) Main graph from a test sentence.

Figure 1: Sample dependency graphs from two sentences expressing a relation of type "causation" between two entities.

the two graphs, like in a typical exact isomorphism search. Instead, we compute the difference between these edges to get an approximate subgraph matching (ASM) distance. The ASM distance is a weighted summation of 3 components, namely structural distance, label distance and directionality distance. These are described below, with the aid of notations described in Table 1. Note that edge directions are interpreted as special *directional labels* of type "forward" or "backward".

The structural distance (SD), label distance (LD) and the directionality distance (DD) for a path $P^r_{x,y}$ is defined as:

$$
\begin{aligned}
\mathrm{SD}(P^r_{x,y}, P^m_{x',y'}) &= \ |\mathrm{Len}(P^r_{x,y}) - \mathrm{Len}(P^m_{x',y'})| \\
\mathrm{LD}(P^r_{x,y}, P^m_{x',y'}) &= \ \#\mathrm{EL}(P^r_{x,y}) \triangle \mathrm{EL}(P^m_{x',y'}) \\
\mathrm{DD}(P^r_{x,y}, P^m_{x',y'}) &= \ \#\mathrm{DL}(P^r_{x,y}) \triangle \mathrm{DL}(P^m_{x',y'})
\end{aligned}
\tag{1}
$$

Essentially, these distances reflect the differences in the structure of the two graphs, focussed at one vertex pair at a time. Notice that the above distances are defined for a given shortest path between two vertices. However, there could be multiple shortest paths of equal length between two vertices in a graph. The distances for a given vertex pair is taken to be the minimum distance over all possible choices for a shortest path.

If $SP(x, y)$ and $SP(x', y')$ denote the set of shortest paths for x, y in the rule graph and x', y' in the main graph respectively, the distance measures for the vertex pair x, y are defined as:

Symbol	Meaning
$G^m = <V^m, E^m>$	Main graph
$G^r = <V^r, E^r>$	Rule graph
$M = \{(x, x'), \ldots\}$, $\forall x \in V^r$ s.t, $\mathrm{label}(x) = \mathrm{label}(x')$ and $x' \in V^m$.	M is the injective mapping scheme, i.e $M(x) = x'$
$P^g_{x,y}$	Shortest path in graph g between the vertices x, y.
$\mathrm{Len}(P)$	The length of the path P.
$\mathrm{EL}(P)$	The multiset of edge labels on the path P.
$\mathrm{DL}(P)$	The multiset of directional labels on the path P.
$S_1 \triangle S_2$	The set symmetric difference of sets S_1 and S_2 .
$|r_1 - r_2|$	The absolute difference of real numbers r_1 and r_2
$\#S$	The cardinality of set S.

Table 1: Notations used in this paper

$$SD(x,y) = \min_{\forall P \in SP(x,y), P' \in SP(x',y')} SD(P,P')$$

$$LD(x,y) = \min_{\forall P \in SP(x,y), P' \in SP(x',y')} LD(P,P')$$

$$DD(x,y) = \min_{\forall P \in SP(x,y), P' \in SP(x',y')} DD(P,P')$$

$$(2)$$

The (unnormalized) distance measure between two graphs G^r and G^m is obtained from the distances between all possible vertex pairs:

$$SD(G^r, G^m) = \sum_{\forall x,y \in V^r} SD(x,y)$$

$$LD(G^r, G^m) = \sum_{\forall x,y \in V^r} LD(x,y) \qquad (3)$$

$$DD(G^r, G^m) = \sum_{\forall x,y \in V^r} DD(x,y)$$

The final classical ASM distance in its unnormalized form is a weighted summation of the above 3 components:

$$\begin{aligned} ASM(G^r, G^m) =\,& w_1 \times SD(G^r, G^m) \\ &+ w_2 \times LD(G^r, G^m) \qquad (4) \\ &+ w_3 \times DD(G^r, G^m) \end{aligned}$$

The classic ASM distance includes a normalization process that we have not described, as it is not central to our discussion. Notice that this distance does not meet the conditions of a positive semidefinite kernel. Trivially, it is an asymmetric distance and undefined when an injective matching is unavailable. In the next section, we describe a modified form of ASM that is shown to be a $||L_2||$ norm in a valid feature space.

2.2 Modified ASM distance

Classical ASM distance measure evaluates distances between two pairs of vertices $x, y \in G^r$ and $x', y' \in G^m$ where $x' = M(x)$ and $y' = M(y)$ and M is the injective matching scheme. Recall that the simplest injective matching scheme maps vertices with identical labels. We assume that node labels in a graph are all distinct. Further, for all missing labels in a graph G, we (virtually) insert a single disconnected dummy node with that label. These steps ensure that all labels in the label vocabulary are represented in the graph G and map to unique vertices. We can

Symbol	Meaning
$P^g_{x,y}$	The representative shortest path in graph g between the vertices x, y.
$EL(P)$	The bag of words representation of edge labels on the path P.
$DL(P)$	The bag of words representation of directional labels on the path P.
$||V_1 - V_2||_2$	The $||L_2||$ norm of the vector difference $V_1 - V_2$
$L = \{a, an, the, \ldots\}$	The vocabulary of all node labels (lemmas)

Table 2: Additional notations for the modified ASM

now define the modified ASM distance over label pairs, instead of vertex pairs. Next, in the modified ASM distance, we consider only a single shortest path between a label pair x, y. For example, in Figure 1a the shortest path $P_{\text{"caused"},\text{"by"}} = $ ("caused", "Entity2", "by"). When more than one such shortest path is available (due to cycles), we simply choose the first of such paths as the representative shortest path. Finally, we transform the set of edge labels in each path into a vector representation (i.e, a bag of words representation). For example, $EL(P_{\text{"caused"},\text{"by"}}) = $ ("nmod:by" : 1, "case" : 1). We use the euclidean distance between these vectors, instead of the cardinality of set symmetric difference used in the classical ASM label distance. Directionality distance is modified similarly.

The modified distances, namely structural distance (SD), label distance (LD) and directionality distance (DD) are defined below, following a few additional notations in Table 2:

$$\mathrm{SD}(G^r, G^m) =$$
$$\sum_{\forall l_1, l_2 \in L \times L} (\mathrm{Len}(P^r_{x,y}) - \mathrm{Len}(P^m_{x',y'}))^2$$

$$\mathrm{LD}(G^r, G^m) =$$
$$\sum_{\forall l_1, l_2 \in L \times L} \|\mathrm{EL}(P^r_{x,y}) - \mathrm{EL}(P^m_{x',y'})\|_2 \qquad (5)$$

$$\mathrm{DD}(G^r, G^m) =$$
$$\sum_{\forall l_1, l_2 \in L \times L} \|\mathrm{DL}(P^r_{x,y}) - \mathrm{DL}(P^m_{x',y'})\|_2$$

$$\text{where} \quad \mathrm{label}(x) = \mathrm{label}(x') = l_1$$
$$\text{and} \quad \mathrm{label}(y) = \mathrm{label}(y') = l_2$$

The final modified ASM distance in its unnormalized form is a weighted summation of the above 3 components:

$$\begin{aligned}\mathrm{ASM}(G^r, G^m) =\ & w_1 \times \mathrm{SD}(G^r, G^m) \\ & + w_2 \times \mathrm{LD}(G^r, G^m) \qquad (6) \\ & + w_3 \times \mathrm{DD}(G^r, G^m)\end{aligned}$$

2.3 ASM Kernel: Validity and Semantics

A valid kernel function is required to be symmetric and positive semidefinite (Burges, 1998). Also, from Mercer's condition (Burges, 1998), we note that such a kernel is essentially equivalent to a dot product ($K(x,y) = \sum_i \phi(x)_i \phi(y)_i$) in a euclidean (or a general RKHS) "feature" space and a valid mapping function(ϕ) exists, that transforms the input object to the feature space. Kernel validity can be directly established by deriving the underlying feature map (ϕ), and computing the kernel directly as a dot product of the mapped vectors ($\langle \phi(x), \phi(y) \rangle$). Also, this feature map directly relates to the semantics of the kernel and helps to interpret the resulting model. We follow this approach, to first derive the feature space ϕ underlying the modified ASM distance and show it to be equivalent to the $\|L_2\|$ norm in this feature space. That is, modified ASM distance$(x,y) = \sum_i (\phi(x)_i - \phi(y)_i)^2$. The ASM kernel can then be obtained by replacing the sum of squared differences with sum of products. That is, the ASM kernel$(x,y) = \sum_i \phi(x)_i \phi(y)_i$.

The feature space of structural distance can be indexed by the set $\{L \times L\}$ where L is the vocabulary of node labels. Each feature value is just the length of the shortest path between a label pair corresponding to the feature index. Similarly, the directionality distance corresponds to two sets of features indexed by $\{L \times L\}$. The first feature set counts the number of "forward" edges and the second set counts the number of "backward" edges in the shortest path corresponding to the feature index. Finally, the label distance can be seen as an extension of directionality distance, obtained by extending the set of edge labels from a limited set of two symbols {"forward", "backward"} to the finite set of all possible dependency edge labels.

Consider the example illustrated in Figure 1a. The ASM kernel transforms the rule graph in the above example, to an explicit set of features as described below. The set of node labels for this example is $L' = \{$"Entity1", "caused", "by", "Entity2"$\}$. The set of edge labels for this example is $EL' = \{$"acl", "nmod:by", "case"$\}$. The features corresponding to this example can be indexed by the set $L' \times \{EL' \cup \{$"distance", "forward", "backward"$\}\}$. Tuples such as ("Entity1", "caused", "distance") and ("Entity1", "by", "distance") represent structural distance features. The values for these are 1 and 3 respectively. Tuples such as ("Entity1", "caused", "forward") and ("Entity1", "by", "forward") denote the forward directionality features. The values for these are 1 and 2 respectively. Similarly, features for label distance are generated by considering the elements of EL'. For example, the edge label "acl" is associated with the tuples such as ("Entity1", "caused", "acl") and ("Entity1", "by", "acl"). The values for these features are 1 and 1 respectively. This is because, there is exactly one instance of the edge label "acl" in the shortest path from "Entity1" to "caused" and from "Entity1" to "by".

To summarize, we note that the modified ASM distance is a sum of squared differences of feature counts (real numbers) and the corresponding feature space is a finite and enumerable set as shown above. By replacing the sum of squares with sum of products of the feature counts, we obtain the dot product in the same valid feature space, which forms the ASM kernel.

2.4 Running times

The classical ASM distance has an exponential time complexity, typically brought about by the search for subgraph isomorphism. Still, it was shown to be practical, as text with very long sentences and therefore large dependency graphs are quite rare. However, the current ASM kernel evaluation is polynomial in runtime as there is no requirement for an isomorphism test.

Consider two graphs with m and n vertices and $m \leq n$ without loss of generality. We first identify the vertices with common labels across the graph, via a sort merge of label lists. This step takes $O(n \cdot \log(m))$. Next, note that there are at most m^2 label pairs that are common to two graphs. Each label pair corresponds to a path in the graph with at most n nodes. Enumerating the features of this graph involves a single traversal of each such path, which translates to a complexity bound of $O(n \cdot m^2)$ or simply $O(n^3)$ (a looser upper bound). Finding the shortest paths across all node pairs can be done in $O(n^3)$ time using standard graph algorithms (Seidel, 1995).

2.5 Implementation details

We used the Java based Kelp framework (Filice et al., 2015) for implementing and testing the ASM kernel with SVM. For this paper, the weights associated with the ASM method (w_1, w_2, w_3) are all set to 1. The feature set for each graph can be computed in parallel and cached. In practice, we found that SVM train-test cycle with ASM kernel took about a day for some of the largest datasets described in this paper. For classic ASM distance, we used the implementation[2] made freely available by the authors.

3 Evaluation

We described the classic ASM distance in the context of a binary relation extraction task in Section 2.1. In this section, we report the performance of this approach over two relation extraction tasks, namely the Chemical-induced-Disease (CID) task (Wei et al., 2015) and the Seedev-Binary relation extraction task (Chaix et al., 2016). Note that it is a rule based with a single parameter being the distance threshold. We determine the optimal threshold value with a grid search over the validation set. We compare this rule based system with a supervised classification approach for relation extraction. The dependency graph of a sentence is made entity aware, by setting the labels of the two nodes corresponding to entities as "Entity1" and "Entity2". Relation extraction is cast as the task of graph labelling using a multiclass SVM

[2]http://asmalgorithm.sourceforge.net

Kernel	P	R	F1
Classical ASM system	35.1	81.1	49.0
PTK with LCT	43.3	77.3	55.5
SSTK with CP	42.6	72.8	53.7
ASM Kernel with DP	46.4	77.7	**58.1**

Table 3: Results on CID test data for sentence level relations. Key: LCT= Location Centered Tree, CP = Constituency Parse, DP = Dependency Parse

with ASM kernel. We extend the comparison to two well known tree kernels, namely Subset Tree Kernel (SSTK) and the Partial Tree Kernel (PTK) that have been shown to be effective for relation extraction (Zelenko et al., 2002; Moschitti, 2006; Chowdhury et al., 2011). Note that unlike constituency parse trees, dependency trees have edge labels which cannot be handled by these tree kernels. Therefore, the edge labels are converted into node labels of specially inserted nodes in the original dependency graph, to get a modified structure referred to as the *Location Centered Tree* (LCT) (Lan et al., 2009).

Finally, we compare the ASM kernel with tree kernels in a sentence classification task. This is a straightforward application of kernels in a graph classification problem, over the unmodified dependency graphs of the corpus.

3.1 Chemical induced Disease (CID) task

The goal of the CID shared task (Wei et al., 2015) is to infer the "induces" relation between Chemicals and Disease from biomedical publications. The shared task has provided a corpus of 1500 PubMed abstracts, divided equally into training, development and test datasets. The corpus includes non-sentence relations, i.e. Chemical-Disease pairs whose relationship cannot be inferred by a single sentence and requires analyzing the whole abstract. We omit such relations and focus on extracting sentence level relations only. We compare ASM kernel against Subset tree kernels (SSTK) and Partial tree kernels (PTK) and report the results in Table 3.

3.2 Seedev Binary

The Seedev Binary task (Chaix et al., 2016) addresses the extraction of genetic and molecular mechanisms that regulate plant seed development from biomedical literature. The task organizers

Kernel	P	R	F1
Classical ASM	8.8	41.7	14.5
PTK with DP	11.6	38.0	17.8
SSTK with DP	14.4	24.6	18.2
SSTK with CP	14.8	32.6	20.3
ASM Kernel	25.0	27.9	**26.4**

Table 4: Aggregate results over the development dataset of the Seedev Binary task. Key:CP = Constituency Parse, DP = Dependency Parse

Kernel	Accuracy (% age)
Bag of Words	86.2
Partial Tree Kernel with LCT	90.6
Subset Tree Kernel with GRCT	**91.4**
ASM Kernel	89.6

Table 5: Results on Question Classification dataset.

provided paragraphs from manually selected full text publications on seed development of *Arabidopsis thaliana* annotated with mentions of biological entities like *proteins* and *genes*, and binary relations like *Exists_In_Genotype* and *Occurs_In_Genotype*. The Seedev task involves extraction of 22 different binary relations over 16 entity types. The corpus provided consists of a total of $7,082$ entities and $3,575$ binary relations, divided into training, development and test datasets. Entity mentions within a sentence and the events between them are provided in the gold standard annotations. We created 22 separate classifiers for detecting each of these relation types. A special feature of this task is that each relation type is associated with a type signature, that specifies which entity types are allowed for the given relation, as its two arguments. We use this type signature, to filter the corpus to create 22 separate training and test sets, for each of the 22 classifiers. In Table 4 aggregate results over the 22 event types are reported for the development set (the annotations for the test set are not available).

3.3 Question Classification

This task deals with classifying general questions expressed in natural language, into one of 6 categories such as HUMAN and LOCATION, a first step in a question answering system. For example, "What is the width of a football field?" is to be classified as a NUMBER. The corpus for this task is the UIUC dataset (Li and Roth, 2002) that consists of $5,542$ questions for training and 500 questions for test[3].

Tree kernels were shown to offer state of the art classification accuracy for this dataset. More details about tree kernels for question classification can be found in (Annesi et al., 2014). In this work, we are concerned with exploiting lex-

[3] http://cogcomp.cs.illinois.edu/Data/QA/QC/

ical and syntactic information only and therefore choose SSTK and PTKs for comparison with ASM and exclude Semantic Partial Tree Kernel (SPTK) that incorporates semantic word similarity (via clustering or word2vec (Goldberg and Levy, 2014)). In Table 5, we report the accuracy of these kernels for the question classification task.

4 Discussion

Evaluation over the two relation extraction tasks reveals that the ASM kernel outperforms both the tree kernels and the classical ASM rule based system. For a more general sentence classification task, we note that the ASM kernel performs competitively to tree kernels but not better. A study of the final scores attained also reveals that the relation extraction tasks are more difficult than general sentence classification tasks. We infer that the flexibility of the ASM kernel such as ability to handle edge labels and directions, is more advantageous in a relation extraction task than a general sentence classification task. This may be due to the fact that relation extraction is primarily focussed on the interaction between two entities in a sentence, which is best described by the edge labels on the shortest dependency path. In contrast, sentence classification is more general and considers the overall properties of a sentence.

Feature selection A closer study of the relation extraction tasks revealed that a simple linear classifier with bag of words and few syntactic features (the lemmas and POS tags of the neighbors of entity nodes in the dependency graph) outperforms any of the kernel methods discussed in this paper. These results are presented in Table 6. This observation suggests that kernel methods are likely to benefit by a simplification or pruning of their feature sets. The clearly defined feature space underlying the ASM kernel makes it amenable to intelligent feature selection techniques such as principal component analysis (PCA) that we plan to explore in future.

Semantic matching ASM relies on comparing properties of paths or graph walks, that are indexed by label pairs. In the simplest case, node labels are taken to be word lemmas instead of word tokens, to improve generalization across minute variations in word usage (such as "cured" and "curing"). We hypothesize that the generalizability of ASM can be further improved by choosing node labels on word classes. Node labels may be set to cluster ids, post word clustering. A semantic matching of lemmas (such as "cured" and "improved"), based on word semantics using distributional word similarities may allow for improved generalization (Saleh et al., 2014).

Task	Kernel	P	R	F1
Seedev	ASM Kernel	25.0	27.9	26.4
Seedev	Linear (hand crafted features)	30.0	34.9	**32.3**
CID	ASM Kernel	46.4	77.7	58.1
CID	Linear(hand crafted features)	54.8	81.5	**65.6**

Table 6: Comparison of ASM kernel with a linear classifier with hand crafted features.

5 Related Work

The closest work to ours is the classical ASM distance (Liu et al., 2013) that has been successfully used in several shared tasks (Kim et al., 2011). Tree kernels in NLP have been studied extensively in (Collins and Duffy, 2001). Relation extraction has been of particular importance within biomedical domain and has been studied in different contexts such as drug-drug interaction (Bjorne et al., 2011) and protein-protein interaction (Lan et al., 2009). Kernels that use constituent parses or dependency structures are studied in (Chowdhury et al., 2011; Airola et al., 2008) for the protein-protein interaction extraction. All path graph (APG) kernel (Airola et al., 2008) over dependency graph is a related work, that has different semantics as compared to ASM. The APG kernel considers all paths between a vertex pair and not just single shortest path as done in the ASM kernel. The primary feature in the

APG kernel is the strength of connection between a vertex pair, which is computed as the product of edge weights along the path. Note that edge labels and not edge weights are the natural properties of a dependency graph. APG proposes modifications to the dependency graph to accommodate edge labels and heuristically driven assignment of edge weights to the dependency graph. An other recent approach in kernel design (Saleh et al., 2014), has been the efforts to include word similarity such as distributional word similarity given by word2vec (Goldberg and Levy, 2014). Incorporating semantic word similarity in ASM is likely to further improve its performance.

6 Summary and Conclusion

In this work, we defined a graph kernel from a previously studied Approximate Subgraph Matching (ASM) distance measure. We demonstrate the effectiveness of this new kernel by experimenting over standard datasets for question classification and relation extraction. Results indicate that the ASM kernel is of comparable performance to the tree kernels for sentence classification, but outperforms tree kernels in relation extraction tasks. We show the validity of the ASM kernel by deriving its feature space and illuminating the semantics of the kernel. Following on these steps, we identify several improvements to the ASM kernel that are likely to further boost its performance.

References

Antti Airola, Sampo Pyysalo, Jari Björne, Tapio Pahikkala, Filip Ginter, and Tapio Salakoski. 2008. A graph kernel for protein-protein interaction extraction. In *Proceedings of the workshop on current trends in biomedical natural language processing*, pages 1–9. Association for Computational Linguistics.

Paolo Annesi, Danilo Croce, and Roberto Basili. 2014. Semantic compositionality in tree kernels. In *Proceedings of the 23rd ACM International Conference on Conference on Information and Knowledge Management*, CIKM '14, pages 1029–1038, New York, NY, USA. ACM.

Jari Bjorne, Antti Airola, Tapio Pahikkala, and Tapio Salakoski. 2011. Drug-drug interaction extraction from biomedical texts with SVM and RLS classifiers. *CEUR Workshop Proceedings*, 761:35–42.

Razvan C Bunescu and Raymond J Mooney. 2005. A shortest path dependency kernel for relation extraction. In *Proceedings of the conference on Human Language Technology and Empirical Methods in Natural Language Processing*, pages 724–731. Association for Computational Linguistics.

Christopher JC Burges. 1998. A tutorial on support vector machines for pattern recognition. *Data mining and knowledge discovery*, 2(2):121–167.

Estelle Chaix, Bertrand Dubreucq, Abdelhak Fatihi, Dialekti Valsamou, Robert Bossy, Mouhamadou Ba, Louise Delger, Pierre Zweigenbaum, Philippe Bessires, Loc Lepiniec, and Claire Ndellec. 2016. Overview of the regulatory network of plant seed development (seedev) task at the bionlp shared task 2016. In *Proceedings of the 4th BioNLP Shared Task workshop*, Berlin, Germany, August. Association for Computational Linguistics.

Faisal Mahbub Chowdhury, Alberto Lavelli, and Alessandro Moschitti. 2011. A study on dependency tree kernels for automatic extraction of protein-protein interaction. In *Proceedings of BioNLP 2011 Workshop*, BioNLP '11, pages 124–133, Stroudsburg, PA, USA. Association for Computational Linguistics.

Michael Collins and Nigel Duffy. 2001. Convolution kernels for natural language. In *Advances in neural information processing systems*, pages 625–632.

Danilo Croce, Alessandro Moschitti, and Roberto Basili. 2011. Structured lexical similarity via convolution kernels on dependency trees. In *Proceedings of the Conference on Empirical Methods in Natural Language Processing*, pages 1034–1046. Association for Computational Linguistics.

Simone Filice, Giuseppe Castellucci, Danilo Croce, and Roberto Basili. 2015. Kelp: a kernel-based learning platform for natural language processing. In *Proceedings of ACL-IJCNLP 2015 System Demonstrations*, pages 19–24, Beijing, China, July. Association for Computational Linguistics and The Asian Federation of Natural Language Processing.

Yoav Goldberg and Omer Levy. 2014. word2vec explained: deriving mikolov et al.'s negative-sampling word-embedding method. *arXiv preprint arXiv:1402.3722*.

Jin-Dong Kim, Sampo Pyysalo, Tomoko Ohta, Robert Bossy, Ngan Nguyen, and Junichi Tsujii. 2011. Overview of bionlp shared task 2011. In *Proceedings of the BioNLP Shared Task 2011 Workshop*, pages 1–6. Association for Computational Linguistics.

Man Lan, Chew Lim Tan, and Jian Su. 2009. Feature generation and representations for protein-protein interaction classification. *Journal of Biomedical Informatics*, 42:866–872.

Xin Li and Dan Roth. 2002. Learning question classifiers. In *Proceedings of the 19th international conference on Computational linguistics-Volume 1*, pages 1–7. Association for Computational Linguistics.

Haibin Liu, Lawrence Hunter, Vlado Kešelj, and Karin Verspoor. 2013. Approximate subgraph matching-based literature mining for biomedical events and relations. *PloS one*, 8(4):e60954.

Christopher D Manning, Mihai Surdeanu, John Bauer, Jenny Finkel, Steven J Bethard, and David Mc-Closky. 2014. The stanford corenlp natural language processing toolkit. In *Proceedings of 52nd Annual Meeting of the Association for Computational Linguistics: System Demonstrations*, pages 55–60.

Alessandro Moschitti. 2006. Efficient convolution kernels for dependency and constituent syntactic trees. In *European Conference on Machine Learning*, pages 318–329. Springer.

I Saleh, Alessandro Moschitti, Preslav Nakov, L Màrquez, and S Joty. 2014. Semantic Kernels for Semantic Parsing. *Proceedings of the 2014 Conference on Empirical Methods in Natural Language Processing (EMNLP)*, pages 436–442.

Raimund Seidel. 1995. On the all-pairs-shortest-path problem in unweighted undirected graphs. *Journal of computer and system sciences*, 51(3):400–403.

Philippe Thomas, Mariana Neves, Illés Solt, Domonkos Tikk, and Ulf Leser. 2011. Relation extraction for drug-drug interactions using ensemble learning. *Training*, 4(2,402):21–425.

Chih-Hsuan Wei, Yifan Peng, Robert Leaman, Allan Peter Davis, Carolyn J Mattingly, Jiao Li, Thomas C Wiegers, and Zhiyong Lu. 2015. Overview of the biocreative v chemical disease relation (cdr) task. In *Proceedings of the fifth BioCreative challenge evaluation workshop, Sevilla, Spain*.

Yan Xu, Lili Mou, Ge Li, Yunchuan Chen, Hao Peng, and Zhi Jin. 2015. Classifying relations via long short term memory networks along shortest dependency paths. In *Proceedings of Conference on Empirical Methods in Natural Language Processing (to appear)*.

Dmitry Zelenko, Chinatsu Aone, and Anthony Richardella. 2002. Kernel methods for relation extraction. *Journal of Machine Learning Research*, 3:1083–1106.

Daojian Zeng, Kang Liu, Siwei Lai, Guangyou Zhou, Jun Zhao, et al. 2014. Relation classification via convolutional deep neural network. In *COLING*, pages 2335–2344.

N-ary Biographical Relation Extraction using Shortest Path Dependencies

Gitansh Khirbat   **Jianzhong Qi**   **Rui Zhang**
Department of Computing and Information Systems
The University of Melbourne
Australia
gkhirbat@student.unimelb.edu.au
{jianzhong.qi, rui.zhang}@unimelb.edu.au

Abstract

Modern question answering and summarizing systems have motivated the need for complex n-ary relation extraction systems where the number of related entities (n) can be more than two. Shortest path dependency kernels have been proven to be effective in extracting binary relations. In this work, we propose a method that employs shortest path dependency based rules to extract complex n-ary relations without decomposing a sentence into constituent binary relations. With an aim of extracting biographical entities and relations from manually annotated datasets of Australian researchers and department seminar mails, we train an information extraction system which first extracts entities using conditional random fields and then employs the shortest path dependency based rules along with semantic and syntactic features to extract n-ary affiliation relations using support vector machine. Cross validation of this method on the two datasets provides evidence that it outperforms the state-of-the-art n-ary relation extraction system by a margin of 8% F-score.

1   Introduction

Information extraction (IE) is the process of extracting factual information from unstructured and semi-structured data and storing it in a structured queryable format. Two important components of an IE system are entity extraction and relation extraction. These components are sequential and together form the backbone of a classic IE system. Entity extraction systems have achieved a high accuracy in identifying certain entities such as mention of people, places and organizations (Finkel et al., 2005). However, such *named entity recognition* (NER) systems are domain-dependent and do not scale up well to generalize across all entities.

Relation extraction systems utilize the identified entities to extract relations among them. Past two decades have witnessed a significant advancement in extracting binary domain-dependent relations (Kambhatla, 2004), (Zhao and Grishman, 2005) and (Bunescu and Mooney, 2005a). However, modern question answering and summarizing systems have triggered an interest in capturing detailed information in a structured and semantically coherent fashion, thus motivating the need for complex n-ary relation extraction systems (where the number of entities, $n \geq 2$). Some notable n-ary relation extraction systems are (McDonald et al., 2005) and (Li et al., 2015). McDonald et al. (2005) factorized complex n-ary relation into binary relations, representing them in a graph and tried to reconstruct the complex relation by making tuples from selected maximal cliques in the graph. While they obtained reasonable precision and recall using a maximum entropy binary classifier on a corpus of 447 selected abstracts from MEDLINE, they have not explored the constituency and dependency parse features which have been proven to be efficient in relation extraction. Li et al. (2015) make use of lexical semantics to train a model based on distant-supervision for n-ary relation extraction. However, the applicability of this method on other datasets is not clear.

We design an algorithm for extracting n-ary relations from biographical data which extracts entities using conditional random fields (CRF) and n-ary relations using support vector machine (SVM) from two manually annotated datasets which contain biography summaries of Australian researchers. Shortest path dependency kernel (Bunescu and Mooney, 2005a) has been proven to be the most efficient in extracting binary relations. In this work, we propose the use of shortest path

Gitansh Khirbat, Jianzhong Qi and Rui Zhang. 2016. N-ary Biographical Relation Extraction using Shortest Path Dependencies. In *Proceedings of Australasian Language Technology Association Workshop*, pages 74–83.

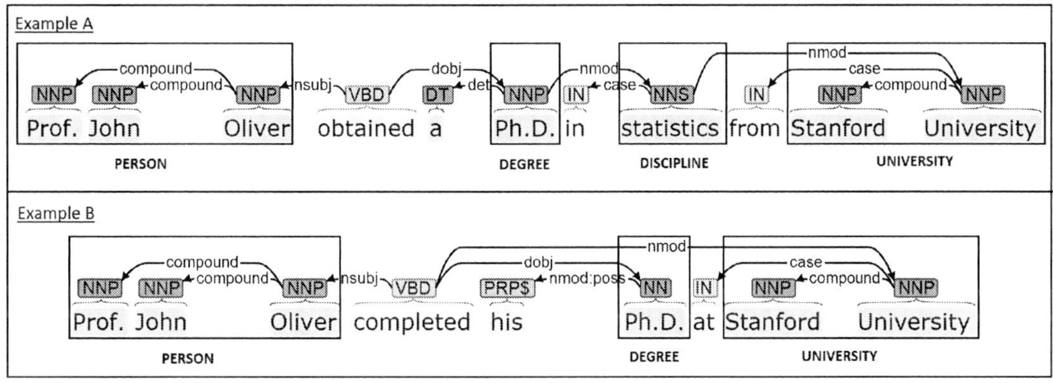

Figure 1: Example sentences with their dependency parses

dependency based rules to extract complex n-ary relations without decomposing the sentences into binary relations. These rules are based on the hypothesis which stipulates that the contribution of the sentence dependency graph to establish a relationship is almost exclusively concentrated in the shortest path connecting all the entities such that there exists a single path connecting any two entities at a given time. We present a thorough experimental evaluation and error analysis, making the following contributions:

- We propose a new approach to handle n-ary relation extraction using shortest path dependency-based rules.

- We conducted a thorough empirical error analysis of using CRF-based entity extractor coupled with SVM-based relation extractor.

- We present two manually annotated corpora containing biographical entities and relation annotations, which can be used for research or to augment existing knowledge bases.

The rest of the paper is organized as follows. Section 2 defines the problem. Section 3 reviews related studies. Section 4 discusses our methodology. Section 5 introduces the corpora. Section 6 presents the experiments. Section 7 presents an error analysis and Section 8 concludes this paper.

2 Preliminaries

2.1 *N*-ary Relation Extraction

We study the problem of n-ary relation extraction. A relation is defined in the form of a tuple $t = < e_1, e_2, \ldots, e_n >$ where e_i is an entity, which can be mention of a person, place, organization, etc. The most studied relations are binary relations, which involve two entities. If more than two entities exist in a relation, it becomes a complex relation which is called an n-ary relation. McDonald et al. (2005) define a complex relation as any n-ary relation among n entities which follows the schema $< t_1, \ldots, t_n >$ where t_i is an entity type. An instance of this complex relation is given by a list of entities $< e_1, e_2, \ldots, e_n >$ such that either type$(e_i) = t_i$, or $e_i = \perp$ indicating that the ith element of the tuple is missing. Here, type(e_i) is a function that returns the entity type of entity e_i.

For example, assume that the entity types are E={*person (PER), degree (DEG), discipline (DISC), position (POS), university (UNI)*} and we are interested to find a n-ary relation with schema *<PER, DEG, DISC, UNI>* that provides information of a *person* affiliated to a *university*, studying a *degree* in a *discipline*. In example A shown in Figure 1, the expected extracted tuple is <Prof. John Oliver, Ph.D., statistics, Stanford University>. In example B, the expected extracted tuple is <Prof. John Oliver, Ph.D., $\perp$, Stanford University>, since the *discipline* entity is not mentioned. Thus, n-ary relation extraction systems aim to identify all instances of a complete and partially complete relations of interest.

2.2 Problem Definition

Given a set of D documents containing biographical data, we classify words in a document $d_i \in D$ into entities $< e_1, e_2, \ldots, e_j >$ and n-ary relations given by dataset R, such that $r_k \in R$ is a tuple $t = < e_1, e_2, \ldots, e_n >$ where $n \geq 2$. In particular, we are interested in extracting affiliation relations such as the one mentioned in Section 2.1.

75

3   Related Work

Information extraction is a sequential confluence of two processes - entity extraction and relation extraction. Entity extraction refers to the task of NER wherein the task is to correctly classify an entity (like person, location, organization, etc.) out of a given sentence in a textual document. Past two decades have seen a massive body of work which aimed to improvise the entity extraction systems (Bikel et al., 1997), (Cunningham et al., 2002) and (Alfonseca and Manandhar, 2002). It is a well-explored research area which has reached maturity (Finkel et al., 2005). Most NER systems are domain dependent and require training with a new annotated corpus for a new task.

Relation extraction refers to the task of finding relations among the entities which were obtained during entity extraction. A huge body of work addresses the task of extracting binary relations wherein a relation exists between two entities only. Feature-based supervised learning methods like (Kambhatla, 2004) and (Zhao and Grishman, 2005) leverage the syntactic and semantic features. Exploration of a large feature space in polynomial computational time motivated the development of kernel based methods like tree kernels (Zelenko et al., 2003) and (Culotta and Sorensen, 2004), subsequence kernels (Bunescu and Mooney, 2005b) and dependency tree kernel (Bunescu and Mooney, 2005a). Open IE system (Banko et al., 2007) gives a sound method to generalize the relation extraction process, however the system does not give any insights to extract complex n-ary relations.

With advances in biomedical text mining and modern question answering systems, complex n-ary relation extraction is gaining attention wherein the task is to detect and extract relations existing between two or more entities in a given sentence. McDonald et al. (2005) attempt to solve this problem by factorizing complex relations into binary relations which are represented as a graph. This graph is then used to reconstruct the complex relations by constructing tuples from selected maximal cliques scored on the graph. Li et al. (2015) make use of lexical semantics to train a model based on distant-supervision for n-ary relation extraction. However, both these systems are computationally expensive and do not scale up efficiently.

Bunescu and Mooney (2005a) advocate the use of shortest path between the entities in a dependency parse to compute the cartesian product of dependencies clubbed with respective POS tags. This method has been proven to be the best among all kernel methods to extract binary relations. However, it is yet to be confirmed if it works for extracting complex n-ary relations.

4   Methodology

4.1   Shortest path dependency: binary to *n-ary* relations

We use dependency parsing (Manning et al., 2014) to help extract n-ary relations. Dependency parse provides information about word-word dependencies in the form of directed links. These dependencies capture the predicate-argument relations present in the sentence. The finite verb is taken to be the structural centre of the clause structure. All other syntactic units (words) are connected either directly (to the predicate) or indirectly (through a preposition or infinitive particle) to the verb using directed links, which are called dependencies. Each dependency consists of a *head* from where the directed link originates and a *dependent* where the link terminates. Dependencies can be classified into two categories - local and non-local dependencies. Local dependencies refer to the dependencies which occur within a sentence and can be represented by predicate-argument structure. Non-local dependencies refer to long-range dependencies involving two positions in a phrase structure whose correspondence can not be captured by invoking predicate-argument structure.

Bunescu and Mooney (2005a) successfully demonstrated the use of shortest path dependencies between two entities to extract *located (at)* relation. We extend this hypothesis to form shortest path dependency based rules for n-ary relation extraction. If a sentence has n entities $e_1, e_2, \ldots, e_n$ such that there exists a relation r among them, our hypothesis stipulates that dependency graph can be used to establish the relationship $r(e_1, e_2, \ldots, e_n)$ by leveraging the shortest path connecting all the entities such that there exists a single path connecting any two entities at a given time.

Entities are considered as one unit. In order to determine entity-level dependency of an entity e_i, the compound dependencies are discarded and the dependency between a word $\in e_i$ and the surrounding word $\notin e_i$ is considered. For any two consecutive entities in a sentence,

- If there exists a direct dependency between the two words belonging to two entities e_1 and e_2, it is represented as ($NER(e_1)$–$dependency\ name$–$NER(e_2)$). This happens mostly in the case of local dependencies. In Example A, it can be illustrated by (*Degree–nmod–Discipline*).

- If there exists a common word connecting e_1 and e_2 but not belonging to either, it is represented by including this common word along with its dependencies for e_1 and e_2. This is usually the case of non-local dependencies. In Example A, it can be illustrated by (*Person–nsubj–obtained–dobj–Degree*).

4.2 Entity Extraction using CRF

The first stage of IE is entity extraction. An entity is defined as a token or a group of tokens which belong to some predefined categories depending on the task. Since our main goal is to extract affiliation relations, we identify six relevant entity types namely *Person*, *Degree*, *University*, *Discipline*, *Organization* and *Position*.

Person and *Organization* entities were classified using Stanford's NER software (Finkel et al., 2005) which makes use of a CRF classifier. For the remaining entities, we train a CRF-based classifier similar to the Stanford's NER, making using of features as described below.

1. Surface tokens (bag of words): For each word token w, all the words in a window size of five, with two words on either side of w are considered. Unigrams, bigrams and trigrams are taken into account.

   In Example A, the surface token features spanning the first five words ("Prof.", "John", "Oliver", "obtained" and "a") are:

   - Unigrams: `Prof., John, Oliver, obtained, a`
   - Bigrams: `(Prof., John), (John, Oliver), (Oliver, obtained), (obtained, a)`
   - Trigrams: `(Prof., John, Oliver), (John, Oliver, obtained), (Oliver, obtained, a)`

2. Part of Speech (POS) Tags: The part of speech for a token like NNP (noun), PRP (pronoun) and IN (preposition) is a strong syntactic feature. For each word token w, POS tags for all the tokens in a window size of five, with two words on either side of w are considered. The POS tags for unigrams, bigrams and trigrams are also taken into account. In Example A, the POS tag features spanning the first five words are:

   - Unigrams: `NNP, NNP, NNP, VBD, DT`
   - Bigrams: `(NNP, NNP), (NNP, NNP), (NNP, VBD), (VBD, DT)`
   - Trigrams: `(NNP, NNP, NNP), (NNP, NNP, VBD), (NNP, VBD, DT)`

3. Presence in word list: We have created gazetteers of degrees, positions, disciplines and universities by crawling the web. Presence of a word w in the respective gazetteer indicating a potential entity mention is used as a feature.

   For example: Lemmatized form of degrees `(PhD, BEng, BA, etc.)`, positions `(Professor, Associate Professor, Assistant, etc.)` and Universities with their abbreviations `(University of Melbourne, Unimelb, ANU, etc.)`

We considered all the permutations of these features in an incremental fashion to train CRF models using the scikit-learn toolkit (Pedregosa et al., 2011) as described in Section 6.

4.3 Complex *n*-ary Relation Extraction using SVM

The second stage of IE system is relation extraction. A relation links two or more entities based on predefined rules to render meaningful information. In this work, we are interested in extracting n-ary affiliation relations ($n \geq 2$).

We classify each candidate entity pairs or a group of entities within a sentence into three affiliation relation categories namely *binary (2-ary)*, *ternary (3-ary)* and *quaternary (4-ary)* as described in Section 5. We train a SVM with radial basis function (RBF) kernel to classify groups of entities within a sentence using these features:

1. Bag of verbs: All the verbs present in between the entities of a sentence. For example, "obtained", "completed", "graduated".

2. Extracted entities: The entities extracted for each sentence from Stage 1 are strong indicators of presence of a relation. The six entity categories correspond to six different features while training a SVM. If either of the six entity categories is present in a candidate sentence, the corresponding feature is set to 1. Since our entity extraction system is not 100% accurate, there might be some entities in a few sentences which might not be identified correctly. For such instances, we just use the entities which are identified correctly and leave the ones which are not.

   For example: In example A, the entities identified in stage 1 are: (e1, Prof. John Oliver), (e2, Ph.D.), (e3, statistics) and (e4, Stanford University). The entity features corresponding to *Person*, *Degree*, *Discipline* and *University* are set to 1, while the features corresponding to other entity categories remain 0.

3. Part of Speech (POS) sequence: The part of speech sequence connecting the entity type acts as a pattern, the presence of which is used as a feature for the SVM classifier. This feature is important as it makes use of the syntactic structure coupled with the entity information. We observe that many of the POS sequence patterns occur frequently for many documents in our dataset, which rules out the possibility of pattern sparsity.

   In Example A, the POS sequence is (*Person-VBD-DT-Degree-IN-Discipline-DT-University*).

   In cases where an entity is not identified by our entity extractor, we consider the POS tag sequence of the missed entity in lieu of the actual entity type.

   In Example B with *Discipline* not being identified, the POS sequence is (*Person-VBD-DT-Degree-IN-NN-DT-University*).

4. Shortest path dependency information:

   The shortest path dependency based rules are essentially patterns, which act as features for the SVM. This feature is used as described in Section 4.1. The shortest path dependency based rules for each candidate group of entities identified in a given sentence are represented as patterns across all the documents in the corpus. The dependency parse of each candidate sentence is checked for the presence of these patterns. If a pattern is present, the corresponding feature is set to 1.

For Example A, some of the patterns are: (*Person–nsubj–obtained–dobj–Degree*), (*Person–nsubj–obtained–dobj–Degree–nmod–Discipline*) and (*Person–nsubj–obtained–dobj–Degree–nmod–Discipline–nmod–University*).

For Example B, some of the patterns are: (*Person–nsubj–completed–dobj–Degree*), (*Person–nsubj–completed–dobj–Degree–nmod–University*)

We considered all the permutations of these features in an incremental fashion to train SVM models using RBF kernel. The predicted tags are compared against the manually annotated gold relation data from AuRes and AuSem datasets described in Section 5. Depending on the number of identified entities (n) within a sentence and the association of these n entities, the relation for a given sentence is categorized into binary, ternary or quaternary relation. We adopted a grid search on C and γ using 10-fold cross validation to prevent overfitting. The experiments are described in Section 6.

5 AuRes and AuSem Corpora

The standard datasets like ACE do not provide annotations for complex *n*-ary relations where $n > 2$. The general affiliation relation category in ACE 2005 dataset contains annotations for only binary relations between entities like *Organization* and *Location*, e.g., <Microsoft, Redmond>. This makes it hard for complex *n*-ary relation extraction where the number of related entities is more than two, which gave rise to the development of two new datasets [1] with annotations for complex relations.

1. AuRes - A collection of 400 documents containing biographical information retrieved from the webpages of researchers and faculty of Australian universities, contains 4092 entities and 1152 relations.

2. AuSem - A collection of 300 seminar announcement mails containing speaker's biography from the department mailing list of the University of Melbourne, contains 2864 entities and 983 relations.

[1] https://github.com/gittykhirbat/nary_datasets

5.1 Label Description

Both AuRes and AuSem are manually annotated with entities and relations following the same annotation guidelines as described below.

5.1.1 Entities

We have identified six different entities which describe the biographical information of a person. We make use of Stanford NER system (Finkel et al., 2005) to classify entities like *Person* and *Organization* as the classification accuracy is very high. For the remaining four entities, we annotate the documents using the following guidelines.

- *Degree*: Token having information related to a degree like B.Sc, PhD, masters or identifiers like undergrad, postrgad, doctoral.

- *University*: Token indicating name of a university or its abbreviation, like "University of Melbourne", "Unimelb", "USyd"

- *Discipline*: Token containing information about a subject or discipline, e.g., Computer Science, Mathematics, Economics.

- *Position*: Token indicating the position of a person in the university of an organization, e.g., Software Engineer, Lecturer, Teacher.

5.1.2 Relations

The documents are annotated for affiliation relations spanning the six entities. The affiliation relation types can be categorized into three classes:

1. *Binary*: When only two entities out of all the identified entities within a sentence are related. For example, in the sentence "Prof. John Oliver did his Ph.D. under the supervision of Prof. Henkel", there are only two entities which satisfy the affiliation relation, <Prof. John Oliver, Ph.D.>.

2. *Ternary*: When three out of all the identified entities within a sentence are related. For example, in the sentence "Prof. John Oliver obtained his Ph.D. in statistics under the supervision of Prof. Henkel", only three entities satisfy the affiliation relation, <Prof. John Oliver, Ph.D., statistics>

3. *Quaternary*: When four out of all the identified entities within a sentence are related. For example, in the sentence "Prof. John Oliver obtained a Ph.D. in statistics from Stanford University under the supervision of Prof. Henkel", four entities satisfy the affiliation relation, <Prof. John Oliver, Ph.D., statistics, Stanford University>

5.2 Annotation

We used Brat annotation tool (Stenetorp et al., 2012) to annotate the document for entities and relations. The annotation task was carried out by two annotators with high proficiency in English. The gold standard was created by detecting annotation overlaps by the two annotators. Legitimate disagreements were resolved by adding an extra attribute to the annotation guidelines which seeks the confidence of annotation on a categorical scale consisting of three values - high, medium and low. The inter-annotator agreement, as computed by Cohen's Kappa measure (Cohen, 1960), was 0.86 for entity annotations and 0.81 for relation annotations.

6 Experiments

6.1 Entity Extraction

For both AuRes and AuSem datasets, we split the data into 70% training and 30% testing datasets. The training data is further split into 90% training and 10% development datasets. The features mentioned in Section 4.2 are employed to train a CRF model using 10-fold cross validation. We train the model in an incremental fashion. Model **M1** makes use of surface tokens which forms baseline for entity extraction. Model **M2** adds POS tag information to M1. Model **M3** adds word list presence feature to M1 and finally model **M4** combines all the features to train the CRF.

These models are used for predictions on the testing dataset, results (F-score in %) for which are shown in Table 1. The best result is obtained when surface tokens, POS tags and presence in word list features are used together. The F-scores for *Person* and *Organization* which are identified using Stanford's NER system are 83.31% and 86.79% respectively.

6.2 *N*-ary Relation Extraction using SVM

We conduct two experiments for relation extraction. First, we run the relation extractor on gold standard entity annotations. This is followed by running the relation extractor on the entities identified by our system in the Stage 1. For both the

Table 1: Entity Extraction Results

Entity	AuRes				AuSem			
	M1	**M2**	**M3**	**M4**	**M1**	**M2**	**M3**	**M4**
Degree	84.85	83.88	85.37	**95.63**	80.31	82.97	84.48	**92.16**
University	79.02	81.27	81.38	**93.88**	78.53	79.92	80.69	**93.33**
Discipline	83.14	91.65	92.22	**92.41**	80.78	86.32	87.18	**88.43**
Position	59.44	61.51	61.02	**93.27**	59.18	60.86	61.19	**89.27**

experiments, we split the data into 70% training and 30% testing datasets. The training dataset is further split into 90% training and 10% testing datasets. We adopted a grid search on C and γ using 10-fold cross validation to prevent overfitting. Pairs of (C, γ) were tried and the one with the best cross-validation accuracy was picked, which in our case turned to be $(2^2, 2^{-3.5})$.

The features mentioned in Section 4.3 are employed incrementally to train a SVM classifier with RBF kernel. The model using bag of words and entity presence features is our baseline system for this task. The SVM models are used for predictions on the testing dataset. Table 2 shows results for both sets of experiments for both the datasets. The columns **Gold** and **Identified** show the results of performing relation extraction using gold standard entity annotations and the system-identified entities respectively. Table 3 gives an account of the performance for extracting binary, ternary and quaternary relations.

7 Discussion

7.1 Error Analysis for Entity Extraction

An account of the entity-wise performance is provided here:

1. *Person*: We used Stanford's NER system for this entity. It was able to classify most of the English names correctly, did well on classifying some non-English names like "Katerina", "Yassaf", "Amit". However, it gave false positives like "Dahab", "Vic" (which are location names); "Rio Tinto", "Leightons" (which are Organization names); "Curtin" (which is a University name); "Dean" (which is a position name) and "Geojournal", "J.J.Immunol." (which are Journal names). These false positives appeared to be a result of the context in which they were being classified. It also resulted in some false negatives like "Cherryl", "Long",

"Wai-Kong", which majorly happened because of uncommon names.

2. *Degree*: We used our CRF model to classify *Degree* entities, which performed well mainly due to an extensive gazetteer of most of the degrees which we used as a feature to train the CRF. It can classify degrees and their abbreviations like "Bachelor of Engineering", "B.E.", "BA (Hons.)", "PhD".

3. *University*: Our CRF model performs well in classifying University entities. This is because of a gazetteer of the university names which contains full names of the universities as well as their abbreviations and aliases. e.g., "The University of Melbourne", "Unimelb", "Melbourne Uni". Some of the false negatives arise in documents where the university name is not mentioned conventionally. e.g., "University of WA" (instead of "University of Western Australia" or "UWA").

4. *Organization*: Stanford's NER system is used for this entity. It did well in classifying most of the Organization entities. However, we witnessed some false negatives. It was not able to classify some not so well-known organizations (like "Action Supermarkets", "Freja Hairstyling", "Strategic Wines") and new companies and startups (like "Tesla Motors", "SpaceX").

5. *Position*: A gazetteer of academic positions like "Professor", "Lecturer" was used to classify such positions. However, more specific positions like "Bankwest Professor", "Inaugural Director" and "Founding member" got missed.

6. *Discipline*: Our CRF model was able to classify most of the higher-level disciplines like "Engineering", "Computer Science", "History" based on our gazetteer. However, it

Table 2: Relation Extraction: Comparison of gold standard with system identified entities

Features	AuRes						AuSem					
	Gold			Identified			Gold			Identified		
	P	R	F1	P	R	F1	P	R	F1	P	R	F1
Bag of words	.64	.59	.62	.57	.53	.55	.59	.54	.56	.54	.48	.51
+ Entity presence (Baseline)	.73	.65	.69	.66	.60	.63	.67	.62	.64	.62	.57	.59
+ POS Tag sequence	.78	.74	.76	.73	.65	.69	.76	.72	.74	.72	.68	.70
+ Shortest path dependency	**.86**	**.82**	**.83**	**.82**	**.73**	**.77**	**.87**	**.82**	**.85**	**.84**	**.73**	**.78**
UPenn System	.76	.71	.73	.66	.73	.69	.76	.73	.74	.65	.74	.69

Table 3: Relation Extraction: Performance across n-ary relations

Features	2-ary			3-ary			4-ary		
	P	R	F1	P	R	F1	P	R	F1
Bag of words	0.61	0.59	0.60	0.58	0.57	0.56	0.52	0.46	0.49
+ Entity presence (Baseline)	0.68	0.64	0.66	0.67	0.61	0.64	0.61	0.55	0.58
+ POS Tag sequence	0.75	0.73	0.74	0.71	0.69	0.70	0.65	0.63	0.64
+ Shortest path dependency	**0.83**	**0.79**	**0.81**	**0.81**	**0.75**	**0.78**	**0.76**	**0.70**	**0.73**
State-of-the-art (UPenn System)	0.74	0.70	0.72	0.71	0.68	0.69	0.69	0.63	0.66

could not classify granular domains within major disciplines like "Equity and Tax", "Shakespearean Literature".

7.2 Error Analysis for Relation Extraction

An account of the n-ary relation extraction system is provided here. Shortest path dependency-based rules prove to be the most effective feature for the trained SVM.

7.2.1 What Worked Well

- Simple relations: Sentences in which the entities are present in a non-complex way. For example, in the sentence "Corinne Fagueret has a Master of Environmental studies completed at Macquarie University", our system extracts *<Person, Degree, University, Discipline>* = <Corinne Fagueret, Master, Macquarie University, Environmental Studies>.

- Complex relations: Sentences in which the entities are present in a non-conventional way. For example, in the sentence "After getting the University of Sydney Science Achievement Prize in 2000 for getting the best weighted average mark for a BSc student, Peter graduated with first class honours and a medal in 2001", our system can extract *<Person, Degree, University>* = <Peter, BSc, University of Sydney>.

- Multiple relations spanning multiple entities: Our system can extract multiple relations from sentences. For example, in the sentence "Angeline is the President of the Lane Cove Bushland and Convener of the better Planning Network", our system can extract *<Person, Position, Organization>* = <Angeline, President, Lane Cove Bushland> and *<Person, Position, Organization>* = <Angeline, Convener, Better Planning Network>.

- Multiple relations spanning same entities: For example, in the sentence "Dr. John Oliver is an Assoc. Prof. and Head in the Department of Finance", our system can extract *<Person, Position, Organization>* = <John Oliver, Assoc. Prof., Department of Finance> and *<Person, Position, Organization>* = <John Oliver, Head, Department of Finance>.

7.2.2 What Did Not Work Well

- Limitation of entity extractor: One bottleneck for our system is the entity extractor sub-system. Even though we have managed to achieve high F-scores for entity extraction, there are cases in which a few entities are missed due to data sparsity. This prohibits the relation extraction. For a given sentence containing n entities, if x entities are identified by our entity extraction sub-system then our relation extraction sub-system makes use of the features to learn valid subset of relations occurring among the $n - x$ entities.

- Limitation of parser: Our system faces ambiguity in cases where an appositive dependency occurs between two entities. For example, in the sentence "Associate Professor Christoff Pforr (PhD) is Course Coordinator for Tourism and Hospitality and Group Leader of the Research Focus Area Sustainable and Health Tourism with the School of Marketing, Curtin Business School", School of Marketing and Curtin Business School are both classified as University entities with an appositive relation between the two because of the common word "School". While extracting relation, it is not clear which entity should be considered.

- Ambiguity in choosing correct entity: Sentences containing multiple entities with the same context cause an ambiguity. For example, in the sentence "Sarah is currently co-investigator with Professor Fiona Haslam for a study commissioned by Rio Tinto through the University of Adelaide". In this sentence, there are two associations for Sarah - Rio Tinto and University of Adelaide. The system renders both, giving us a false positive <Sarah, co-investigator, Rio Tinto>.

- Unknown words from other language: For example, in the sentence "Marios holds a PhD in Political Science from Northern Territory University and a Staatsexamen in Geography and Political Science as well as a Teaching Certificate from the University of Tübingen (Germany). Staatsexamen and Tübingen are not detected, thereby causing errors.

- Inference-based relations: Inference of relation from previous sentences in the paragraph can not be done as our system lacks long distance dependency information. For example, in the sentence "Ruhul words as a tutor for Biotechnology at RMIT University. He also worked in a similar position at the University of Melbourne.", we are unable to infer what "similar position" mean. This would be explored in the future.

7.3 Comparison with other state-of-the-art IE systems

A comparison with the UPenn system (McDonald et al., 2005) is provided in Table 2 and 3. We re-implement this system and train it on our training and development datasets using 10-fold cross validation. The learnt system is used to predict the relations for testing dataset. At the time of this work, this system is the state-of-the-art in complex n-ary relation extraction, with an F1-score of 69.42% on a dataset of 447 abstracts selected from MEDLINE. On our datasets of AuRes and AuSem, their technique achieved F1-Score of 69.44% and 69.22% respectively as compared to 77.49% and 78.38% respectively using shortest path dependency based rules, which shows an improvement of 8% F1-score. Our technique obtained far less false positives and a comparable recall.

8 Conclusions and Future Work

Through this paper, we show a new approach to n-ary relation extraction using shortest path dependency based rules which provides an improvement of 8% F1-score over the state-of-the-art. Two stage extraction procedure involving CRF-based entity extraction and SVM-based relation extraction is proposed to extract affiliation relations. An empirical analysis is conducted over two manually annotated datasets to validate this method. The manually annotated datasets could be used for the advancement of natural language processing research in the future.

For future work, it would be interesting to investigate the usage of shortest path parse tree for n-ary relation extraction since sentence parsing provides a semantically rich information about a sentence. It would also be interesting to explore n-ary relation extraction spanning across multiple sentences. Finally, future use of the introduced corpora in research to augment existing knowledge bases could yield interesting insights.

Acknowledgments

Jianzhong Qi is supported by the Melbourne School of Engineering Early Career Researcher Grant (project reference number 4180-E55), and the University of Melbourne Early Career Researcher Grant (project number 603049).

References

Enrique Alfonseca and Suresh Manandhar. 2002. An unsupervised method for general named entity recognition and automated concept discovery. In *In: Proceedings of the 1 st International Conference on General WordNet*.

Michele Banko, Michael J. Cafarella, Stephen Soderland, Matt Broadhead, and Oren Etzioni. 2007. Open information extraction from the web. In *Proceedings of the 20th International Joint Conference on Artifical Intelligence*, IJCAI'07, pages 2670–2676, San Francisco, CA, USA. Morgan Kaufmann Publishers Inc.

Daniel M. Bikel, Scott Miller, Richard Schwartz, and Ralph Weischedel. 1997. Nymble: A high-performance learning name-finder. In *Proceedings of the Fifth Conference on Applied Natural Language Processing*, ANLC '97, pages 194–201, Stroudsburg, PA, USA. Association for Computational Linguistics.

Razvan C. Bunescu and Raymond J. Mooney. 2005a. A shortest path dependency kernel for relation extraction. In *Proceedings of the Conference on Human Language Technology and Empirical Methods in Natural Language Processing*, HLT '05, pages 724–731, Stroudsburg, PA, USA. Association for Computational Linguistics.

Razvan C. Bunescu and Raymond J. Mooney. 2005b. Subsequence kernels for relation extraction. In *Proceedings of the 19th Conference on Neural Information Processing Systems (NIPS)*. Vancouver, BC, December.

J. Cohen. 1960. A Coefficient of Agreement for Nominal Scales. *Educational and Psychological Measurement*, 20(1):37.

Aron Culotta and Jeffrey Sorensen. 2004. Dependency tree kernels for relation extraction. In *Proceedings of the 42Nd Annual Meeting on Association for Computational Linguistics*, ACL '04, Stroudsburg, PA, USA. Association for Computational Linguistics.

Hamish Cunningham, Diana Maynard, Kalina Bontcheva, and Valentin Tablan. 2002. A framework and graphical development environment for robust nlp tools and applications. In *ACL*, pages 168–175.

Jenny Rose Finkel, Trond Grenager, and Christopher Manning. 2005. Incorporating non-local information into information extraction systems by gibbs sampling. In *Proceedings of the 43rd Annual Meeting on Association for Computational Linguistics*, ACL '05, pages 363–370, Stroudsburg, PA, USA. Association for Computational Linguistics.

Nanda Kambhatla. 2004. Combining lexical, syntactic, and semantic features with maximum entropy models for extracting relations. In *Proceedings of the ACL 2004 on Interactive Poster and Demonstration Sessions*, ACLdemo '04, Stroudsburg, PA, USA. Association for Computational Linguistics.

Hong Li, Sebastian Krause, Feiyu Xu, Andrea Moro, Hans Uszkoreit, and Roberto Navigli. 2015. Improvement of n-ary relation extraction by adding lexical semantics to distant-supervision rule learning. In *ICAART 2015 - Proceedings of the 7th International Conference on Agents and Artificial Intelligence*. SciTePress.

Christopher D. Manning, Mihai Surdeanu, John Bauer, Jenny Finkel, Steven J. Bethard, and David McClosky. 2014. The Stanford CoreNLP natural language processing toolkit. In *Association for Computational Linguistics (ACL) System Demonstrations*, pages 55–60.

Ryan McDonald, Fernando Pereira, Seth Kulick, Scott Winters, Yang Jin, and Pete White. 2005. Simple algorithms for complex relation extraction with applications to biomedical ie. In *Proceedings of the 43rd Annual Meeting on Association for Computational Linguistics*, ACL '05, pages 491–498, Stroudsburg, PA, USA. Association for Computational Linguistics.

F. Pedregosa, G. Varoquaux, A. Gramfort, V. Michel, B. Thirion, O. Grisel, M. Blondel, P. Prettenhofer, R. Weiss, V. Dubourg, J. Vanderplas, A. Passos, D. Cournapeau, M. Brucher, M. Perrot, and E. Duchesnay. 2011. Scikit-learn: Machine learning in Python. *Journal of Machine Learning Research*, 12:2825–2830.

Pontus Stenetorp, Sampo Pyysalo, Goran Topić, Tomoko Ohta, Sophia Ananiadou, and Jun'ichi Tsujii. 2012. Brat: A web-based tool for nlp-assisted text annotation. In *Proceedings of the Demonstrations at the 13th Conference of the European Chapter of the Association for Computational Linguistics*, EACL '12, pages 102–107, Stroudsburg, PA, USA. Association for Computational Linguistics.

Dmitry Zelenko, Chinatsu Aone, and Anthony Richardella. 2003. Kernel methods for relation extraction. *J. Mach. Learn. Res.*, 3:1083–1106, March.

Shubin Zhao and Ralph Grishman. 2005. Extracting relations with integrated information using kernel methods. In *Proceedings of the 43rd Annual Meeting on Association for Computational Linguistics*, ACL '05, pages 419–426, Stroudsburg, PA, USA. Association for Computational Linguistics.

Phonotactic Modeling of Extremely Low Resource Languages

Andrei Shcherbakov[1] and Ekaterina Vylomova[2] and Nick Thieberger[1]
[1]School of Languages and Linguistics
[2]Department of Computing and Information Systems
The University of Melbourne
ultrasparc@yandex.ru evylomova@gmail.com thien@unimelb.edu.au

Abstract

This paper presents a novel approach to low resource language modeling. Here we propose a model for word prediction which is based on multi-variant ngram abstraction with weighted confidence level. We demonstrate a significant improvement in word recall over "traditional" Kneser-Ney back-off model for most of the examined low resource languages.

1 Introduction

For a dictionary in the course of being created, a problem for the linguist/lexicographer is how to find words that are not already recorded in the dictionary. Linguists working on small languages may extract as many lexemes as they can from texts they record, and then add to that with elicitation of items unlikely to appear in texts, especially paradigmatic information (like verb inflections, pronouns, kin terms and so on), place names, and biological names. They are now also using experimental stimuli to get at more nuanced meanings. However, once they have exhausted these sources, they need some way to discover other possible forms in the language. In this paper we discuss a method for creating possible word forms that can be confirmed by speakers (or not) as being words in the language. A general approach that has been used before is to apply the phonotactics to generate other possible forms (Prince and Tesar, 2004; Dell et al., 2000; Goldrick, 2004; Heinz, 2007). This was done with flip charts of possible sequences of phonemes, and then computationally, generating forms on the basis of known permissible combinations.[1]

This task could also be viewed from the perspective of machine learning, representing a particular case of language modeling. We can state the task as follows. The model gets an initially collected vocabulary of a given language as an input and has to predict likely undiscovered words as accurately as possible. There are many approaches to this task. The most powerful ones known today are based on neural networks, including deep learning techniques (Sundermeyer et al., 2012; Kim et al., 2015; Sundermeyer et al., 2015; Hwang and Sung, 2016; Oparin et al., 2012). Unfortunately, the ability of such algorithms to capture knowledge depends heavily on the amount of training data, and generally they aren't usable for a real language unless one provides at least several thousand training instances to them. Although, theoretically, such algorithms are able to learn many sophisticated rules not obvious even for a human analyst, the rules are hard to validate.

Typically, for low resource languages we are not able to obtain a training vocabulary of sufficient size. In the current research, we consider a practical task where an initial vocabulary of 300+ basic words has to be extended with more or less proper candidate words. For an optimal likelihood of hitting new words, we need to produce more diverse word forms while keeping compliance to phonotactical rules of word formation. Many researchers (Onishi et al., 2002; Blevins, 2003; Warker and Dell, 2006; Edwards et al., 2004; Chambers et al., 2003; Luce and Large, 2001; Vitevitch and Luce, 2005) have identified the importance of phonotactics in the process of word prediction.

Fortunately, pattern-based language modeling is a well explored topic in NLP. A pattern, e.g. an ngram, here may mean a sequence of some language units (phrases, words, characters, phonemes); these approaches mainly rely on probabilistic evaluation of various sequence likelihood based on training set statistics. A text corpus or vocabulary may be used for pattern distribution evaluation. However, as we will see in our experiments, such algorithms are too simplistic for really

---

[1]See e.g. `http://billposer.org/Software/WordGenerator.html`

Andrei Shcherbakov, Ekaterina Vylomova and Nick Thieberger. 2016. Phonotactic Modeling of Extremely Low Resource Languages. In *Proceedings of Australasian Language Technology Association Workshop*, pages 84–93.

small vocabularies.

A recurrent back-off to an $(n-1)$-gram suffix of a given n-gram is the most common strategy. In the context of smoothing for language models, back-off n-gram models have been well studied (Chen and Goodman, 1999). Among the myriad of proposed approaches, the Kneser-Ney approach is widely considered to be the best approach. Therefore, we consider Kneser-Ney smoothing as a baseline for evaluating the proposed algorithm.

We demonstrate that suffix gram-based back-off approaches may lack predictive power for small vocabularies, and go on to propose two major new methods: (1) multi-variant abstraction in n-grams, and (2) a distributional confidence metric for abstracted n-gram likelihood estimation. The algorithm based on these methods has been successfully realized in the Word Generator application[2] that is being currently used in field linguistics studies of endangered languages.

The paper is structured as follows. In Section 2 we provide a description of the system's architecture. Then in Section 3 we describe the languages we used and the corresponding vocabularies. In Section 4 we provide our experiments settings. And, finally, we discuss the results and observations in Section 5.

2 Architecture

2.1 Multi-Variant abstraction

In the context of our work, a word is considered as a sequence of phonemes that is expected to obey latent phonotactical rules. The rules are estimated based on the training data. The choice of phonemes (vs. characters) is primarily based on the fact that many low resource languages simply didn't have any script system during active phases of their evolution, and modern scripts merely follow their phonetic representation. We also note that our experiments with English have shown that phonetic representation enables better prediction results than orthographic one.

We now describe the process of generating abstracted forms in more detail. First, we add beginning (^) and finishing ($) quasi-phonemes to each word. Then the system parses the source vocabulary and records frequency of each observed

---

ngram. The length N of a gram is limited by a parameter $MaxNG$. In our experiments $MaxNG$ is chosen to be 5 since it yields the best results for the majority of tested languages.

We then augment the list of *concrete* ngrams with *k-abstracted* ones, where k is set of abstracted positions.[3] Each position $p \in k$ should satisfy the following two conditions. First, the pth phoneme in the original *concrete* ngram should be **abstractable**. *Abstractable* here means that it's known either as a vowel or a consonant phoneme; quasi-phonemes and specials, such as pauses or phoneme modifiers, are not abstractable. Second, the tail phoneme in a ngram is exempt of abstraction always being treated as concrete; thus, the following inequality should be true: $1 \leq p \leq N - 1$. We will further refer to the final list of *concrete* and *abstracted* ngrams as V^+. As an example, suppose we observed a 5-gram `^bats` in the training vocabulary. The system generates the following abstracted 5-grams: `^Ⓒats`, `^bⓋts`, `^baⒸs`, `^ⒸⓋts`, `^bⓋⒸs`, `^ⒸaⒸs`, and `^ⒸⓋⒸs` where Ⓥ and Ⓒ are abstract vowel and consonant, respectively. Again, note the first pseudo-phoneme is not abstracted here as it's neither vowel nor a consonant.

At the next step ngrams that differ by the last phoneme only, are grouped into a structure referred to as *selector* over some prefix $(n-1)$-gram.

Then the algorithm builds a candidate word starting with a single `^` and adds phonemes one by one. A word is complete once a `$` is appended. This assumption is based on the observation that word boundaries are tied to some phonotactical patterns as well (McQueen, 1998; Brent and Cartwright, 1996; Friederici and Wessels, 1993). We now take a closer look at the process of a word formation. Let w be a word prefix that has been generated up to this point, and L be its length. The algorithm takes into consideration a $(n-1)$-gram consisting of $N-1$ trailing phonemes of w, where $N = \max(L, MaxNG)$. The next phoneme is actually produced in two steps. Firstly, we randomly choose a single *selector* from V^+ which prefix $(n-1)$-gram matches w. The probability of each candidate is proportional to its abstraction confidence level (see below) as well as a direct function of its vocabu-

---

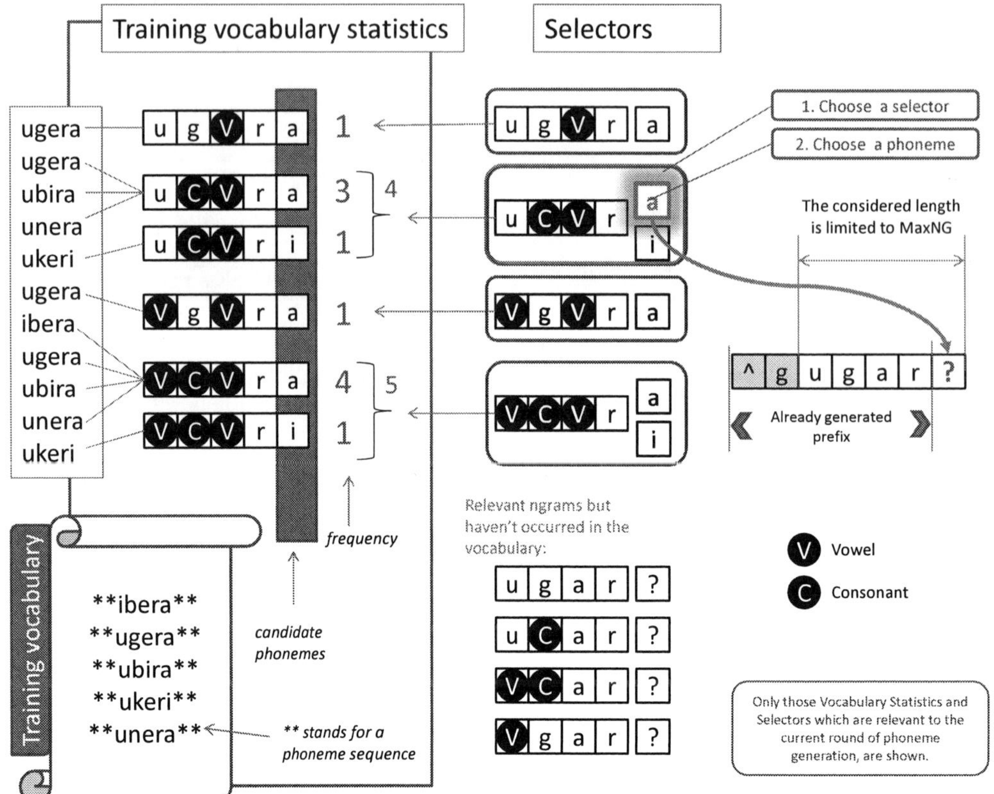

Figure 1: An example of phoneme generation. A prefix '^gugar' is assumed to be already generated at this point. The next phoneme choice is based on a fraction of our toy vocabulary relevant to the 'ugar' trailing $(n-1)$-gram, $n = 5$

lary frequency. Secondly, we choose an n-gram from the given *selector* content with the probability proportional to its frequency. The trailing phoneme of chosen n-gram is nominated to be the next phoneme of the generated word. Indeed, this procedure assigns smoothed conditional probability of y phoneme addition to a given $(n-1)$-gram $\tilde{w}$ as follows:

$$p(y|\tilde{w}) = \sum_{g \in \tilde{w}^+} \left(\frac{c(g, y)}{c(g)} \cdot \frac{F(g) f_s(c(g))}{S} \right) \quad (1)$$

where $c(x)$ is a count of x gram occurrences in the training vocabulary; S is a normalizing constant; f_s is a frequency squashing function; in our experiments, $f_s(n) = \log_2(1+n)$; F(g) is the confidence level of g gram which is discussed in more detail in 2.2; x^+ is abstract closure of x gram, i.e. set of concrete or/and abstract grams known in training vocabulary statistics (V^+) that satisfy

x gram:

$$x^+ = \{x' \in V^+ : x' \models x\} \quad (2)$$

Equation 1 generally looks like a "traditional" back-off probability but with more potentially contributing terms and with confidence levels introduced. Figure 1 illustrates candidate phoneme selection process in a toy vocabulary example.

2.2 Confidence level

As shown above, we apply various abstracted ngrams in order to predict the next phoneme. Although such an approach has an advantage of multiple pattern usage, it's pretty clear that soundness of each abstraction may differ. For example, consider 'xxoxx', 'xxaxx', 'xxexx', 'xxixx' grams that occur uniformly in the vocabulary. Here it's likely that any vowel is suitable to appear in the middle position of these grams. However, if we observe just a single pattern 'xxaxx' then we consider 'a' as an immutable phoneme at its position. Taking into account such considerations, we attempt to evaluate the 'appropriateness' of each abstracted ngram and avoid over-generalization. We used an entropy-like metric representing the uniformity of more concrete sequences distribution over an embracing abstracted ngram. For an n-gram g containing $a(g) > 0$ abstracted phonemes, the following formula denotes a confidence level:

$$F(g) = \alpha^{a(g)-1} \cdot z(F'(g)) \qquad (3)$$

Here α is a constant found to have the optimum value $\alpha \approx 0.9$; z is a simple piece-wise function which setting is considered in 4.2 ; $F'(g)$ is a confidence metric itself calculated as follows.

$$F'(g) = \left\langle F'(h_i) \log_2 \left(1 + \frac{c(h_i)F'(h_i)}{\langle c(h_j)F'(h_j) \rangle} \right) \right\rangle \qquad (4)$$

Averages $\langle \ldots \rangle$ here are taken over all satisfying ngrams h_k having one less abstracted phonemes, i.e over

$$\forall h_k : g \models h_k \wedge a(h_k) = a(g) - 1$$

For concrete ngrams, we assume that confidence levels equal to one:

$$a(g) = 0 \implies F(g) = F'(g) = 1 \qquad (5)$$

3 Data set

In our study we consider two language families: Oceanic (Austronesian) and Pama-Nyungan. For the first group we take three languages spoken in Vanuatu: South Efate (Central Vanuatu), Vurës (Northern Vanuatu), and Tamambo (Northern Vanuatu). Phonologically they are quite different to those spoken in Australia. Their sound system consists of around 15 consonants and 5 vowels ([a], [i], [u], [o], [e]).

Languages of the second group are spoken in Australia. Pama-Nyungan presents the most widely spread language group in Australia and covers 7/8 of its territory. Most Australian languages present quite similar phonology comprising 15-17 consonants and 3 vowels with variative length ([i], [i:], [u], [u:], [a], [a:]) (Baker, 2014; Hamilton, 1996; Busby, 1980). Gamilaraay (northern New South Wales), Kukatja (Western Desert), and Wik-Mungkan (Cape York Peninsula) belongs to Pama-Nyungan family.

The number of speakers varies from as low as 35 (Gamilaraay, 2006) up to 6,000 (South Efate, 2005).

Table 1 summarizes the basic sizes of language vocabularies used in our experiments.

Language	#Words	#Vowels	#Cons.
Gamilaraay	2423	5	15
Kukatja	8632	5	12
South Efate	2575	5	15
Tamambo	2067	5	15
Vurës	2166	9	16
Wambaya	1195	3	17
Wik-Mungkan	3884	10	17

Table 1: Explored low resource languages vocabulary summary

4 Experiments

4.1 Method and Measure

In our experiments we randomly split the data into the training and the test parts. We run cross-validation several times, each time shuffling the data. In each run the model generates a fixed size set of samples (words). To evaluate the model's quality, we measure the recall over the test vocabulary, i.e. the ratio of generated word hits out of the test vocabulary. We suppose that such an evaluation procedure would model adequately an exploration of unknown words as well, projecting a train set and a test set into a today's known part of a language vocabulary and its yet undiscovered part, respectively. In order to emphasize the dictionary incompleteness and the extrapolation intent, we'll use the *Recall rate* term in place of mere *Recall*. Note that the maximum theoretically reachable recall value is below one in most of the reported experiments, due to a relatively low number of generated words; nevertheless, we do use such a convenient metric unless that limitation really affects the result.

4.2 A study on confidence level

We use a simplex optimization method to find the best approximation of z function in Equation (3) that maps confidence into the likelihood. We approximate it as a piece-wise linear function. The objective is to achieve the best mean recall rate for low resources languages we examined; we repeated measurements with various sizes of training vocabularies taken in a uniform proportion.

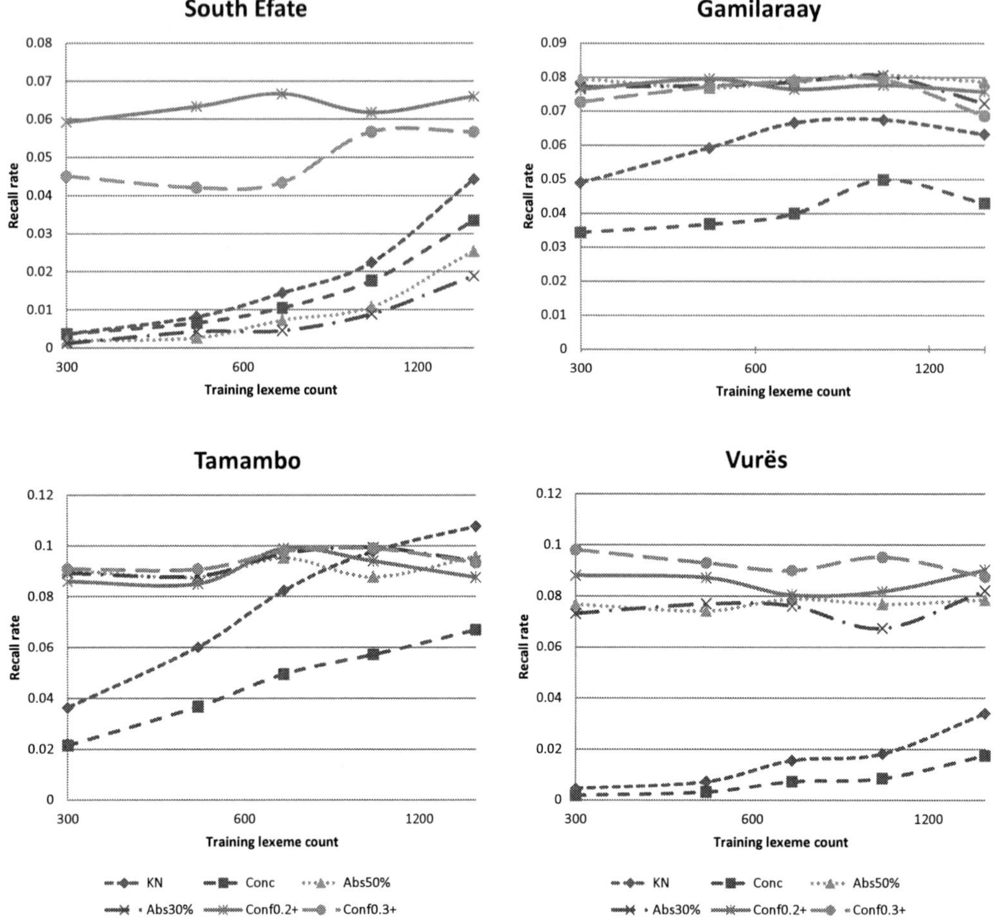

Figure 2: Recall rate vs. training vocabulary size ($300\ldots1500$ words) for low resource languages

Surprisingly, the optimal function was (almost) linear at the middle range of its domain; after validating a series of solving results and some non-affecting rounding of digits we have chosen the following two options for further experiments. The first one, referred to as $\mathbf{CONF}_{0.3+}$, yields the best mean result as well as best results for most of languages explored:

$$z(x) = \left\{ \begin{array}{ll} 0, & \text{iff } x < 0.3 \\ 0.6, & \text{iff } 0.3 \leq x < 0.4 \\ 0.8, & \text{iff } 0.4 \leq x < 0.5 \\ 1, & \text{iff } x \geq 0.5 \end{array} \right\} \quad (6)$$

The second one, $\mathbf{CONF}_{0.2+}$, was preferable in some cases:

$$z(x) = \left\{ \begin{array}{ll} 0, & \text{iff } x < 0.2 \\ \min(\frac{100x-2}{45}, 1), & \text{iff } x \geq 0.2 \end{array} \right\} \quad (7)$$

4.3 Options

In our contrastive experiments we use the following algorithms and options (the identifiers correspond to those found in graph legends).

$\mathbf{CONC}$ - concrete ngrams only used for word generation, i.e. no vowel or consonant abstraction is allowed at all.

$\mathbf{KN}$ - Kneser-Ney back-off, $\delta = 1$

$\mathbf{ABS50\%}$, $\mathbf{ABS30\%}$ denote multi-variant abstractions with fixed uniform confidence ($F' \equiv 0.5$ and $F' \equiv 0.3$ in Equation 3, respectively.)

$\mathbf{CONF0.3+}$, $\mathbf{CONF0.2+}$ represent multi-variant abstraction with variable confidence computed according to Equation 6 or Equation 7, respectively.

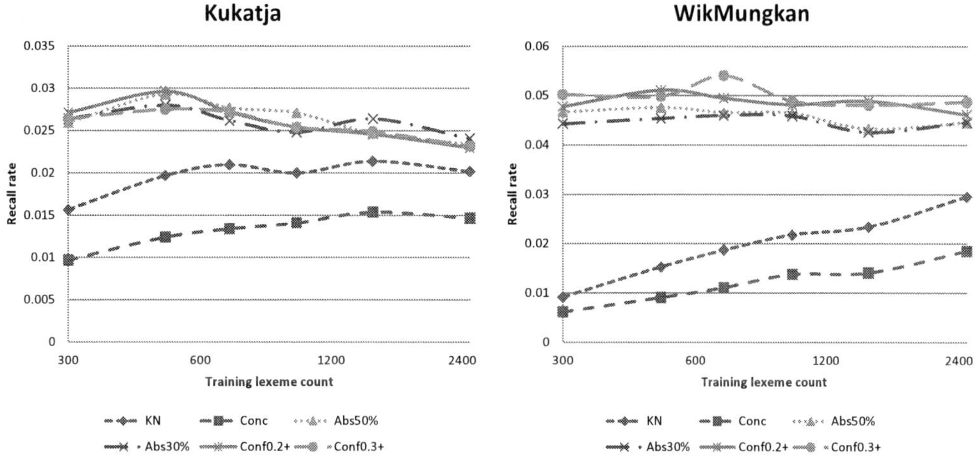

Figure 3: Recall rate vs. training vocabulary size (300 . . . 2500 words) for low resource languages

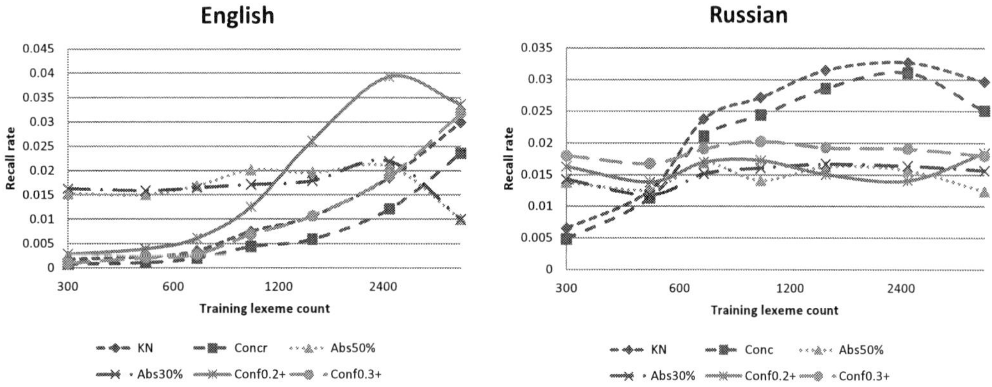

Figure 4: Recall rate vs. training vocabulary size (300 . . . 4000 words) for high resource languages

4.4 Recall & Precision vs. Training word count

In each trial we generate 1000 words for each language and measure the recall rate as described in 4.1. Figure 2 shows how the recall rate depends on the training vocabulary size at various options for South Efate, Gamilaraay, Tamambo and Vurës languages. We tried training vocabularies of 300, 500, 700 and 1500 words. For Kukatja and Wik-Mungan, we also examined a larger training word list, of 2500 words (see Figure 3)

For the comparison, we built similar graphs for two very high resource languages, Russian and English[4] (Tabain et al., 2004; Kipyatkova and Kar-

pov, 2015), restricting the total vocabulary used in experiments to 5000 most frequently used words of each languages. In such a way we were simulating a low resource environment. The results are presented at Figure 4. Also, in order to catch a picture of models' predictive power in a large resource vocabulary context, we attempted predicting words of a large vocabulary having the models trained on a given number of most frequently used words. We generated 1000 non-learned words each time and measured precision[5] of vocable pre-

---

[4]English words were broken into phoneme-representing character sequences before the training.

[5]At fixed counts of generated and test words, the precision is proportional to the recall. Thus, these two metrics are of similar sense for comparing the algorithms quality. We prefer the precision here just because the test vocabulary is vastly larger in volume than a generated word set, which fact lowers the maximum recall value terribly.

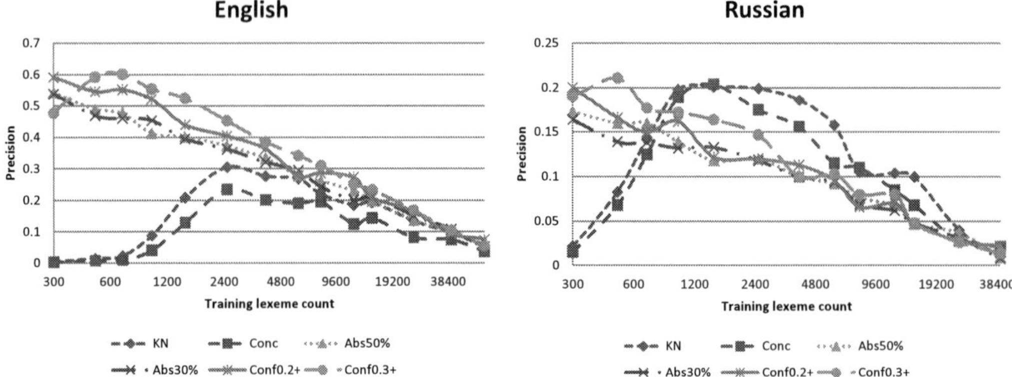

Figure 5: Precision against a large vocabulary vs. count of (most frequent) training words for high resource languages

diction (see Figure 5). We used Wiktionary top 100,000 most frequently-used English words and the frequency dictionary of modern Russian language (Lyashevskaya and Sharov, 2009) as large dictionaries.

4.5 Recall vs. Generated word count

In this experiment we evaluate the recall value achieved upon k words has been generated, $k \in [1 \dots 10,000]$. We use training vocabularies of 1500 words each. The idea here is to check the ability of each method to hit less easily derivable 'fractions' of vocabulary content.

Some of the graphs are shown on Figure 7. As we see, the proposed multi-variant abstraction methods keep hitting new words pretty well even when thousands of test dictionary words are nailed and excluded of further targeting; in contrast, concrete ngram approach and even Kneser-Ney backoff tend to decline yielding an equally high hit rate at some point (and sometimes nearly stop hitting at all), despite any possible advantage they may possess at the start.

4.6 Inflected words Recall

We roughly estimated the recall of inflected word forms for South Efate language. To get a collection of inflected words, we extracted all words of stories collected in (Thieberger, 2011). Then we filtered out known lemmas as well as proper nouns. The rest has been used a test set for the inflected word hit detection. We used random 1500 vocable samples to train the generator and varied the number of generated words, exactly as we did

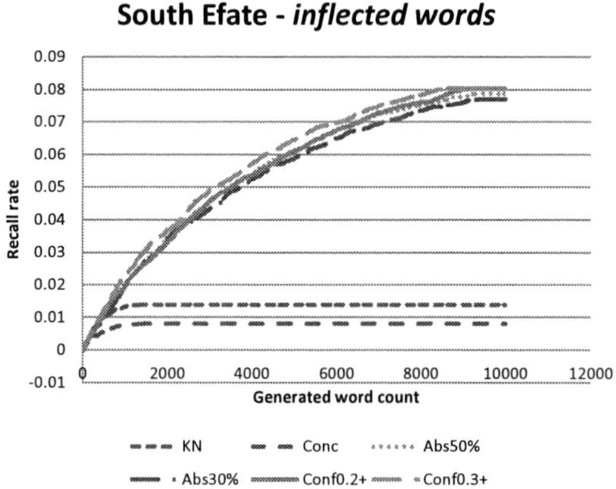

Figure 6: Recall rate of inflected words found in "Stories from South Efate" vs. generated word count

in 4.5. The recall curves displayed at Figure 6 appear to be similar to ones at Figure 7 (for South Efate), demonstrating an approximately constant ratio of about 3.6 between lemmas and inflected forms over generated words.[6]

5 Discussion

Unsurprisingly, the increase of the training vocabulary yields more chances to produce meaningful words merely attempting to reuse concrete sequences, and power of abstraction gradually decreases with training vocabulary size increase.

---

[6]This should be respected as an overestimation since not all possible inflected forms are present in the text corpus

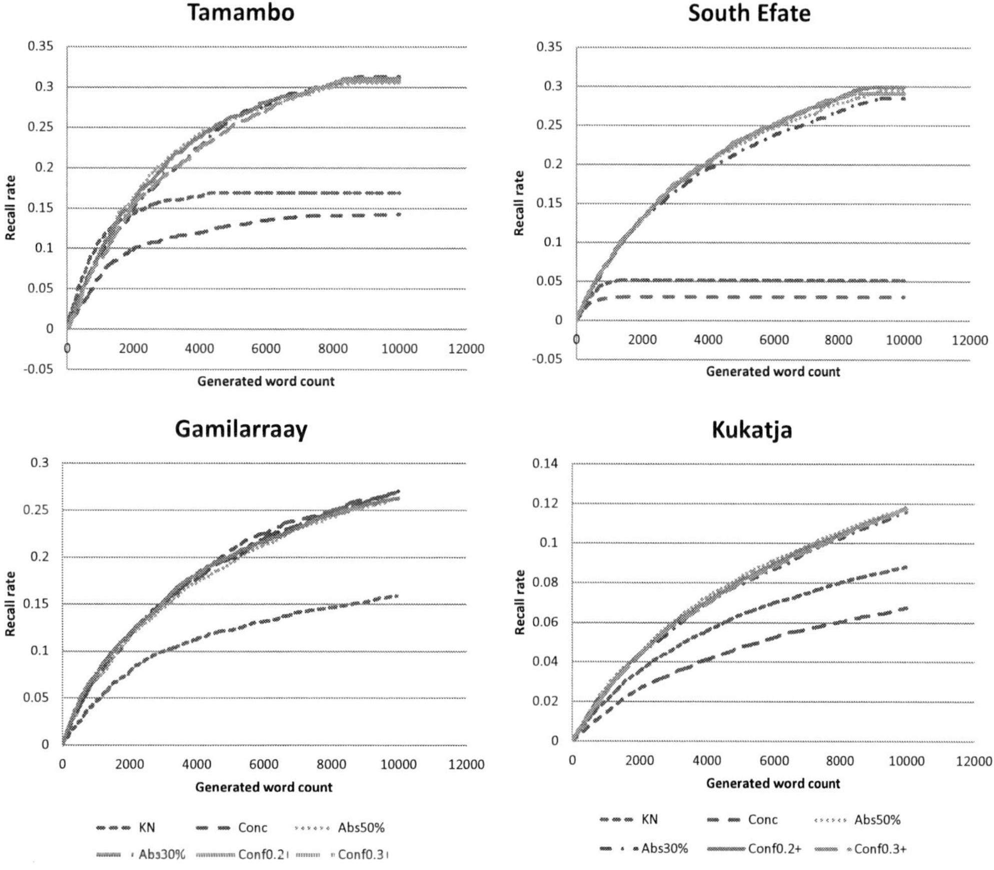

Figure 7: Recall rate as a function of generated word count for training vocabularies of 1500 words

The level of necessary concreteness may essentially vary over languages. Most languages demonstrate strong preference towards the abstracted approach. This feature doesn't quite correlate to a language family, it's more related to each language's own phonotactics instead. For example, two of three examined Austronesian languages follow that rule, but the third one doesn't. For such languages, the proposed multi-variant abstraction algorithm works fine, and with `Conf0.3+` option it outperforms the Kneser-Ney approach significantly, especially for very small vocabularies: its recall is higher in about 1.3 to 8 times.

However, some language vocabularies still tend to be much more predictable by following concrete ngrams, except for cases of really tiny training sets. At those "phonotactically concrete" languages the proposed technique may play either around the the same or somewhat less efficient than Kneser-Ney smoothing (which one indeed reproduces continues concrete grams); still, in such cases increasing the weight of concrete ngrams may more directly address the issue than merely adjusting the smoothing and abstraction mode.

In hunting more unusual words (at the cost of precision), when one generates large number of candidate words, the proposed algorithm demonstrates its advantages almost regardless of language and training set size.

During the experiments with word generator it was reported that the generator rather frequently produces inflected forms of known words. In this view, usage of existing text corpora for filtering out such forms, as well as learning of inflection rule patterns may effectively increase the precision of word prediction algorithm w.r.t. vocabularies.

6 Conclusions

We proposed a novel abstraction technique and confidence metric in probabilistic language modeling and demonstrated its advantage for different families of low resource languages. We also outlined two primary areas for further research. They include finding a self-adjustable balance between concrete and abstracted consideration, and improving vocable prediction by filtering out inflection patterns (Tesar and Prince, 2003).

Acknowledgments

We thank Catriona Malau for Vurës dictionary, Dorothy Jauncey for Tamambo dictionary and John Giacon for Gamilaraay dictionary.We thank reviewers for their valuable comments. Word Generator has been written as part of a project funded by ARC Future Fellowship FT140100214.

References

Frans Adriaans and René Kager. 2010. Adding generalization to statistical learning: The induction of phonotactics from continuous speech. *Journal of Memory and Language*, 62(3):311–331.

Brett Baker. 2014. 4 word structure in australian languages. *The Languages and Linguistics of Australia: A comprehensive guide*, 3:139.

Juliette Blevins. 2003. The independent nature of phonotactic constraints: an alternative to syllable-based approaches. *The syllable in optimality theory*, pages 375–403.

Michael R Brent and Timothy A Cartwright. 1996. Distributional regularity and phonotactic constraints are useful for segmentation. *Cognition*, 61(1):93–125.

Peter A Busby. 1980. The distribution of phonemes in australian aboriginal languages. *Pacific Linguistics. Series A. Occasional Papers*, (60):73.

Kyle E Chambers, Kristine H Onishi, and Cynthia Fisher. 2003. Infants learn phonotactic regularities from brief auditory experience. *Cognition*, 87(2):B69–B77.

Stanley F Chen and Joshua Goodman. 1999. An empirical study of smoothing techniques for language modeling. *Computer Speech & Language*, 13(4):359–394.

Gary S Dell, Kristopher D Reed, David R Adams, and Antje S Meyer. 2000. Speech errors, phonotactic constraints, and implicit learning: a study of the role of experience in language production. *Journal of Experimental Psychology: Learning, Memory, and Cognition*, 26(6):1355.

Jan Edwards, Mary E Beckman, and Benjamin Munson. 2004. The interaction between vocabulary size and phonotactic probability effects on children's production accuracy and fluency in nonword repetition. *Journal of speech, language, and hearing research*, 47(2):421–436.

Angela D Friederici and Jeanine MI Wessels. 1993. Phonotactic knowledge of word boundaries and its use in infant speech perception. *Perception & psychophysics*, 54(3):287–295.

Matthew Goldrick. 2004. Phonological features and phonotactic constraints in speech production. *Journal of Memory and Language*, 51(4):586–603.

Philip James Hamilton. 1996. Phonetic constraints and markedness in the phonotactics of australian aboriginal languages (1996). *Toronto Working Papers in Linguistics*.

Jeffrey Nicholas Heinz. 2007. *Inductive learning of phonotactic patterns*. ProQuest.

Kyuyeon Hwang and Wonyong Sung. 2016. Character-level language modeling with hierarchical recurrent neural networks. *arXiv preprint arXiv:1609.03777*.

Yoon Kim, Yacine Jernite, David Sontag, and Alexander M Rush. 2015. Character-aware neural language models. *arXiv preprint arXiv:1508.06615*.

Irina Kipyatkova and Alexey Karpov. 2015. A comparison of rnn lm and flm for russian speech recognition. In *International Conference on Speech and Computer*, pages 42–50. Springer.

Paul A Luce and Nathan R Large. 2001. Phonotactics, density, and entropy in spoken word recognition. *Language and Cognitive Processes*, 16(5-6):565–581.

O Lyashevskaya and S Sharov. 2009. The frequency dictionary of modern russian language. *Azbukovnik, Moscow*.

James M McQueen. 1998. Segmentation of continuous speech using phonotactics. *Journal of memory and language*, 39(1):21–46.

Kristine H Onishi, Kyle E Chambers, and Cynthia Fisher. 2002. Learning phonotactic constraints from brief auditory experience. *Cognition*, 83(1):B13–B23.

Ilya Oparin, Martin Sundermeyer, Hermann Ney, and Jean-Luc Gauvain. 2012. Performance analysis of neural networks in combination with n-gram language models. In *2012 IEEE International Conference on Acoustics, Speech and Signal Processing (ICASSP)*, pages 5005–5008. IEEE.

Alan Prince and Bruce Tesar. 2004. Learning phonotactic distributions. *Constraints in phonological acquisition*, pages 245–291.

Martin Sundermeyer, Ralf Schlüter, and Hermann Ney. 2012. Lstm neural networks for language modeling. In *Interspeech*, pages 194–197.

Martin Sundermeyer, Hermann Ney, and Ralf Schlüter. 2015. From feedforward to recurrent lstm neural networks for language modeling. *IEEE/ACM Transactions on Audio, Speech and Language Processing (TASLP)*, 23(3):517–529.

Marija Tabain, Gavan Breen, and Andrew Butcher. 2004. Vc vs. cv syllables: a comparison of aboriginal languages with english. *Journal of the International Phonetic Association*, 34(02):175–200.

Bruce Tesar and Alan Prince. 2003. Using phonotactics to learn phonological alternations. In *Proceedings from the annual meeting of the Chicago Linguistic Society*, volume 39, pages 241–269. Chicago Linguistic Society.

Nick Thieberger. 2011. Natrauswen nig efat: stories from south efate.

Michael S Vitevitch and Paul A Luce. 2005. Increases in phonotactic probability facilitate spoken nonword repetition. *Journal of memory and language*, 52(2):193–204.

Jill A Warker and Gary S Dell. 2006. Speech errors reflect newly learned phonotactic constraints. *Journal of Experimental Psychology: Learning, Memory, and Cognition*, 32(2):387.

The Role of Features and Context on Suicide Ideation Detection

Yufei Wang[*]
School of ITEE
The University of Queensland
Brisbane, Australia
`Yufei.Wang1@uq.net.au`

Stephen Wan and Cécile Paris
CSIRO Data61
Sydney, Australia
`firstname.lastname@data61.csiro.au`

Abstract

There is a growing body of work studying suicide ideation, expressions of intentions to kill oneself, on social media. We explore the problem of detecting such ideation on Twitter, focusing on the impact of a set of features drawn from the literature and on the role of discussion context for this task. Our experiments show a significant improvement upon the previously published results for the O'Dea et al. (2015) dataset on suicide ideation. Interestingly, we found that stylistic features helped while social media metadata features did not. Furthermore, discussion context was useful. To further understand the contributions of these different features and of discussion context, we present a discussion of our experiments in varying the feature representations, and examining their effects on suicide ideation detection on Twitter.

1 Introduction

According to World Health Organisation, a suicide occurs every 40 seconds worldwide (WHO, 2014). Suicidal death has destructive effect on both family (Cerel et al., 2008) and community (Levine, 2008) level. Tragically, many suicide cases can be prevented (Bailey et al., 2011). As social media platforms, such as Twitter[1], are often used as channels to discuss mental health topics, there is a need for new technologies to deliver online mental health support (Daine et al., 2013). Such services may be particular important for the youth, well represented on social media, for whom suicide is the second leading cause of death (WHO, 2014).

Consequently, there is a growing body of work that studies suicide ideation, expressions of intentions to kill oneself, on platforms such as Twitter. For example, O'Dea et al. (2015) describe a data set of Twitter posts that has been annotated by mental health and social media experts for (i) the presence of suicide ideation, and (ii) the level of severity of the ideation. In that text classification work, lexical features alone were used. However, intuitively, one might expect that information, such as the discussion context, might each provide valuable information to detect cases of suicide ideation.

For example, information from the surrounding discussion context, perhaps by friends, might indicate the presence of genuine suicide ideation. Two examples, Post A and Post B and their respective replies, are shown below.[2]

Post-A: *Okay goodbye, im going to kill myself tomorrow @ the retreat thing.*
Reply-A: *@ANON No plz dont.*

Post-B: *Listening to ultra live stream rn in ANON's car da gonna kill myself*
Reply-B: *@ANON I was watching it at work!!*

Although both cases contain the key phrase "kill myself", the replies indicate that Post-A is a more concerning post than Post-B, as the respondent answers sympathetically and supportively. However, the reply to Post-B focuses on the topic of the "live stream", seemingly dismissing the phrase "kill myself" as a colloquialism.

In this paper, we describe our exploration of these different feature sets for suicide ideation detection. We perform this study using the data set of O'Dea et al. (2015) as it contains annotations of suicide ideation and also of the severity of that ideation. That is, it also includes cases of non-genuine suicide ideation (based on uses of

---

[*]This work was performed while Yufei Wang was on a CSIRO Student Vacation Scholarship, 2015-2016

[1]www.twitter.com

[2]Examples have been modified to remove Twitter handles.

Yufei Wang, Stephen Wan and Cecile Paris . 2016. The Role of Features and Context on Suicide Ideation Detection. In *Proceedings of Australasian Language Technology Association Workshop*, pages 94–102.

the word "suicide" for metaphorical or humorous purposes). In addition, the data set also includes metadata for each Twitter post and the discussion context following each annotated post.

Our contributions are as follows.

1. We improve on the results published in O'Dea et al. (2015);

2. We describe a unified feature set drawn from the literature of mental health and suicide ideation analytics; and

3. We present a novel analysis on the impact of discussion level features for suicide ideation detection on Twitter.

Interestingly, we find that the literature-inspired feature sets only marginally improved upon the classification results. Specifically, for this work, stylistic features helped but social media features did not. Furthermore, discussion context was useful but only provided a small gain in performance. This is a surprising outcome, and so we investigate the roles of these features and of the discussion context further.

In the remainder of this paper, we describe the O'Dea et al. (2015) dataset and the previously published results in Section 2. We survey the related work from which our feature set was inspired in Section 3. Section 4 outlines the stylistic and social media metadata features used in this work, as well as providing an analysis about the contributions of these feature types. We examine the role of discussion context in Section 5. Finally, we present concluding remarks in Section 6.

2 The O'Dea et al. (2015) Dataset and Classification Results

In this work, we base our study of features relevant in suicide ideation detection on an existing Twitter dataset that contains judgements on the severity of the suicide ideation and also a rich collection of supplementary data for the post in question, such as the following discussion and the Twitter metadata (O'Dea et al., 2015). In this section, we will briefly describe the dataset, along with the machine learning features and algorithm used to obtain published performance results.

2.1 The Dataset

Twitter data was collected by O'Dea et al. (2015) using queries based on words relating to general

Attribute	SI	PC	SC	All
Num. Twitter posts	534	1029	258	1821
Num. Unique words	2545	3016	694	4750
Avg. Num. words	17.5	14.9	10.9	15.1

Table 1: Descriptive summary statistics about each class label.

English words about suicide ideation (Jashinsky et al., 2014), such as: suicidal; suicide; kill myself; my suicide note; never wake up; better off dead; suicide plan; tired of living; die alone; go to sleep forever.

Of these, 2000 Twitter posts occurring between February and April 2014 were randomly sampled and annotated using three categories of severity listed here from least to most severe: "Safe to Ignore"(SI), "Possibly Concerning"(PC) and "Strongly Concerning"(SC) according to their suicide risk (O'Dea et al., 2015). Table 1 presents summary statistics about each class.

2.2 Prior classification results

The best performing system found by O'Dea et al. (2015) was a Support Vector Machine (SVM) (Joachims, 1999) with a feature set of unigrams weighted by TF-IDF scores. For these features, casing was ignored. To focus on the impact of using different feature types, we continue using SVM as the classifier and TF-IDF for lower-cased unigram features.

We successfully replicated the previous result reported by O'Dea et al. (2015), built using the Python Scikit-learn package[3]. We achieved a 10-fold cross-validation accuracy of 66% that is slightly better than the reported result of 63% in O'Dea et al. (2015).

We suspect this difference is due to variations in the text preprocessing. We thus experimented with different text preprocessing variants for n-gram lexical features. These are as follows:

- **N-gram** We extended the feature set to include uni-, bi- and tri-gram, where longer n-grams potentially captures phasal information.

- **Text Preprocessing** We tokenised the text using the Twokenize tool from Carnegie Melon University (CMU), which provides a

---

[3] http://scikit-learn.org/stable/index.html

Features	Accuracy	Macro-F1 (p-value)
Baseline	66.4%	58.6 (-)
1-3 NGrams	66.0%	57.7 (p = 0.275)
CMU	66.6%	59.0 (p = 0.432)

Table 2: Accuracy and macro-F1 scores for different variants of our baseline.

treatment of social media conventions such as emoji.[4].

We summarise thse results in Table 2 Given our multi-class scenario, a more informative metric than accuracy is the macro-F1 score, which we present here (scaled to lie from 0 to 100) and use in the remainder of this paper. For this experiment and in the remainder of this paper, we consistently report on 10-fold cross-validation results, using the same fold splits each time. For significance tests, we use the Wilcoxon Signed Ranks (Wilcoxon, 1945) test. Following the evaluation procedure of the 2016 CL Psych shared task, (Milne et al., 2016), we use macro-F1 as it gives "more weight to infrequent yet more critical labels", noting that the shared task and the classification task described in this paper shared much in common, albeit for different data sets. In this paper, significant results are in **bold** font.

We found that using a larger n-gram size did not help, decreasing the macro-F1 score to 57.7. We suspect this is due to the short nature of Twitter. Using the CMU tool provided a small improvement in macro-F1 (59.0), which we attribute to Twokenise's more comprehensive treatment of social media text conventions.

We note that character n-grams have also been explored in the literature, as a means to abstract beyond the noisy nature of social media. This has been experimented in the past by Coppersmith et al. (2016) and Malmasi et al. (2016). We focus on unigram features here to allow a straightforward comparison with the previously published results for the dataset.

In the remainder of this paper, as our baseline, we use our re-implementation of the O'Dea et al. (2015) classifier, using the Twokenise tool to create unigram features.

3 Features used in Suicide-related Research

3.1 A Survey

One recent focus of computational linguistics research community has been on natural language processing tools to facilitate mental health research. This has been coordinated as shared tasks in the 2011 i2b2 Medical NLP Challenge[5] as well as the recent 2015 and 2016 shared tasks in the Computational Linguistics and Clinical Psychology (CL Psych) series (Coppersmith et al. (2015b) and Milne et al. (2016), respectively).

In this short survey, we focus on related work that examines different facets of text studied that help to characterise mental illness, with a particular focus on work on detecting suicide ideation. We can characterise features used as being: (i) **stylistic**, or (ii) **social media metadata**:

The **stylistic** features for analysing suicide-related text often uses features from the Linguistics Inquirer Word Count (LIWC) (Tausczik and Pennebaker, 2010). LIWC provides features such as articles, auxiliary verbs, conjunctions, adverbs, personal pronouns, prepositions, functional words, assent, negation, certainty and quantifier and have been used by Coppersmith et al. (2014) and De Choudhury et al. (2013) to study mental health signals in Twitter. Coppersmith et al. (2015a) employ the features to characterise mental illness, such Attention Deficit/Hyperactivity Disorder (ADHD) and Seasonal Affective Disorder (SAD).

These have also been applied to other data sources besides Twitter. For analyses of text on suicide ideation, Matykiewicz et al. (2009), uses LIWC to study suicide notes of suicide completers. Kumar et al. (2015) look at Reddit discussions following a celebrity suicide. Cohan et al. (2016) use the features to categorise mental health forum data in the 2016 CL Psych shared task.

In addition to LIWC, other stylistic features are possible. For example, Pestian et al. (2010) examines the use of readability metrices, such as the Flesch and Kincaid readability scores. Liakata et al. (2012) describe the role of features such as grammatical subject and object, grammatical triples, and negation in detecting emotion in the i2b2 dataset.

Social media metadata features have also pre-

---

[4]https://github.com/myleott/ark-twokenize-py

[5]https://www.i2b2.org/NLP/Coreference/Call.php

viously been explored in the analysis of mental health related content. For example, metadata such as the time of post has previously been studied by Huang et al. (2015) and De Choudhury et al. (2013). Interestingly, De Choudhury et al. (2013) link time of posting to an insomnia index.

De Choudhury et al. (2013) also examines Twitter discussions, looking at the proportion of reply posts and the fraction of retweets as features. Related features are possible with other data sources besides Twitter. For example, Cohan et al. (2016) examine the role of discussion thread length for forum data.

A more complex set of features derived from the social media platform are network-related features. Colombo et al. (2016) perform social network analysis and examine the friend vs follower distributions in their analysis of Twitter networks and suicide ideation.

4 Evaluating Literature-Inspired Features

In this section, we describe our literature-inspired feature set covering (i) stylistic features and (ii) social media features. Our focus is on Twitter data which differs from other text given its short length, its informality in style, spelling and grammaticality. Consequently, instead of LIWC, we use a range of tools that are optimised for Twitter analytics, such as the CMU preprocessing tools, which provides Part-of-Speech tags for Twitter, and our own Twitter specific versions of the stylistic features listed above.

4.1 Stylistic Features

Following related work in examining stylistic linguistic features in analysing the language of mental health discussions (for example, Kumar et al. (2015) and Coppersmith et al. (2015a)), we examine a set of features that capture the linguistics attributes associated with the style of writing, such as orthography or words that have a strong syntactic element like pronouns. Similar features have been proven successful in sentiment analysis domain (for example, Mohammad et al. (2013) look at part-of-speech features and Brody and Diakopoulos (2011) examines orthographic features).

The features we explored are as follows:

- **Generic Text Attributes** The number of *chars*, *tokens* in the Twitter message.

- **Orthographic** This feature group includes the number of *all-upper-letter word*, *all-lower-letter word*, *words starting with upper letter*, *words containing continuously repeated letters* and *ratio of all uppercase to all lowercase* words in one tweet.

- **Sympathy Response Words** The number of words associated with a sympathetic response. We use the following categories:

    - please: *please, pls, plz*
    - no: *no, not, none, nope*

- **Punctuation** The number of *question marks*, *exclamation marks* and *colons* in the tweet.

- **Personal Pronoun** Three Boolean features to indicate the presence of 1st, 2nd and 3rd person pronouns. We define these as:

    - 1st: *I, me, myself, im, I'm*
    - 2nd: *u, you, yourself*
    - 3rd: *she, he, hers, his, her, him, herself, himself*

- **Question Words** The number of question words, such as: *why, what, whats, what's, when, where,* and *how*.

- **Time References** The number of time references, searching keywords including: *tomorrow, today, yesterday, now*, and the names of days (including abbreviations).

- **Auxiliary Verbs** The number of auxiliary and modal verbs, including: *am, is, are, do, does, have, has, going, gonna, was, were, did, had, gone, shall, can, may, might, could, would, should, will, must.*

- **Part-of-Speech (POS) features** The counts for POS tags provided by the CMU Twitter NLP tool (Gimpel et al., 2011).

4.2 Social Media Features

The Twitter Application Programming Interface (API)[6] provides additional metadata in addition to the message content. Some of these features capture elements of the social environment of the Twitter user posting the message, such as the size of their Twitter community (through the follower

---

[6]For full documentation, please view the Twitter Developer documentation: http://dev.twitter.com

and followee counts), and the level of conversational interaction for the current discussion, as given by the number of replies or retweets (Boyd et al., 2010).

The features we examined and our intuitions for using them were as follows:

- **Number of replies** The number of replies could indicate if the content was concerning enough to evoke one or more responses.

- **The timestamp of the post** Tweets posted at certain hours, for example late in the night, may be potentially more concerning.

- **Account features** These features capture the extent to which the Twitter user has personalised their Twitter account. The degree of personalisation could indicate the presence of spam accounts. We use 5 types of features: (i) whether the author has changed the default profile, (ii) whether author uses the default image, (iii) whether the author has provided a personal web URL; (iv) the number of followers; and (v) the number of friends (where both parties follow each other).

- **Tweet Special Elements** The count of special elements in a tweet, including: *retweet* flags, *favourite* flags, *hashtags*, *URLs present*, *user mentions*. This could indicate the style of communication.

- **Message Truncation** If the message is truncated, this could indicate that the content has been copied or reposted, potentially indicating that the content did not originate with the author.

4.3 Feature Normalization

So far, we introduced features with different units and scaling. In a linear model, such as the SVM, features with larger scale will be assigned higher weight during training stage. To avoid this, we normalised each feature independently by removing mean and scaling them to unit variance, as shown in following equation:

$$X_{norm} = \frac{X - \mu}{\sigma}$$

4.4 Results

In Table 3, we present 10-fold cross validation results for the dataset using the baseline features, as

Model	Macro-F1 (P-value)
Baseline (1-gram TFIDF)	58.6 (-)
+ Stylistic	60.2 (p = 0.084)
+ Social Media	58.5 (p = 1.000)

Table 3: Classification performance for different feature types.

Features	Macro-F1 (P-Value)
All	38.7 (-)
All - Style. Ling.	27.7 ($p = 0.002$)
All - POS	36.6 ($p = 0.010$)
All - Social Media	38.7 ($p = 1.000$)

Table 4: Metadata Features Performance

well as variants of the classifier that combine the stylistic and social media metadata features outlined above with the baseline features. The results show that performance is relatively unchanged when using social media features and stylistic features seem to help marginally. However, these results are not statistically significant.

The lack of improvement was surprising, given the prevalence of these features in the literature. We thus performed a feature ablation study for social media features and the stylistic linguistic features. To gain insights on the contribution of these features types, this study was done without unigram features.

The results are presented in Table 4. The lower overall score indicates that the baseline classifier heavily relies on the unigram features, indicating that this is a strongly lexical task. We note that stylistic features capture textual cues, such as auxiliary verbs and pronouns, that may overlap somewhat with the unigram features. This is why we see so little benefit when they are added to the unigram features, as shown earlier in Table 3.

Removing POS features, as a subcategory of the stylistic features, only drops performance marginally, We infer that features to do with content, such as pronouns and sympathetic features are thus more useful cues in detecting suicide ideation.

Again, we find that social media features do not contribute greatly. One reason why this result may differ from related work is the nature of the data set, which may differ substantially from other data studied in related work. For example, it may be the case that timestamps do not matter for this Twitter dataset, which was collected under different conditions than the work of De Choud-hury et al. (2013), where Twitter content is much more strongly aligned to suicide attempts.

In addition, although the number of replies was useful in related work, in this data set most posts only had a single response, as shown in Figure 1. Furthermore Figure 2 shows that there is little difference in the length of discussion across different class labels.

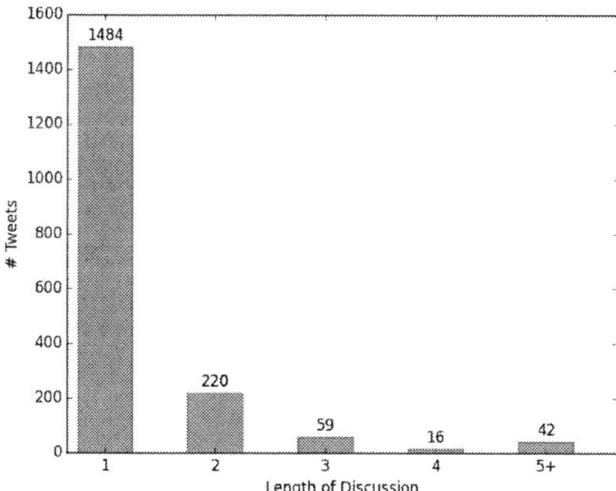

Figure 1: Distribution of Discussion Length

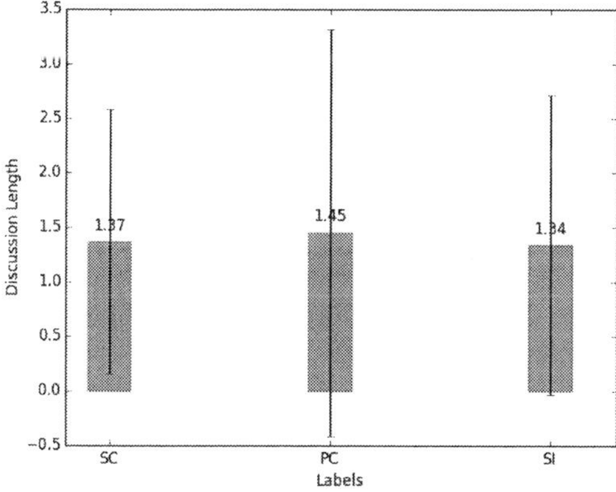

Figure 2: Averaged discussion length for each class label.

5 Discussion Context

One facet of the O'Dea et al. (2015) dataset is that it contains the responses to the annotated post. Although in a real-world intervention system that classifies a newly created Twitter post, responses may not be available, it may still be useful to gauge their role in suicide ideation detection.

Our motivation here in examining the responses is that these could lead to alternative methods for labelled data acquisition. For example, if responses turn out to be strongly correlated with the level of concerns for suicide ideation, perhaps by virtue of containing sympathetic content, we can explore methods that capitalise on this. Our aim here is to understand the feasibility of data acquisition approaches based on responses.

In exploring the role of the text in responses for suicide ideation detection, our work is similar to the recent 2016 CL Psych shared task, where forum discussions were the main source data. As a result, many participants explored the discussion as extra text context from which to derive features. For example, Malmasi et al. (2016) used the discussion structure to look at the posts preceding and following the discussion post in question. Pink et al. (2016) look at concatenations of discussion reply chains as a source of features. We used a similar approach in this work, except that we focus on the much shorter Twitter discussions.

We incorporate information about the discussion context by examining the responses to the Twitter post in question, or the "triggering post". When using the additional context of discussion responses, the feature representation of the triggering post can be augmented with feature representations based on the text of the responses. Given the results of the preceding section, we focus on unigram features for responses.

The two methods we explored are:

- **Merge Text** In the simplest approach, the text of original Twitter post and all responses are merged together into one text. Unigram features are extracted from this combined text. The length of this feature $|V|$ where V is the vocabulary size.

- **Split Text** In this representation, we keep the text of the triggering post and the text of the responses separate, resulting in two sets of unigram features. The size of this feature vector is $2|V|$.

5.1 Results

In Table 5, we present the results for the discussion features, showing that performance increases when maintaining some discussion structure (using the split text variant). Indeed, by collapsing the discussion, the triggering post and the responses, into a single text block, which one might want to do for the purposes of simplifying the model, the results are negatively affected.

Model	Macro-F1 (P-value)
Baseline (1-gram TFIDF)	58.6 (-)
+ Disc. (Merge Text)	57.1 (p = 0.375)
+ Disc. (Split Text)	60.7 (p = 0.084)
Disc. Split Text + Stylistic	**61.7 (p = 0.010)**
All	62.3 (p = 0.193)

Table 5: Classification performance for different feature types. All means "Disc. Split Text + Stylistic + Social media"

If we combine this with the stylistic features for the triggering post and for the responses, the gains are culminative with performance increasing to 61.7 (+3.1 macro-F1 points), a significant improvement above the baseline ($\alpha = 0.05$). We also conduct experiment including both stylistic features and social media features with results shown in All in Table 5. As we expected, by incorporating social media features, we only gain mild 0.6% F1 score improvement which is not statistical significant ($\alpha = 0.193 > 0.05$) compared with "Disc. Split Text + Stylistic".

5.2 The Role of the First Response

We observed a statistically significant positive improvement of 3.1 macro-F1 points. Although this is a positive improvement, it is slight. This is a surprise given the motivating example above. In particular, we expected that content-based features from the responses would help more in labelling the triggering post.

We performed subsequent experiments to see whether additional features that capture more of the discussion structure would help. For the results reported in Table 5, responses were treated as single amalgamated unit. However, one might expect that it is the first response that potentially sheds the most light as to whether there is a severe suicide ideation in the triggering post, since the subsequent responses may contain divergent topics.

Approach	Macro-F1 (P-Value)
Baseline	58.6 (-)
All Responses	60.7 (p = 0.084)
First Response	60.5 (p = 0.105)

Table 6: Investigating the role of the first response

We investigated this by creating variants of the system that would use just the first response, com-

	Resp.	SC	PC	SI	All
Chars	FR	55.8	62.0	69.1	63.2
	OR	69.8	57.7	69.2	62.1
Words	FR	10.8	12.0	13.4	12.2
	OR	13.2	10.5	12.4	11.31

Table 7: Average lengths of the first response (FR) vs. other responses (OR) in terms of characters and words.

Class	Words
SC	you, i, **don't**, to, **no**, it, **do**, me, that, **please**
PC	you, i, to, that, it, the, me, a, and, **don't**
SI	you, i, to, the, a, it, that, is, and, me

Table 8: Top 10 most frequent words in the first response (ordered by rank).

pared to the system described above, which uses all responses. The results are presented in Table 6. We observe that the performance is almost identical, if not marginally worse. We believe that this is because, while the first response may indicate the severity of the ideation, sympathetic responses tend to be shorter. Thus segmenting the discussion after the first response means that the feature representations is less rich.

To explore this negative result further, we checked to see if indeed the first responses were shorter. Table 7 presents the average length of the first responses (compared to other responses) in terms of characters and words. Interestingly, for the SC class, the length of the first response is indeed shorter than the other responses. Furthermore, this is not the case for the other class labels.

This shorter length was associated with sympathetic responses. Table 8 provides a summary view of these responses by showing the top 10 words for the first response for each class label, with sympathetic terms bolded (terms that correspond to responses like "no, don't do it please"). The SC case has more of these words in its top 10 list, compared to the other class labels.

As the SVM was not able to utilise this information, we checked to see if a partially heuristic approach would work. We implemented a variant of the suicide ideation detection system that would first check the length of the first response. If this was less than a certain threshold, it would be deemed to be of the SC class. Otherwise, we

Thres.	6	8	10	12	14
F1	38	33	29	27	25

Table 9: A partially heuristic approach based on the length of the first response (in words). *thresh.* stands for threshold.

used the trained model (with the combination of the discussion split text features and the stylistic feature set, see Table 5) select the best class label.

In Table 9, we present the cross-validation results for this heuristic approach. The results show that this manual heuristic does not perform well. Thus, we are unable to beat the simpler model that simply treats the entire set of responses as single text. Unfortunately, given that we were not able to detect any stronger boost in performance, we conclude that basing an alternative mechanism for automatic data acquisition on the use of responses is not feasible.

6 Conclusion

In this paper, we explored a range of literature-inspired features that for the task of detecting suicide ideation on Twitter. We focused on stylistic linguistic and social media metadata features for use in addition to unigram features, finding that it was the stylistic features that helped for our dataset. We described a number of further investigations on the role of discussion context for this classification task, finding that discussion context helps. Furthermore, both discussion context and stylistic features can be combined to achieve a significant improvement in performance, compared with the previously published performance on this dataset. We also explored the contributions of different feature types and variations in representing the discussion context. We found that a simple representation that does not make a distinction between the first and following responses worked best. From these results, we conclude that unigram features still represent a strong baseline, reflecting perhaps that suicide ideation detection is a task that is heavily influenced by lexical cues.

Acknowledgments

We would like to thank the anonymous reviewers for their valuable feedback. This work is supported by CSIRO Undergraduate Vacation Scholarships.

References

Rahn K. Bailey, Tejas C. Patel, Jaymie Avenido, Milapkumar Patel, Mohammad Jaleel, Narviar C. Barker, Jahanzeb Ali Khan, Shahid All, and Shagufta Jabeen. 2011. Suicide: Current trends. *Journal of the National Medical Association*, 103(7):614 – 617.

Danah Boyd, Scott Golder, and Gilad Lotan. 2010. Tweet, tweet, retweet: Conversational aspects of retweeting on twitter. In *System Sciences (HICSS), 2010 43rd Hawaii International Conference on*, pages 1–10. IEEE.

Samuel Brody and Nicholas Diakopoulos. 2011. Cooooooooooooooolllllllllllllll!!!!!!!!!!!!!! using word lengthening to detect sentiment in microblogs. In *Proceedings of the 2011 Conference on Empirical Methods in Natural Language Processing*, pages 562–570, Edinburgh, Scotland, UK., July. Association for Computational Linguistics.

Julie Cerel, John R. Jordan, and Paul R. Duberstein. 2008. The impact of suicide on the family. *Crisis*, 29(1):38–44. PMID: 18389644.

Arman Cohan, Sydney Young, and Nazli Goharian. 2016. Triaging mental health forum posts. In *Proceedings of the Third Workshop on Computational Lingusitics and Clinical Psychology*, pages 143–147, San Diego, CA, USA, June. Association for Computational Linguistics.

Gualtiero B. Colombo, Pete Burnap, Andrei Hodorog, and Jonathan Scourfield. 2016. Analysing the connectivity and communication of suicidal users on twitter. *Computer Communications*, 73(Pt B):291–300, jan.

Glen Coppersmith, Mark Dredze, and Craig Harman. 2014. Quantifying mental health signals in twitter. In *Proceedings of the Workshop on Computational Linguistics and Clinical Psychology: From Linguistic Signal to Clinical Reality*, pages 51–60, Baltimore, Maryland, USA, June. Association for Computational Linguistics.

Glen Coppersmith, Mark Dredze, Craig Harman, and Kristy Hollingshead. 2015a. From ADHD to SAD: Analyzing the Language of Mental Health on Twitter through Self-Reported Diagnoses. *the 2nd Workshop on Computational Linguistics and Clinical Psychology: From Linguistic Signal to Clinical Reality*, pages 1–10.

Glen Coppersmith, Mark Dredze, Craig Harman, Kristy Hollingshead, and Margaret Mitchell. 2015b. Clpsych 2015 shared task: Depression and ptsd on twitter. In *Proceedings of the 2nd Workshop on Computational Linguistics and Clinical Psychology: From Linguistic Signal to Clinical Reality*, pages 31–39, Denver, Colorado, June 5. Association for Computational Linguistics.

Glen Coppersmith, Kim Ngo, Ryan Leary, and Anthony Wood. 2016. Exploratory analysis of social media prior to a suicide attempt. In *Proceedings of the Third Workshop on Computational Linguistics and Clinical Psychology*, pages 106–117, San Diego, CA, USA, June. Association for Computational Linguistics.

Kate Daine, Keith Hawton, Vinod Singaravelu, Anne Stewart, Sue Simkin, and Paul Montgomery. 2013. The Power of the Web: A Systematic Review of Studies of the Influence of the Internet on Self-Harm and Suicide in Young People. *PLoS ONE*, 8(10):e77555, oct.

Munmun De Choudhury, Michael Gamon, Scott Counts, and Eric Horvitz. 2013. Predicting Depression via Social Mcdia. *Proceedings of the Seventh International AAAI Conference on Weblogs and Social Media*, 2:128–137.

Kevin Gimpel, Nathan Schneider, Brendan O'Connor, Dipanjan Das, Daniel Mills, Jacob Eisenstein, Michael Heilman, Dani Yogatama, Jeffrey Flanigan, and Noah A Smith. 2011. Part-of-speech tagging for twitter: Annotation, features, and experiments. In *Proceedings of the 49th Annual Meeting of the Association for Computational Linguistics: Human Language Technologies: short papers-Volume 2*, pages 42–47. Association for Computational Linguistics.

Xiaolei Huang, Xin Li, Tianli Liu, David Chiu, Tingshao Zhu, and Lei Zhang. 2015. Topic model for identifying suicidal ideation in chinese microblog. In *Proceedings of the 29th Pacific Asia Conference on Language, Information and Computation, PACLIC 29, Shanghai, China, October 30 - November 1, 2015*.

Jared Jashinsky, Scott H Burton, Carl L Hanson, Josh West, Christophe Giraud-Carrier, Michael D Barnes, and Trenton Argyle. 2014. Tracking suicide risk factors through twitter in the us. *Crisis*.

Thorsten Joachims. 1999. Making large-scale support vector machine learning practical. pages 169–184.

Mrinal Kumar, Mark Dredze, Glen Coppersmith, and Munmun De CHoudhury. 2015. Detecting Changes in Suicide Content Manifested in Social Media Following Celebrity Suicides. *Proceedings of the 26th ACM Conference on Hypertext & Social Media*, pages 85–94.

Heidi Levine. 2008. Suicide and its impact on campus. *New Directions for Student Services*, 2008(121):63–76.

Maria Liakata, Jee-Hyub Kim, Shyamasree Saha, Janna Hastings, and Dietrich Rebholz-Schuhmann. 2012. Three Hybrid Classifiers for the Detection of Emotions in Suicide Notes. *Biomedical Informatics Insights*, 5(1):175–184.

Shervin Malmasi, Marcos Zampieri, and Mark Dras. 2016. Predicting Post Severity in Mental Health Forums. pages 133–137.

Pawel Matykiewicz, W Duch, and John P Pestian. 2009. Clustering semantic spaces of suicide notes and newsgroups articles. *Proceedings of the Workshop on Current Trends in Biomedical Natural Language Processing*, (June):179–184.

David N. Milne, Glen Pink, Ben Hachey, and Rafael A. Calvo. 2016. Clpsych 2016 shared task: Triaging content in online peer-support forums. In *Proceedings of the Third Workshop on Computational Linguistics and Clinical Psychology*, pages 118–127, San Diego, CA, USA, June. Association for Computational Linguistics.

Saif M Mohammad, Svetlana Kiritchenko, and Xiaodan Zhu. 2013. Nrc-canada: Building the state-of-the-art in sentiment analysis of tweets. *arXiv preprint arXiv:1308.6242*.

Bridianne O'Dea, Stephen Wan, Philip J Batterham, Alison L Calear, Cecile Paris, and Helen Christensen. 2015. Detecting suicidality on twitter. *Internet Interventions*, 2(2):183–188.

John Pestian, Henry Nasrallah, Pawel Matykiewicz, Aurora Bennett, and Antoon Leenaars. 2010. Suicide Note Classification Using Natural Language Processing: A Content Analysis. *Biomedical informatics insights*, 2010(3):19–28.

Glen Pink, Will Radford, and Ben Hachey. 2016. Classification of mental health forum posts. In *Proceedings of the Third Workshop on Computational Linguistics and Clinical Psychology*, pages 180–182, San Diego, CA, USA, June. Association for Computational Linguistics.

Yla R. Tausczik and James W. Pennebaker. 2010. The psychological meaning of words: Liwc and computerized text analysis methods.

WHO. 2014. Preventing suicide: A global imperative. Technical report, World Health Organisation, Geneva, Switzerland.

Frank Wilcoxon. 1945. Individual comparisons by ranking methods. *Biometrics Bulletin*, 1(6):80–83.

Featureless Domain-Specific Term Extraction with Minimal Labelled Data

Rui Wang
The University of
Western Australia
35 Stirling Highway, Crawley,
W.A. 6009, Australia
`rui.wang@research.`
`uwa.edu.au`

Wei Liu[*]
The University of
Western Australia
35 Stirling Highway, Crawley,
W.A. 6009, Australia
`wei.liu@uwa.edu.au`

Chris McDonald
The University of
Western Australia
35 Stirling Highway, Crawley,
W.A. 6009, Australia
`chris.mcdonald@`
`uwa.edu.au`

Abstract

Supervised domain-specific term extraction often suffers from two common problems, namely labourious manual feature selection, and the lack of labelled data. In this paper, we introduce a weakly supervised bootstrapping approach using two deep learning classifiers. Each classifier learns the representations of terms separately by taking word embedding vectors as inputs, thus no manually selected feature is required. The two classifiers are firstly trained on a small set of labelled data, then independently make predictions on a subset of the unlabeled data. The most confident predictions are subsequently added to the training set to retrain the classifiers. This co-training process minimises the reliance on labelled data. Evaluations on two datasets demonstrate that the proposed co-training approach achieves a competitive performance with limited training data as compared to standard supervised learning baseline.

1 Introduction

Domain-specific terms are essential for many knowledge management applications, such as clinical text processing, risk management, and equipment maintenance. Domain-specific term extraction aims to automatically identify domain relevant technical terms that can be either unigram words or multi-word phrases. Supervised domain-specific term extraction often relies on the training of a binary classifier to identify whether or not a candidate term is relevant to the domain (da Silva Conrado et al., 2013; Foo and Merkel, 2010; Nazar and Cabré, 2012). In such approaches, term extraction models are built upon

---

Corresponding author

manually selected features including the local statistical and linguistic information (e.g. frequency, co-occurrence frequency, or linguistic patterns), and external information form third-party knowledge bases (e.g. WordNet, DBpedia). Designing and evaluating different feature combinations turn the development of term extraction models into a time-consuming and labor-intensive exercise. In addition, these approaches require a large amount of labelled training data to generalise the learning. However, labelled data is often hard or impractical to obtain.

In this paper, our first objective is to minimise the usage of labelled data by training two classifiers in a co-training fashion. Co-training is a weakly supervised learning mechanism introduced by Blum and Mitchell (1998), which tackles the problem of building a classification model from a dataset with limited labelled data among the majority of unlabelled ones. It requires two classifiers, each built upon separate *views* of the data. Each view represents a separate set of manually selected features that must be sufficient to learn a classifier. For example, Blum and Mitchell classify web pages based on words appearing in the content of a web page, and words in hyperlinks pointing to the web page. Co-training starts with training each classifier on a small labelled dataset, then each classifier is used to predict a subset of the unlabelled data. The most confident predictions are subsequently added to the training set to re-train each classifier. This process is iterated a fixed number of times. Co-training algorithms have been applied to many NLP tasks where labelled data are in scarce, including statistical parsing (Sarkar, 2001), word sense disambiguation (Mihalcea, 2004), and coreference resolution (Ng and Cardie, 2003), which demonstrate that it generally improves the performance without requiring additional labelled data.

Our second objective is to eliminate the ef-

Rui Wang, Wei Liu and Chris McDonald. 2016. Featureless Domain-Specific Term Extraction with Minimal Labelled Data.
In *Proceedings of Australasian Language Technology Association Workshop*, pages 103–112.

fort of feature engineering by using deep learning models. Applying deep neural networks directly to NLP tasks without feature engineering is also described as NLP from scratch (Collobert et al., 2011). As a result of such training, words are represented as low dimensional and real-valued vectors, encoding both semantic and syntactic features (Mikolov et al., 2013). In our model, word embeddings are pre-trained over the corpora to encode word features that are used as inputs to two deep neural networks to learn different term representations (corresponding to the concept of *views*) over the same dataset. One is a convolutional neural network (CNN) to learn term representations through a single convolutional layer with multiple filters followed by a max pooling layer. Each filter is associated with a region that essentially corresponds to a sub-gram of a term. The underlying intuition is that the meaning of a term can be learnt from its sub-grams by analysing different combinations of words. The other is a Long Short-Term Memory (LSTM) network which learns the representation of a term by recursively composing the embeddings of an input word and the composed value from its precedent, hypothesising that the meaning of a term can be learnt from the sequential combination of each constituent word. Each network connects to a logistic regression layer to perform classifications.

Our model is evaluated on two benchmark domain-specific corpora, namely GENIA (biology domain) (Kim et al., 2003), and ACL RD-TEC (computer science domain) (Handschuh and QasemiZadeh, 2014). The evaluation shows that our model outperforms the C-value algorithm (Frantzi et al., 2000) that is often treated as the benchmark in term extraction. We also trained two classifiers using the standard supervised learning approach, and demonstrate that co-training deep neural networks is an effective approach to reduce the usage of labelled data while maintaining a competitive performance.

This paper is organised as follows. In Section 2, we briefly review the related work. Section 3 introduces our proposed model, and in Section 4 we describe our evaluation datasets and discuss the experimental results. Section 5 summarises our study with an outlook to the future work.

2 Related Work

2.1 Supervised Term Extraction

Supervised machine learning approaches for domain-specific term extraction start with candidate identification, usually by employing a phrase chunker based on pre-identified part-of-speech (POS) patterns, then uses manually selected features to train a classifier. The feature may include linguistic, statistical, and semantic features (Foo and Merkel, 2010; Nazar and Cabré, 2012; da Silva Conrado et al., 2013). The work closely related to ours is *Fault-Tolerant Learning* (FTL) (Yang et al., 2010) inspired by Transfer Learning (Ando and Zhang, 2005) and Co-training (Blum and Mitchell, 1998). FTL builds two *support vector machine* (SVM) classifiers using manually selected features, whereas our model uses deep neural networks taking pre-trained word embeddings as inputs, without using any manually selected feature.

2.2 Learning Representations of Words and Semantic Compositionality

Word embeddings are proposed to overcome the *curse of dimensionality* problem by Bengio et al. (2006), who developed a probabilistic neural language model using a feed-forward multi-layer neural network, which demonstrates how word embeddings can be induced. Recently, Mikolov et al. (2013) presented a shallow network architecture that is specifically for learning word embeddings, known as the *word2vec* model. Their work reveals that word embeddings are capable of representing the meaning of words to a certain degree through analogy test.

Semantic composition is to understand the meaning of a multi-word expression by composing the meanings of each constituent word. For example, given the word embeddings of *pet* and *doctor*, the compositional representation of *pet doctor* is expected to have the high cosine similarity or small Euclidian distance to the vector of *veterinarian*. Such characteristics help classifiers to recognise the semantically related expressions or equivalent counterparts of a term, which offers significant advantages for term extraction. Popular deep neural networks for modelling semantic compositionality include *convolutional*, *recurrent*, *recursive*, and *hybrid* networks. Kim (2014) reported a number of experiments of applying a convolutional network with one single

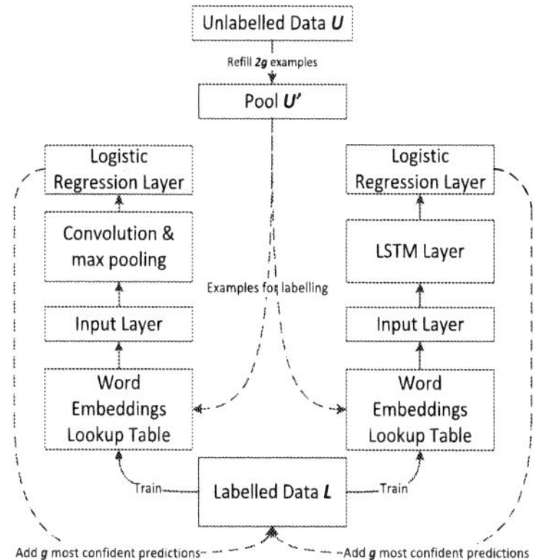

Figure 1: Co-training Network Architecture Overview: Solid lines indicate the training process, dashed lines indicate prediction and labelling processes.

convolutional and 1-Max pooling layer for *Sentiment Analysis* and *Topic Categorisation* tasks producing the state-of-the-art performance on 4 out of 7 datasets, which shows the power of the convolutional architecture. Recurrent neural network is efficient on encoding sequential combinations of data with various lengths, which naturally offers an advantage for capturing semantic compositionality of multi-word terms. Using recurrent neural networks modelling natural languages and their long-term dependencies was attempted by Mikolov et al. (2010). More recently, Sutskever et al. (2014) use LSTM network, and Cho et al. (2014) use *Gated Recurrent Unit* (GRU) network to encode and decode the semantic compositionality of sentences for machine translation. Chung et al. (2015) propose an even deeper architecture named Gated Feedback Recurrent network that stacks multiple recurrent layers for character-level language modelling. Other network architectures for learning semantic compositionality include recursive networks (Socher et al., 2010; Socher et al., 2012), which require using POS tagging texts to produce syntactical tree structures as a prior. Hybrid networks, such as recurrent-convolutional network (Kalchbrenner and Blunsom, 2013; Lai et al., 2015), are designed for capturing document-level semantics.

3 Proposed Model

The model consists of two classifiers, as shown in Figure 1. The left classifier is a CNN network,

and the right one is a LSTM network. Both networks take pre-trained word embedding vectors as inputs to learn the representations of terms independently. The output layer is a logistic regression layer for both networks. Two neural networks are trained using the Co-training algorithm.

The Co-training algorithm requires two separate views of the data, which traditionally are two sets of manually selected features. In our model, however, there is no manually selected features. Thus, two views of the data are carried by our two hypotheses of learning the meaning of terms. The meaning of a term can be learnt by 1) analysing different sub-gram compositions, and 2) sequential combination of each constituent word. The hypotheses are implemented via the CNN and LSTM network. We expect that the rules of composing words can be captured by the networks. The CNN network analyses different regions of a input matrix that is constructed by stacking word embedding vectors, as shown in Figure 2, where the size of regions reflect different n-grams of a term. By scanning the embedding matrix with different region sizes, we expect that the CNN network can learn the meaning of a term by capturing the most representative sub-gram. The LSTM network, on the other hand, learns the compositionality by recursively composing an input embedding vector with the precedent or previously composed value, as shown in Figure3. We expect the LSTM network to capture the meaning of a term through its gates that govern the information flow – how much information (or meaning) of an input word can be added in to the overall meaning, and how much information should be dismissed from the previous composition.

3.1 Term Representation Learning

The objective is to learn a mapping function f that outputs the compositional representation of a term given its word embeddings. Concretely, let V be the vocabulary of a corpus with the size of v. For each word $w \in V$, there is a corresponding d dimensional embedding vector. The collection of all embedding vectors in the vocabulary is a matrix, denoted as C, where $C \in \mathbb{R}^{d \times v}$. C can be thought of as a look-up table, where $C(w_i)$ represents the embedding vectors of word w_i. Given a term $s = (w_1, w_2, ..., w_n)$, the goal is to learn a mapping function $f(C(s))$ that takes the individual vector representation of each word as in-

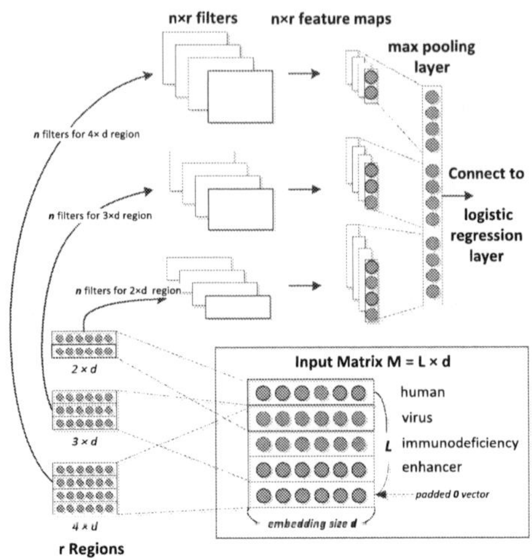

Figure 2: Convolutional Model

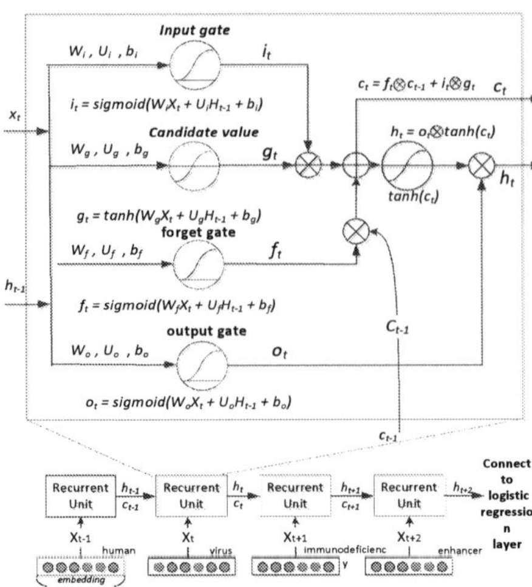

Figure 3: LSTM Model

puts, and output a composed value that represent the compositional meaning of s.

3.1.1 Convolutional Model

We adopt the CNN network used by Kim (2014), and Zhang and Wallace (2015), which has only one convolutional layer, shown in Figure 2. The inputs $C(s)$ to the network are vertically stacked into a matrix M, where the rows are word embeddings of each $w \in s$. Let d be the length of word embedding vectors, and l be the length of a term, then M has the dimension of $d \times l$ where d and l are fixed. We pad zero vectors to the matrix if the number of tokens of an input term is less than l. The convolutional layer has r predefined regions, and each region has n filters. All regions have the same width d, because each row in the input matrix M represents a word and the goal is to learn the composition of them. However, the regions have various heights h, which can be thought of as different *n-gram* models. For example, when $h = 2$, the region is to represent bigram features. Let W be the weights of a filter, where $W \in \mathbb{R}^{d \times h}$. The filter outputs a feature map $c = [c_1, c_2, ..., c_{l-h+1}]$, and c_i is computed as:

$$c_i = f(W \cdot M[i : i + h - 1] + b) \qquad (1)$$

where $M[i : i + h - 1]$ is a sub-matrix of M from row i to row $i + h - 1$, f is an activation function – we use hyperbolic tangent in this work, and b is a bias unit. A pooling function is then applied to extract values from the feature map. We

use the *1*-Max pooling as suggested by Zhang and Wallace (2015) who conduct a sensitivity analysis on one-layer convolutional network showing that *1*-Max pooling consistently outperforms other pooling strategies in sentence classification task. The total number of feature maps in the network is $m = r \times n$, so the output from the max pooling layer $y \in \mathbb{R}^m$ is computed as:

$$y = \max_{i=1}^{m}(c^i) \qquad (2)$$

3.1.2 LSTM Model

We use a LSTM network that is similar to the *vanilla* LSTM (Greff et al., 2015) without peephole connections, shown in Figure 3. The LSTM network features memory cells at each timestamp. A memory cell is to store, read and write information passing through the network at a timestamp t, which consists of four elements, an input gate i, a forget gate f, a candidate g for the current cell state value, and an output gate o. At t, the inputs to the network are the previous cell state value c_{t-1}, the previous hidden state value h_{t-1}, and the input value x_t. The outputs are current cell state c_t and the current hidden state value h_t, which will pass to the next timestamp $t + 1$. At time t, the candidate g for the current cell state value compose the newly input x_t and the previously composed value h_{t-1} to generate a new state value as:

$$g_t = \tanh(W_g \cdot x_t + U_g \cdot h_{t-1} + b_g) \qquad (3)$$

where W_g and U_g are shared weights, and b_i is the bias unit.

The input gate i in the LSTM network decides how much information can pass through from g_t to the actual computation of the memory cell state using a *sigmoid* function $\sigma = \dfrac{1}{1+e^{-x}}$ that outputs a value between 0 and 1 indicating the percentage, as:

$$i_t = \sigma(W_i \cdot x_t + U_i \cdot h_{t-1} + b_i) \tag{4}$$

where W_i and U_i are shared weights, and b_i is the bias unit. Likewise, the forget gate f governs how much information to be filtered out from the previous state c_{t-1}:

$$f_t = \sigma(W_f \cdot x_t + U_f \cdot h_{t-1} + b_f) \tag{5}$$

The new cell state value is computed as taking a part of information from the current inputs and the previous cell state value:

$$c_t = i_t \otimes g_t + f_t \otimes c_{t-1} \tag{6}$$

where $\otimes$ is the element-wise vector multiplication. c_t will be passed to the next timestamp $t+1$, which remains constant from one timestamp to another, representing the *long-short term* memory.

The output gate o can be thought of as the filter that prevents any irrelevant information that may be passed to the next state. The output gate o_t and the hidden state value h_t are computed as:

$$\begin{aligned} o_t &= \sigma(W_o \cdot x_t + U_o \cdot h_{t-1} + b_o) \\ h_t &= o_t \otimes \tanh(c_t) \end{aligned} \tag{7}$$

where h_t is the composed representation of a word sequence from time 0 to t.

3.2 Training Classifier

To build the classifiers, each network is connected to a logistic regression layer for the binary classification task – we are only concerned whether a term is domain relevant or not. The logistic regression layer, however, can be simply replaced by a *softmax* layer for multi-class classification tasks, such as *Ontology Categorisation*.

Overall, the probability that a term s is relevant to the domain is:

$$p(s) = \sigma(W \cdot f(C(s)) + b) \tag{8}$$

where σ is the sigmoid function, W is the weights for logistic regression layer, b is the bias unit, and f is the mapping function that is implemented by the CNN or the LSTM network.

The parameters of convolutional classifier are $\theta = (C,\ W^{conv},\ b^{conv},\ W^{convlogist},\ b^{convlogist})$ where W^{conv} are weights for all m filters, and b^{conv} is the bias vectors. For LSTM classifier, $\theta = (C,\ W^{lstm},\ b^{lstm},\ W^{lstmlogist},\ b^{lstmlogist})$ where $W^{lstm} = (W_i, W_g, W_f, W_o, U_i, U_g, U_f, U_o)$, and $b^{lstm} = (b_i, b_g, b_f, b_o)$. Given a training set D, the learning objective for both of the classifiers is to maximise the log probability of correct labels for $s \in D$ by looking for parameters θ:

$$\underset{\theta}{\operatorname{argmax}} \sum_{s \in D} \log p(s_{label}|s; \theta) \tag{9}$$

θ is updated using *stochastic gradient descent* (SGD) to minimise the negative log likelihood error:

$$\theta := \theta - \varepsilon \frac{\partial \log p(s_{label}|s; \theta)}{\partial \theta} \tag{10}$$

where ε is the learning rate.

3.3 Pre-training Word Embedding

We use the SkipGram model (Mikolov et al., 2013) to learn word embeddings. Given a word w, the SkipGram model predicts the context (surrounding) words $S(w)$ within a pre-defined window size. Using the *softmax* function, the probability of a context word $s \in S$ is:

$$p(s|w) = \frac{e^{v'_w{}^\top \cdot v_s}}{\sum_{t=1}^{V} e^{v'_t{}^\top \cdot v_s}} \tag{11}$$

where V is the vocabulary, v'_w is the output vector representations for w, v_s is the input vector representations for contexts s, respectively. The learning objective is to maximise the conditional probability distribution over vocabulary V in a training corpus D by looking for parameters θ:

$$\underset{\theta}{\operatorname{argmax}} \sum_{w \in D} \sum_{s \in S(w)} \log p(s|w; \theta) \tag{12}$$

3.4 Co-training Algorithm

Given the unlabelled data U, a pool U' of size p, and a small set of labelled data L, firstly each classifier $c \in C$ are trained over L. After training, the classifiers make predictions on U', then choose the most confident g predictions from each classifier and add them to L. The size of U' now becomes $p - 2g$, and $L := L + 2g$. U' then is refilled by randomly selecting $2g$ examples from U. This process iterates k times. Algorithm 1 documents the details.

Algorithm 1 Co-training

Input: L, U, C, p, k, g

   create U' by randomly choosing p example from U

   while $iteration < k$ **do**

      for $c \in C$ **do**

         use L to train C

      end for

      for $c \in C$ **do**

         use c to posit label in U'

         add most confident g example to L

      end for

      refill U' by randomly choosing $2 \times g$ example from U

   end while

4 Experiments

4.1 Datasets

We evaluate our model on two datasets. The first dataset is the GENIA corpus[1]. The current Version 3.02 is a collection of 1,999 article abstracts in the field of *molecular biology* including 451,562 tokens and 30,893 ground truth terms. The second dataset is the ACL RD-TEC corpus[2], which consists of 10,922 articles published between 1965 to 2006 in the domain of *computer science*. The ACL RD-TEC corpus classifies terms into three categories, invalid terms, general terms, and computational terms. We only treat computational terms as ground truth in our evaluation. The dataset has 36,729,513 tokens and 13,832 ground truth terms.

4.2 Preprocessing

We firstly clean the datasets by extracting text content and ground truth terms, removing plurals of nouns, and converting all tokens into lowercases. The ACL RD-TEC corpus provides a pre-identified candidate list, so we only need to identify candidate terms from the GENIA corpus. We build two candidate identifiers. The first identifier uses noun phrase chunking with pre-defined POS patterns, we call it *POS identifier*. We use a common POS pattern `<JJ>*<NN.*>+`, that is, a number of adjectives followed by a number of nouns. The second identifier uses n-gram based chunking, so called *N-gram identifier*, which decomposes a sequence of words into all possible n-grams. However, there would be too many candidates if we simply decompose every sentence into all possible n-grams. Thus, we use stop-words as delimiters to decompose any expression between two stop-words into all possible n-grams as candidates. For example, *novel antitumor antibiotic* produces 6 candidates, *novel antitumor antibiotic*, *novel antitumor*, *antitumor antibiotic*, *novel*, *antitumor*, and *antibiotic*.

4.3 Experiment Settings

The co-training requires a few parameters. We set the small set of labelled data $L = 200$ and the size for the pool U' 500 for all evaluations. The number of iterations k is 800 for POS identified candidates, 500 for N-grams identified candidates in the GENIA dataset, 500 for the ACL RD-TED dataset. The growth size is 20 for POS, 50 for N-grams, and 20 for ACL RD-TED. The evaluation data is randomly selected from candidate sets. For each e in the evaluation set E, $e \notin L$. Table 1 show the class distributions and statistics.

All word embeddings are pre-trained with 300 dimensions on each corpus. The maximum length of terms is 13 on GENIA and 5 on ACL RD-TED, therefore the CNN classifier has 5 different region size , $\{2, 3, 4, 5, 6\}$ for GENIA and 3 region size $\{2, 3, 4\}$ for ACL RD-TED. Each region has 100 filters. There are no specific hyper-parameters required for training the LSTM model. The learning rate for SGD is 0.01.

The model was trained in an *online* fashion. We trained our model on a NVIDIA GeForce 980 TI GPU. The training time linearly increases at each iteration, since the model incrementally adds training examples into the training set. At the beginning, it only took less than a second for one iteration. After 100 iterations, the training set was increased by 1,820 examples that took a few seconds to train. Thus the training time is not critical – even the standard supervised training only took a few hours to converge.

4.4 Evaluation Methodology

We use $precision = \frac{TP}{TP+FP}$, $recall = \frac{TP}{TP+FN}$, $F = 2 \times \frac{precision \times recall}{precision+recall}$ and $accuracy = \frac{TP+TN}{TP+FP+FN+TN}$ for our evaluation. We illustrate the set relationships of *true postive* (TP) , *true negative* (TN), *false postive* (FP), and *false negative* (FN) in Figure 4.

---

[1] publicly available at http://www.geniaproject.org/

[2] publicly available at https://github.com/languagerecipes/the-acl-rd-tec

	Test Examples	Positive	Negative
GENIA POS	5,000	2558 (51.0%)	2442 (49.0%)
GENIA N-gram	15,000	1,926 (12.8%)	13,074 (87.2%)
ACL RD-TEC	15,000	2,416 (16.1%)	12,584 (83.9%)

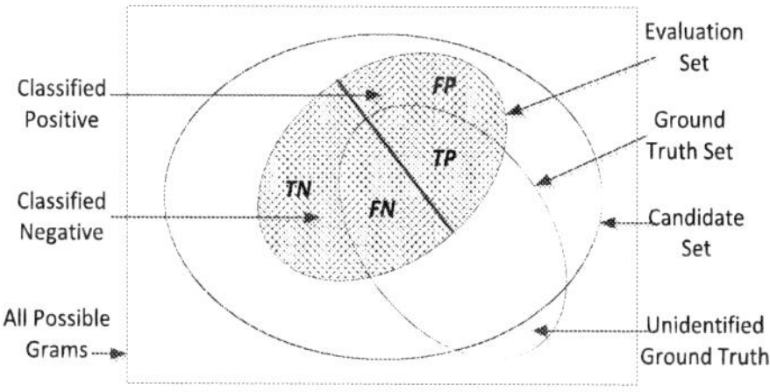

Figure 4: Relationships in TP, TN, FP, and FN for Term Extraction.

4.5 Result and Discussion

We use C-value (Frantzi et al., 2000) as our baseline algorithm. C-value is an unsupervised ranking algorithm for term extraction, where each candidate term is assigned a score indicating the degree of domain relevance. We list the performance of C-value by extracting top scored terms. Since we treat the task as a binary classification task, we also list random guessing scores for each dataset, where recall and accuracy scores are always 50% and precisions correspond to the distribution of positive class of each evaluation set. As a comparison to the Co-training model, we also trained each classifier individually using the standard supervised machine learning approach. The training is conducted by dividing the candidate set into 40% for training, 20% for validation, and 40% for evaluation. For Co-training model, we found that the CNN classifier outperforms the LSTM classifier in all the evaluation, so we only present the performance of the CNN classifier, as shown in Table 2.

The supervised approach unsurprisingly produces the best results on all evaluation sets. However, it uses much more labelled data than the Co-training model, while delivering only 2 percent better performance (F-score) on the GENIA corpus, and 6 percent on the ACL RD-TEC corpus. In comparison to standard supervised machine learning approach, Co-training is more "cost-effective" since it only requires 200 labelled data as seed terms.

On the GENIA corpus, all algorithms produce much better F-score for the POS evaluation set. This is because of different class distributions – on the POS evaluation set, the proportion of positive (ground truth) terms is 50.5% whereas only 12.8% positive terms in the N-gram evaluation set. Therefore, we consider that the results from POS and N-gram evaluation sets are not directly comparable. However, the actual improvements on F-score over random guessing on both evaluation sets are quite similar, suggesting that evaluating performance of a classifier should not only consider the F-score, but should also analyse the actual improvement over random guessing.

It is also interesting to note that the GENIA N-gram evaluation set has 12.8% positive examples, which has similar unbalanced class distribution as ACL RD-TED, 16.1% positives. However, all algorithms produce much better performance on the ACL RD-TEC corpus. We found that in the ACL RD-TEC corpus, the negative terms contain a large number of invalid characters (e.g. ˜), mistakes made by the tokeniser (e.g. `evenunseeneventsare`), and none content-bearing words (e.g. `many`). The classifiers can easily spot these noisy data. Another reason might be that the ACL RD-TEC corpus is bigger than GENIA, which not only allows C-value to produce better performance, but also enables the *word2vec* algorithm to deliver more precise word embedding vectors which are required inputs to our deep learning model.

Although the accuracy measure is commonly used in classification tasks, it does not reflect the true performance of a model when classes are not evenly distributed in an evaluation set. For example, on the N-gram evaluation set, the positive examples are about 12.8% whereas the *negative* examples are about 87.2%. At the beginning of the training, both models tend to classify most of the examples as negative thus the accuracy score is close to 87%. While the training progress, the accuracy starts dropping. However, it is still difficult

Table 2: Evaluation Results

	Labelled Data	Precision	Recall	F-score	Accuracy
GENIA POS					
Random Guessing	–	51%	50%	50.5%	50%
C-value (Top 1000)	–	62.4%	24.4%	35.1%	–
C-value (Top 2500)	–	53.7%	52.5%	53.1%	–
Supervised	16,400	**64.7%**	**78.0%**	**70.7%**	67.1%
Co-training	200	64.1%	76.0%	69.5%	65.5%
GENIA N-gram					
Random Guessing	–	12.8%	50%	20.4%	50%
C-value (Top 2500)	–	12.9%	16.7%	14.6%	–
C-value (Top 7500)	–	11.4%	44.3%	18.1%	–
Supervised	91,924	**35.0%**	**59.1%**	**44.0%**	81.4%
Co-training	200	34.3%	56.6%	42.7%	75.5%
ACL RD-TEC					
Random Guessing	–	16.1%	50%	24.4%	50%
C-value (Top 2500)	–	14%	14.6%	14.3%	–
C-value (Top 7500)	–	21.8%	68.2%	33.3%	–
Supervised	33,538	**70.8%**	**67.7%**	**69.2%**	85.2%
Co-training	200	66%	60.5%	63.1%	79.7%

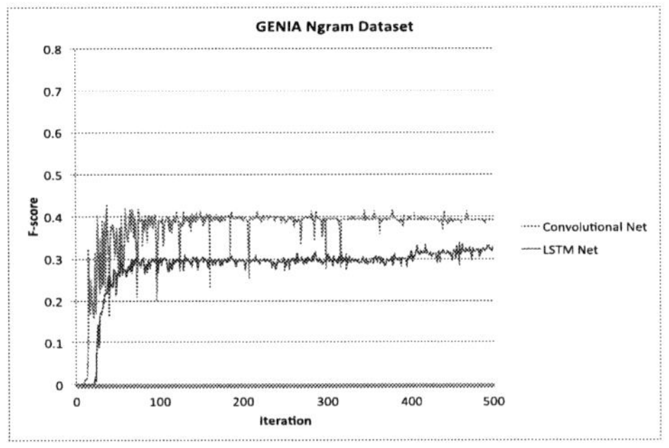

Figure 5: Performance on Ngram evaluation set

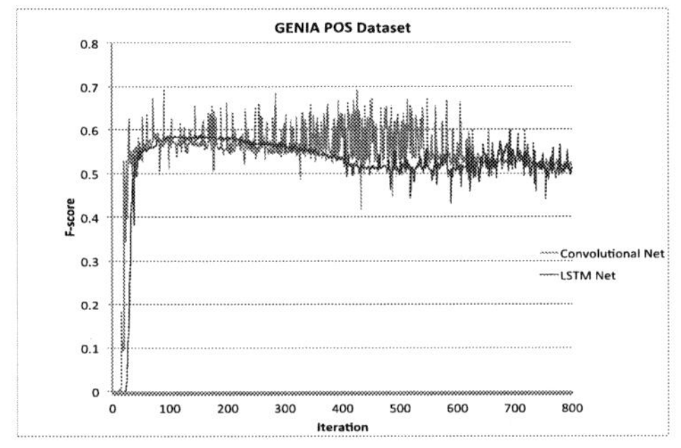

Figure 6: Performance on POS evaluation set

to understand how exactly the model performs according to the accuracy score. On the other hand, because the classes are evenly distributed on POS evaluation set, we can clearly identify how the accuracy measure corresponds to F-scores.

The CNN classifier outperforms the LSTM on all evaluation sets. It also requires much fewer iterations to reach the best F-score. We plot F-score for both classifiers over a few hundreds iterations on the GENIA corpus, shown in Figure 5 and 6. Both classifiers reach their best performance within 100 iterations. For example, the CNN classifier on POS evaluation set, produced a good F-score around 62% at just about 30 iterations, then reached its best F-score 69.5% after 91 iterations. However, the size of the training set is still quite small – by 91 iterations, the training set only grows by 1,820 examples. This phenomenon leads us to consider two more questions 1) what is the exact performance boosted by Co-training? 2) How different numbers of training examples affect the performance of a deep learning model, and do deep learning models still need large amount of labelled training examples to produce the best performance? In the rest of the paper, we will answer the first question, and leave the second question for our future work.

To investigate how Co-training boosts the performance of classifiers, we trained our model using only 200 seed terms over 800 iterations, results are shown in Figure 7. The best F-score is from the convolutional model, about 53%, just slightly

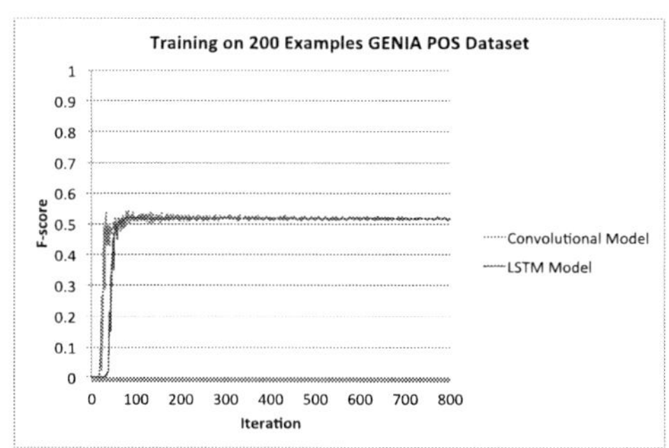

Figure 7: Convolutional and LSTM Classifier Training on 200 Examples on POS Evaluation set

higher than random guessing. On the other, by applying Co-training we obtain the best F-score of 69.5% which is a 16.5% improvement. In fact, the improvement achieved by just adding a small number of training examples to the training set was also report by (Clark et al., 2003). Consequently, it is clear that our co-training model is an effective approach to boost the performance of deep learning models without requiring much training data.

5 Conclusion

In this paper, we have shown a deep learning model using Co-training – a weakly supervised bootstrapping paradigm, for automatic domain-specific term extraction. Experiments show that our model is a "cost-effective" way to boost the performance of deep learning models with very few training examples. The study also leads to further questions such as how the number of training examples affects the performance of a deep learning model, and whether deep learning models still need as many labelled training examples as required in other machine learning algorithms to reach their best performance. We will keep working on these question in the near future.

6 Acknowledgment

This research was funded by the Australian Postgraduate Award (APA), Safety Top-Up Scholarships from The University of Western Australia, and partially funded by Australian Research Council grants DP150102405 and LP110100050.

References

Rie Kubota Ando and Tong Zhang. 2005. A framework for learning predictive structures from multiple tasks and unlabeled data. *Journal of Machine Learning Research*, 6(Nov):1817–1853.

Yoshua Bengio, Holger Schwenk, Jean-Sébastien Senécal, Fréderic Morin, and Jean-Luc Gauvain. 2006. Neural probabilistic language models. In *Innovations in Machine Learning*, pages 137–186. Springer.

Avrim Blum and Tom Mitchell. 1998. Combining labeled and unlabeled data with co-training. In *Proceedings of the eleventh annual conference on Computational learning theory*, pages 92–100. ACM.

Kyunghyun Cho, Bart Van Merriënboer, Caglar Gulcehre, Dzmitry Bahdanau, Fethi Bougares, Holger Schwenk, and Yoshua Bengio. 2014. Learning phrase representations using rnn encoder-decoder for statistical machine translation. *arXiv preprint arXiv:1406.1078*.

Junyoung Chung, Caglar Gülçehre, Kyunghyun Cho, and Yoshua Bengio. 2015. Gated feedback recurrent neural networks. *CoRR, abs/1502.02367*.

Stephen Clark, James R Curran, and Miles Osborne. 2003. Bootstrapping pos taggers using unlabelled data. In *Proceedings of the seventh conference on Natural language learning at HLT-NAACL 2003-Volume 4*, pages 49–55. Association for Computational Linguistics.

Ronan Collobert, Jason Weston, Léon Bottou, Michael Karlen, Koray Kavukcuoglu, and Pavel Kuksa. 2011. Natural language processing (almost) from scratch. *The Journal of Machine Learning Research*, 12:2493–2537.

Merley da Silva Conrado, Thiago Alexandre Salgueiro Pardo, and Solange Oliveira Rezende. 2013. A machine learning approach to automatic term extraction using a rich feature set. In *HLT-NAACL*, pages 16–23.

Jody Foo and Magnus Merkel. 2010. Using machine learning to perform automatic term recognition. In *LREC 2010 Workshop on Methods for automatic acquisition of Language Resources and their evaluation methods, 23 May 2010, Valletta, Malta*, pages 49–54.

Katerina Frantzi, Sophia Ananiadou, and Hideki Mima. 2000. Automatic recognition of multi-word terms:. the c-value/nc-value method. *International Journal on Digital Libraries*, 3(2):115–130.

Klaus Greff, Rupesh Kumar Srivastava, Jan Koutník, Bas R Steunebrink, and Jürgen Schmidhuber. 2015. Lstm: A search space odyssey. *arXiv preprint arXiv:1503.04069*.

Siegfried Handschuh and Behrang QasemiZadeh. 2014. The acl rd-tec: A dataset for benchmarking terminology extraction and classification in computational linguistics. In *COLING 2014: 4th International Workshop on Computational Terminology*.

Nal Kalchbrenner and Phil Blunsom. 2013. Recurrent convolutional neural networks for discourse compositionality. *arXiv preprint arXiv:1306.3584*.

J-D Kim, Tomoko Ohta, Yuka Tateisi, and Junichi Tsujii. 2003. Genia corpusa semantically annotated corpus for bio-textmining. *Bioinformatics*, 19(suppl 1):i180–i182.

Yoon Kim. 2014. Convolutional neural networks for sentence classification. *arXiv preprint arXiv:1408.5882*.

Siwei Lai, Liheng Xu, Kang Liu, and Jun Zhao. 2015. Recurrent convolutional neural networks for text classification. In *AAAI*, pages 2267–2273.

Rada Mihalcea. 2004. Co-training and self-training for word sense disambiguation. In *CoNLL*, pages 33–40.

Tomas Mikolov, Martin Karafiát, Lukas Burget, Jan Cernockỳ, and Sanjeev Khudanpur. 2010. Recurrent neural network based language model. In *INTERSPEECH*, volume 2, page 3.

Tomas Mikolov, Ilya Sutskever, Kai Chen, Greg S Corrado, and Jeff Dean. 2013. Distributed representations of words and phrases and their compositionality. In *Advances in neural information processing systems*, pages 3111–3119.

Rogelio Nazar and Maria Teresa Cabré. 2012. Supervised learning algorithms applied to terminology extraction. In *Proceedings of the 10th Terminology and Knowledge Engineering Conference*, pages 209–217.

Vincent Ng and Claire Cardie. 2003. Weakly supervised natural language learning without redundant views. In *Proceedings of the 2003 Conference of the North American Chapter of the Association for Computational Linguistics on Human Language Technology-Volume 1*, pages 94–101. Association for Computational Linguistics.

Anoop Sarkar. 2001. Applying co-training methods to statistical parsing. In *Proceedings of the second meeting of the North American Chapter of the Association for Computational Linguistics on Language technologies*, pages 1–8. Association for Computational Linguistics.

Richard Socher, Christopher D Manning, and Andrew Y Ng. 2010. Learning continuous phrase representations and syntactic parsing with recursive neural networks. In *Proceedings of the NIPS-2010 Deep Learning and Unsupervised Feature Learning Workshop*, pages 1–9.

Richard Socher, Brody Huval, Christopher D Manning, and Andrew Y Ng. 2012. Semantic compositionality through recursive matrix-vector spaces. In *Proceedings of the 2012 Joint Conference on Empirical Methods in Natural Language Processing and Computational Natural Language Learning*, pages 1201–1211. Association for Computational Linguistics.

Ilya Sutskever, Oriol Vinyals, and Quoc V Le. 2014. Sequence to sequence learning with neural networks. In *Advances in neural information processing systems*, pages 3104–3112.

Yuhang Yang, Hao Yu, Yao Meng, Yingliang Lu, and Yingju Xia. 2010. Fault-tolerant learning for term extraction. In *PACLIC*, pages 321–330.

Ye Zhang and Byron Wallace. 2015. A sensitivity analysis of (and practitioners' guide to) convolutional neural networks for sentence classification. *arXiv preprint arXiv:1510.03820*.

An Effect of Background Population Sample Size on the Performance of a Likelihood Ratio-based Forensic Text Comparison System: A Monte Carlo Simulation with Gaussian Mixture Model

Shunichi Ishihara

Department of Linguistics, The Australian National University

`shunichi.ishihara@anu.edu.au`

Abstract

This is a Monte Carlo simulation-based study that explores the effect of the sample size of the background database on a likelihood ratio (LR)-based forensic text comparison (FTC) system built on multivariate authorship attribution features. The text messages written by 240 authors who were randomly selected from an archive of chatlog messages were used in this study. The strength of evidence (= LR) was estimated using the multivariate kernel density likelihood ratio (MVKD) formula with a logistic-regression calibration. The results are reported along two points: the system performance (= accuracy) and the stability of performance based on the standard metric for LR-based systems; namely the log-likelihood-ratio cost (C_{llr}). It was found in this study that the system performance and its stability improve as a function of the sample size (= author count) in the background database in a non-linear manner, and that the more features used for modelling, the more background data the system generally requires for optimal results. The implications of the findings to the real casework are also discussed.

1 Introduction

1.1 Forensic text comparison and the likelihood-ratio framework

The conceptual framework of likelihood ratio (LR) has received or has started receiving wide support from various areas of forensic comparative sciences as the logically and legally correct framework for assessing forensic evidence, and presenting the strength of the evidence (Balding, 2005; Evett et al., 1998; Marquis et al., 2011; Morrison, 2009; Neumann et al., 2007). Although forensic text comparison (FTC) is lagging behind other areas of forensic comparative sciences, studies in which the LR framework was applied to authorship attribution have started emerging (Ishihara, 2012, 2014b).

As expressed in equation (1), the LR, the quantified strength of evidence, is a ratio of two conditional probabilities: one is the probability (p) of observed evidence (E) assuming that the prosecution hypothesis is true (H_p) and the other is the probability of the same observed evidence assuming that the defence hypothesis (H_d) is true (Robertson & Vignaux, 1995).

$$LR = \frac{p(E|H_p)}{p(E|H_d)} \tag{1}$$

For FTC, for instance, it will be the probability of observing the difference (referred to as the evidence, E) between the offender's and the suspect's text messages if they had been produced by the same author (H_p) relative to the probability of observing the same evidence (E) if they had come from different authors (H_d).

In practice, an LR is estimated as a ratio of two terms: similarity and typicality, which correspond to the numerator and denominator of equation (1). Similarity means the similarity (or difference) between the offender and the suspect samples (e.g. text messages). Typicality means, in general terms, the typicality (or atypicality) of the offender sample against the relevant population. If the offender and the suspect samples are more similar or more atypical, the LRs will be greater than when the same samples are more different or more typical.

It is important to emphasise that for example, LR = 100 does not mean that it is 100 times more likely that the offender and the suspect are the same person, but it means that the evidence is 100 times more likely to arise if the offender and the s-

Shunichi Ishihara. 2016. An Effect of Background Population Sample Size on the Performance of a Likelihood Ratio-based Forensic Text Comparison System: A Monte Carlo Simulation with Gaussian Mixture Model. In *Proceedings of Australasian Language Technology Association Workshop*, pages 113–121.

uspect samples had been produced by the same individual, than by different individuals.

As can be well understood from the concept of typicality, besides the offender and the suspect samples, it is an essential part of the LR framework to have samples from a relevant population for typicality. It goes without saying that an appropriate amount of data is required as relevant population data (= background data) to build an accurate model for typicality. Yet, how much do we need?

1.2 Research question

Having briefly outlined the key concepts of the LR framework, the present study investigates how the sample size of the background data influences the performance of the LR-based FTC system.

For this, a series of experiments was repeatedly carried out with the synthetic background data generated by the Monte Carlo technique, which are different in sample size (= different numbers of authors). The performance of the FTC system was assessed by the log likelihood ratio cost (C_{llr}) (Brümmer & du Preez, 2006). Three different lengths: 500, 1000 and 1500 words and four feature vectors: two, four, six and eight features were used in the experiments to see how these factors also contribute to the performance.

1.3 Previous studies

It can be considered that the greater the amount of representative data, the more accurate the model of the reference population, leading to a more accurate estimate of strength of evidence. A small number of studies have investigated the effect of sample size in the background database on the system performance, in particular, in the field of forensic voice comparison (Hughes et al., 2013; Ishihara & Kinoshita, 2008), and reported a similar outcome that the performance of a system becomes stable with greater than 20 reference individuals. However, those studies are voice/speech as evidence and did not consider the number of features in vectors.

Features	Two	Four	Six	Eight
Unusual word ratio	√	√	√	√
Punctuation character ratio	√	√	√	√
Type-token ratio (TTR)		√	√	√
Average word count per message line		√	√	√
Honoré's R			√	√
Digit character ratio			√	√
Average character count per message line				√
Special character ratio (, . ? ! ; : ' ")				√

Table 1: List of eight features and four different feature vectors. √ = feature used.

2 Research Design

2.1 Database

An archive of chatlog messages[1], which is a collection of real pieces of chatlog evidence used to prosecute paedophiles, was employed in this study. From the archive, 240 authors were randomly selected. Two non-overlapping fragments (in other words, two message groups) of 500 words were extracted from each author's messages so that one fragment can represent the offender and the other the suspect. The same was repeated for 1000 and 1500 words. As a result, there are altogether 480 message groups (= 240 authors × 2 message groups). The chatlog messages were tokenised into word tokens using WhitespaceTokenizer() stored in the *Natural Language Tool Kit* (*NLTK*) (version 2.0)[2].

The 240 authors were further divided into mutually-exclusive test (50 authors), background (140 authors) and development (50 authors) databases. The test database is used to assess the performance of the FTC system by comparing the message groups with the derived LRs. A more detailed explanation for testing is given in §2.4. The background database is used as the reference database (in terms of typicality) for calculating LRs. The development database is to calculate weights for calibrating the derived LRs from the test database. §2.5 explains calibrations in detail.

2.2 Features

In this study, the four different feature vectors given in Table 1 were used for modelling each message group. These four vectors consist of either two, four, six or eight features. These were select-

---

[1] http://pjfi.org/
[2] http://www.nltk.org/

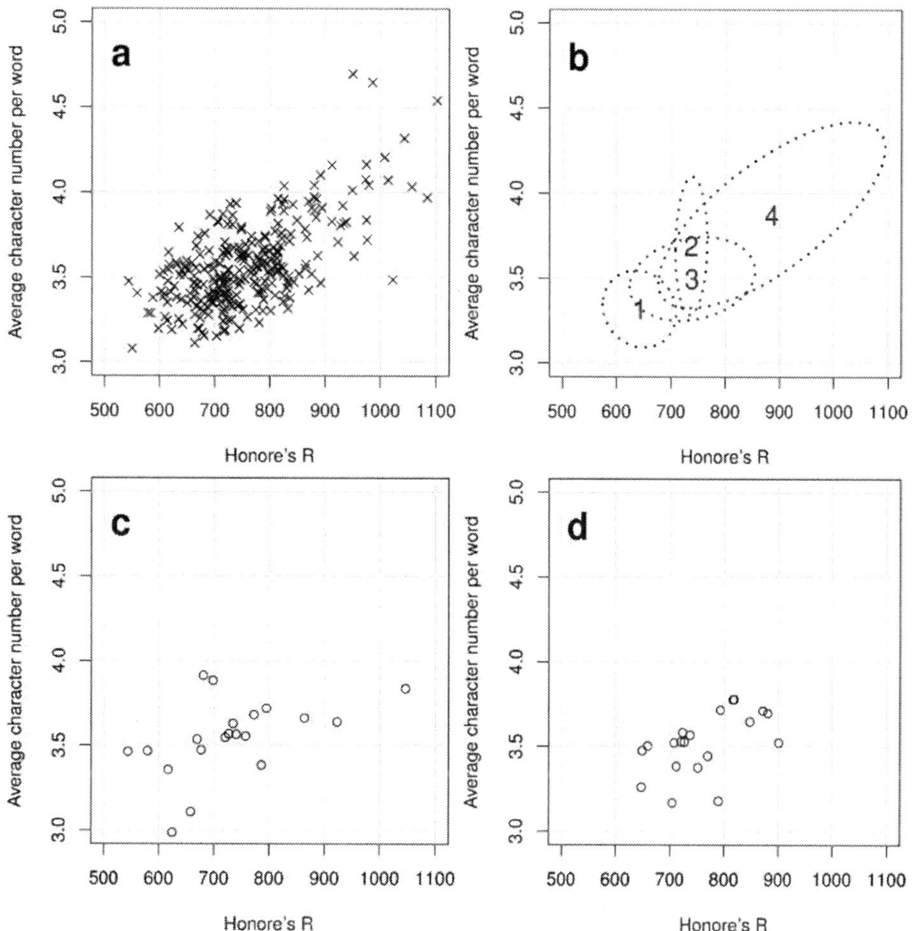

Figure 1: Panel a = the distribution of the two features: 'Honoré's R' and 'Average character count per message line'; Panel b = A GMM (four components) of the distribution; Panels c and d = two sets of randomly generated feature values (20 samples) based on the GMM.

ed from 11 features, which were previously reported as carrying good authorial information (De Vel et al., 2001; Iqbal et al., 2010; Zheng et al., 2006). They are: 1) Yule's I (the inverse of Yule's K), 2) Type-token ratio (TTR), 3) Honoré's R, 4) Average word count per message line, 5) Unusual word ratio, 6) Average character count per message line, 7) Upper case character ratio, 8) Digit character ratio, 9) Average character count per word, 10) Punctuation character ratio and 11) Special character ratio (, . ? ! ; : ' "). Based on these, a series of FTC experiments was carried out with all possible combinations of two, four, six and eight features in order to identify which combinations perform best. The combinations listed in Table 1 returned the best C_{llr} values, respectively for the sets of two, four, six and eight features.

Many of the features given in Table 1 are self-explanatory. The unusual_words() function[3] of the *NLTK* was used to obtain "Unusual word ratio" (e.g. unusual and misspelt words). TTR and Honoré's R are so-called vocabulary richness features.

2.3 Repeated experiments using Monte Carlo techniques

If the current study had been conducted with natural data, sufficiently large amounts of text messag-

---

[3] http://www.nltk.org/book/ch02.html#code-unusual

es written by a substantial number of authors would have been required. However, due to a lack of such a database of extensively large natural data, the Monte Carlo simulations were employed for this study (Fishman, 1995). The Monte Carlo simulations enable us to generate synthetic values from the specified statistical properties of a distribution. It is common to use a single Gaussian component to model a distribution in the Monte Carlo simulations. However, the Gaussian mixture model (number of components = 4) was utilised in this study. This is because the distributional patterns of the features concerned in the current study do not always conform to a normal distribution as can be seen in Panel a of Figure 1, in which the sampled values of 'Honoré's R' and 'Average character count per message line' are plotted.

The process of the Monte Carlo simulation is illustrated in Figure 1, using the feature values of 'Honoré's R' and 'Average character count per message line', as an example. First of all, the distributional pattern of the two features are modelled using four Gaussian components as shown in Figure 1b. Figure 1c and Figure 1d are two examples of synthetic data, each of which contains randomly generated 20 values of the two features based on the model given in Figure 1b. The number of Gaussian components was set as four because the log likelihood value remains relatively stable with four components. Thus, in this study, the feature values of the X number of authors (X = (10, 20, 30, 40, 50, 60, 70, 80, 90, 100, 110, 120, 130, 140)) were randomly generated 200 times for building the background model using the necessary statistics (the mean vectors, covariance matrices and mixture weights from all component densities) obtained from the original background database of 140 authors. A single GMM (a dimension of eight) was used in all experiments (even when features of less than eight are evaluated). The mixtools and mixAK libraries of R statistical package were used for the Monte Carlo simulations.

2.4 Testing

In order to assess the performance of an FVC system, two types of comparisons, namely same-author (SA) and different-author (DA) comparisons, are necessary. In SA comparisons, the two groups of messages produced by the same individuals are compared and evaluated with the derived LRs. Given their same origin, it is expected that the derived LRs are higher than 1, to the extent that the features are valid. In DA comparisons, *mutatis mutandis*, they are expected to receive LRs lower than 1.

Out of the 50 authors in the test database, in total, 50 SA comparisons and 2450 (= $_{50}C_2 \times 2$) DA comparisons are possible. The LRs were calculated for these comparisons with the synthetic background databases which are different in the author count. Following the common practice, a logarithmic scale (base 10) was used in this study, in which case unity is $\log_{10}LR = 0$.

2.5 Likelihood ratio calculation and calibration

LRs were estimated using the Multivariate Kernel Density Likelihood Ratio (MVKD) formula, which is one of the methods that can be used in FTC (Ishihara, 2012, 2014d). A full mathematical exposition of the MVKD formula is given in Aitken & Lucy (2004). One of the advantages of this formula is that an LR can be estimated from multiple variables (e.g. the eight features given in Table 1), considering the correlation between them. The MVKD formula assumes normality for within-group (within-author) variance while it uses a kernel-density model for between-group (between-author) variance.

2.6 Logistic-regression calibration

The outputs of the MVKD formula explained in §2.5 are actually *scores* (not LRs) (Rose, 2013). Scores are logLRs in that their values indicate degrees of similarity between two samples in comparison having taken into account their typicality against a background population (Morrison, 2013, p. 2). A logistic-regression calibration (Brümmer & du Preez, 2006) was applied to the outputs (scores) of the MVKD formula in order to convert them to interpretable logLRs. The conversion is carried out by linearly shifting and scaling the scores in the logged odd space, relative to a decision boundary. The FoCal toolkit[4] was used for the logistic-regression calibration in this study (Brümmer & du Preez, 2006). The logistic-regression weight was obtained from the development database.

---

[4] https://sites.google.com/site/nikobrummer/focal

2.7 Performance evaluation

It is common to use metrics based on the accuracy or error rate in order to assess the systems which carry identification or classification tasks. However, accuracy or error rate is binary and categorical (e.g. correct or not correct), and it is not suited for the nature of LR, which is gradient and continuous. It has been argued that a more appropriate metric for assessing LR-based systems is the log-likelihood-ratio cost (henceforth C_{llr}) (Brümmer & du Preez, 2006). C_{llr} can be calculated using (2).

$$C_{llr}$$
$$= \frac{1}{2}\left(\frac{1}{N_{H_p}} \sum_{i \, for \, H_p=true}^{N_{H_p}} log_2\left(1 + \frac{1}{LR_i}\right) + \frac{1}{N_{H_d}} \sum_{j \, for \, H_d=true}^{N_{H_d}} log_2\left(1 + LR_j\right) \right) \quad (2)$$

N_{H_p} and N_{H_d} refer to the numbers of SA and DA comparisons. LR_i and LR_j refer to the LRs derived from these SA and DA comparisons, respectively. In this approach, LRs are given penalties in proportion to their magnitudes, and, in particular, the LRs which support the counter-factual hypotheses are more severely penalised. The C_{llr} is based on information theory, and if the C_{llr} value is higher than 1, the system is performing worse than not utilising the evidence at all. The FoCal toolkit[4] was used for calculating C_{llr} values in this study.

3 Pre-analysis

Before presenting the results of the Monte Carlo simulations, it is useful to see how the system performs with the original raw data (test database = 50 authors; development database = 50 authors and the background database = 140 authors). As described in §2.2, four different feature vectors: two, four, six or eight features, were trialled. Furthermore, each message group was modelled using three different amounts of data: 500, 1000 and 1500 words. The results of the pre-analysis are given in Table 2 in terms of C_{llr}.

As can be well expected, the performance improves as the sample size increases; for example, C_{llr} = 0.6765 (500 words) → 0.5992 (1000 words) → 0.5448 (1500 words) for the two features. More data in the background database will naturally lead to building a better and more accurate background model for typicality; consequently the experimental result improves. This result aligns with the general rule of thumb in statistics: "more is better".

	two	four	six	eight
500	0.6765	<u>0.5774</u>	0.5812	0.7590
1000	0.5992	<u>0.4690</u>	0.4694	0.4835
1500	0.5448	0.3697	0.3817	<u>0.3619</u>

Table 2: C_{llr} values of the experiments with the original raw data, but differing in the sample size (500, 1000 or 1500 words) for modelling each message group and the number of features (two, four, six or eight). The underlined figures = the best C_{llr} values for the sample sizes.

The results given in Table 2 also show that having more features does not necessarily lead to an improvement in performance. For example, the system performed best with four features for 500 and 1000 words.

4 Results and discussions

The experimental results of the Monte Carlo simulations are given in Figure 2. In the left column of Figure 2 (Panels a, b, c and d), the mean C_{llr} values (of the 200 repeated experiments) are plotted as a function of the author count in the background database (10, 20, 30, 40, 50, 60, 70, 80, 90, 100, 110, 120, 130 and 140 authors), but separately for the sample size (word lengths) of either 500, 1000 or 1500 words. Panels a, b, c and d of Figure 2 are for the two, four, six and eight features, respectively. The panels on the left-hand side of Figure 2 show how the performance of the system changes as a function of the author count in the background database.

In the right column of Figure 2 (Panels e, f, g and h), the standard deviation (sd) values of the pooled C_{llr} values are plotted against the number of authors in the background database, but separately for the different word counts. Panels e, f, g and h of Figure 2 are again for two, four, six and eight features, respectively. Panels e, f, g and h show how the stability of the system performance fluctuates as the author count increases in the background database.

First of all, conforming to the results of the pre-analysis given in §3, as can be seen from the left panels of Figure 2, the results of the simulated experiments also show that the performance of the system improves as the word count increases. The

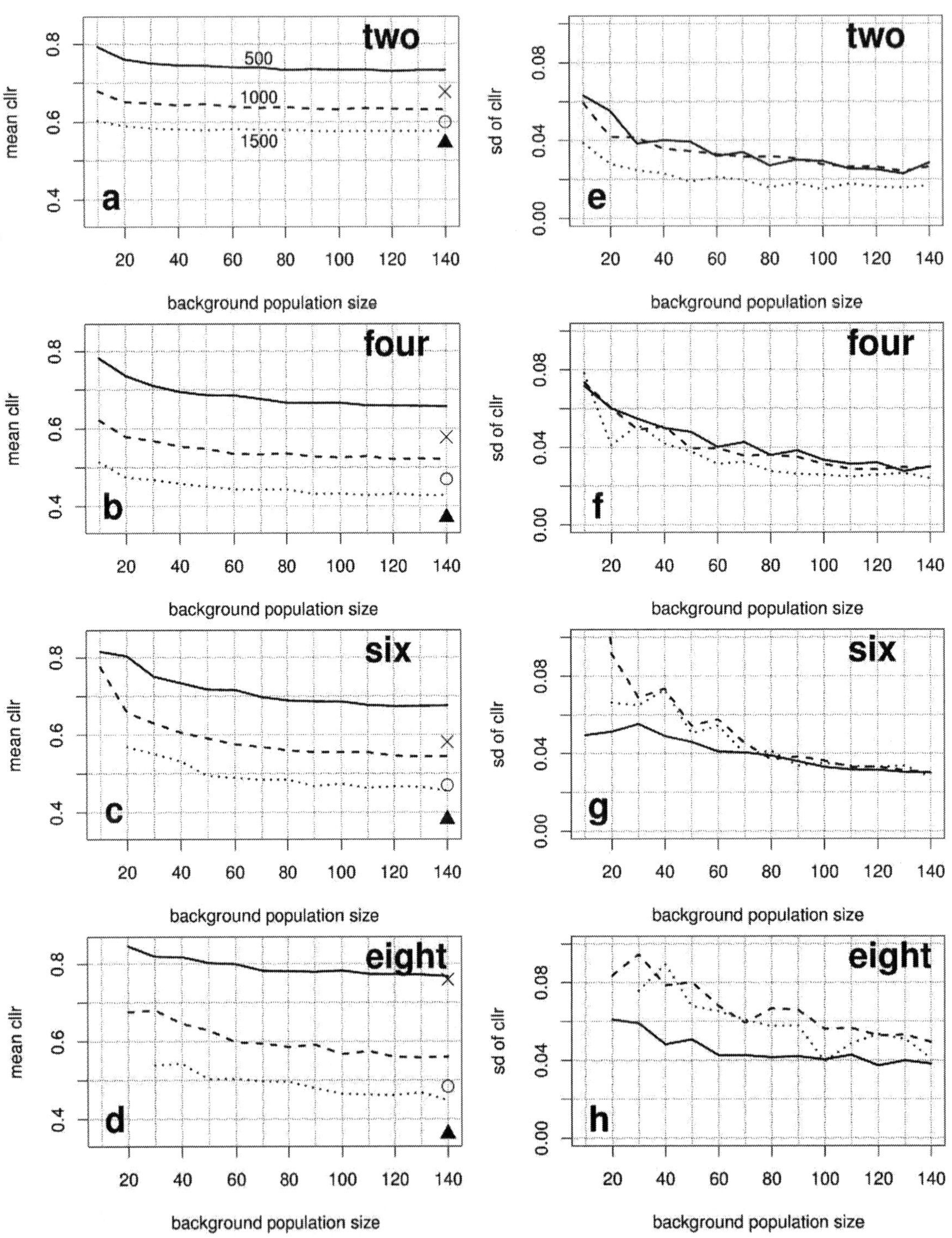

Figure 2: Mean C_{llr} (Panels a, b, c and d) and standard deviation values of the pooled C_{llr} values (Panels e, f, g and h) are plotted as the function of the author count in the background database (10 ~ 140 authors) (x-axis), separately for the word counts: 500 (solid), 1000 (dashed) and 1500 (dotted). Note that some values are missing in Panels c, d, g and h. ×, ○, ▲ = the C_{llr} values with the raw original data (background database = 140 authors).

above observation is not surprising, but it is novel to see that the three curves included in each of Panels a, b, c and d are more or less parallel to each other within the same feature number. This means that the degree of improvement which resulted from the increase in word count is there or thereabouts constant, regardless of the author count in the background database.

Further relating to the left panels of Figure 2, although there are some minor ups and downs, the system performance improves, regardless of the number of words and features, as the author count increases in the background database. More precisely speaking, the improvement is in a decelerating manner; there is a large improvement at the beginning, after which the performance starts converging or continues to improve to a (far) less degree. In the case of the feature number of two (Panel b), for example, there is a minor improvement from the author count of 10 to that of 20-30, after which the C_{llr} values almost remain unchanged. Whereas for the feature number of four (Panel b), there is a large drop in C_{llr} value between the author counts of 10 and 50-60, but with 60 authors or more, the degree of improvement is small and linear. That is to say, the more features used for modelling, the more data is required in the background database for the system performance to start converging. However, if the discriminating potential of each feature differs significantly, the above point may not be valid. Thus, the variance ratio (between-speaker sd^2/mean within-speaker sd^2) (Rose et al., 2006); the greater the ratio is, the higher the discriminating potential of the feature, was calculated for each feature, and given in Table 3.

Features	Ratios
Unusual word ratio	7.01
Punctuation character ratio	63.06
Type-token ratio (TTR)	13.38
Average word count per message line	11.40
Honoré's R	9.51
Digit character ratio	4.00
Average character count per message line	11.87
Special character ratio (, . ? ! ; : ' ")	1.71

Table 3: Variance ratios.

As can be seen from Table 3, the features of "Digit character ratio" and "Special character ratio" are relatively low in variance ratio in comparison to the other features. These poor-performing features (variance ratio: 4.00 and 1.71, respectively) may have functioned as noise features in the six and eight features, and the inclusion of them may not have contributed to the improvement of the system performance; thus consequently the system may have required more samples to continue to improve in the six and eight features. This entails further study.

Some values are missing in Panels c (six features) and d (eight features) – and consequently in Panels g and h – with the author counts of 10 and 20. This is because all of the relevant 200 repeated experiments returned one or more $\log_{10}LR$ = inf or –inf, which is an ill-condition for the calculation of C_{llr}. It is well known that for the higher the dimension of the feature vector, the more data is required to appropriately model the multi-dimensional density (Silverman, 1986, pp. 93-94). The occurrence of $\log_{10}LR$ = inf or –inf indicates that having only 10-20 authors in the background database is not large enough to accurately model the multi-dimensional density of the background population with the feature numbers of six and eight.

As for the stability of the system, an unexpected observation can be made from the right-hand side panels of Figure 2 in that the system does not necessarily become more stable in performance (= smaller sd values) with more words in each message group. This somehow disagrees with the earlier observation regarding the system performance and the word count in each message group. For example, the three curves included in Panel f overlap with each other to a reasonable extent, which means that the system shares a similar degree of stability in performance across the three different word counts, whereas in Panel h, the system with 500 words exhibits smaller sd values (better stability) on the whole than the systems with 1000 and 1500 words.

These results are counter-intuitive as one would ideally expect that the performance will be more stable with more samples. However, Morrison (2011) notes that in practice this is not often the case. There seems to be some degree of trade-off between the performance in accuracy (which can be represented by C_{llr}) and the stability of the system.

In light of the background population size, it is evident from the downward-trend of the curves included in the right-hand panels of Figure 2 that the system performance becomes more stable as the sample size in the background database increases; a large improvement in stability at the beginning, but the degree of improvement in stability becomes less and less with more authors included in the background database. Additionally, similar to the system performance, it appears in many cases that for the stability to start converging, the system needs more authors in the background database with more features. This point can be seen in Panels e, f and g (1000 and 1500 words), in which the degree of falling in sd values becomes sharper as the feature number increases.

Although the usefulness of the GMM-based Monte Carlo simulation was discussed for the purpose of the current study, there is always the possibility that the GMM model did not accurately approximate the true nature of the original raw data. In particular, it needs to be pointed out that the system with the synthesised data, on average, underperformed the system with the original raw data (refer to Figure 2). However, it is not clear at this stage to what extent and how this possible inaccuracy of the GMM model influenced the results.

5 Conclusion

By generating synthetic data for the background database by means of the Monte Carlo technique, this study looked into how the performance of the system and its stability are subject to the sample size (= the number of authors) in the background database. The effect of the background sample size on the system performance and stability may differ with the dimensions of the feature vector and the number of words used for modelling. Thus, four different vectors consisting of two, four, six and eight features were tested in this study. Furthermore, the number of words used for modelling each message group was also altered as 500, 1000 and 1500 words.

Regardless of the number of features (two, four, six and eight) and words (500, 1000 and 1500), the performance of the system improved in a decelerating manner as the sample size (the number of authors) increases in the background database. This result conforms to previous studies on other types of evidence (Hughes et al., 2013; Ishihara & Kinoshita, 2008). Moreover, in general terms, it was found that the more features included in the vector, the more authors the system needs in the background database for the performance to start converging. However, other potential factors which may have contributed to the outcomes of the current study have also been discussed.

Although there are a large number of potential features that can be used in casework – according to Abbasi and Chen (2008), the total number of features tested in previous studies exceeds 1000, the results of the current study indicate that more features may only deteriorate the performance of the system unless an appropriate amount of background data is available for the dimension of the feature vector, and that the number of features should be determined according to the size of the available background data. These two points are important, in particular, as data scarcity is a common issue in FTC casework. Some drawbacks arising from the use of the GMM-based approximation were also discussed.

It was also pointed out that the model is likely to be inaccurately built only with 10 or 20 authors when the feature number is six or more, resulting in the system returning erroneous LR values. Together with other observations, it can be judged that a system with 20 or less authors in the background database is not admissible in court in terms of performance.

In terms of the stability of the system performance, it is interesting to know that having more words in each message group does not necessarily lead to an improvement in stability. This point was in fact reported in previous studies (Frost, 2013; Ishihara, 2014a; Morrison, 2011). On the other hand, like the case of system performance, regardless of the number of features and words, it was shown that the system becomes more stable along with the number of authors in the background database.

The MVKD formula was used in this study. However, there are other methods for estimating LRs (e.g. word or character N-grams) (cf. Ishihara, 2014a; Ishihara, 2014c). This warrants further studies on the same topic as the current study with other methods for LR estimations.

This study focused on the performance (= accuracy) and stability of the system in order to investigate the effect of the background sample size. However, it is equally important to investigate to what extent the LR value fluctuates depending on the sample size in the background database. This also entails a future study.

Acknowledgments

The author thanks the three anonymous reviewers for their valuable comments.

References

Abbasi, A., & Chen, H. (2008). Writeprints: A stylometric approach to identity-level identification and similarity detection in cyberspace. *ACM Transactions on Information Systems, 26*(2), 1-29.

Aitken, C. G. G., & Lucy, D. (2004). Evaluation of trace evidence in the form of multivariate data. *Journal of the Royal Statistical Society Series C-Applied Statistics, 53*, 109-122.

Balding, D. J. (2005). *Weight-of-evidence for Forensic DNA Profiles*. Hoboken, N.J.: John Wiley & Sons.

Brümmer, N., & du Preez, J. (2006). Application-independent evaluation of speaker detection. *Computer Speech and Language, 20*(2-3), 230-275.

De Vel, O., Anderson, A., Corney, M., & Mohay, G. (2001). Mining e-mail content for author identification forensics. *ACM Sigmod Record, 30*(4), 55-64.

Evett, I., Lambert, J., & Buckleton, J. (1998). A Bayesian approach to interpreting footwear marks in forensic casework. *Science & Justice, 38*(4), 241-247.

Fishman, G. S. (1995). *Monte Carlo: Concepts, Algorithms, and Applications*. New York: Springer.

Frost, D. (2013). *Likelihood Ratio-based Forensic Voice Comparison on L2 Speakers.* (Unpublised Honours thesis), The Australian National University, Canberra.

Hughes, V., Brereton, A., & Gold, E. (2013). Reference sample size and the computation of numerical likelihood ratios using articulation rate. *York Papers in Linguistics, 13*, 22-46.

Iqbal, F., Binsalleeh, H., Fung, B., & Debbabi, M. (2010). Mining writeprints from anonymous e-mails for forensic investigation. *Digital Investigation, 7*(1), 56-64.

Ishihara, S. (2012). Probabilistic evaluation of SMS messages as forensic evidence: Likelihood ration based approach with lexical features. *International Journal of Digital Crime and Forensics, 4*(3), 47-57.

Ishihara, S. (2014a). A comparative study of likelihood ratio based forensic text comparison procedures: Multivariate kernel density with lexical features vs. word N-grams vs. character N-grams. *Proceedings of the 5th Cybercrime and Trustworthy Computing Conference*, 1-11.

Ishihara, S. (2014b). A likelihood ratio-based evaluation of strength of authorship attribution evidence in SMS messages using N-grams. *International Journal of Speech Language and the Law, 21*(1), 23-50.

Ishihara, S. (2014c). A likelihood ratio based forensic text comparison in SMS messages: A fused system with lexical features and N-grams. In H. R. Nemati (Ed.), *Analyzing Security, Trust, and Crime in the Digital World* (pp. 208-224): IGI Global.

Ishihara, S. (2014d). Predatory Chatlog messages as forensic evidence in court: A comparison of two different procedures for estimating the weight of evidence. *Proceedings of the 45th Australian Linguistic Society Conference*, 131-152.

Ishihara, S., & Kinoshita, Y. (2008). How many do we need? Exploration of the population size effect on the performance of forensic speaker classification. *Proceedings of Interspeech 2008*, 1941-1944.

Marquis, R., Bozza, S., Schmittbuhl, M., & Taroni, F. (2011). Handwriting evidence evaluation based on the shape of characters: Application of multivariate likelihood ratios. *Journal of Forensic Sciences, 56*(Supplement 1), S238-242.

Morrison, G. S. (2009). Forensic voice comparison and the paradigm shift. *Science & Justice, 49*(4), 298-308.

Morrison, G. S. (2011). Measuring the validity and reliability of forensic likelihood-ratio systems. *Science & Justice, 51*(3), 91-98.

Morrison, G. S. (2013). Tutorial on logistic-regression calibration and fusion: Converting a score to a likelihood ratio. *Australian Journal of Forensic Sciences, 45*(2), 173-197.

Neumann, C., Champod, C., Puch-Solis, R., Egli, N., Anthonioz, A., & Bromage-Griffiths, A. (2007). Computation of likelihood ratios in fingerprint identification for configurations of any number of minutiae. *Journal of Forensic Sciences, 52*(1), 54-64.

Robertson, B., & Vignaux, G. A. (1995). *Interpreting Evidence: Evaluating Forensic Science in the Courtroom*. Chichester: Wiley.

Rose, P. (2013). More is better: Likelihood ratio-based forensic voice comparison with vocalic segmental cepstra frontends. *International Journal of Speech Language and the Law, 20*(1), 77-116.

Rose, P., Kinoshita, Y., & Alderman, T. (2006). Realistic extrinsic forensic speaker discrimination with the diphthong /ai/. *Proceedings of the 11th Australian International Conference on Speech Science and Technology*, 329-334.

Silverman, B. W. (1986). *Density Estimation for Statistics and Data Analysis*. London; New York: Chapman and Hall.

Zheng, R., Li, J. X., Chen, H. C., & Huang, Z. (2006). A framework for authorship identification of online messages: Writing-style features and classification techniques. *Journal of the American Society for Information Science and Technology, 57*(3), 378-393.

Short papers

How Challenging is Sarcasm versus Irony Classification?: An Analysis From Human and Computational Perspectives

Aditya Joshi[1,2,3]**, Vaibhav Tripathi**[1]**, Pushpak Bhattacharyya**[1]**, Mark James Carman**[2]
Meghna Singh[1]**, Jaya Saraswati**[1]**, Rajita Shukla**[1]
[1]Indian Institute of Technology Bombay, India, [2]Monash University, Australia
[3]IITB-Monash Research Academy, India
{adityaj, pb}@cse.iitb.ac.in, mark.carman@monash.edu
mohan.meghnasingh@gmail.com, jaya.saraswati@gmail.com
rajita.shukla38@gmail.com

Abstract

Sarcasm and irony, although similar, differ in that sarcasm has an impact on sentiment (because it is used to ridicule a target) while irony does not. Past work treats the two interchangeably. In this paper, we wish to validate if sarcasm versus irony classification is indeed a challenging task. To this end, we use a dataset of quotes from English literature, and conduct experiments from two perspectives: the human perspective and the computational perspective. For the former, we show that three human annotators have lower agreement for sarcasm versus irony as compared to sarcasm versus philosophy. Similarly, sarcasm versus irony classification performs with a lower F-score as compared to another classification task where labels are not related: sarcasm versus philosophy classification. Another key point that our paper makes is that features designed for sarcasm versus non-sarcasm classification do not work well for sarcasm versus irony classification.

1 Introduction

Irony is a situation in which something which was intended to have a particular result has the opposite or a very different result[1]. On the other hand, sarcasm is a form of verbal irony that is intended to express contempt or ridicule. In other words, sarcasm has an element of ridicule and a target of ridicule, which is absent in irony (Lee and Katz, 1998). For example, '*He invented a new cure for a heart disease but later, died of the same disease himself*' is ironic but not sarcastic. However, '*I didn't make it big in Hollywood because I don't write bad enough*' is sarcastic where the target of ridicule is Hollywood.

Past work in sarcasm detection considers it as a sarcastic versus non-sarcastic classification (Kreuz and Caucci, 2007; Davidov et al., 2010; González-Ibáñez et al., 2011). Alternately, Reyes et al. (2012) consider classification of irony/sarcasm versus humor. In many past approaches, sarcasm and irony are treated interchangeably (Buschmeier et al., 2014; Joshi et al., 2015;

---

[1]Source: The Cambridge Dictionary

Maynard and Greenwood, 2014). However, since sarcasm has a target that is being ridiculed, it is crucial that sarcasm be distinguished from mere irony. This is because when the target is identified, the sentiment of the target can be appropriately assigned. Owing to the two above reasons, sarcasm versus irony detection is a useful task.

In this paper, we investigate sarcasm versus irony classification. To do so, we compare sarcasm versus irony classification with sarcasm versus philosophy classification. In case of former, the two classes are similar (where sarcasm is hurtful/contemptuous). In case of sarcasm versus philosophy, the two classes are likely to be diverse. Thus, the goal of this paper is to *to establish the challenging nature of sarcasm versus irony detection*. The novelty of this paper is that we present our findings from two perspectives: human and computational perspectives. We first describe agreement statistics and challenges faced by human annotators to classify between sarcasm and irony. Then, to validate computational challenges of the task, we compare sarcasm versus irony classification with sarcasm versus philosophy classification. Our dataset consists of book snippets, annotated with one among three labels: sarcasm, irony and philosophy. The dataset is available on request. Our results show that for both humans and computers, detecting sarcasm versus irony in literature is more challenging than detecting sarcasm versus philosophy. Our experiments also suggest that the set of features generated in past works for sarcasm versus non-sarcasm tasks work well for sarcasm versus philosophy but not as much for sarcasm versus irony.

2 Related Work

Several approaches have been proposed for sarcasm detection, with context incongruity as the basis of sarcasm detection. Joshi et al. (2015) present features based on explicit and implicit incongruity for sarcasm detection. Maynard and Greenwood (2014) use contrasting sentiment between hashtag and text of a tweet as an indicator of sarcasm. Davidov et al. (2010) rely on Wallace and Do Kook Choe (2014) use properties of reddit comments to add contextual information. Recent work uses deep learning-based techniques for sarcasm detection (Poria et al., 2016; Joshi et al., 2016).

The work closest to ours is by Ling and Klinger

Aditya Joshi, Vaibhav Tripathi, Pushpak Bhattacharyya, Mark Carman, Meghna Singh, Jaya Saraswati and Rajita Shukla. 2016. How Challenging is Sarcasm versus Irony Classification?: A Study With a Dataset from English Literature. In *Proceedings of Australasian Language Technology Association Workshop*, pages 123–127.

A1		Sarcasm	Philosophy	Irony
		Original Labels		
	Sarcasm	27	18	6
	Philosophy	5	222	17
	Irony	2	7	12
	Cannot say	13	24	14

Table 1: Confusion matrix for Annotator 1

A2		Sarcasm	Philosophy	Irony
		Original Labels		
	Sarcasm	30	20	9
	Philosophy	9	227	18
	Irony	4	16	16
	Cannot say	3	7	6

Table 2: Confusion matrix for Annotator 2

A3		Sarcasm	Philosophy	Irony
		Original Labels		
	Sarcasm	16	13	6
	Philosophy	6	180	17
	Irony	4	33	11
	Cannot say	22	44	15

Table 3: Confusion matrix for Annotator 3

	All Three	Sarcasm-Irony	Sarcasm-Philosophy
A1	0.532	0.624	0.654
A2	0.479	0.537	0.615
A3	0.323	0.451	0.578

Table 4: Cohen's Kappa Values for the three annotators

(2016). They present an empirical analysis of difficulty of understanding sarcasm and irony. They use a wide set of features for the classification task, and show that word-based features are good candidate features for the task. However, our analysis from both human and computational perspectives is novel, along with our observations.

Another novelty of this work is the domain of our dataset. Majority of the past works in sarcasm detection use tweets. Riloff et al. (2013a) and Maynard and Greenwood (2014) label these tweets manually whereas Bamman and Smith (2015) and Davidov et al. (2010) rely on hashtags to produce annotations. Some works in the past also explore long text for the task of sarcasm detection. Wallace and Do Kook Choe (2014) download posts from Reddit [2] for irony detection, whereas Lukin and Walker (2013) work with reviews. One past work by Tepperman et al. (2006) performs sarcasm detection on spoken dialogues as well. There are past works using literary quotes corpora for a variety of other NLP problems. Elson and McKeown (2010) extract quotes from popular literary work, for the task of quote attribution[3]. Søgaard (2012) perform the task of detecting famous quotes in literary works, gathered from the *Gutenberg Corpus*. Skabar and Abdalgader (2010) cluster famous quotations by improving sentence similarity measurements. This dataset consists of quotes from a quotes website. In terms of a dataset of literary snippets for sarcasm detection, we use the approach by Joshi et al. (2016) by using user-defined tags as labels.

3 Our Dataset of Quotes from English Literature

Goodreads[4] is a book recommendation website that allows users to track their friends' reads and obtain recommendations. We use a specific section of the website. The website has a section containing quotes from books added by the users of the website. These quotes are accompanied with user-assigned tags such as philosophy, experience, crying, etc. We download a set of 4306 quotes with three tags: philosophy, irony and sarcasm. These tags are assigned as the labels. The label-wise distribution is: (a) Sarcasm: 753, (b) Irony: 677, (c) Philosophy: 2876. We ensure that quotes marked with one of the three labels are not marked with another label. The dataset is available on request. Some examples in our dataset are:

1. **Sarcasm**: *A woman needs a man like a fish needs a bicycle.*

2. **Irony**: *You can put anything into words, except your own life.*

3. **Philosophy**: *The best way to transform a society is to empower the women of that society.*

The first quote is sarcastic towards a man, and implies that women do not need men. The victim of sarcasm in this case is 'a man'. On the other hand, the second quote is ironic because the speaker thinks that a person's own life cannot be put in words. It, however, does not express contempt or ridicule towards life or another entity. Finally, the last quote is philosophical and talks about transforming a society.

It is interesting to note that a sarcastic quote can be converted to a philosophical quote by word replacement. For example, converting the first quote to '*A woman needs a man like a fish needs water*' makes it

---

[2]Reddit (`www.reddit.com`) is an entertainment, social news networking service, and news website.

[3]Quote Attribution is the computational task of attributing a quote to the most likely speaker.

[4]`www.goodreads.com`

non-sarcastic (and arguably philosophical). The converse is also true. A philosophical quote can be converted to a sarcastic quote by word replacement. For example, converting the third (*i.e.*, philosophical) quote to '*The best way to transform a society is to empower the criminals of that society*' makes it sarcastic.

4 The Human Perspective

This section describes the human perspective of sarcasm versus irony classification. In the forthcoming subsections, we describe our annotation experiments followed by the quantitative and qualitative observations from these experiments.

4.1 Annotation Experiment

Three annotators, with annotation experience of 8k+ hours each, participate in our annotation experiment. We refer to them as A1, A2, and A3.

For a subset of 501 quotes as described in the previous subsection[5], we obtain exactly one label out of four labels: sarcasm, irony, philosophy and 'cannot say'. The last label 'cannot say' is a fall-back label that indicates that the annotator could not determine the label as one among sarcasm, philosophy and irony. The three annotators annotate the dataset separately. The annotators are provided definitions of the three classes as from the Free Dictionary. They are aware that sarcasm has an element of ridicule which irony lacks. In addition to these definitions, the annotators are instructed that a statement 'about' sarcasm/irony/philosophy (e.g. 'People use sarcasm when they are tired') must not be marked as sarcastic/ironic/philosophical.

4.2 Evaluation

The confusion matrices for the three annotators are shown in Tables 1, 2 and 3. The rows indicate labels assigned by an annotator, whereas columns indicate the 'gold' label *i.e.*, the label as extracted from the source website.

Table 4 compares Cohen's Kappa values for the three annotators with the gold label. In case of annotator A1, the agreement of the annotator with the gold labels for the three-label task is 0.532. The agreement of A1 with the gold labels for the Sarcasm-Irony task is 0.624. The corresponding value for sarcasm-philosophy task is higher: 0.654. This trend holds for the two other annotators as well. In general, an annotator agrees with the gold label in case of sarcasm versus philosophy classification, as compared to sarcasm versus irony classification.

4.3 Error Analysis

The following situations are where our annotators did not agree with the gold label, for each of the two pairs. These categories highlight the difficulties they faced during annotation.

---

[5]This subset was selected randomly.

	Precision (%)	Recall (%)	F-Score (%)
Sarcasm versus irony			
Average	65.4	65.4	65.4
Weighted Average	65.2	65.3	65.2
(b) Sarcasm versus philosophy			
Average	85	84.8	84.6
Weighted Average	76.5	77.7	77
(c) Sarcasm versus philosophy (class-balanced)			
Average	80.2	80	80
Weighted Average	80.2	80.1	80.1

Table 5: Average and weighted average values for three configurations: sarcasm versus philosophy, sarcasm versus philosophy (class-balanced) and sarcasm versus irony; Weighted average indicates that the values were weighted according to class label skews.

1. **Confusion between sarcasm and irony**: Consider the example '*... And I wondered if we had disappointed God so much, that he wrote us off as pets, just alive to entertain.*' Annotator A1 labeled this quote as sarcastic whereas the gold label was ironic. The annotators felt that the quote was a self-deprecating post where the speaker was being sarcastic towards themselves.

2. **Confusion between sarcasm and philosophy**: Consider another example '*Business people - Your business - is your greatest prejudice: it ties you to your locality, to the company you keep, to the inclinations you feel. Diligent in business - but indolent in spirit, content with your inadequacy, and with the cloak of duty hung over this contentment: that is how you live, that is how you want your children to live!*'. This example was labeled as philosophical according to the gold labels. However, Annotator A2 labeled it as sarcastic towards business people. Although the quote expresses contempt towards business people, it does not use positive words to express this contempt.

Config.	Precision (%)	Recall (%)	F-Score (%)
(a)	67.2	66.6	67.2
(b)	62.2	65.8	63.8
(c)	80.2	80.2	80.2

Table 6: Average Precision, Recall, and F-score values for the label 'sarcasm' for the three configurations

5 The Computational Perspective

In this section, we describe our results from training automatic classifiers to perform the two classification tasks: sarcasm versus irony and sarcasm versus philosophy.

5.1 Classifier & Features

We use LibSVM[6] to train our classifier. We use default parameters, and report five-fold cross-validation values. For features, we use features given in Joshi et al. (2015). These features were used to distinguish between sarcastic and non-sarcastic text. It is interesting to note that in our case, sarcasm versus philosophy is likely to indicate the 'sarcastic versus non-sarcastic' divide, but sarcasm versus irony is not as distant.

The features proposed by Joshi et al. (2015) are:

1. Unigrams

2. Pragmatic features: Capitalization, emoticons, punctuation marks

3. Implicit sentiment phrases: These are phrases that are indicative of sarcasm. They are extracted from a separate dataset of sarcastic tweets based on algorithm given in Riloff et al. (2013b).

4. Explicit sentiment features: # positive and negative words, largest positive/negative subsequences, lexical polarity

We consider three classification tasks: (a) Sarcasm versus irony, (b) Sarcasm versus philosophy, and (c) Sarcasm versus philosophy (data-balanced). The configuration in (c) neutralizes the effects of data skew on performance of classification since it is known that the performance on skewed datasets may not be reliable (Akbani et al., 2004). This configuration is motivated by the fact that (a) does not contain substantial skew. In case of (c), we undersample from philosophy class by randomly eliminating some training instances, as given in (Tang et al., 2009). This ensures that there are equal number of training and test instances from both classes for all folds.

5.2 Evaluation

Table 5 shows average and weighted average Precision, Recall, and F-score values for three sets of experiments. Weighted average indicates that the average is computed by weighting according to the class imbalance. On the other hand, average indicates that class imbalance is not taken into consideration.

The average F-score for sarcasm versus philosophy is 84.6%. In the class-balanced configuration as well, the F-score reduces to 80%. This F-score is 15% higher than that for sarcasm versus irony, where it is 65.4%. Also, the weighted average is 77% in case of sarcasm versus philosophy and 80.1% in case of sarcasm versus philosophy (class-balanced). The value is 12% higher

---

than that for sarcasm versus irony, where it is 65.2%. The trend is common for both precision and recall. It must be noted that the features used in the classifier were generated initially for sarcasm versus non-sarcasm task. The results show that these features can be used for sarcasm versus philosophy as well, but not for sarcasm versus irony task. This points to the fact that for sarcasm versus irony classification, a new set of features will be required in the future.

To understand how the three configurations compare, it is also important to compare their performance for the sarcasm label. We, therefore, show the average values for the three configurations for the sarcasm class in Table 6. For the class-balanced sarcasm versus philosophy configuration, the F-score for sarcasm class is 80.2%. The corresponding value for sarcasm versus irony is 67.2%. This highlights that sarcasm versus irony proves to be challenging in general and specifically for sarcastic quotes.

6 Conclusion & Future Work

The focus of this paper is to highlight challenges of the sarcasm versus irony classification task, because sarcasm and irony are closely related to one another. We compare this classification formulation with sarcasm versus philosophy. To describe the challenging nature of the sarcasm versus irony classification task, we present our findings from two perspectives: human and computational perspective.

In terms of the human perspective, our three annotators have a lower Kappa score for sarcasm-irony as compared to sarcasm-philosophy and sarcasm-philosophy-irony classification. In the computational perspective, we observe that for the features reported for sarcasm versus non-sarcasm classification, sarcasm versus irony classification performs 12-15% lower than sarcasm versus philosophy. Even in case of the sarcasm class, the difference is 13%. Our findings show that although these features work well for sarcasm versus philosophy classification, they do not work well for sarcasm versus irony classification. This means that novel features are imperative for the task of sarcasm versus irony classification.

Our findings show the non-triviality and challenges underlying sarcasm versus irony classification. Since a key distinction between sarcasm and irony is a target of ridicule, having techniques for the detection of sarcasm targets, like in the case of sentiment target identification, may be helpful. Our results will also act as a baseline for future work in sarcasm versus irony classification. Additionally, features that distinguish between the two will be useful.

References

Rehan Akbani, Stephen Kwek, and Nathalie Japkowicz, 2004. *Machine Learning: ECML 2004: 15th European Conference on Machine Learning, Pisa,*

---

[6]https://www.csie.ntu.edu.tw/ cjlin/libsvm/

Italy, September 20-24, 2004. Proceedings, chapter Applying Support Vector Machines to Imbalanced Datasets, pages 39–50. Springer Berlin Heidelberg, Berlin, Heidelberg.

David Bamman and Noah A Smith. 2015. Contextualized sarcasm detection on twitter.

Konstantin Buschmeier, Philipp Cimiano, and Roman Klinger. 2014. An impact analysis of features in a classification approach to irony detection in product reviews.

Dmitry Davidov, Oren Tsur, and Ari Rappoport. 2010. Semi-supervised recognition of sarcastic sentences in twitter and amazon. In *Proceedings of the Fourteenth Conference on Computational Natural Language Learning*, pages 107–116. Association for Computational Linguistics.

David K Elson and Kathleen McKeown. 2010. Automatic attribution of quoted speech in literary narrative. In *AAAI*. Citeseer.

Roberto González-Ibáñez, Smaranda Muresan, and Nina Wacholder. 2011. Identifying sarcasm in twitter: A closer look. In *Proceedings of the 49th Annual Meeting of the Association for Computational Linguistics: Human Language Technologies: Short Papers - Volume 2*, HLT '11, pages 581–586, Stroudsburg, PA, USA. Association for Computational Linguistics.

Aditya Joshi, Vinita Sharma, and Pushpak Bhattacharyya. 2015. Harnessing context incongruity for sarcasm detection. In *Proceedings of the 53rd Annual Meeting of the Association for Computational Linguistics and the 7th International Joint Conference on Natural Language Processing*, volume 2, pages 757–762.

Aditya Joshi, Kevin Patel, Vaibhav Tripathi, Pushpak Bhattacharyya, and Mark J Carman. 2016. Are word embedding-based features useful for sarcasm detection? In *EMNLP*.

Roger J. Kreuz and Gina M. Caucci. 2007. Lexical influences on the perception of sarcasm. In *Proceedings of the Workshop on Computational Approaches to Figurative Language*, FigLanguages '07, pages 1–4, Stroudsburg, PA, USA. Association for Computational Linguistics.

Christopher J Lee and Albert N Katz. 1998. The differential role of ridicule in sarcasm and irony. *Metaphor and Symbol*, 13(1):1–15.

Jennifer Ling and Roman Klinger. 2016. An empirical, quantitative analysis of the differences between sarcasm and irony. In *Semantic Web: ESWC 2016 Satellite Events*.

Stephanie Lukin and Marilyn Walker. 2013. Really? well. apparently bootstrapping improves the performance of sarcasm and nastiness classifiers for online dialogue.

Diana Maynard and Mark A Greenwood. 2014. Who cares about sarcastic tweets? investigating the impact of sarcasm on sentiment analysis.

Soujanya Poria, Erik Cambria, Devamanyu Hazarika, and Prateek Vij. 2016. A deeper look into sarcastic tweets using deep convolutional neural networks. *arXiv preprint arXiv:1610.08815*.

Antonio Reyes, Paolo Rosso, and Davide Buscaldi. 2012. From humor recognition to irony detection: The figurative language of social media. *Data Knowl. Eng.*, 74:1–12, April.

Ellen Riloff, Ashequl Qadir, Prafulla Surve, Lalindra De Silva, Nathan Gilbert, and Ruihong Huang. 2013a. Sarcasm as contrast between a positive sentiment and negative situation.

Ellen Riloff, Ashequl Qadir, Prafulla Surve, Lalindra De Silva, Nathan Gilbert, and Ruihong Huang. 2013b. Sarcasm as contrast between a positive sentiment and negative situation. In *EMNLP*, volume 13, pages 704–714.

Andrew Skabar and Khaled Abdalgader. 2010. Improving sentence similarity measurement by incorporating sentential word importance. In *AI 2010: Advances in Artificial Intelligence*, pages 466–475. Springer.

Anders Søgaard. 2012. Mining wisdom. *NAACL-HLT 2012*, page 54.

Yuchun Tang, Yan-Qing Zhang, Nitesh V Chawla, and Sven Krasser. 2009. Svms modeling for highly imbalanced classification. *Systems, Man, and Cybernetics, Part B: Cybernetics, IEEE Transactions on*, 39(1):281–288.

Joseph Tepperman, David R Traum, and Shrikanth Narayanan. 2006. " yeah right": sarcasm recognition for spoken dialogue systems.

Byron C Wallace and Laura Kertz Do Kook Choe. 2014. Humans require context to infer ironic intent (so computers probably do, too).

Learning cascaded latent variable models for biomedical text classification

Ming Liu   **Gholamreza Haffari**   **Wray Buntine**
Faculty of Information Technology, Monash University
`ming.m.liu, gholamreza.haffari, wray.buntine @ monash.edu`

Abstract

In this paper, we develop a weakly supervised version of logistic regression to help to improve biomedical text classification performance when there is limited annotated data. We learn cascaded latent variable models for the classification tasks. First, with a large number of unlabelled but limited amount of labelled biomedical text, we will bootstrap and semi-automate the annotation task with partially and weakly annotated data. Second, both coarse-grained (document) and fine-grained (sentence) levels of each individual biomedical report will be taken into consideration. Our experimental work shows this achieves higher classification results.

1 Introduction

In recent years, large amounts of biomedical text have become available with the development of electronic medical record (EMR) systems. The type of biomedical text ranges from reports of CT scans to doctoral notes and discharge summaries. Based on these biomedical text, there are medical tasks such as disease identification, diagnostic surveillance and evaluation and other clinical support services. Manual extraction and classification for these medical tasks from biomedical text is a time-consuming and often costly effort.

Biomedical text classification systems which consider both manual effort (e.g. annotation) and predictive performance are more appropriate in the medical context than those which only consider classification predictive performance. Early biomedical classification methods are rule-based (Tinoco et al., 2011; Matheny et al., 2012), which requires medical experts to develop logical rules to identify reports consistent with some diseases.

The main advantages of such rule-based systems is that high precision can be achieved, but the weakness lies in the fact that the process is not easily transferable to similar tasks, because medical experts have to carefully develop specific types of rules and formulas for different kinds of diseases. In recent years, machine learning methods have been widely used in disease identification from biomedical text(Ehrentraut et al., 2012; Bejan et al., 2012; Martinez et al., 2015; Hassanpour and Langlotz, 2015), which also ask medical experts to do some annotation work for building training data. Unlabelled free biomedical text in hospitals and other clinical organizations is abundant but manual annotation is very expensive.

Exploiting fine-grained sentence level properties for coarse-grained document level classification has attracted large amounts of attention. Pang(Pang and Lee, 2004) first explored subjectivity extraction methods based on a minimum cut formulation, in which they performed subjectivity detection on individual sentences and implemented document level polarity classification by leveraging those extracted subjective sentences. McDonald(Täckström and McDonald, 2011) proposed a structured model for jointly classifying the sentiment of text at varying levels of granularity, they showed that this task can be reduced to sequential classification with constrained inference. Yessenalina(Yessenalina et al., 2010) described a joint two-level approach for document level sentiment classification that simultaneously extracts useful sentences, and Fang(Fang and Huang, 2012) extended it by incorporating aspect information to the structured model to aspect level sentiment analysis.

In this paper, we propose a cascaded latent variable model for biomedical text classification that combines logistic regression and EM, which is trained with a large number of unlabelled but limited amount of labelled biomedical text. Exper-

Ming Liu, Gholamreza Haffari and Wray Buntine. 2016. Learning cascaded latent variable models for biomedical text classification. In *Proceedings of Australasian Language Technology Association Workshop*, pages 128–132.

imental results show that the combined cascaded model is efficient in biomedical text classification tasks.

2 Methodology

In this section, we propose variants developed from a cascaded logistic regression model: the partially supervised model called as logistic regression with hard EM (LREM) and the weakly supervised model named as weak logistic regression with hard EM (WLREM). LREM is trained with part of the fully-annotated data and all of the partially-annotated data. WLREM is trained with the same part of the fully-annotated data and all of the weakly annotated data.

2.1 Preliminaries

Let d be a document consisting of n sentences, $\mathbf{X} = (X_i)_{i=1}^n$, with a document-sentence-sequence pair denoted $\mathbf{d} = (d, \mathbf{X})$. Let y^d denote the document level polarity and $\mathbf{Z} = (Z_i)_{i=1}^n$ be the sequence of sentence level polarity. In what follows, we assume that there are three types of training sets: a small set of fully labeled instances D_F which are annotated at both sentence and document levels, another small set of partially labeled instances D_P which are annotated only at the document level, and a large set of weakly annotated instances D_U (explained later). Besides, we assume that all Z_i take values in $\{POS(+1), NEG(-1), NEU(0)\}$ while y^d is in $\{POS(+1), NEG(-1)\}$.

The following three cascaded models are based on logistic regression, with the following standard parametrization

$$P_\theta\left(y^d|\mathbf{X}\right) = \sum_{\mathbf{Z}} P_\alpha(y^d|\mathbf{Z})P_\beta(\mathbf{Z}|\mathbf{X}) \quad (1)$$

where $\theta = \{\alpha, \beta\}$, and α and β are the parameters of document and sentence level classifiers respectively.

2.2 The partially supervised model

The partially supervised model (LREM) is trained from the sets of fully labeled data D_F and partially labelled data D_P. Since the sentence polarity is unknown in D_P, a hard EM algorithm is used to iteratively estimate $\mathbf{Z}$ and maximize the cascaded goal function. Figure 1 outlines LREM. The parameters, α and β, of this model can be es-

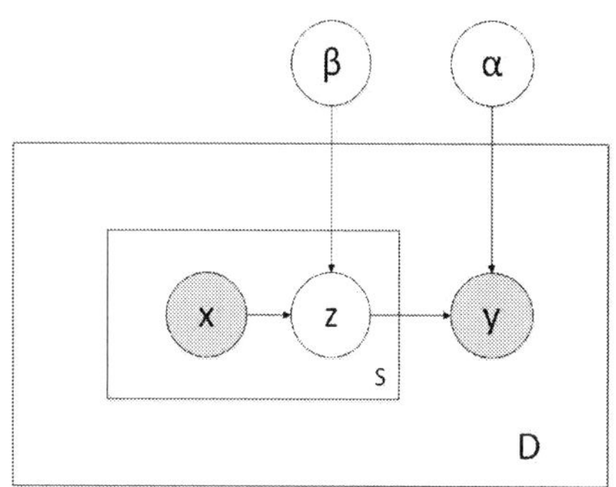

Figure 1: A partially supervised model.

timated by maximizing the joint conditional likelihood function

$$\alpha, \beta = \arg\max_{\alpha,\beta} \left(\sum_{d=1}^N \log P_\theta(y^d|\mathbf{X}) \right) \quad (2)$$

where $N = |D_F \cup D_P|$.

2.3 The weakly supervised model

The weakly supervised model (WLREM) is trained from the sets of fully labeled data D_F and weakly labelled data D_U. In our case, the document polarity is unknown from D_U, while U represents the patient level diagnostic result in the treating hospital. Generally, if a patient is diagnosed with positive infection in the hospital, the reports of this patient are more likely to be positive. We get this estimated probability from a confusion matrix of D_F as shown in table 1. We

Table 1: Confusion matrix of fully-annotated dataset

D_F	y=POS	y=NEG
U=POS	167	68
U=NEG	41	82

notice that $P(U = POS|y = POS) = 0.803$, which is a trustful prior information for guessing y, thus we can extend the previous partially supervised model into a weakly one. Figure 2 shows WLREM. The parameters, α and β, of this model can be estimated by maximizing the joint conditional likelihood function

$$P_\theta(U^d|\mathbf{X}) = \sum_{y,\mathbf{z}} P_\beta(\mathbf{Z}|\mathbf{X})P_\alpha(y^d|\mathbf{Z})P(U^d|y^d)$$
$$\alpha, \beta = \arg\max_{\alpha,\beta} \left(\prod_{d=1}^M P_\theta(U^d|\mathbf{X}) \right) \quad (3)$$

where $M = |D_F \cup D_U|$.

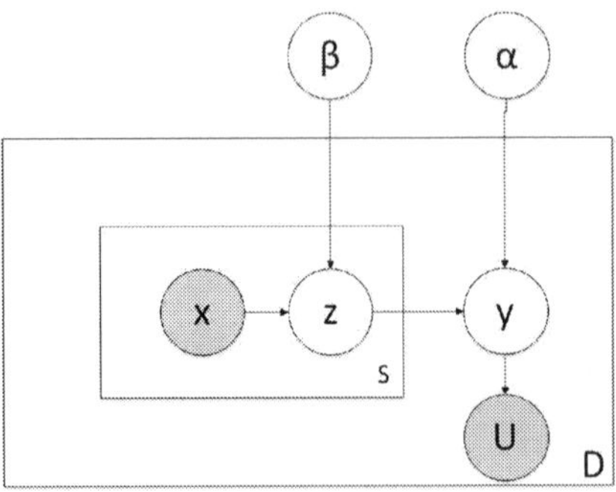

Figure 2: A weakly supervised model.

3 Combining partial and weak supervision

The partially and weakly supervised models both have their merits. The former requires document level annotation, while the latter can be used directly with available documents except for an initial guess of the document level polarity. In order to achieve the best predictive performance, we propose to combine the merits of these two models.

3.1 A combined cascaded latent variable model

Given in Algorithm 1, ComLREM is an integration of the above two models (LREM+WLREM), which can make full use of the partially and weakly annotated data.

Algorithm 1 ComLREM

$\alpha, \beta \leftarrow$ update for data D_F via Eqn (2)

$Z_i \leftarrow 0$ for all the sentences in $D_P \cup D_U$

$y \leftarrow 1$ for all the documents in D_U

while the convergence condition is meet **do**

    for every document $d \in D_P$ **do**

        $n_d \leftarrow$number of sentences of d

        for $k = 1$ to n_d in d **do**

            $Z_k^d = \arg\max_{Z_k^d} P_\theta \left(y^d | \mathbf{X} \right)$

                       $\triangleright$ from Equation (1)

    for every document $d \in D_U$ **do**

        $n_d \leftarrow$number of sentences in d

        for $k = 1$ to n_d in d **do**

            $Z_k^d, Y^d = \arg\max_{Z_k^d, Y^d}$

                $P_\beta(\mathbf{Z}|\mathbf{X}) P_\alpha(y^d|\mathbf{Z}) P(U^d|y^d)$

    $\alpha, \beta \leftarrow$ update for all data via Eqns (2), (3)

Table 2: Feature representation

Feature level	Discription
Sentence-level	Uni-gram tokens + MetaMap concepts
Report-level	Pos sentence exists or not
	Neg sentence exists or not
	No. of pos sentences
	No. of neg sentences
	No. of other sentences
	Polarity of the first sentence
	Polarity of the last sentence
	Percentage of pos sentences
	Percentage of neg sentences
	Pos sentence exists in the beginning
	Pos sentence exists in the end
	Neg sentence exists in the beginning
	Neg sentence exists in the end

3.2 Feature representation

Two main types of features are explored: Bag and Structural. Bag features are applied to the sentence-level classification, while structural features are built on the results of sentence-level classification.

Dates, time and numbers are normalised into DATE, TIME, and NUM symbols. Reports are segmented into sentences using the JulieLab (Tomanek et al., 2007) automatic sentence segmentor. Stop words are terms and phrases which are regarded as not conveying any significant semantics to the sentences and reports, NLTK stop word list was chosen to do the filtering. The Genia Tagger (Tsuruoka et al., 2005) is used to do tokenization and lemmatization. The MetaMap concepts (Aronson, 2001) come from the mappings of biomedical knowledge representation. Table 1 illustrates the feature representation at the sentence and report levels.

4 Experiment

As shown in (Martinez et al., 2015), CT reports for fungal disease detection were collected from three hospitals. For each report, only the free text section were used, which contains the radiologist's understanding of the scan and the reason for the requested scan as written by clinicians. Every report was de-identified: any potentially identifying information such as name, address, age/birthday, gender were removed. Table 2 shows the number of distribution of reports over fully-annotated, partially-annotated and verified data sets.

Receiver operating characteristic (ROC) curve and Precision recall (PR) curve are used for the model evaluation. Area under ROC curve and

Table 3: Fully-annotated, partially-annotated and weakly annotated datasets

Datasets	D_F	D_P	D_U
Pos fungal	150	51	431
Neg fungal	208	53	816

PR curve is an estimated measure of the test accuracy. The results presented here are 5-fold cross validation outcomes on the fully-annotated data.

Fig. 3 and 4 show the ROC curves and PR curves of the four models: LR is the baseline algorithm, LREM is trained based on part of the fully-annotated data and all of the partially-annotated data, WLREM is trained based on part of the fully-annotated data and all of the unannotated data, and ComLREM is an integration of the above two models.

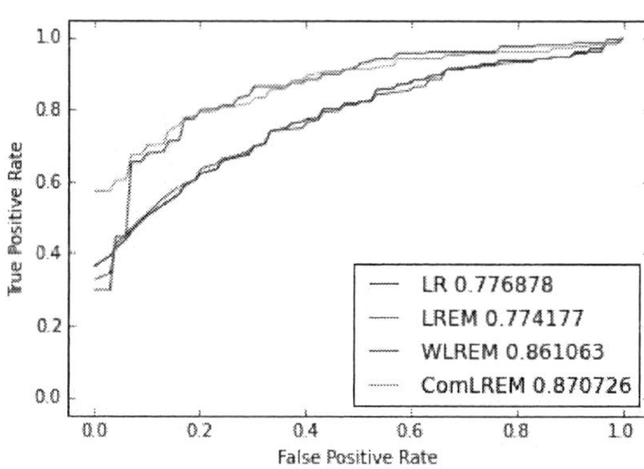

Figure 3: ROC curve of LR, LREM, WLREM and ComLREM.

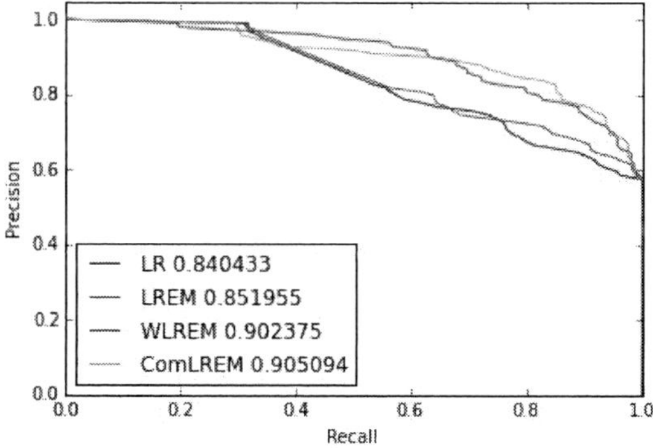

Figure 4: PR curve of LR, LREM, WLREM and ComLREM.

We can see from Fig. 3 that WLREM obtained higher ROC score than LR, the area under LREM and WLREM ROC curve is 0.774 and 0.861, which shows that the involvement of weakly annotated data contributes higher than that of partially annotated data to the improvement of classification performance. It is noticed WLREM achieved greater improvement than LREM, because the D_U contains big volume and trustful prior information. The highest ROC score (0.870) was achieved with a combination of the above two models, which is within our expectation. Fig. 4 shows the PR curves of the four models, there is a trade-off between precision and recall with recall as the most important metric. When the threshold is set to obtain a high recall (> 0.9), ComLREM obtained higher precision than other models. Overall, with true positive rate or recall as the first priority, the combined model ComLREM achieved the best classification performance.

We also compared our model with Martinez's system (Martinez et al., 2015), in which they applied conservative rules over sentence-classification output. Their sentence-level classifier used SVMs with Bag-of-words and Bag-of-concepts features. Since the conservative rules indicate that a report is labeled as positive if any sentence in it is labeled positive, the report-level prediction is not probabilistic and the PR curve can not be drawn accordingly. In order to make some comparison, we adjusted the threshold of our report-level logistic regression classifier to make our recall the same as theirs (0.930), and see whether the precision improves. Table 3 shows the compared results, we noticed that both WLREM and ComLREM outperforms the Conservative SVM approach, which indicates that the estimation we made from the unlabelled data is trustful and can be used to improve classification performance.

Table 4: Comparison of the experimental results

Models	Recall	Precision	F score
Conservative SVM	0.930	0.694	0.795
LR	0.930	0.646	0.762
LREM	0.930	0.656	0.769
WLREM	0.930	0.703	0.801
ComLREM	0.930	0.707	0.802

5 Conclusion

Learning classification models in a fully supervised manner is expensive in the biomedical domain. We therefore proposed a combined cascaded latent variable model, which effectively combines both partial and weak supervision for biomedical text classification. Sentence label is regarded as a latent variable in this model, and both fine-grained and coarse-grained features are considered in the learning process. In the future, we consider to develop active learning methods towards our cascaded latent variable model and further reduce manual annotation cost.

References

Alan R Aronson. 2001. Effective mapping of biomedical text to the umls metathesaurus: the MetaMap program. In *Proceedings of the AMIA Symposium*, page 17. American Medical Informatics Association.

Cosmin Adrian Bejan, Fei Xia, Lucy Vanderwende, Mark M Wurfel, and Meliha Yetisgen-Yildiz. 2012. Pneumonia identification using statistical feature selection. *Journal of the American Medical Informatics Association*, 19(5):817–823.

Claudia Ehrentraut, Hideyuki Tanushi, Hercules Dalianis, and Jörg Tiedemann. 2012. Detection of hospital acquired infections in sparse and noisy Swedish patient records. *A machine learning approach using Naïve Bayes, Support Vector Machines and C*, 4.

Lei Fang and Minlie Huang. 2012. Fine granular aspect analysis using latent structural models. In *Proceedings of the 50th Annual Meeting of the Association for Computational Linguistics: Short Papers-Volume 2*, pages 333–337. Association for Computational Linguistics.

Saeed Hassanpour and Curtis P Langlotz. 2015. Information extraction from multi-institutional radiology reports. *Artificial intelligence in medicine*.

David Martinez, Michelle R Ananda-Rajah, Hanna Suominen, Monica A Slavin, Karin A Thursky, and Lawrence Cavedon. 2015. Automatic detection of patients with invasive fungal disease from free-text computed tomography (CT) scans. *Journal of biomedical informatics*, 53:251–260.

Michael E Matheny, Fern FitzHenry, Theodore Speroff, Jennifer K Green, Michelle L Griffith, Eduard E Vasilevskis, Elliot M Fielstein, Peter L Elkin, and Steven H Brown. 2012. Detection of infectious symptoms from va emergency department and primary care clinical documentation. *International journal of medical informatics*, 81(3):143–156.

Bo Pang and Lillian Lee. 2004. A sentimental education: Sentiment analysis using subjectivity summarization based on minimum cuts. In *Proceedings of the 42nd annual meeting on Association for Computational Linguistics*, page 271. Association for Computational Linguistics.

Oscar Täckström and Ryan McDonald. 2011. Semi-supervised latent variable models for sentence-level sentiment analysis. In *Proceedings of the 49th Annual Meeting of the Association for Computational Linguistics: Human Language Technologies: short papers-Volume 2*, pages 569–574. Association for Computational Linguistics.

Aldo Tinoco, R Scott Evans, Catherine J Staes, James F Lloyd, Jeffrey M Rothschild, and Peter J Haug. 2011. Comparison of computerized surveillance and manual chart review for adverse events. *Journal of the American Medical Informatics Association*, 18(4):491–497.

Katrin Tomanek, Joachim Wermter, Udo Hahn, et al. 2007. A reappraisal of sentence and token splitting for life sciences documents. In *Medinfo 2007: Proceedings of the 12th World Congress on Health (Medical) Informatics; Building Sustainable Health Systems*, page 524. IOS Press.

Yoshimasa Tsuruoka, Yuka Tateishi, Jin-Dong Kim, Tomoko Ohta, John McNaught, Sophia Ananiadou, and Junichi Tsujii. 2005. Developing a robust part-of-speech tagger for biomedical text. *Advances in informatics*, pages 382–392.

Ainur Yessenalina, Yisong Yue, and Claire Cardie. 2010. Multi-level structured models for document-level sentiment classification. In *Proceedings of the 2010 Conference on Empirical Methods in Natural Language Processing*, pages 1046–1056. Association for Computational Linguistics.

Temporal Modelling of Geospatial Words in Twitter

Bo Han[1], Antonio Jose Jimeno Yepes[2], Andrew MacKinlay[2,3], Lianhua Chi[2]
Hugo AI[1]
IBM Research Australia[2]
University of Melbourne[3]
bhan@hugo.ai, {antonio.jimeno, admackin, lianhuac}@au1.ibm.com

Abstract

Twitter text-based geotagging often uses geospatial words to determine locations. While much work has been done in word geospatiality analysis, there has been little work on temporal variations in the geospatial spread of word usage. In this paper, we investigate geospatial words relative to their temporal locality patterns by fitting periodical models over time. The model jointly captures inherent geospatial locality and periodical factor for a word. The resultant factorisation enables better understanding of word temporal trends and improves geotagging accuracy by only using inherent geospatial local words.

1 Introduction

Automatically inferring geographical location of social media data has become increasingly popular, as geospatial information plays a vital role in applications such as advertising, influenza detection and disaster management. Due to a lack of abundant reliable geospatial information (Cheng et al., 2010), various text-based geotagging methods have been proposed (Cheng et al., 2010; Eisenstein et al., 2010; Wing and Baldridge, 2014).[1] The main idea is to leverage geospatial words such as dialects and location names embedded in Twitter text to infer geographic locations. For instance, *yinz* is primarily used in Pittsburgh, *#auspol* is a popular hashtag in Australia, and *@TransLink* is frequently mentioned by Vancouver users.

Social media data often comes as a stream, and its contents and topics change over time. This implies geospatial words in social media can be fur-

---

[1]Indeed there is a way that a user can turn on their location sharing options which offers accurate location information, however, the ratio of such users are pretty low (Cheng et al., 2010).

ther distinguished based on their temporal patterns of locality (i.e. how location-indicative a word is). Some time-invariant geospatial words (e.g. *CalTech*) are consistently associated with a location, while other words like *#ALTA216* are only transiently associated with a location (e.g. during the conference).

In this paper, we investigate the word locality pattern over time. First, we bin streaming tweet data into a series of sliding time windows and calculate the locality estimators in each window. The time-indexed locality estimators are then fed into periodical models which jointly capture the inherent geospatial locality and periodical factor. We show that by removing the periodical factor, we can obtain improved geotagging accuracy. Furthermore, we demonstrate the utility of fitted model parameters in explaining some intuitive observations for reoccurring words.

2 Background

Text-based geotagging is often formulated as a classification task (Cheng et al., 2010) which involves predicting a location from a set of predefined geographical partitions. It exploits words in tweets on the grounds that some of them carry geographical information. The accuracy is often measured by the agreement of the predicted locations with true oracle locations (Wing and Baldridge, 2011).

Earlier work in geotagging exploits language models identified from textual data from different locations (Cheng et al., 2010; Wing and Baldridge, 2011; Kinsella et al., 2011). It selects the location with the most similar language model relative to the input tweet text. However, these methods also include irrelevant words such as stop words (e.g. *the*) and common hashtags (e.g. *#iphone*), meaning they capture imperfect geospatial signals.

Cheng et al. (2010) improved language model-based methods by augmenting local words for

Bo Han, Antonio Jimeno Yepes, Andrew MacKinlay and Lianhua Chi. 2016. Temporal Modelling of Geospatial Words in Twitter. In *Proceedings of Australasian Language Technology Association Workshop*, pages 133–137.

geotagging. Words with sharply-peaked frequency distributions with respect to location are categorised as local words, and only local words are used in geotagging. Furthermore, ranking geospatial words by their locality in the decreasing order has been proposed (Chang et al., 2012; Laere et al., 2013; Han et al., 2014), however the categorisation of local and non-local words is still binary. Hierarchical models and regularisation have also shown to be effective in geotagging (Ahmed et al., 2013; Wing and Baldridge, 2014).

With much progress in identifying and utilising geospatial words, the temporal variance of geospatial words has not been under studied. In this paper, we study the impact of this temporal aspect for geospatial words.

3 Temporal Geospatial Word Modelling

To analyse the temporal pattern of geospatial words, we first define a fixed-length sliding time window. The collected data within a time window is then aggregated for computing locality variances for each word. The same calculations are performed for each consecutive time window and the location scores are collectively incorporated in a periodical model, and the geospatial words are then ranked and categorised based on this model. Top ranked words are assumed to be consistently location-indicative over time and should therefore be preferred when building geotagging models.

3.1 Measurement of Word Locality

The locality variances of a word are computed on basis of time windows (e.g. one week). For each word found in a time window, we obtain a list of locations (i.e. GPS coordinates) from tweets containing the word. Then we draw random samples of paired locations without replacement (non-exhaustive to improve tractability), and compute the distances between paired locations following Cook et al. (2014), yielding a list of paired location distances. The mean and median of these distances serve as locality variances and are used in subsequent experiments. Permanent location-indicative words should have consistently low locality variances as they are likely to occur in geographically close regions in most time windows. The metric of median distance reduces the influence of outlier locations (e.g. caused by people mentioning their home city while travelling).

3.2 Sinusoidal Modelling

We assume that a word's observed geospatial pattern is jointly influenced by its inherent locality and periodical factor. A general sinusoidal model is applied to capture both factors in Equation 1.

$$f(t) = \underbrace{C}_{\text{Inherent locality}} + \underbrace{\alpha \sin(\omega t + \phi)}_{\text{Periodical factor}} \quad (1)$$

$f(t)$ denotes the geospatial locality variance over time and t is the time window index. C, which is constant with respect to time, models the inherent permanent locality, while the periodic factor is captured by the time-dependent $\alpha \sin(\omega t + \phi)$ in Equation 1.

A smaller C suggests the corresponding word is more inherently location-indicative since the periodic effects are factored out into the other term.

The time component $\alpha \sin(\omega t + \phi)$ is dependent on the time window index t and parameterised by the amplitude α, angular frequency ω and phase ϕ. α represents the maximum impact of periodic component on a word's locality, with a larger value suggesting the word is strongly time-dependent.

ω denotes the frequency of this periodic component. It is inversely proportional to the period, which is important for categorising the geospatial patterns of a word. Ideally, for transient geospatial words, lower locality variances will occur in a tight cluster of time windows giving a large period (and hence low ω), while recurring geospatial words will have a smaller period corresponding to lower locality variances appearing at more regular intervals.

ϕ is the phase of the wave and reflects the point, such as a day of the week, within a time window and it is crucial for curve fitting.

4 Experiments and Discussion

4.1 Datasets

We collected 10% 2014 Twitter stream data from Gnip.[2] Tweets are lowercased and non-English data is removed according to Gnip-provided language code. We use `APR-DEC` geotagged tweets as the training data and `JAN-MAR` users (by aggregating all their tweets) for test.[3] To ensure the

---

[2] `https://gnip.com/`
[3] Because we had a major data collection interruptions between March and April, we chose the larger of two datasets for training and the other for test.

quality of test data, we only include users who have more than 10 English tweets that are within 150 km of a city centre according to the geotag coordinates of the tweets, with at least 80% of these tweets having the same closest city. The closest city is stored as the user's true location.[4] The datasets after applying the above process are shown in Table 1.[5]

Datasets	Data size
`Train(APR-DEC)`	45.4M tweets
`Test(JAN-MAR)`	373K users

Table 1: Filtered Twitter dataset

4.2 Fitting Sinusoidal Models

We estimate parameters for Equation 1 using *Nonlinear Least Square* for each word. The initial values for important factors are set as follows:[6]

- C is set to the mean of the "10%-trimmed" (5th-95th percentile) locality variance numbers.
- α is determined by taking the root mean square of the 10%-trimmed locality variance numbers and dividing by $\sqrt{2}$.
- ω is set to the dominant frequency in *Discrete-Time Fourier Transformation*.

We further check the model validity by checking p-values for each C, and only keeping geospatial words with models that are significant at $p < 0.05$. We also only keep words that occur at least 20 times in at least 20 time windows due to efficiency considerations and because rare words have less impact in terms of analysis and building statistical models.

4.3 Impact on Geotagging

One advantage of temporal modelling of geospatial words is that the geotagging accuracy is expected to improve by teasing out transient and recurring location-indicative words. We set a benchmark multinomial naive Bayes classifier with the

following settings to test the impact.[7]

- WHOLE: This baseline uses the whole training data collection period to calculate the locality median score in training without specifying time windows, which is roughly equivalent to conventional word-based non-temporal geotagging model.
- SIN-MEAN: This setting uses a fourteen-day sliding time window with one day as the sliding step.[8] Random location pairs are generated three times with each sample size equal to 20. Mean numbers are used to fit the sinusoidal model and the initial parameters are estimated as described in Section 4.2.
- SIN-MEDIAN: Similar to SIN-MEAN, but we use medians as locality variances to reduce the negative impact of outliers.

We then rank words by the C value from (3.2) and evaluate the accuracy of the geotagging models produced by using the top n words. The experiment range starts from the top 5K with a next 5K increment up to 40K.[9] As shown in Figure 1, we found (1) As expected, the more features, the better the performance of the geotagger; (2) With the same number of features, both SIN-MEAN and SIN-MEDIAN outperform WHOLE consistently by 2.0-4.7% error reduction (with an absolute accuracy 5.3-9.3%); (3) The differences between WHOLE and each of the SIN methods are all statistically significant ($p < 0.0001$). In contrast, the difference between SIN methods is indistinguishable. Overall this indicates that using only permanent location indicative words (as determined by C) allows us to build more accurate models for text-based geotagging.

4.4 Post Analysis and Discussions

The fitted model parameters also imply some interesting patterns for geospatial words. As explained in Section 3.2, C provides an indication of inherent locality (as shown in Table 2).

---

[4]We adopted the 3709 city partitions of Han et al. (2014)

[5]Pavalanathan and Eisenstein (2015) mentioned geotagging results are influenced by demographics and where the true location source being used. These influencing factors are less of our concern when analysing the impact of temporal factors.

[6]The remaining parameters for data fitting are set as follows: $\phi = 1$, $maxIter = 500$.

[7]The objective is to analyse the impact of temporal geospatial word modelling instead of building state-of-the-art geotagging systems. Advanced models including a regularised logistic regression as discussed by Wing and Baldridge (2014) are preferred in building geotaggers for better accuracy.

[8]In theory, we can choose other window sizes, however shorter time windows would produce sparse location distributions and unreliable samples.

[9]The total feature number is around 43K.

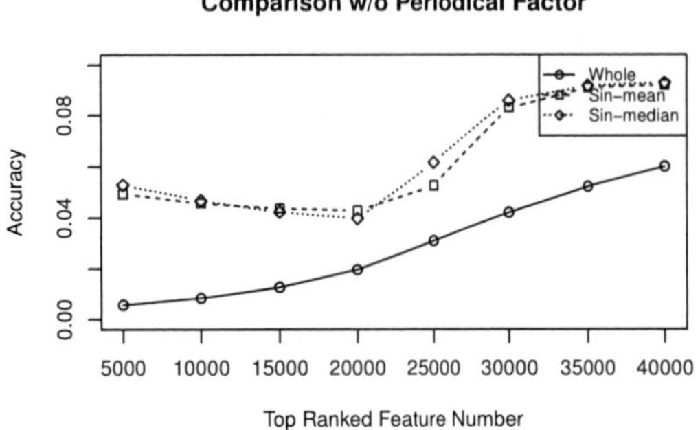

Figure 1: Geotagging performance comparisons (over 373K test users)

$C \geq 10^5$	$C \leq 10^{-3}$
siya	*@zeling97*
#thankyoulord	*@seandasheepdog*
@armorogod	*#xiomaraforugirlperu*
@aquariusquotez	*@parazetsalive*
@shainedawson	*@mishecollins*

Table 2: Examples of large and small C values

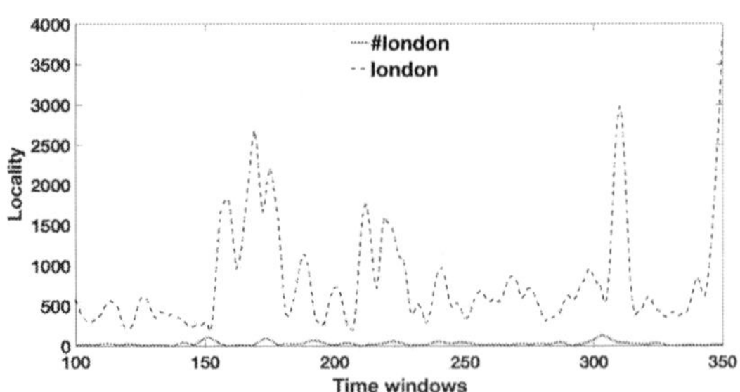

Figure 2: Locality comparison: locations versus location hashtags

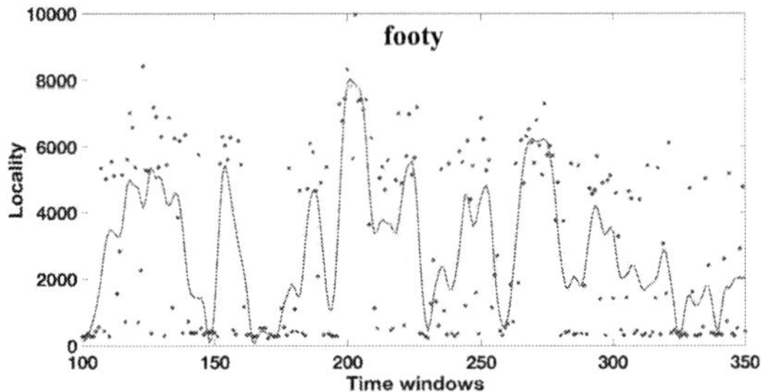

Figure 3: Recurring pattern for local sports

We found words with lower C values are often user names and hashtags which are used in specific regions. For instance, *#telpadmovienight* and *#xiomaraforugirlperu* are popular in Philippines and Peru. Large C values are associated with popular people (e.g. *siya* and *@shainedawson*) or common expressions (e.g. *#thankyoulord*).

Metropolitan city names are often not consistent local words over time, as they might be mentioned across the world. In contrast, the hashtag versions seem to be more permanent location indicative (e.g. Figure 2).[10] Some local sport terms (e.g. Figure 3) share (modest) recurring locality patterns over time as captured by the temporal modelling. Theoretically, it is possible to have location indicative words that are local to one location at certain times, while local to other locations at other times, however, we have not found such examples in our selected features.

The current modelling approach also has several limitations. Some infrequent location-indicative words may be missed due to the minimum frequency threshold in Section 4.2 and the relatively small datasets we used for experiments. Further-

more, we may obtain unreliable fitted parameters due to insufficient data points, because as few as 20 locality variances may be available. Using a training data set which covers a longer time span would partially mitigate this problem and help learn parameters for words with longer periods. We could also increase the time window size (e.g. to a month) to incorporate more words, however this may make it difficult to capture monthly recurring words.

5 Conclusion and Future Work

In this paper, we investigated the temporal variance of geospatial words over time. Specifically, a sinusoidal model is applied to jointly capture the inherent permanent locality along with time-dependent component representing changes which occur in word usage with respect to particular locations over time. This model factors out permanent location indicative words which are shown to be able to improve geotagging accuracy. The fitted parameters also confirm intuitive geospatial locality patterns. In general, we believe such temporal modelling of geospatial words benefits both predictive tasks and geospatial data analysis.

Sinusoidal models are effective in capturing strict recurring patterns, however, this assumption

---

[10]All figures are smoothed using "loess" with $span = 0.06$ (Cleveland and Devlin, 1988).

is often not satisfied due to the nature of periodical patterns and noise in the data. In future work, we plan to experiment with more advanced periodical models for data fitting, e.g. employ a number of superposed periodical models, instead of using only the dominant frequency model. Inspired by Dredze et al. (2016) that periodical patterns have impacts on geotagging results, we also plan to compare test results based on datasets collected over different periods.

References

Amr Ahmed, Liangjie Hong, and Alexander J. Smola. 2013. Hierarchical geographical modeling of user locations from social media posts. In *Proceedings of the 22nd International Conference on the World Wide Web (WWW 2013)*, pages 25–36, Rio de Janeiro, Brazil.

Hau-wen Chang, Dongwon Lee, Eltaher Mohammed, and Jeongkyu Lee. 2012. @Phillies tweeting from Philly? Predicting Twitter user locations with spatial word usage. In *2012 IEEE/ACM International Conference on Advances in Social Networks Analysis and Mining (ASONAM)*, pages 111–118, Istanbul, Turkey.

Zhiyuan Cheng, James Caverlee, and Kyumin Lee. 2010. You are where you tweet: a content-based approach to geo-locating Twitter users. In *Proceedings of the 19th ACM Conference on Information and Knowledge Management (CIKM 2010)*, pages 759–768, Toronto, Canada.

William S Cleveland and Susan J Devlin. 1988. Locally weighted regression: an approach to regression analysis by local fitting. *Journal of the American statistical association*, 83(403):596–610.

Paul Cook, Bo Han, and Timothy Baldwin. 2014. Statistical methods for identifying local dialectal terms from gps-tagged documents. *Dictionaries*, 35:248–271.

Mark Dredze, Miles Osborne, and Prabhanjan Kambadur. 2016. Geolocation for twitter: Timing matters. In *Proceedings of the 2016 Conference of the North American Chapter of the Association for Computational Linguistics: Human Language Technologies*, pages 1064–1069, San Diego, California, June. Association for Computational Linguistics.

Jacob Eisenstein, Brendan O'Connor, Noah A. Smith, and Eric P. Xing. 2010. A latent variable model for geographic lexical variation. In *Proceedings of the 2010 Conference on Empirical Methods in Natural Language Processing (EMNLP 2010)*, pages 1277–1287, Cambridge, USA.

Bo Han, Paul Cook, and Timothy Baldwin. 2014. Text-based Twitter user geolocation prediction. *Journal Artificial Intelligence Research (JAIR)*, 49:451–500.

Sheila Kinsella, Vanessa Murdock, and Neil O'Hare. 2011. "I'm eating a sandwich in Glasgow": Modeling locations with tweets. In *Proceedings of the 3rd International Workshop on Search and Mining User-Generated Contents*, pages 61–68, Glasgow, UK.

Olivier Van Laere, Jonathan Quinn, Steven Schockaert, and Bart Dhoedt. 2013. Spatially-aware term selection for geotagging. *IEEE Transactions on Knowledge and Data Engineering*, 99:221–234.

Umashanthi Pavalanathan and Jacob Eisenstein. 2015. Confounds and consequences in geotagged Twitter data. In *Proceedings of the 2015 Conference on Empirical Methods in Natural Language Processing (EMNLP)*, pages 2138–2148, Lisbon, Portugal.

Benjamin P. Wing and Jason Baldridge. 2011. Simple supervised document geolocation with geodesic grids. In *Proceedings of the 49th Annual Meeting of the Association for Computational Linguistics: Human Language Technologies (ACL HLT 2011)*, pages 955–964, Portland, USA.

Benjamin Wing and Jason Baldridge. 2014. Hierarchical discriminative classification for text-based geolocation. In *Proceedings of the 2014 Conference on Empirical Methods in Natural Language Processing (EMNLP)*, pages 336–348, Doha, Qatar, October. Association for Computational Linguistics.

NER for Medical Entities in Twitter using Sequence to Sequence Neural Networks

Antonio Jimeno Yepes◇ **and Andrew MacKinlay**◇♠
◇ IBM Research – Australia, Melbourne, VIC, Australia
♠ Dept of Computing and Information Systems, University of Melbourne, Australia
`{antonio.jimeno,admackin}@au1.ibm.com`

Abstract

Social media sites such as Twitter are attractive sources of information due to their combination of accessibility, timeliness and large data volumes. Identification of medical entities in Twitter can support tasks such public health surveillance. We propose an approach to perform annotation of medical entities using a sequence to sequence neural network. Results show that our approach improves over previous work based on CRF in the annotation of two medical entities types in Twitter.

1   Introduction

Public health surveillance (Nsubuga et al., 2006) is the systematic collection, analysis and monitoring of population health for the public good using a variety of tools. Governments rely mostly on aggregated health data from health care centres, which cannot be used in real-time scenarios such as syndromic surveillance.

Twitter is a promising source of information due to its availability and the large quantity of information published, with more than 500 million posts published each day. It can be potentially used to mine information about the status of the population (Jimeno Yepes et al., 2015a), and can then be used in combination with other sources to empower government decision makers.

Natural language processing can leverage the short messages in Twitter by extracting pieces of structured information from them which can be aggregated for data analysis. Identifying entities of interest in tweets is relevant for several tasks, including public health surveillance. Several approaches have been used to perform named entity recognition in Twitter, which range from dictionary matching approaches to machine learning methods. Named entity recognition (NER) in

Twitter has unique challenges compared to many other sources of text. Tweets are short (with at most 140 characters), and often contain highly informal language, idioms, humour, typos and grammatical errors (Baldwin et al., 2013; Jimeno Yepes et al., 2015b).

Effective biomedical NER methods for Twitter rely on machine learning methods such as conditional random fields (CRF) (Lafferty et al., 2001). Learning algorithms like CRF typically consider a limited span of one token before and/or after the token being annotated, which may omit valuable contextual information in order to work within the limitations of the learning algorithms.

We use a recurrent neural network under the assumption that it can manage dependencies in language better than traditional methods such as CRF. The proposed approach uses a sequence to sequence network (Sutskever et al., 2014) to analyse text in a tweet producing an encoding vector which is then used to perform the annotation by a second LSTM (Long Short Term Memory) node. Word embeddings generated from several million tweets are used to represent the tokens in text, which is the only feature engineering required in this neural network approach.

This approach improves over previous work based on CRF in the annotation of two medical entity types in Twitter. It also takes advantage of word embeddings, thus reducing the domain-specificity of the NE recogniser, i.e. no domain-specific lexicon is used by the LSTM approach.

2   Methods

In this section, we describe the generation of word embeddings and the recurrent network structure used. We describe the data set used and the CRF baseline method.

Antonio Jimeno Yepes and Andrew MacKinlay. 2016. NER for Medical Entities in Twitter using Sequence to Sequence Neural Networks. In *Proceedings of Australasian Language Technology Association Workshop*, pages 138–142.

2.1 Word embeddings

Bag-of-words representations for natural language processing are typically high-dimensional (with dimension equal to the vocabulary size) and very sparse, since just the words in the represented document will have non-zero values. This representation is a problem for deep neural networks and recently word embeddings have been used. Word embeddings map this high dimensional space into a lower dimensionality space which is dense rather than sparse and has some interesting properties that allow, for instance, identifying words with a similar meaning (Mikolov et al., 2013).

The data set used in this work to generate the word embeddings consists of 148 million tweets randomly selected from years 2012 and 2013. We used word2vec[1] to generate word vectors using the continuous bag-of-words (CBOW) approach (Mikolov et al., 2013) with 200 dimensions and other parameters set to default values.

Tweet text was lowercased and then tokenised using the TweetNLP package[2].

2.2 Sequence to sequence neural network

Typically recurrent neural networks suffer from the *vanishing gradient* problem (Bengio et al., 1994; Pascanu et al., 2013) when trained on long dependencies. These networks rely on gradient descent methods and *backpropagation through time*, thus gradients after long dependencies might be very small. As an effect, the time needed to train a network might be quite large. It can even make a problem difficult to learn since the signal for important events might be missed. LSTM (Hochreiter and Schmidhuber, 1997) memory cells were developed to overcome the vanishing gradient limitation and it can learn to retain information for a long period of time.

LSTM memory cells introduce mechanisms to avoid the vanishing gradient problem using, for a given time t, an input gate i_t, an output gate o_t, a forget gate f_t and a cell c_t. The weights for these three gates and memory cell are trained using backpropagation using training data. The input to the LSTM cell is the vector x_t and the hidden output is h_t. The ability of LSTM to effectively deal with long-range dependencies (such as syntactic dependencies) may be useful for NLP tasks such as disambiguation.

---

[1]https://code.google.com/archive/p/word2vec
[2]www.cs.cmu.edu/ ark/TweetNLP

We adopt the definition of LSTM memory cell introduced in (Graves, 2013), which follows the diagram in Figure 1. Equations 1 to 5 show how the values in different LSTM components get calculated. Weights matrices W have subscripts that indicate the components being related. For instance W_{hi} is the weight matrix between the hidden output and the input gate.

$$i_t = \sigma(W_{xi}x_t + W_{hi}h_{t-1} + W_{ci}c_{t-1} + b_i) \quad (1)$$
$$f_t = \sigma(W_{xf}x_t + W_{hf}h_{t-1} + W_{cf}c_{t-1} + b_f) \quad (2)$$
$$c_t = f_tc_{t-1} + i_t tanh(W_{xc}x_t + W_{hc}h_{t-1} + b_c) \quad (3)$$
$$o_t = \sigma(W_{xo}x_t + W_{ho}h_{t-1} + W_{co}c_t + b_o) \quad (4)$$
$$h_t = o_t tanh(c_t) \quad (5)$$

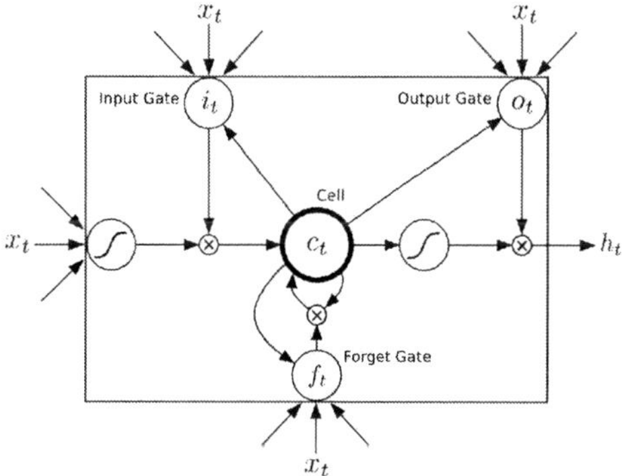

Figure 1: LSTM memory cell unit diagram (Graves, 2013)

Our network design is inspired by the previously-mentioned sequence to sequence learning network for machine translation of Sutskever et al. (2014).

In our network, we have two LSTM nodes with n units each. The first one (LSTMe) is used encoded to encode the text into a vector representation. The second one (LSTMa) takes as input an input vector and the current token and generates an annotation. The output of LSTMa is processed by a linear classifier trained using multiclass hinge loss. In this stage, one of three categories is predicted, corresponding to IOB tags common in NER: B(eginning), I(nside entity) and O(ut of entity).

Training relies on AdaGrad (Duchi et al., 2011), and the learning rate has been set to 0.01 for all iterations, with the number of iterations set to 300.

A lookup table was used to translate each token into a vector representation. Word embedding vec-

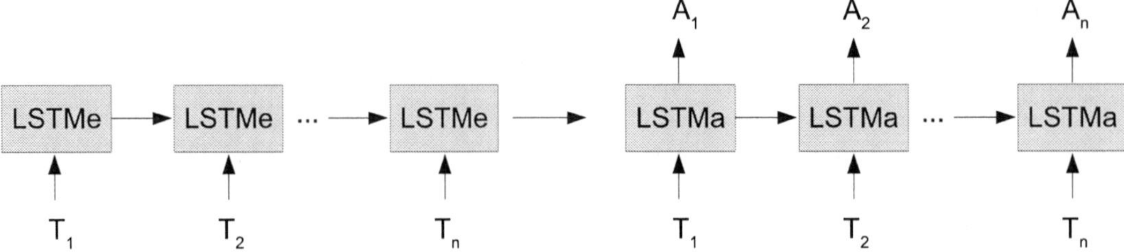

Figure 2: Recurrent network layout. LSTMe performs encoding of tweets while LSTMa performs B(eginning), I(n entity) and O(ut of entity) annotation.

tors of 200 dimensions for each token were generated. The LSTM memory cells have been configured to use 200 units each, which matches the dimensions of the vectors generated with word2vec.

The vocabulary for word embeddings is finite, as it is dependent on the training data we supply to word2vec training data; in addition, words with less than 20 occurrences in the training set are removed to reduce the size of the vocabulary. This means that some tokens in the NER training and test sets might not be found in the word embedding lookup table. In these cases, a vector with all dimensions equal to zero is provided to the LSTM nodes for both training and evaluation.

2.3 Micromed data set

We have used the Micromed[3] data set described in Jimeno Yepes et al. (2015b), which contains 1300 tweets from May 2014 manually annotated with mentions of diseases, pharmacological substances and symptoms. In addition, the annotations include parts-of-speech for some of the entities, since adjectives have been considered for symptoms and it includes references to either figurative terms or entities that look as medical terms but are used in a figurative meaning (e.g. mentions of *heart attack* when someone is anxious).

Non medical entities were removed and the JSON format was converted into IOB format for training the recurrent network system based on Torch[4] and then converted into BRAT format[5] for evaluation. As in the generation of word embeddings, Tweet text was lowercased and then tokenized using the TweetNLP package.

2.4 CRF baseline method

As an informed comparative baseline, we used previously published work (Jimeno Yepes et al., 2015a) based on a linear-chain CRF system with the following features: part-of-speech, token surface form and window relative position, token prefix and suffix character n-grams of all lengths up to eight, whether the token appears in a list of terms extracted from the UMLS (Unified Medical Language System) (Bodenreider, 2004) corresponding to the entity type. This is currently the method with best performance on this data set.

3 Results

The Micromed data set is split in 13 subsets of 100 tweets each, which are used to train and test the machine learning methods using 13-fold cross validation.

Results are presented in tables 1 and 2. Previous results published on Micromed (Jimeno Yepes et al., 2015a) are compared to the proposed LSTM approach with word embeddings as features. We report precision, recall and F1 results for each method, for both exact match (boundaries exactly match the gold standard) and partial match (the postulated entity overlaps at all with the gold standard). Statistical significance was determined using a randomisation version of the paired sample t-test (Cohen, 1996).

Our approach improves the performance for both pharmacological substance and symptom entity types against the CRF comparison method. However, the performance on the disease entity type is decreased, particularly with exact match.

4 Discussion

The proposed method improves the F-score in the annotation of pharmacological substances due to a boost in recall. It improves the accuracy on the

---

[3] https://github.com/IBMMRL/medinfo2015
[4] http://torch.ch
[5] http://brat.nlplab.org/standoff.html

	Disease			Pharm.Substance			Symptom		
Method	Prec	Rec	F1	Prec	Rec	F1	Prec	Rec	F1
Baseline	**0.796**	**0.527**	**0.634**[†]	**0.821**	0.396	0.535	0.720	0.608	0.659
LSTMe+LSTMa	0.600	0.439	0.507	0.694	**0.476**	**0.565**	**0.744**	**0.619**	**0.676**

Table 1: Exact match NER results. Precision (Prec), recall (Rec) and F1 are used for evaluation. Baseline tagger and the proposed approach (LSTMe+LSTMa) are trained and evaluated for the three entity types: disease, pharmacological substance (Pharm.Substance) and symptom. † denotes statistically significant different of $p < 0.05$ against the alternate method.

	Disease			Pharm.Substance			Symptom		
Method	Prec	Rec	F1	Prec	Rec	F1	Prec	Rec	F1
Baseline	**0.845**	0.562	**0.675**	**0.854**	0.415	0.558	0.746	0.630	0.683
LSTMe+LSTMa	0.795	**0.572**	0.665	0.838	**0.575**	**0.682**[†]	**0.793**	**0.656**	**0.718**[†]

Table 2: Partial match Named entity recognition results. Precision (Prec), recall (Rec) and F1 are used for evaluation. Baseline tagger and the proposed approach (LSTMe+LSTMa) are trained and evaluated for the three entity types: disease, pharmacological substance (Pharm.Substance) and symptom. † denotes statistically significant difference of $p < 0.05$ against the alternate method.

annotation of symptoms to a lesser extent. On the other hand, the accuracy decreases for the annotation of diseases, mostly in the exact match evaluation.

A manual examination of the neural network annotation shows that for entities with multiple tokens, annotations are sometimes incorrect for one of the tokens in the entity.

The recall is typically higher in our NER system, even though the CRF baseline uses external domain-specific terminological resources such as the UMLS. In fact, the CRF baseline heavily relies on the term lists extracted from the UMLS, which represent extensive domain-specific customisation, while our LSTM approach does not depend on anything specific to the medical domain apart from the relatively small training corpus. The external knowledge comes solely from word embeddings derived from a general Twitter corpus, which would only contain a very small amount of domain-specific information, suggesting that the LSTM approach is more robust and domain-agnostic.

Even with higher recall, there are some terms that are missed by the neural network tagger and a larger data set or domain knowledge based on the UMLS could provide a boost in the recall. Infrequent terms might cause problems – for example, *valerian* did not appear in the word embeddings generated using word2vec. A larger Twitter corpus and/or a domain corpus based on MED-LINE might be considered to generate the word embeddings to make them more robust and encode more relevant domain knowledge including rarer phenomena such as these.

5 Related work

CRF has become the standard tool for NER, including for Twitter (Ritter et al., 2011; Ritter et al., 2012). Previous work in biomedical natural language processing (NLP) has explored using CRF methods to several manually annotated data sets (Jimeno Yepes et al., 2015b; Nikfarjam et al., 2015).

Initial work using convolutional neural networks (Collobert et al., 2011) showed state-of-the-art performance on standard general English data sets. There is recent work on named entity recognition using bidirectional LSTM based recurrent networks that are enhanced using CRFs (Lample et al., 2016) and complemented with CNNs (Ma and Hovy, 2016), which show state-of-the-art performance in standard data sets. These works use word-based features as we do here but also features at the character level.

6 Conclusions and Future work

The proposed method improves the annotation of biomedical entities in Twitter based on a previously state-of-the-art method based on CRF. For future work, we may consider additional neural network designs. For example, to alleviate the aforementioned problem of tokens only partially aligning with ground truth, we could use methods discussed in a preprint (Lample et al., 2016) to combine the output of a bigraph neural network with CRF to improve the annotation of the beginning of the entity (B). We may also consider additional neural network designs inspired by other work on deep learning for NER, and combining external domain knowledge from a terminology such as the UMLS, which may improve accuracy while making it more targeted to the medical domain and this particular corpus.

NER over medical entities is a potentially useful part of a public health surveillance system; further normalisation of these terms, and detecting figurative or non-medical uses would further enhance their utility and could also benefit from a deep neural network approach.

References

Timothy Baldwin, Paul Cook, Marco Lui, Andrew MacKinlay, and Li Wang. 2013. How noisy social media text, how diffrnt social media sources? In *IJCNLP*, pages 356–364.

Yoshua Bengio, Patrice Simard, and Paolo Frasconi. 1994. Learning long-term dependencies with gradient descent is difficult. *Neural Networks, IEEE Transactions on*, 5(2):157–166.

Olivier Bodenreider. 2004. The unified medical language system (umls): integrating biomedical terminology. *Nucleic acids research*, 32(suppl 1):D267–D270.

Paul R Cohen. 1996. Empirical methods for artificial intelligence. *IEEE Intelligent Systems*, (6):88.

Ronan Collobert, Jason Weston, Léon Bottou, Michael Karlen, Koray Kavukcuoglu, and Pavel Kuksa. 2011. Natural language processing (almost) from scratch. *The Journal of Machine Learning Research*, 12:2493–2537.

John Duchi, Elad Hazan, and Yoram Singer. 2011. Adaptive subgradient methods for online learning and stochastic optimization. *The Journal of Machine Learning Research*, 12:2121–2159.

Alex Graves. 2013. Generating sequences with recurrent neural networks. *arXiv preprint arXiv:1308.0850*.

Sepp Hochreiter and Jürgen Schmidhuber. 1997. Long short-term memory. *Neural computation*, 9(8):1735–1780.

Antonio Jimeno Yepes, Andrew MacKinlay, and Bo Han. 2015a. Investigating public health surveillance using twitter. *ACL-IJCNLP 2015*, page 164.

Antonio Jimeno Yepes, Andrew MacKinlay, Bo Han, and Qiang Chen. 2015b. Identifying diseases, drugs, and symptoms in twitter. In *MEDINFO 2015: eHealth-enabled Health - Proceedings of the 15th World Congress on Health and Biomedical Informatics, São Paulo, Brazil, 19-23 August 2015*, pages 643–647.

John Lafferty, Andrew McCallum, and Fernando Pereira. 2001. Conditional random fields: Probabilistic models for segmenting and labeling sequence data. In *Proceedings of the eighteenth international conference on machine learning, ICML*, volume 1, pages 282–289.

Guillaume Lample, Miguel Ballesteros, Sandeep Subramanian, Kazuya Kawakami, and Chris Dyer. 2016. Neural architectures for named entity recognition. *arXiv preprint arXiv:1603.01360*.

Xuezhe Ma and Eduard Hovy. 2016. End-to-end sequence labeling via bi-directional lstm-cnns-crf. *arXiv preprint arXiv:1603.01354*.

Tomas Mikolov, Ilya Sutskever, Kai Chen, Greg S Corrado, and Jeff Dean. 2013. Distributed representations of words and phrases and their compositionality. In *Advances in neural information processing systems*, pages 3111–3119.

Azadeh Nikfarjam, Abeed Sarker, Karen OConnor, Rachel Ginn, and Graciela Gonzalez. 2015. Pharmacovigilance from social media: mining adverse drug reaction mentions using sequence labeling with word embedding cluster features. *Journal of the American Medical Informatics Association*, 22(3):671–681.

Peter Nsubuga, Mark E. White, Stephen B. Thacker, Mark A. Anderson, Stephen B. Blount, Claire V. Broome, Tom M. Chiller, Victoria Espitia, Rubina Imtiaz, Dan Sosin, Donna F. Stroup, Robert V. Tauxe, Maya Vijayaraghavan, and Murray Trostle. 2006. Public health surveillance: a tool for targeting and monitoring interventions. In *Disease Control Priorities in Developing Countries. 2nd edition*. World Bank.

Razvan Pascanu, Tomas Mikolov, and Yoshua Bengio. 2013. On the difficulty of training recurrent neural networks. *ICML (3)*, 28:1310–1318.

Alan Ritter, Sam Clark, Mausam, and Oren Etzioni. 2011. Named entity recognition in tweets: An experimental study. In *EMNLP*.

Alan Ritter, Mausam, Oren Etzioni, and Sam Clark. 2012. Open domain event extraction from twitter. In *KDD*.

Ilya Sutskever, Oriol Vinyals, and Quoc V Le. 2014. Sequence to sequence learning with neural networks. In *Advances in neural information processing systems*, pages 3104–3112.

An empirical study for Vietnamese dependency parsing

Dat Quoc Nguyen, Mark Dras and **Mark Johnson**
Department of Computing
Macquarie University, Australia
`dat.nguyen@students.mq.edu.au, {mark.dras, mark.johnson}@mq.edu.au`

Abstract

This paper presents an empirical comparison of different dependency parsers for Vietnamese, which has some unusual characteristics such as copula drop and verb serialization. Experimental results show that the neural network-based parsers perform significantly better than the traditional parsers. We report the highest parsing scores published to date for Vietnamese with the labeled attachment score (LAS) at 73.53% and the unlabeled attachment score (UAS) at 80.66%.

1 Introduction

Dependency parsing has become a key research topic in natural language processing in the last decade, boosted by the success of the CoNLL 2006 and 2007 shared tasks on multilingual dependency parsing (Buchholz and Marsi, 2006; Nivre et al., 2007a). McDonald and Nivre (2011) identify two types of approaches for dependency parsing: graph-based approaches (McDonald et al., 2005) and transition-based approaches (Nivre et al., 2007b). Most traditional graph- or transition-based dependency parsers (McDonald et al., 2005; Nivre et al., 2007b; Bohnet, 2010; Zhang and Nivre, 2011; Martins et al., 2013; Choi and Mc-Callum, 2013) manually define a set of core and combined features associated with one-hot representations.

Recent work shows that neural network-based parsers obtain the state-of-the-art parsing results across many languages. Chen and Manning (2014), Weiss et al. (2015), Pei et al. (2015), and Andor et al. (2016) represent the core features with dense vector embeddings and then feed them as inputs to neural network-based classifiers, while Dyer et al. (2015), Kiperwasser and Goldberg (2016a), and Kiperwasser and Goldberg

(2016b) propose novel neural network architectures to solve the feature-engineering problem.

Dependency parsing for Vietnamese has not been actively explored. One main reason is because there is no manually labeled dependency treebank available. Thi et al. (2013) and Nguyen et al. (2014b) propose constituent-to-dependency conversion approaches to automatically translate the manually built constituent treebank for Vietnamese (Nguyen et al., 2009) to dependency treebanks. The converted dependency treebanks are then used in later works on Vietnamese dependency parsing, including Vu-Manh et al. (2015), Le-Hong et al. (2015) and Nguyen and Nguyen (2015). All of the previous research works use either the MSTparser (McDonald et al., 2005) or the Maltparser (Nivre et al., 2007b) for their parsing experiments. Among them, Nguyen et al. (2014b) report the highest results with LAS at 71.66% and UAS at 79.08% obtained by MSTparser. However, MSTparser and Maltparser are no longer considered state-of-the-art parsers.

In this paper, we present an empirical study of Vietnamese dependency parsing. We make comparisons between neural network-based parsers and traditional parsers, and also between graph-based parsers and transition-based parsers. We show that the neural network-based parsers obtain significantly higher scores than the traditional parsers. Specifically, we report the highest up-to-date scores for Vietnamese with LAS at 73.53% and UAS at 80.66%. We also examine potential problems specific to parsing Vietnamese, and point out potential solutions for improving the parsing performance.

2 Experimental setup

Dataset: There are two Vietnamese dependency treebanks which are automatically converted from the manually-annotated Vietnamese constituent

Dat Quoc Nguyen, Mark Dras and Mark Johnson. 2016. An empirical study for Vietnamese dependency parsing. In
Proceedings of Australasian Language Technology Association Workshop, pages 143–149.

Dep. labels		POS tags		Sent. length	
Type	Rate	Type	Rate	Length	Rate
adv	5.9	A	6.0	$1-10$	19.0
amod	2.4	C	3.7	$11-20$	35.4
conj	1.9	E	6.5	$21-30$	25.6
coord	1.9	M	3.6	$31-40$	12.2
dep	3.1	N	24.6	$41-50$	4.9
det	6.2	Nc	2.4	>50	2.9
dob	6.0	Np	4.2	–	–
loc	2.3	P	4.0	–	–
nmod	19.0	R	7.4	–	–
pob	5.6	V	19.4	–	–
punct	13.9	–	–	–	–
root	4.7	–	–	–	–
sub	6.8	–	–	–	–
tmp	2.2	–	–	–	–
vmod	14.8	–	–	–	–

Table 1: VnDT statistics by most frequent dependency and part-of-speech (POS) labels, and sentence length (i.e. number of words). "Rate" denotes the percentage occurrence in VnDT. Dependency labels: *adv* (adverbial), *amod* (adjectival modifier), *conj* (conjunct), *coord* (coordinating conjunction), *dep* (unspecified dependency), *det* (determiner), *dob* (direct object), *loc* (location), *nmod* (noun modifier), *pob* (object of a preposition), *punct* (punctuation), *sub* (subject), *tmp* (temporal), *vmod* (verb modifier). POS tags: A (Adjective), C (Conjunction), E (Preposition), M (Quantity), N (Noun), Nc (Classifier noun), Np (Proper noun), P (Pronoun), R (Adjunct), V (Verb).

treebank (Nguyen et al., 2009), using conversion approaches proposed by Thi et al. (2013) and Nguyen et al. (2014b). In Thi et al. (2013)'s conversion approach, it is not clear how the dependency labels are inferred; also, it ignores grammatical information encoded in grammatical function tags. In addition, Thi et al. (2013)'s approach is unable to handle cases of coordination and empty category mappings, which frequently appear in the Vietnamese constituent treebank. Nguyen et al. (2014b) later proposed a new conversion approach to handle those cases, with a better use of existing information in the Vietnamese constituent treebank. So we conduct experiments using VnDT, the high quality Vietnamese dependency treebank produced by Nguyen et al. (2014b). The VnDT treebank consists of 10,200 sentences (about 219K words). Table 1 gives some basic statistics of VnDT. We use the last 1020 sentences of VnDT

for testing while the remaining sentences are used for training, resulting in an out-of-vocabulary rate of 3.3%.

Dependency parsers: We experiment with four parsers: the graph-based parsers BIST-bmstparser[1] (**BistG**) and MSTparser[2] (**MST**), and the transition-based parsers BIST-barchybrid[3] (**BistT**) and Maltparser[4] (**Malt**). The state-of-the-art BistG and BistT parsers (Kiperwasser and Goldberg, 2016b) employ a bidirectional LSTM RNN architecture (Schuster and Paliwal, 1997; Hochreiter and Schmidhuber, 1997) to automatically learn the feature representation. In contrast, the traditional parsers MST (McDonald et al., 2005) and Malt (Nivre et al., 2007b) use a set of predefined features. For training these parsers, we used the default settings.

Evaluation metrics: The metrics are the labeled attachment score (LAS), unlabeled attachment score (UAS) and label accuracy score (LS). LAS is the percentage of words which are correctly assigned both dependency arc and label while UAS is the percentage of words for which the dependency arc is assigned correctly, and LS is the percentage of words for which the dependency label is assigned correctly.

3 Main results

3.1 Overall accuracy

Table 2 compares the parsing results obtained by the four parsers. The first four rows report the scores with gold part-of-speech (POS) tags while the last four rows present the scores with automatically predicted POS tags.[5]

As expected the neural network-based parsers BistG and BistT perform significantly better than the traditional parsers MST and Malt.[6] Specifically, we find $2^+\%$ absolute improvements in LAS and UAS scores in both graph- and transition-based types. In most cases, there are no significant differences between the LAS and UAS scores of BistG and BistT, except LAS scored on gold POS

---

[1] https://github.com/elikip/bist-parser/tree/master/bmstparser

[2] http://www.seas.upenn.edu/~strctlrn/MSTParser/MSTParser.html

[3] https://github.com/elikip/bist-parser/tree/master/barchybrid

[4] http://www.maltparser.org

[5] We adapted the RDRPOSTagger toolkit (Nguyen et al., 2014a; Nguyen et al., 2016) to automatically assign POS tags to words in the test set with an accuracy of 94.58%.

[6] Using McNemar's test, the differences are statistically significant at $p < 0.001$.

System		With punctuation						Without punctuation					
		Overall			Exact match			Overall			Exact match		
		LAS	UAS	LS	LAS	UAS	LS	LAS	UAS	LS	LAS	UAS	LS
Gold POS	BistG	**73.17**	**79.39**	**84.22**	**11.27**	**19.71**	15.20	**73.53**	80.66	**81.86**	**11.96**	**20.88**	15.20
	BistT	72.53	79.33	83.71	**11.27**	19.41	**16.18**	72.91	**80.73**	81.29	11.67	20.29	**16.18**
	MST	70.29	76.47	83.23	8.43	12.94	14.02	71.61	78.71	80.72	9.80	16.37	14.02
	Malt	69.10	74.91	81.72	9.22	14.80	13.92	70.39	77.08	79.33	9.71	17.16	13.92
Auto POS	BistG	**68.40**	76.28	**80.56**	9.12	16.18	11.76	**68.50**	77.55	**77.65**	9.71	**17.25**	11.76
	BistT	68.22	**76.56**	80.22	**9.80**	**16.27**	**13.24**	68.31	**77.91**	77.27	**10.00**	17.06	**13.24**
	MST	65.99	73.94	79.78	6.86	10.78	10.88	66.99	76.12	76.75	7.84	13.33	10.88
	Malt	64.94	72.32	78.43	7.35	12.25	10.20	65.88	74.36	75.56	7.55	14.02	10.20

Table 2: Parsing results. "Without punctuation" denotes parsing results where the punctuation and other symbols are excluded from evaluation. "Exact match" denotes the proportion of sentences whose predicted dependency trees are entirely correct.

tags (73.17% against 72.53%, and 73.53% against 72.91%).[7] Compared to the previous highest results (LAS at 71.66% and UAS at 79.08%) scored without punctuation on gold POS tags in Nguyen et al. (2014b), we obtain better scores (LAS at 73.53% and UAS at 80.66%) with BistG.

Next, Section 3.2 gives a detailed accuracy analysis on gold POS tags **without** punctuation, and Section 3.3 discusses the source of some errors and possible improvements.

3.2 Accuracy analysis

Sentence length: Figures 1 and 2 detail LAS and UAS scores by sentence length in bins of length 10. It is not surprising that all parsers produce better results for shorter sentences. For sentences shorter than 10 words, all LAS and UAS scores are around 80% and 85%, respectively. However, the scores drop by $10^+\%$ for sentences longer than 50 words. The Malt parser obtains the lowest LAS and UAS scores across all sentence bins. BistG obtains the highest scores for sentences shorter than 20 words while BistT obtains highest scores for sentences longer than 40 words. BistG, BistT and MST perform similarly on 30-to-40-word sentences. For shorter sentences from 20 to 30 words, BistG and BistT produce similar results but higher than obtained by MST.

Dependency distance: Figures 3 and 4 show F_1 scores in terms of the distance from each dependent word to its head. Similar to English (Choi et al., 2015), we find better predictions for the left dependencies than for the right dependencies. Unlike in English where the lower scores are associated with longer distances, we find a different pattern when predicting the left dependencies

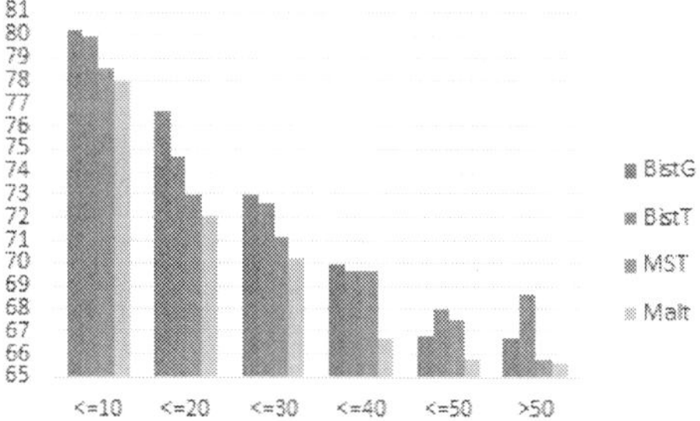

Figure 1: LAS by sentence length.

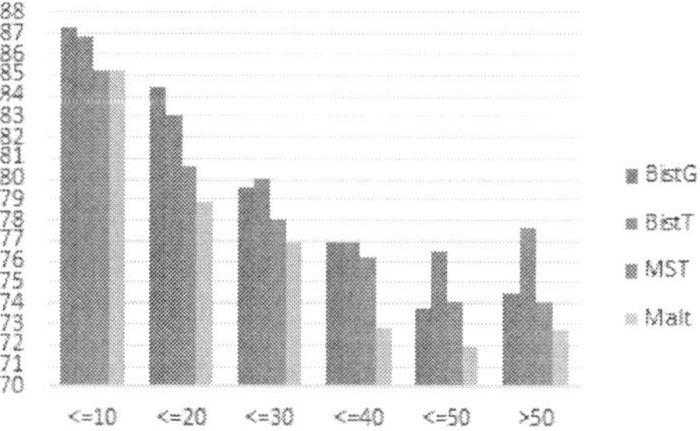

Figure 2: UAS by sentence length

in Vietnamese. In a distance bin of 3, 4 and 5 words with respect to the left dependencies, three over four parsers including BistG, BistT and Malt generally obtain better predictions for longer distances. Compared to English, Vietnamese is head-initial, so finding a difference with respect to left dependencies is not completely unexpected. In addition, for this distance bin, the transition-based parser does better than the graph-based parser in both neural net-based and traditional categories (i.e. BistT > BistG and Malt > MST). In both those categories, however, the graph-based parser does better than the transition-based parser for 5-word-longer distances (i.e. BistG > BistT and MST > Malt), while they produce similar results on dependency distances of 1 or 2 words.

---

[7]The differences are statistically significant at $p < 0.02$.

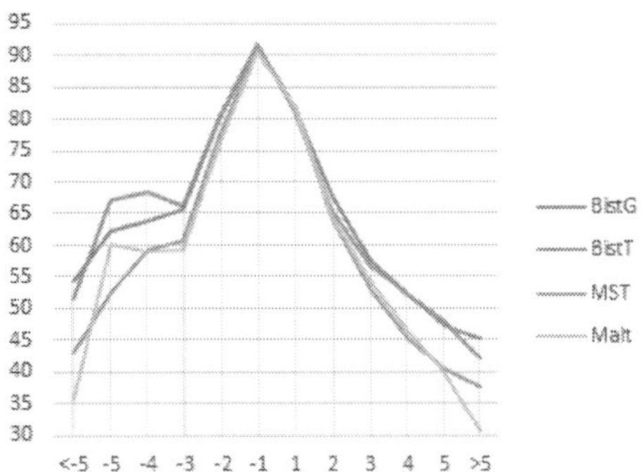

Figure 3: F_1 scores by dependency distance for labeled attachment

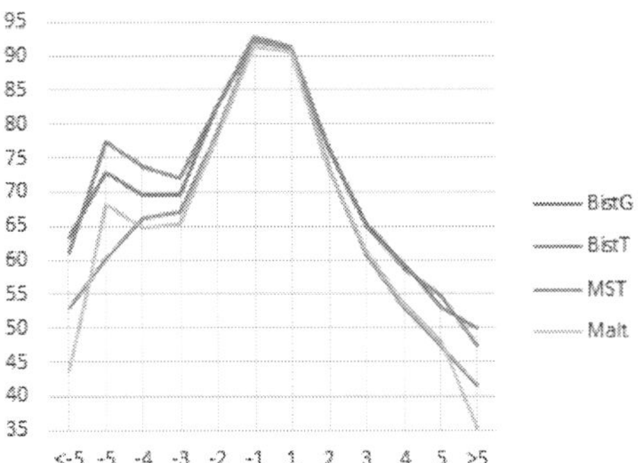

Figure 4: F_1 scores by dependency distance for unlabeled attachment

Because the dependency distance of 3, 4 or 5 occurs quite frequently in long sentences, so the results here are consistent with the results shown in Figures 1 and 2 where BistT obtains the highest scores for long sentences.

Dependency labels: Table 3 presents LAS scores for the most frequent dependency labels. The labels with higher than 90% accuracy are *adv*, *det* and *pob* in which surprisingly MST obtains the best results on all these labels and even on both *conj* and *dob* labels. BistT obtains the best scores on the two most frequent labels *nmod* and *vmod*, and also on the *loc* label. BistG performs best on the remaining labels. Biggest ranges ($> 10\%$) of obtained scores across parsers associate to labels *coord*, *dep*, *sub* and *tmp*.

Table 3 also shows that the label with the lowest LAS scores ($< 50\%$) across all parsers is *dep* which is a very general label. Those with LAS scores ranging from 50% to about 60% are *coord*, *loc*, *tmp* and *vmod* in which *coord*, *loc* and *tmp* are among the least frequent labels, while *vmod* is the second most frequent label.

Type	BistG	BistT	MST	Malt	Avg.
adv	92.09	**92.40**	**92.40**	92.33	92.31
amod	**77.30**	73.89	76.11	73.21	75.13
conj	74.82	73.11	**78 .00**	71.64	74.39
coord	**57.49**	49.52	46.14	52.66	51.45
dep	**47.83**	46 .00	32.54	42.08	42.11
det	94.15	94.30	**95.27**	94.52	94.56
dob	73.01	70.81	**78.62**	76.35	74.70
loc	52.54	**53.86**	51.43	50.77	52.15
nmod	79.34	**79.51**	78.10	76.67	78.41
pob	94.35	95.27	**96.18**	95.85	95.41
root	**85.69**	82.55	82.06	74.41	81.18
sub	**73.34**	72.61	66.49	62.67	68.78
tmp	**60.68**	57.05	44.66	41.45	50.96
vmod	61.51	**62.02**	60.79	60.23	61.14

Table 3: LAS by most frequent dependency labels. "Avg." denotes the averaged score of four parsers.

POS	LAS				UAS			
	BistG	BistT	MST	Malt	BistG	BistT	MST	Malt
A	68.32	**70.31**	69.89	66.83	73.01	**75.50**	74.86	70.88
C	**55.90**	50.00	44.94	50.00	**61.33**	56.87	50.60	54.94
E	**55.47**	53.87	50.91	49.96	**72.27**	71.54	68.86	64.45
M	92.11	91.05	**93.03**	91.18	93.42	93.16	**94.21**	91.71
N	**74.37**	73.58	73.77	71.30	**83.95**	83.86	82.58	80.48
Nc	69.86	**72.02**	68.49	67.12	78.47	**79.26**	76.13	74.17
Np	84.69	84.47	**84.80**	82.84	**88.49**	**88.49**	88.06	86.43
P	79.34	**80.16**	79.69	77.23	85.45	**85.92**	84.62	82.39
R	91.94	**93.08**	92.42	92.60	92.90	**93.87**	92.96	93.27
V	**68.01**	66.49	63.78	63.13	**75.05**	74.95	71.83	70.49

Table 4: Results by most frequent POS tags.

POS tags: In Table 4 we analyze the results by the POS tag of the dependent. BistG achieves the highest results on the two most frequent POS tags *N* and *V* and also on *C* and *E*. BistT achieves the highest scores on the remaining POS tags except *M* for which MST produces the highest score.

3.3 Discussions

Linguistic aspects: One surprising characteristic of the results is the poor performance of verb-related dependencies: *vmod* accuracy is low, as are scores associated with the second most frequent POS tag *V* (Verb). For the latter, we find significantly lower scores for verbs in Vietnamese (around 65% as shown in Table 4) against scores for verbs (about $80^+\%$) obtained by MST and Malt parsers on 13 other languages reported in McDonald and Nivre (2011), and also much worse performance in terms of rank relative to other POS.

This may be related to syntactic characteristics of Vietnamese (Thompson, 1987). First, Vietnamese is described as a copula-drop language. Consider *Cô Hà có nhà đẹp* "Miss Hà has a beautiful house", where the attributive adjective *đẹp*

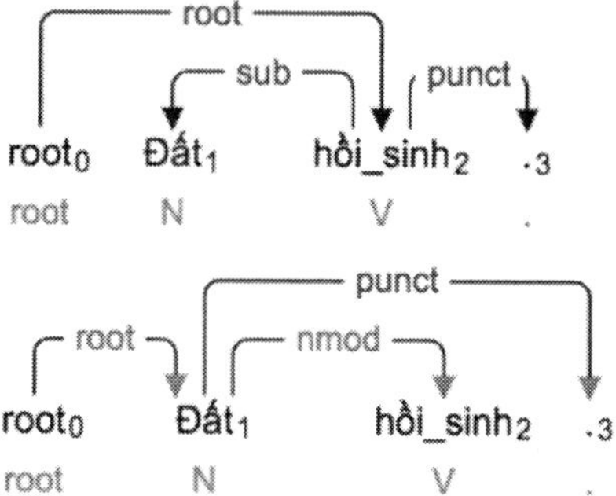

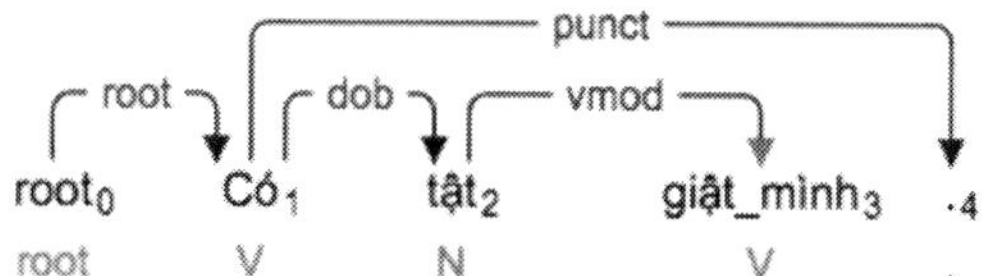

Figure 5: An example of a Vietnamese sentence with copula-drop. The first parsed tree is the gold one while the second parsed tree is the same output produced by all parsers. This sentence is translated to English as "the land$_{\#1}$ is revived$_{\#2}$.", in which the copula "is" is dropped in Vietnamese. The subscripts in the English-translated sentence refer to alignments with the word indexes in the Vietnamese sentence.

"beautiful" postmodifies the noun *nhà* "house". Adjectives can also be predicative, where they are conventionally labelled *V* (Verb), and a copula is absent: with Vietnamese's SVO word order, this is also *nhà đẹp* "the house is beautiful." Figure 5 presents an example from the treebank: all four parsers produce the incorrect structure, which is what would be expected for the attributive adjectival use in an NP. This construction is quite common in Vietnamese.

Second, Vietnamese permits verb serialization, as in Figure 6: *giật_mình* "accuses" should be a *vmod* dependent of *có* "excuses"; such a construction is analogous to the more familiar *nmod* in other languages. Verb dependencies in Vietnamese might thus be less predictable than in other languages, with a more varied distribution of dependents.

Other aspects: Generally, one reason for low overall scores on Vietnamese dependency parsing when compared to the scores obtained on the other languages (McDonald and Nivre, 2011) is probably because of the complex structures of many long sentences in the VnDT treebank (e.g. 45% of the sentences in VnDT consist of more than 20 words). So we can only obtain 60% and 50% for left and right dependency distances larger than 5 as shown in Figure 4, respectively, while for English both left and right dependencies with distances larger than 5 have greater than 70% accuracy (Choi et al., 2015).

Figure 6: An example of a Vietnamese sentence with verb serialization (and pronoun-dropping), parsed by BistT. The gold parsed tree is when the indexed-3 word is attached to the indexed-1 word by *vmod*, instead of the indexed-2 word. For this sentence, BistG, MST and Malt attach the indexed-3 word to be dependent to the indexed-2 word by the label *nmod*. This sentence is translated to English as "He who excuses$_{\#1}$ himself$_{\#2}$, accuses$_{\#3}$ himself ."

Oracle	With punct.			Without punct.		
	LAS	UAS	LS	LAS	UAS	LS
Tree	79.20	85.22	88.38	79.33	86.24	86.66
Arc	85.98	90.50	92.67	85.96	91.14	91.57

Table 5: Upper bound of ensemble performance.

One simple approach to improve parsing performance for Vietnamese is to separately use the graph-based parser BistG for short sentences and the transition-based parser BistT for longer sentences. Another approach is to use system combination (Nivre and McDonald, 2008; Zhang and Clark, 2008), e.g. building ensemble systems (Sagae and Tsujii, 2007; Surdeanu and Manning, 2010; Haffari et al., 2011). Table 5 presents an upper bound of oracle ensemble performance, using the DEPENDABLE toolkit (Choi et al., 2015). DEPENDABLE assumes that either the best tree or the best arc can be determined by an oracle.

4 Conclusions

We have presented an empirical comparison for Vietnamese dependency parsing. Experimental results on the Vietnamese dependency treebank VnDT (Nguyen et al., 2014b) show that the neural network-based parsers (Kiperwasser and Goldberg, 2016b) obtain significantly higher scores than the traditional parsers (McDonald et al., 2005; Nivre et al., 2007b). More specifically, in each graph- or transition-based type, we find a 2% absolute improvement of the neural network-based parser over the traditional one.

We report the highest performance up to date for Vietnamese dependency parsing with LAS at 73.53% and UAS at 80.66%.

Acknowledgments

The first author is supported by an International Postgraduate Research Scholarship and a NICTA NRPA Top-Up Scholarship.

References

Daniel Andor, Chris Alberti, David Weiss, Aliaksei Severyn, Alessandro Presta, Kuzman Ganchev, Slav Petrov, and Michael Collins. 2016. Globally Normalized Transition-Based Neural Networks. In *Proceedings of the 54th Annual Meeting of the Association for Computational Linguistics*, pages 2442–2452.

Bernd Bohnet. 2010. Very high accuracy and fast dependency parsing is not a contradiction. In *Proceedings of the 23rd International Conference on Computational Linguistics*, pages 89–97.

Sabine Buchholz and Erwin Marsi. 2006. CoNLL-X shared task on multilingual dependency parsing. In *Proceedings of the Tenth Conference on Computational Natural Language Learning, CoNLL-X*, pages 149–164.

Danqi Chen and Christopher Manning. 2014. A fast and accurate dependency parser using neural networks. In *Proceedings of the 2014 Conference on Empirical Methods in Natural Language Processing*, pages 740–750.

Jinho D. Choi and Andrew McCallum. 2013. Transition-based dependency parsing with selectional branching. In *Proceedings of the 51st Annual Meeting of the Association for Computational Linguistics*, pages 1052–1062.

Jinho D. Choi, Joel Tetreault, and Amanda Stent. 2015. It Depends: Dependency Parser Comparison Using A Web-based Evaluation Tool. In *Proceedings of the 53rd Annual Meeting of the Association for Computational Linguistics and the 7th International Joint Conference on Natural Language Processing*, pages 387–396.

Chris Dyer, Miguel Ballesteros, Wang Ling, Austin Matthews, and Noah A. Smith. 2015. Transition-Based Dependency Parsing with Stack Long Short-Term Memory. In *Proceedings of the 53rd Annual Meeting of the Association for Computational Linguistics and the 7th International Joint Conference on Natural Language Processing*, pages 334–343.

Gholamreza Haffari, Marzieh Razavi, and Anoop Sarkar. 2011. An ensemble model that combines syntactic and semantic clustering for discriminative dependency parsing. In *Proceedings of the 49th Annual Meeting of the Association for Computational Linguistics: Human Language Technologies*, pages 710–714.

Sepp Hochreiter and Jürgen Schmidhuber. 1997. Long short-term memory. *Neural Computation*, 9(8):1735–1780.

Eliyahu Kiperwasser and Yoav Goldberg. 2016a. Easy-first dependency parsing with hierarchical tree lstms. *Transactions of the Association for Computational Linguistics*, 4:445–461.

Eliyahu Kiperwasser and Yoav Goldberg. 2016b. Simple and Accurate Dependency Parsing Using Bidirectional LSTM Feature Representations. *Transactions of the Association for Computational Linguistics*, 4:313–327.

Phuong Le-Hong, Thi-Minh-Huyen Nguyen, Thi-Luong Nguyen, and My-Linh Ha. 2015. Fast dependency parsing using distributed word representations. In *Proceedings of the PAKDD 2015 Workshops*, pages 261–272.

Andre Martins, Miguel Almeida, and Noah A. Smith. 2013. Turning on the Turbo: Fast Third-Order Non-Projective Turbo Parsers. In *Proceedings of the 51st Annual Meeting of the Association for Computational Linguistics (Volume 2: Short Papers)*, pages 617–622.

Ryan McDonald and Joakim Nivre. 2011. Analyzing and integrating dependency parsers. *Computational Linguistics*, 37(1):197–230.

Ryan McDonald, Koby Crammer, and Fernando Pereira. 2005. Online large-margin training of dependency parsers. In *Proceedings of the 43rd Annual Meeting on Association for Computational Linguistics*, pages 91–98.

Kiet Van Nguyen and Ngan Luu-Thuy Nguyen. 2015. Error Analysis for Vietnamese Dependency Parsing. In *Proceedings of the 2015 Seventh International Conference on Knowledge and Systems Engineering*, pages 79–84.

Phuong Thai Nguyen, Xuan Luong Vu, Thi Minh Huyen Nguyen, Van Hiep Nguyen, and Hong Phuong Le. 2009. Building a Large Syntactically-Annotated Corpus of Vietnamese. In *Proceedings of the Third Linguistic Annotation Workshop*, pages 182–185.

Dat Quoc Nguyen, Dai Quoc Nguyen, Dang Duc Pham, and Son Bao Pham. 2014a. RDRPOSTagger: A Ripple Down Rules-based Part-Of-Speech Tagger. In *Proceedings of the Demonstrations at the 14th Conference of the European Chapter of the Association for Computational Linguistics*, pages 17–20.

Dat Quoc Nguyen, Dai Quoc Nguyen, Son Bao Pham, Phuong-Thai Nguyen, and Minh Le Nguyen. 2014b. From Treebank Conversion to Automatic Dependency Parsing for Vietnamese. In *Proceedings of 19th International Conference on Application of Natural Language to Information Systems*, pages 196–207.

Dat Quoc Nguyen, Dai Quoc Nguyen, Dang Duc Pham, and Son Bao Pham. 2016. A robust transformation-based learning approach using ripple down rules for part-of-speech tagging. *AI Communications*, 29(3):409–422.

Joakim Nivre and Ryan McDonald. 2008. Integrating Graph-Based and Transition-Based Dependency Parsers. In *Proceedings of ACL-08: HLT*, pages 950–958.

Joakim Nivre, Johan Hall, Sandra Kübler, Ryan McDonald, Jens Nilsson, Sebastian Riedel, and Deniz Yuret. 2007a. The CoNLL 2007 Shared Task on Dependency Parsing. In *Proceedings of the CoNLL Shared Task Session of EMNLP-CoNLL 2007*, pages 915–932.

Joakim Nivre, Johan Hall, Jens Nilsson, Atanas Chanev, Gülsen Eryigit, Sandra Kübler, Svetoslav Marinov, and Erwin Marsi. 2007b. MaltParser: A language-independent system for data-driven dependency parsing. *Natural Language Engineering*, 13(January):1.

Wenzhe Pei, Tao Ge, and Baobao Chang. 2015. An effective neural network model for graph-based dependency parsing. In *Proceedings of the 53rd Annual Meeting of the Association for Computational Linguistics and the 7th International Joint Conference on Natural Language Processing*, pages 313–322.

Kenji Sagae and Jun'ichi Tsujii. 2007. Dependency parsing and domain adaptation with LR models and parser ensembles. In *Proceedings of the CoNLL Shared Task Session of EMNLP-CoNLL 2007*, pages 1044–1050.

M. Schuster and K.K. Paliwal. 1997. Bidirectional recurrent neural networks. *IEEE Transactions on Signal Processing*, 45(11):2673–2681.

Mihai Surdeanu and Christopher D. Manning. 2010. Ensemble models for dependency parsing: Cheap and good? In *Human Language Technologies: The 2010 Annual Conference of the North American Chapter of the Association for Computational Linguistics*, pages 649–652.

Luong Nguyen Thi, Linh Ha My, Hung Nguyen Viet, Huyen Nguyen Thi Minh, and Phuong Le Hong. 2013. Building a treebank for Vietnamese dependency parsing. In *Proceedings of 2013 IEEE RIVF International Conference on Computing and Communication Technologies, Research, Innovation, and Vision for the Future*, pages 147–151.

Laurence C. Thompson. 1987. *A Vietnamese Reference Grammar*. University of Hawaii Press.

Cam Vu-Manh, Anh Tuan Luong, and Phuong Le-Hong. 2015. Improving vietnamese dependency parsing using distributed word representations. In *Proceedings of the Sixth International Symposium on Information and Communication Technology*, pages 54–60.

David Weiss, Chris Alberti, Michael Collins, and Slav Petrov. 2015. Structured training for neural network transition-based parsing. In *Proceedings of the 53rd Annual Meeting of the Association for Computational Linguistics and the 7th International Joint Conference on Natural Language Processing*, pages 323–333.

Yue Zhang and Stephen Clark. 2008. A Tale of Two Parsers: Investigating and Combining Graph-based and Transition-based Dependency Parsing. In *Proceedings of the 2008 Conference on Empirical Methods in Natural Language Processing*, pages 562–571.

Yue Zhang and Joakim Nivre. 2011. Transition-based dependency parsing with rich non-local features. In *Proceedings of the 49th Annual Meeting of the Association for Computational Linguistics: Human Language Technologies*, pages 188–193.

📞💀⛵🐋🖐 ; or "Call me Ishmael" – How do you translate emoji?

Will Radford   **Andrew Chisholm**   **Ben Hachey**   **Bo Han**

Hugo.ai

58-62 Kippax Street

Surry Hills

NSW 2010

(wradford|achisholm|bhachey|bhan)@hugo.ai

Abstract

We report on an exploratory analysis of Emoji Dick, a project that leverages crowdsourcing to translate Melville's Moby Dick into emoji. This distinctive use of emoji removes textual context, and leads to a varying translation quality. In this paper, we use statistical word alignment and part-of-speech tagging to explore how people use emoji. Despite these simple methods, we observed differences in token and part-of-speech distributions. Experiments also suggest that semantics are preserved in the translation, and repetition is more common in emoji.

1 Introduction

Emoji are pictographic characters commonly used in informal written communication, originally in SMS messages, but increasingly in all social media. Emoji represents a range of faces, animals, weather, emotions and activities, compensating for a lack of verbal and non-verbal cues in face-to-face communication (Davis and Edberg, 2016; Dresner and Herring, 2010). Widespread support for emoji input on desktops and mobile devices has led to a rapid adoption of emoji as a communication tool and a part of popular culture, spawning a *Word of the Year* in 2015 (Oxford Dictionaries, 2015) and, somewhat dubiously, a feature film slated for a 2017 release (IMDb, 2016). Davis and Edberg (2016) also suggest that the limited coverage and a lack of formal grammar in emoji lead to multiple ambiguous messages, and point out the playful aspect of composing and decoding emoji. At its tersest, this can result in a film plot encoded into a single tweet (MacLachlan, 2016): "🌑💧...⛏...🗡#dune". Despite heavy constraints of its form, emoji are used in some surprising linguistic contexts that merit further study.

TEXT	EMOJI
MOBY DICK; OR THE WHALE	🐋
CHAPTER 1.	🖐1️⃣🐋🐋
Loomings.	👀🍴🐷😮😮
Call me Ishmael.	📞💀⛵🐋🖐

Figure 1: The title and first lines of Emoji Dick.

Most analysis of emoji considers its usual context amongst regular text, focusing on geographic preferences (Swiftkey, 2015; Ljubešić and Fišer, 2016), single-word translations (Dimson, 2015) and sentiment (Kralj Novak et al., 2015). Other work has focused on emoticons (e.g. ":)"), uncovering stylistic variation (Schnoebelen, 2012) and demographic factors associated with usage (Hovy et al., 2015). Different types of ambiguity have also been identified: subjective interpretations of symbols, as well as different renderings of what should be the same symbol (Miller et al., 2016). Mitchell et al. (2015) observe that emoji are less likely to occur in the language of schizophrenics, possibly related to a "flat affect" symptom of the mental disorder.

This paper analyses a specific instance where emoji have been used in a context usually reserved for fully-fledged languages. Emoji Dick (Benenson, 2010) is a fascinating project that used Amazon Mechanical Turk to translate the novel "Moby-Dick; or, The Whale" (Melville, 1851) into emoji (e.g. Figure 1). Three turkers were paid $0.05 to translate each sentence, and a second round of turkers paid $0.02 to vote for the best translation. Funded entirely by donations through the crowdsourcing platform Kickstarter, soft- and hard-bound copies are available for sale. The idiosyncratic nature of the task raises several key questions: how does one translate a work from the English literary canon into emojis? And, what can statistical analysis techniques from natural language processing tell us about it?

Will Radford, Ben Hachey, Bo Han and Andy Chisholm. 2016. :telephone::person::sailboat::whale::okhand: ; or âĂIJCall me IshmaelâĂİ âĂŞ How do you translate emoji? In *Proceedings of Australasian Language Technology Association Workshop*, pages 150–154.

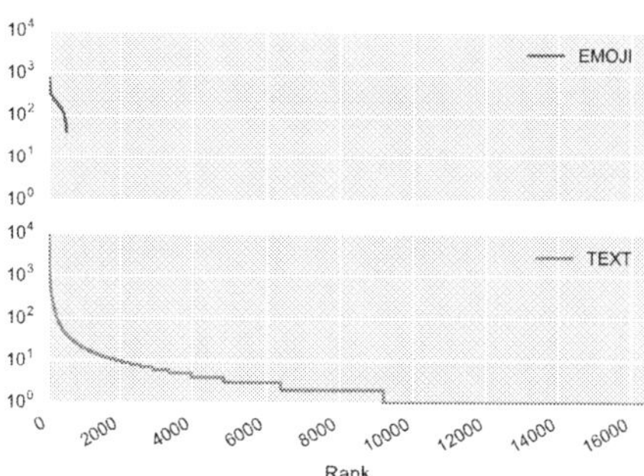

Figure 2: Log-counts of emoji and tokens at different ranks.

2 Corpus Analysis

The dataset contains 9,971 pairs of text and emoji translations. We tokenise the text using the default tokeniser from NLTK (Bird et al., 2009). Digits and stopwords are removed and all tokens are lowercased.

The descriptive statistics of the two corpora, TEXT and EMOJI, show a few differences. TEXT has a larger and sparser vocabulary than EMOJI when constructing sentences. There are 207,194 text tokens (16,454 types) and 93,342 emoji tokens (470 types). Furthermore, emoji sentences are roughly half the length of textual sentences with respective means of 9.4 to 20.8. Figure 2 plots the log-counts of two corpora token or emoji frequencies against their ranks. As is common in Zipfian distributions, the TEXT frequencies quickly reduce with rank, but EMOJI has a heavier tail and no approach to low frequencies.

Table 1 shows the 20 most common tokens and emoji. Unsurprisingly, "whale" is the most common non-stopword token, while other thematic tokens (e.g. "man", "ship", "sea", "boat") and character names (e.g. "ahab", "captain"') are also common. The three most common emoji reference characters: people (e.g. 🐳🐋🐙), and, of course, 🐋. Less obvious emoji include references to objects (e.g. ➖⚓🐟) and places (e.g. 🏯), though not 🐋 or 🐋 as found in the common tokens. Symbols (e.g. ✖❓❗) are also present, as are other non-facial body parts (e.g. •• 👃).

3 Aligning emoji to tokens

The analysis above makes no attempt to characterise how TEXT was translated to EMOJI. To explore this, we learn an IBM translation model one

Token	n	Emoji	n
whale	1029	🐳	743
one	898	🐋	724
like	572	🐋	669
upon	561	➖	637
ahab	511	⚓	626
man	497	🐋	607
ship	464	🔪	598
old	435	⚙	574
ye	433	🏯	556
would	429	✖	537
though	380	❓	511
sea	367	⚓	496
yet	344	❗	442
time	325	••	439
captain	323	🐋	438
long	315	🐋	419
still	312	👃	415
said	299	❗	407
great	288	🐋	399
boat	286	🐋	379

Table 1: The top 20 tokens and emoji by individual frequency.

(Brown et al., 1993) using NLTK's implementation with default parameters. We prepare the parallel text by removing English stopwords and punctuation and filtering pairs missing input or output, leaving 9,734 pairs. We opt for the simplest model with the fewest assumptions about the "language pair", but with the caveat that it does not account well for token phrases aligning to a single emoji, as a phrase-based translation model might allow. We did explore some of the more advanced IBM models and sequence-to-sequence neural models (Sutskever et al., 2014), but these did not seem to yield readily-interpretable results. Recall that despite turkers vote for the best translations, the translations are expected to be extremely noisy, due to the high subjectivity of human emoji comprehension, and the scarcity of native speakers.

Having trained the model over 100 iterations, we examine the translation table and find the most probable alignment from token to emoji. Table 2 shows the top-20 emoji ranked by their strongest individual alignment with the tokens that they align to. The most commonly-aligned emoji, 🐋 aligns to "whale", "sperm" and "whales", as does 🐋. Rather less satisfying is the strong alignments of "whale" to 🐋, and ϵ where a token aligned to

e	t	p	t	p	t	p	e	t	p	t	p	t	p
(emoji)	whale	.23	sperm	.06	whales	.05	(emoji)	man	.07	men	.05	ahab	.02
(emoji)	chapter	.15	book	.05	read	.03	(emoji)	ship	.07	lay	.02	vessel	.02
ϵ	one	.11	whale	.11	like	.06	(emoji)	bed	.06	good	.03	sleeping	.02
(emoji)	chapter	.10	two	.02	one	.02	(emoji)	whale	.06	among	.03	sperm	.03
(emoji)	captain	.08	sir	.06	know	.02	(emoji)	good	.06	things	.03	man	.03
(emoji)	sun	.08	sunrise	.03	air	.03	(emoji)	water	.06	sea	.05	round	.02
(emoji)	chapter	.08	straight	.02	beheld	.01	(emoji)	death	.05	life	.03	dead	.03
(emoji)	see	.08	eyes	.05	seen	.03	(emoji)	whales	.05	sperm	.03	ancient	.02
(emoji)	boat	.07	ship	.03	boats	.03	(emoji)	oh	.05	aye	.02	old	.02
(emoji)	hand	.07	say	.03	stop	.03	(emoji)	whales	.05	starbuck	.02	fossil	.02

Table 2: The top-20 emoji by alignment probability ($p(e|t)$), and the top 3 tokens they align to. We also list ϵ as some tokens (i.e. "one, whale, like") *align away* with relatively high probability.

nothing, showing the extent of the noise and the tendency of the model to align away tokens. Plural forms align well, as do synonyms (e.g. "boat", "ship" and "boats" align to (emoji)). Other alignments cover formal elements such as chapter headings ((emoji)) and characters ((emoji)(emoji)), natural phenomena ((emoji) (emoji) (emoji)), actions ((emoji) (emoji) (emoji)) and sentiments ((emoji)). Overall, most high-probability alignments seem reasonable, suggesting some consistency between translations.

4 Emoji parts-of-speech

We apply the BookNLP pipeline (Bamman et al., 2014) to the original text, which predicts part-of-speech (POS) tags, character clusters and many other linguistic metadata. Again, we expect this to be noisy, as the models are not adapted to 19th century literature. Nonetheless, we are able to create a distribution of noisy POS tags[1] for each token, then induce a distribution of POS for each emoji, by applying the chain rule and alignment probabilities above. Most emoji are NN, with the highest probability (emoji). Only 5 emoji have a different majority POS prefix – VB – including (emoji) (i.e. "see" or "seen" from Table 2). Although the low probabilities and compounded noise of the model mean the results are hardly compelling, it is interesting that some emoji seem to align more strongly to verbs, suggesting their consistent use as actions. This preponderance of NN and VB alignments supports the observation made elsewhere that emoji have features in common with pidgin languages (Rosefield, 2014; Stockton, 2015).

Accumulating the POS probabilities for ac-

Emoji	$p(VB|e)$	Emoji	$p(NN|e)$
(emoji)	.37	(emoji)	.70
(emoji)	.36	(emoji)	.56
(emoji)	.30	(emoji)	.55
(emoji)	.29	(emoji)	.53
(emoji)	.29	(emoji)	.52

Table 3: The top-5 emoji for VB and NN POS.

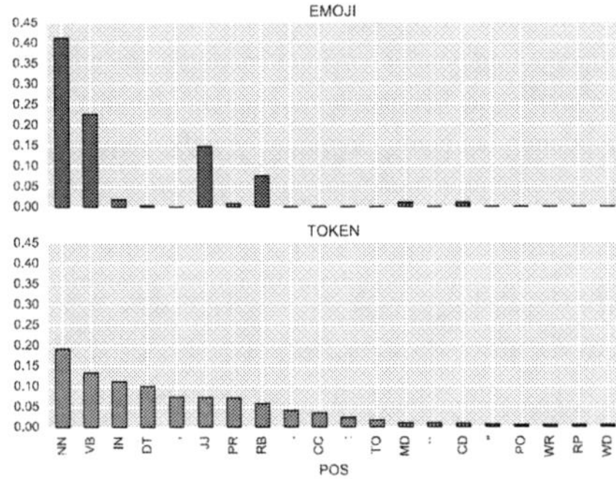

Figure 3: POS probability distributions.

tual occurrence of tokens or emojis, we are able to characterise the whole distribution. Figure 3 shows that emoji concentrate mass into fewer categories: NN, JJ, RB and VB.

5 Modelling repeats in emoji

As emoji are often used to convey extra layers of emotion or context, we examine how emoji are repeated. Counting common bigrams of emoji, the most frequently emoji repeat-bigrams are (emoji)(emoji) followed by (emoji)(emoji), ! ! and (emoji)(emoji). The probability of repeat-bigrams is much higher in emoji at 3.2% as opposed to 0.4% in text, indicating that there is a

---

[1] We attempt to reduce noise by considering the only the first two characters of the POS tag. NNP and NNS as NN.

systematic difference in usage, although it is not clear whether they are used as intensifiers ("very strong") or counting mechanisms ("many boys").

6 Discussion

As intriguing as the dataset is, there are substantial challenges to working with it and drawing strong conclusions. Firstly, the setting is idiosyncratic and unlike standard current emoji usage, as it lacks the textual context in which emoji are usually found. Thus, findings in these contexts may not necessarily hold when applied to emoji found in informal discourse on the web. Indeed, a promising direction seems to be to learn embedding models that allow an elegant fusion of textual and emoji content (Barbieri et al., 2016; Eisner et al., 2016). The constraints of the limited vocabulary foster a creativity that, combined with the desire of the translator to produce a witty translation, only serves to increase the subjectivity of the dataset. This is exacerbated by the small size of the dataset, and while there are ordinal constraints in emoji (Schnoebelen, 2012), whether they hold for longer sequences is not clear.

The next issue to examine in future work is the failure of phrase-based translation models in this context, as this might uncover more interesting translations, as well as shed light on strange alignments (e.g. "whale" to ϵ). Data collection is also important, as lack of data could prohibit more sophisticated models. Moreover, collecting a dataset in a more natural context, such as chat or social message data, might lead to more immediately-applicable conclusions. Exploring whether there is strong evidence for a consistent interpretation of emoji repeats using analysis of the textual corpus would be interesting. Multi-lingual differences in emoji usage are compelling – do certain languages exhibit features that correlate with different emoji usage? Moreover, emoji may be a productive pivot upon which to align web-scale bitext, which may drive other semantic resources such as paraphrase databases (Ganitkevitch et al., 2013). The overarching direction of this work are to characterise broader temporal trends about how people use emoji, how a community of users settles on specific interpretations of emoji and, perhaps, uncover more evidence for or against the hypothesis that emoji is a pidgin.

7 Conclusion

This paper presents a pilot study on how emoji are used in an unusual setting – verbatim translation. We use NLP techniques to compare the statistical properties of the two corpora (EMOJI and TEXT), showing that emoji operate in a far smaller space. Statistical alignment models from machine translation allow us to explore how translators mapped emoji onto tokens, including plural and synonymous forms. We also considered a noisily-induced POS distribution, showing that most emoji are nouns, with a few operating most frequently as verbs, and that the emoji POS distribution places weights on nouns and verbs, a phenomenon that bears some similarity to pidgins. Finally, we briefly explore how emoji are repeated, finding a much higher rate of repetition in emoji than text. Emoji offer a rare opportunity to study a rapidly evolving and increasingly important mode of communication that is complementary to text and speech and has parallels to human languages like pidgins.

Acknowledgments

Many thanks to Fred Benenson and Chris Mulligan for having the wit to create the project and share the data ⚙📖. Thanks also to the reviewers and readers at Hugo.ai for their insightful comments 🙏💬.

References

[Bamman et al.2014] David Bamman, Ted Underwood, and Noah A. Smith. 2014. A bayesian mixed effects model of literary character. In *Proceedings of the 52nd Annual Meeting of the Assoc. for Computational Linguistics (Volume 1: Long Papers)*, pages 370–379, Baltimore, Maryland, June. Assoc. for Computational Linguistics.

[Barbieri et al.2016] Francesco Barbieri, Francesco Ronzano, and Horacio Saggion. 2016. What does this emoji mean? a vector space skip-gram model for twitter emojis. In *Language Resources and Evaluation conference, LREC*, Portoroz, Slovenia, May.

[Benenson2010] Fred Benenson. 2010. Emoji dick. http://www.emojidick.com.

[Bird et al.2009] Steven Bird, Ewan Klein, and Edward Loper. 2009. *Natural Language Processing with Python*. O'Reilly Media.

[Brown et al.1993] Peter F. Brown, Vincent J. Della Pietra, Stephen A. Della Pietra, and Robert L. Mercer. 1993. The mathematics of statistical machine translation: Parameter estimation. *Computational Linguistics*, 19(2):263–311, June.

[Davis and Edberg2016] Mark Davis and Peter Edberg. 2016. Unicode® technical report 51 - unicode emoji. Technical report, Unicode, June.

[Dimson2015] Thomas Dimson. 2015. Emojineering part 1: Machine learning for emoji trends. `http://instagram-engineering.tumblr.com/post/117889701472/emojineering-part-1-machine-learning-for-emoji`.

[Dresner and Herring2010] Eli Dresner and Susan C. Herring. 2010. Functions of the non-verbal in cmc: Emoticons and illocutionary force. *Communication Theory*, 20:249–268.

[Eisner et al.2016] Ben Eisner, Tim Rocktäschel, Isabelle Augenstein, Matko Bosnjak, and Sebastian Riedel. 2016. emoji2vec: Learning emoji representations from their description. In *Proceedings of The Fourth International Workshop on Natural Language Processing for Social Media*, pages 48–54, Austin, TX, USA, November. Association for Computational Linguistics.

[Ganitkevitch et al.2013] Juri Ganitkevitch, Benjamin Van Durme, and Chris Callison-Burch. 2013. PPDB: The paraphrase database. In *Proceedings of NAACL-HLT*, pages 758–764, Atlanta, Georgia, June. Association for Computational Linguistics.

[Hovy et al.2015] Dirk Hovy, Anders Johannsen, and Anders Søgaard. 2015. User review sites as a resource for large-scale sociolinguistic studies. In *Proceedings of the 24th International Conference on World Wide Web*, WWW '15, pages 452–461, New York, NY, USA. ACM.

[IMDb2016] IMDb. 2016. Emojimovie: Express yourself. `http://www.imdb.com/title/tt4877122/`, June.

[Kralj Novak et al.2015] Petra Kralj Novak, Jasmina Smailović, Borut Sluban, and Igor Mozetič. 2015. Sentiment of emojis. *PLoS ONE*, 10(12):1–22, 12.

[Ljubešić and Fišer2016] Nikola Ljubešić and Darja Fišer. 2016. A global analysis of emoji usage, August.

[MacLachlan2016] Kyle MacLachlan. 2016. Tweet in response to "@kyle_maclachlan can you explain dune to me please" by lifeofkeira. `https://twitter.com/Kyle_MacLachlan/status/765390472604971009`.

[Melville1851] Herman Melville. 1851. *Moby-Dick; or, The Whale*. Bentley, Richard.

[Miller et al.2016] Hannah Jean Miller, Jacob Thebault-Spieker, Shuo Chang, Isaac L. Johnson, Loren G. Terveen, and Brent Hecht. 2016. "blissfully happy" or "ready to fight": Varying interpretations of emoji. In *Proceedings of the Tenth International Conference on Web and Social Media, Cologne, Germany, May 17-20, 2016.*, pages 259–268. AAAI Press.

[Mitchell et al.2015] Margaret Mitchell, Kristy Hollingshead, and Glen Coppersmith. 2015. Quantifying the language of schizophrenia in social media. In *Proceedings of the 2nd Workshop on Computational Linguistics and Clinical Psychology: From Linguistic Signal to Clinical Reality*, pages 11–20, Denver, Colorado, June 5. Assoc. for Computational Linguistics.

[Oxford Dictionaries2015] Oxford Dictionaries. 2015. Oxford dictionaries word of the year 2015 is.... `http://blog.oxforddictionaries.com/2015/11/word-of-the-year-2015-emoji/`, November.

[Rosefield2014] Hannah Rosefield. 2014. Could emoji ever be a language? `http://motherboard.vice.com/read/could-emoji-ever-be-a-language`, March.

[Schnoebelen2012] Tyler Schnoebelen. 2012. Do you smile with your nose? stylistic variation in twitter emoticons. *University of Pennsylvania Working Papers in Linguistics*, 18(2).

[Stockton2015] Nick Stockton. 2015. Emoji—trendy slang or a whole new language? `https://www.wired.com/2015/06/emojitrendy-slang-whole-new-language`, June.

[Sutskever et al.2014] Ilya Sutskever, Oriol Vinyals, and Quoc V. Le. 2014. Sequence to sequence learning with neural networks. In Zoubin Ghahramani, Max Welling, Corinna Cortes, Neil D. Lawrence, and Kilian Q. Weinberger, editors, *Advances in Neural Information Processing Systems 27: Annual Conference on Neural Information Processing Systems 2014, December 8-13 2014, Montreal, Quebec, Canada*, pages 3104–3112.

[Swiftkey2015] Swiftkey. 2015. Most-used emoji revealed: Americans love skulls, brazilians love cats, the french love hearts. `https://blog.swiftkey.com/americans-love-skulls-brazilians-love-cats-swiftkey-emoji-meanings-report/`, April.

Presenting a New Dataset for the Timeline Generation Problem

Xavier Holt
University of Sydney
`xhol4115@`
`uni.sydney.edu.au`

Will Radford
Hugo.ai
`wradford@`
`hugo.ai`

Ben Hachey
University of Sydney
`ben.hachey@`
`sydney.edu.au`

Abstract

The timeline generation task summarises an entity's biography by selecting stories representing key events from a large pool of relevant documents. This paper addresses the lack of a standard dataset and evaluative methodology for the problem.

We present and make publicly available a new dataset of 18,793 news articles covering 39 entities. For each entity, we provide a gold standard timeline and a set of entity-related articles. We propose ROUGE as an evaluation metric and validate our dataset by showing that top Google results outperform straw-man baselines.

1 Introduction

Information is more readily available in greater quantities than ever before. Timeline generation is a recent method for summarising data – taking a large pool of entity-related documents as input and selecting a small set that best describe the key events in the entity's life. There are several challenges in evaluation: (1) finding gold-standard timelines, (2) finding corpora from which to draw documents to build timelines, and (3) evaluating system timelines.

Standard practice for the first challenge is to make use of existing timelines produced by news agencies (Chieu and Lee, 2004; Yan et al., 2011a), but these are constrained by the tight editorial focus on prominent entities and depends on well-funded news agencies. Another approach is to annotate new timelines from the web for domains of choice. Wang (2013) do this, but do not make their data available for direct comparison. Regarding the second challenge, access to the document pool used during the annotation process is also important, as any system must have a reasonable set from which to choose.

Previous approaches have used drawn on working in document summarisation, using ROUGE (Lin, 2004) to evaluate timeline generation (Chieu and Lee, 2004; Yan et al., 2011a; Yan et al., 2011b; Ahmed and Xing, 2012; Wang, 2013). This is convenient as each element in a timeline can represent a *story* which can be equivalently described by many different documents. However, previous work has not validated the use of ROUGE for evaluating timeline generation.

We present a general framework for creating a crowd-sourced datasets for evaluating timeline generation, including choosing a set of entities, deriving articles for annotation from Wikipedia, and annotating these articles to generate a gold standard.

The dataset covers a broad range of entities with different levels of news-coverage or publicity. We provide gold-standard timelines for each entity, as well as a larger pool of topically-linked documents for further development. We analyse the dataset, showing some interesting artifacts of crowd-worker importance judgements and use ROUGE evaluation to verify that the crowd-annotations correlate well with Google News[1] rankings. This reflects favourably on Google News, suggesting that it is a strong baseline for timeline generation. We release the dataset generated through this process in the hope that it will be useful in providing common benchmarks for future work on the timeline generation task.[2]

2 Data Collection

We now detail how we choose entities and collect a corpus for annotating gold-standard timelines and evaluating models. We have taken care to design a general experimental protocol that can be used to generate entities from a range of domains.

---

[1] `https://news.google.com`
[2] `https://github.com/xavi-ai/`
`tlg-dataset`

Xavier Holt, Will Radford and Ben Hachey. 2016. Presenting a New Dataset for the Timeline Generation Problem. In *Proceedings of Australasian Language Technology Association Workshop*, pages 155–159.

We begin by choosing a domain (politics) and two regions (The USA/Australia). We motivate this choice of domain by noting its large media interest, polarising entities and diverse range of topics. We choose several entities from each region a priori – 39 in total. The rest of our entity-set is then generated through a process of bootstrapping. At each iteration, we use our current entities as seeds. For each seed-entity, we performed a Google News query. An entity name was defined as either the title of the entity's Wikipedia page or {#Firstname #Lastname} if they did not have a Wiki. We choose five articles from the first page of results. For each article we manually identify all other previously unseen entities and add them to our set. We continue this process of bootstrapping, using our newly included entities as seeds for the next iteration. Once we have a sufficient number of entities, we terminate the process.

This process can be viewed as *bootstrap sampling*, weighted by the probability an entity occurs in one of the articles we retrieve. By doing so we provide a realistic set of entities with varying levels of popularity and coverage. In Section 4 we show that this process results in a wide distribution of mentions and reference-timeline sizes.

As well as relevant entities, we also provide a corpus of relevant documents from which we can construct their timelines. Each document in the corpus includes URL, publishing date and other metadata. These were obtained by performing Google News queries on our entities, and retrieving the resulting URLs. As our timelines should cover a wide range of time, we set the time-range on the query to 'archives'. This has the effect of returning articles from a broader period of time, mitigating the default recency bias.

In total, there are 15,596 articles. The minimum, median and maximum number of articles per entity was 54, 464 and 985 respectively. By including this corpus with our gold-standards we aim to provide a complete dataset for the timeline generation task.

3 Data Annotation and Gold-Standards

We present a general framework for formulating gold-standard timeline generation as an annotation task. This involves two components – using Wikipedia to generate a minimal set of sufficient links, and the formulation of the problem as an annotation task.

3.1 Article Selection

Annotation is cost-sensitive to the size of the task. As such, attempting to annotate the whole corpus of over 15,000 articles is infeasible. We propose a method to reduce the size of our task while maintaining the quality of the underlying timeline. For our article selection process, we need to fulfil the following criteria:

- Coverage: Our set of articles should have good coverage. Timelines should cover a broad range of time-periods and events. As such, the dataset we derive our reference timelines from must also share this property.

- Manageability: Each entity-article pair will be subject to a number of crowd-judgments. As such, it's important to balance coverage with total data-set size.

- Informativeness: Ideally we desire the articles to be of a high quality.

To meet these criteria, we scrape the external (non-Wiki) links from an entity's Wikipedia page. We motivate this decision by first noting the Wikipedia guidelines on verifiability[3]:

> Attribute all quotations and any material challenged or likely to be challenged to a reliable, published source using an inline citation. The cited source must clearly support the material as presented in the article.

These standards of verifiability are not universally followed. Nevertheless, where they are we expect reasonable entity coverage and informativeness. After removing invalid URLS, we identify 3,197 articles for annotation.

3.2 Crowd-task Formulation

We formulate timeline generation as an annotation task by reducing it to a simple classification problem. A single judgment is on the level of an entity-article pair. An annotator is given the first paragraph of, and a link to, the entity's Wikipedia page. They then follow a given link, and perform a two-stage classification task.

The annotators first determine whether a link is valid. A valid article is one that covers a single

---

[3]https://en.wikipedia.org/wiki/Wikipedia:Verifiability

event in the target entity's life. They then indicate the importance of an article's when considering the story of the entity. There was a choice of three labels:

- Very important: key events which would be included in a one-page summary or brief of the entity.

- Somewhat important: newsworthy events that might make it into a broader Biography, but not of critical relevance.

- Not important: events which are mundane or unimportant.

For our annotations, we use the CrowdFlower[4] platform. On average, three judgments by a trusted user were made per row. A trusted user was one whose annotations agreed with our expert's across a validation set ($n = 48$) at least 80% of the time. This was then aggregated into a classification label. In addition, CrowdFlower also provides a confidence measure on each judgment – a score of agreement, weighted by trust of the crowd-worker. Gold standard timelines comprise the articles that are judged to be both 'valid' and 'very important'. There were 2,601 'valid articles' and 217 'very important'.

4 Analysis of Gold-Standards

We see that particularly prominent entities are responsible for a large portion of the articles. 'Barack Obama' and 'Donald Trump' each have over four hundred articles each. In fact, the six most prominent entities account for over half of all total articles (Figure 1).

Very Important Articles The 'very important' articles make up our gold-standard timelines. The mean and median number of articles per entity is 5.56 and 2 respectively.

There are some interesting properties that emerge. 'Barack Obama' and 'Donald Trump' each have around the same number of articles. The former has 14.6% articles deemed 'very important' – the latter only 1.5% (Figure 2). It is a given that certain entity's will be involved in more newsworthy events than others. However, to have such a large[5] discrepancy – considering to that all articles were deemed necessary to reference in an entity's Wiki – is curious. We believe the proportion

---

[4]https://www.crowdflower.com
[5]Or tremendous?

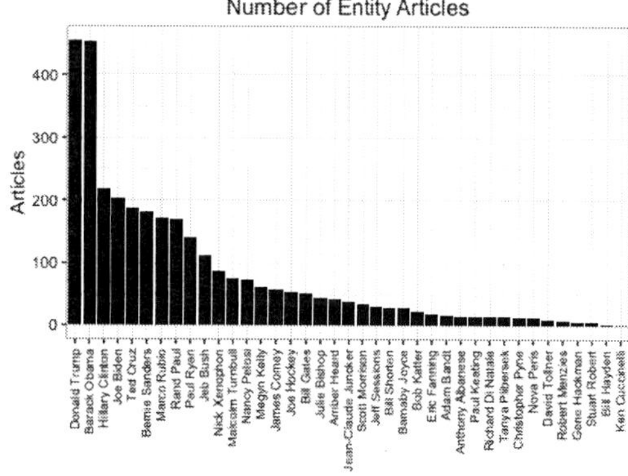

Figure 1: Number of different articles by entity. A small number of entities are responsible for a large number of articles.

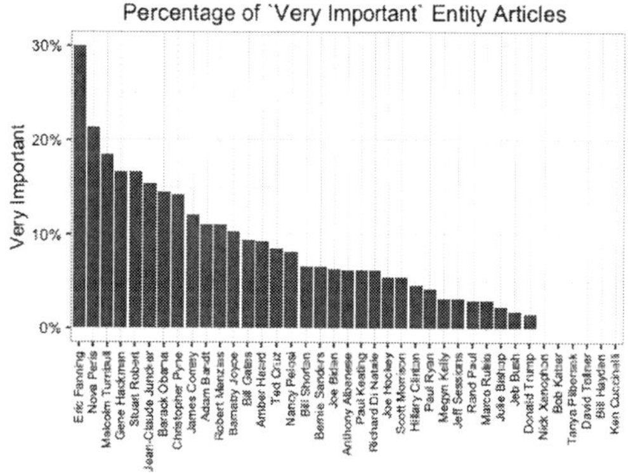

Figure 2: Percentage of very important articles by entity.

of 'very important' articles for a given entity is an interesting avenue of future research.

Confidence 'Very important' articles have a mean confidence of 0.60. Only 4.6% of articles received a unanimous 1.00 confidence score (Figure 3). However, three-quarter of the 'very important articles' had a confidence over 0.50 (Figure 4). 'Somewhat important' articles have the highest overall confidence, with a mean value of 0.76. Over a third of these articles had a confidence score of 1.00 (Figure 3). This is somewhat understandable. Intuitively, 'somewhat important' is the default prior – we would expect most articles to fall in this category.

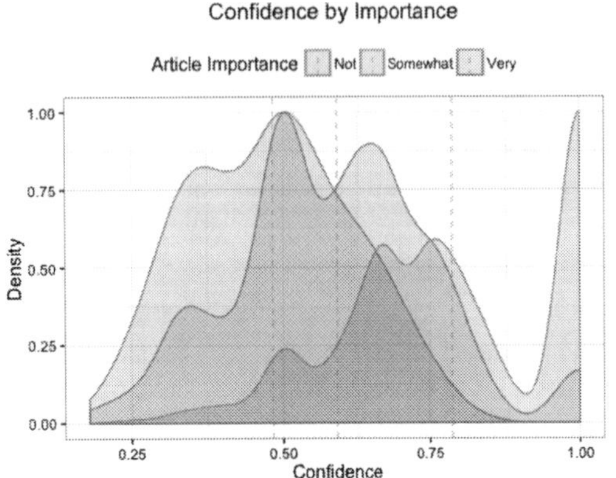

Figure 3: Distribution of confidence for three different levels of article importance. Mean-values are indicated by a dashed line.

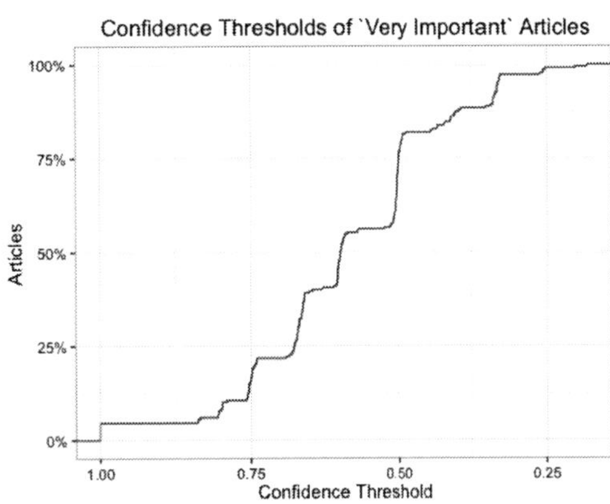

Figure 4: Percentage of 'very important' articles meeting a given confidence threshold.

5 Evaluation

For our evaluation pipeline, we adopt the approach of a number of papers in the field (Wang, 2013; Yan et al., 2011a; Yan et al., 2011b) in using the ROUGE metric (Lin, 2004). ROUGE was first used in automatic summarisation evaluation. It is similar to the BLEU measure for machine translation (Papineni et al., 2002). In terms of timeline evaluation, quality is measured by the amount of overlapping units (e.g. word n-grams) between articles in a system timeline and articles in a reference timeline. For details on how ROUGE scores are calculated, please refer to the original paper (Lin, 2004). For our purposes, articles annotated as 'valid' and 'very important' are taken to be components of an entity's reference timeline. We use the ROUGE F measure over unigrams and bi-

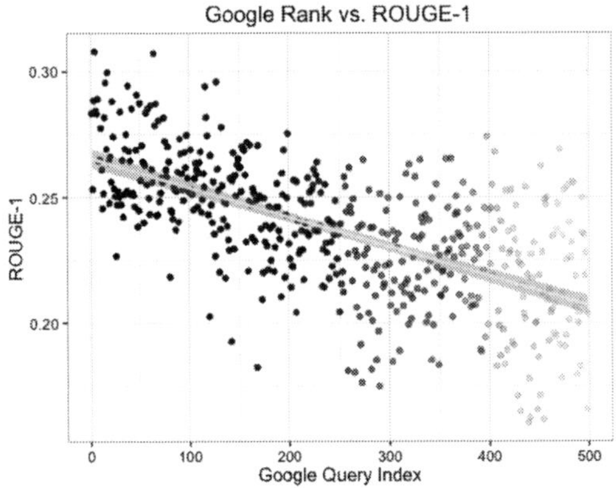

Figure 5: Google search rank for a given article vs. ROUGE score. Each point is an average across entities. The intensity of the point is a measure of confidence

grams ($n = 1, 2$).

6 Benchmarks and System Validation

In this section we use our supplemental dataset of articles generated by Google News to validate and benchmark the task.

ROUGE vs. Search Rank For a given news query, an article's rank is a signal of its important and centrality. It is reasonable to expect then that the better an article's search-rank, the more likely it is to appear in an entity's timeline. This appears to be the case. For both the ROUGE-1 and -2 measures, there is a clear negative correlation between an article's average score and index (Figure 5).

Benchmarks For a given entity timeline, we include the following three benchmarks – Random (R): 15 articles are sampled from the entire corpus. Random+Linked (RL): 15 articles linked to the entity arc sampled. Ordered+Linked (OL): the

	ROUGE-1	ROUGE-2
OL	0.290	0.051
RL	0.248	0.041
R	0.2052	0.027

Table 1: F-Scores for Benchmark Systems

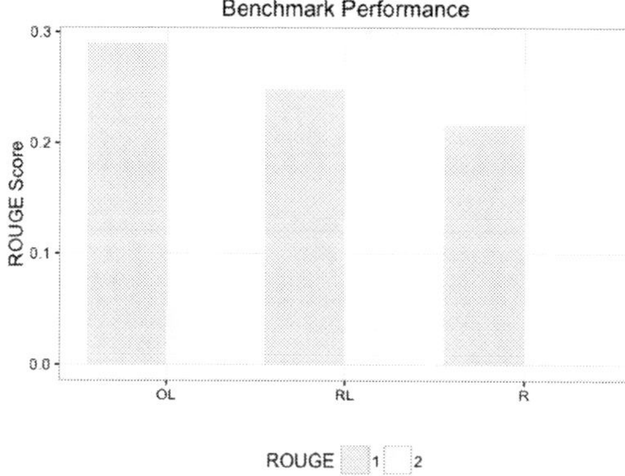

Figure 6: Benchmark performance. As expected, OL outperforms RL which in turn outperforms R for both ROUGE-1 and -2.

15 highest ranked articles for an entity are chosen. Reassuringly, we see that OL outperforms RL which outperforms R for both ROUGE-1 and ROUGE-2 scores (Figure 6). OL received scores of 0.290 (ROUGE-1) and 0.051 (ROUGE-2) (Table 1). This can be taken as a strong benchmark for future timeline generation models trained and evaluated using this dataset.

7 Conclusion and Future Work

In this paper we have developed, analysed and justified a new dataset for the timeline generation problem. There are several interesting avenues for future work. The most obvious is the development of new timeline-generation systems using this dataset. There are also still problems to be solved with the process of evaluating timeline models, but we hope that the framework described above allow researchers to easily generate evaluation datasets for timeline generation.

References

Amr Ahmed and Eric P Xing. 2012. Timeline: A Dynamic Hierarchical Dirichlet Process Model for Recovering Birth/Death and Evolution of Topics in Text Stream. *CoRR abs/1203.3463*.

Hai Leong Chieu and Yoong Keok Lee. 2004. *Query based event extraction along a timeline*. ACM, New York, New York, USA, July.

Chin-Yew Lin. 2004. Rouge: A package for automatic evaluation of summaries. In Stan Szpakowicz Marie-Francine Moens, editor, *Text Summarization Branches Out: Proceedings of the ACL-04 Workshop*, pages 74–81, Barcelona, Spain, July. Association for Computational Linguistics.

Kishore Papineni, Salim Roukos, Todd Ward, and Wei-Jing Zhu. 2002. Bleu: a method for automatic evaluation of machine translation. In *Proceedings of 40th Annual Meeting of the Association for Computational Linguistics*, pages 311–318, Philadelphia, Pennsylvania, USA, July. Association for Computational Linguistics.

Tao Wang. 2013. Time-dependent Hierarchical Dirichlet Model for Timeline Generation. *arXiv preprint arXiv:1312.2244*.

Rui Yan, Liang Kong, Congrui Huang, Xiaojun Wan, Xiaoming Li, and Yan Zhang. 2011a. Timeline Generation through Evolutionary Trans-Temporal Summarization. *EMNLP*, pages 433–443.

Rui Yan, Xiaojun Wan, Jahna Otterbacher, Liang Kong, Xiaoming Li, and Yan Zhang. 2011b. Evolutionary timeline summarization. In *the 34th international ACM SIGIR conference*, page 745, New York, New York, USA. ACM Press.

ALTA Shared Task papers

Overview of the 2016 ALTA Shared Task: Cross-KB Coreference

Andrew Chisholm
Hugo.ai
Sydney, Australia
achisholm@hugo.ai

Ben Hachey
Hugo.ai
Sydney, Australia
bhachey@hugo.ai

Diego Mollá
Macquarie University
Sydney, Australia
diego.molla-aliod@mq.edu.au

Abstract

This paper presents an overview of the 7th ALTA shared task that ran in 2016. The task was to disambiguate endpoints by determining whether two URLs were referring to the same entity. We present the motivation for the task, the description of the data and the results of the participating teams.

1 Introduction

Entity endpoints are URLs which reliably disambiguate named entity mentions on the web. For example, the URL `en.wikipedia.org/wiki/Barack_Obama` may be used in reference to US president Barack Obama. Inlinks to this page are unlikely to refer to some other entity, so we should consider this a disambiguating endpoint.

While Wikipedia has been used extensively for automated entity recognition and disambiguation, many other endpoints may exist for an entity on the web. For example, `nytimes.com/topic/person/barack-obama` and `twitter.com/BarackObama` may be used equivalently. This style of systematic entity indexing is characteristic of social sources (e.g. `facebook.com/*`), news aggregation endpoints (e.g. `nytimes.com/topic/person/*`) and organisation directories (e.g. `gtlaw.com/People/*`). These resources present a valuable and largely untapped source of entity information, both in the content they host and semantic resources that may be extracted from inbound links.

The ALTA 2016 Shared task addresses the problem of Cross-KB coreference resolution. Given two candidate endpoint URLs, systems must determine whether they refer to the same underlying entity. This pairwise version of the task serves as an important precursor to the general problem of clustering web endpoints into coreferent sets.

These clusters act as aggregation points for information about entities, and may used for entity centric information extraction which is not limited by the coverage constraints of any single structured KB.

This paper is structured as follows. Section 2 describes the shared task. Section 3 gives a short survey of related research. Section 4 describes the data set that was used. Section 5 details the evaluation process. Section 6 briefly describes the participating systems. Section 7 presents and discusses the results. Finally, Section 8 concludes this paper.

2 The 2016 ALTA Shared Task

The 2016 ALTA Shared Task is the 7th of the shared tasks organised by the Australasian Language Technology Association (ALTA). Like the previous ALTA shared tasks, it is targeted at university students with programming experience. The general objective of these shared tasks is to introduce university students to the sort of problems that are the subject of active research in a field of natural language processing.

There are no limitations on the size of the teams or the means that they can use to solve the problem, as long as the processing is fully automatic — there should be no human intervention.

There are two categories: a student category and an open category.

- All the members of teams from the **student category** must be university students. The teams cannot have members that are full-time employed or that have completed a PhD.

- Any other teams fall into the **open category**.

The prize is awarded to the team that performs best on the private test set — a subset of the evaluation data for which participant scores are only revealed at the end of the evaluation period (see Section 5).

Andrew Chisholm, Ben Hachey and Diego Mollá. 2016. Overview of the 2016 ALTA Shared Task: Cross-KB Coreference.
In *Proceedings of Australasian Language Technology Association Workshop*, pages 161–164.

3 Related Work

Entity disambiguation work has traditionally focused on the reconciliation of textual mentions to records in a centralised KB like Wikipedia (Cucerzan, 2007) or Freebase (Zheng et al., 2012). In this case, the domain of linkable entities is limited by the coverage of the target knowledge base and those which fall outside this domain are classified as NILs. NIL mention clustering is often addressed separately, and has been the focus of Text Analysis Conference (TAC) Knowledge Base Population shared tasks since 2011 (Ji et al., 2011).

A more generalised approach to resolving mention ambiguity is that of cross-document coreference resolution — where systems cluster mentions of the same entity together without reference to a central KB (Bagga and Baldwin, 1998; Singh et al., 2011). Both NIL clustering and cross-document coreference deal with ambiguity at the mention level. In contrast, the task of cross-KB coreference resolution deals with entity coreference at the KB level, by attempting to cluster entity records across distinct KBs.

This task is similarly structured to that of record linkage (Fellegi and Sunter, 1969; Xu et al., 2013). But, where record linkage commonly operates over structured databases, cross-KB coreference relies primarily on unstructured nodes as input. Cross-KB coreference can draw on the content of the entity endpoint, including the URL, the text and any structured or semi-structured data inside the endpoint page. It can also draw on the web's hyperlink graph, e.g., collecting mentions in context from pages that link to an entity endpoint.

In the web domain, work on finding links associated with existing KB entities (Hachenberg and Gottron, 2012) and web person search (WePS) (Artiles et al., 2007) is also closely related. WePS takes the output of a web search for some entity name and attempts to cluster the results that refer to the same underlying entity. The ultimate aim of cross-KB coreference is also to cluster web pages. By contrast, however, it focuses on clustering entity endpoint pages instead of entity mention pages.

The task builds in part on the Knowledge Base Discovery (KBD) system of Chisholm et al. (2016), where the existence of web endpoints may be inferred from their usage on the web. Shared task data and evaluation are described below.

4 Data

Constructing a balanced corpus of endpoint URL pairs which present non-trivial cases of entity ambiguity is a challenging task. Randomly sampling from a corpus of web links is insufficient as any two URLs are unlikely to refer to the same entity, leading to a highly imbalanced dataset of negative samples. Conversely, if we constrain our sampling to pairs linked from similar anchor text, almost all pairs will be coreferent since entity mentions follow a Zipf-like distribution corresponding to notability.

To address these challenges, we target entity names at the low end of the notability distribution where the ratio of URLs per entity is small in comparison to the general corpus. We train the KBD system of Chisholm et al. (2016) over a corpus of 14.5 million news article outlinks and extract high-confidence endpoints where $P(entity|url) \geq 0.825$. We construct a bipartite anchor-endpoint graph and keep only those anchors that link to only one endpoint URL. These anchors constitute a corpus of long-tail entities names.

We sample 1,000 names from this collection and use the Bing Web Search API[1] to search the web for links corresponding to each anchor span. From each search, we take the first two result URLs which are classified by KBD as entity endpoints and use this as a candidate entity URL pair for the shared task. We also record the page title and search engine snippet returned by the Bing Search API for each instance. Next, we filter out instances of result pairs which both come from the same domain, as these samples typically represent trivial cases of non-coreference. Finally, URL pairs are manually annotated to filter out erroneous endpoint classifications and judge coreference. We randomly sample 200 positive and 200 negative pairs from this set and shuffle them into equal train and test splits.

We observe most endpoints originate from social sources `linkedin.com` and `twitter.com` , while a moderate amount come from more traditional KB-style sites like `imdb.com` and `tripadvisor.com` . The remainder come from a variety of news sources (e.g. `sports.yahoo.com` , `forbes.com`) and small online directories (e.g. `psychology.nova.edu`).

---

[1] http://www.bing.com/toolbox/bingsearchapi

5 Evaluation

The shared task was managed and evaluated using the Kaggle in Class framework, with the name "ALTA 2016 Challenge"[2]. The Kaggle in Class site was created as an invitation-only competition, where the participants could post questions and comments, and submit trial runs and the final submission.

As is standard in Kaggle-in-class competitions, the data set was partitioned into a training set, a public test set, and a private test set. The training set contained 200 pairs of URLs and their labels, and was made available to the participants. The public and private test sets contained 100 new unlabeled pairs of URLs each and were combined into a single test file. The participants were asked to submit the labels of the combined test set. The evaluation results of the public test set were available as soon as the results were submitted, and the evaluation results of the private test set were not made available until after the final deadline. This way, the participants could obtain instant feedback with the public test set, and the risk of overfitting to the final results was diminished.

Evaluation uses the F1 score for the positive class. This is similar to pairwise F1 sometimes used for evaluation of entity resolution (Winkler, 2006), except calculated here over pairs listed in the data only. Precision is the ratio of true positives tp (the number of pairs of endpoints that were correctly labelled as coreferring) to all predicted positives (the total number of pairs of endpoints that the system labelled as coreferring, computed as the sum of true positives and false positives fp). Recall is the ratio of true positives to all actual positives (the number of pairs of endpoints that are coreferring according to the test data, computed as the sum of true positives and false negatives fp). The formula of the F1 score is:

$$F1 = 2\frac{p \cdot r}{p + r}$$

where

$$p = \frac{tp}{tp + fp}, \quad r = \frac{tp}{tp + fn}$$

The product $p \cdot r$ in the numerator of the formula will tend to reward systems that are moderately good in both recall and precision, whereas systems that do extremely well in one and poorly in the other would achieve a lower F1 score.

6 Systems

This section presents short descriptions of some of the participating systems. For further details, refer to the shared task section of the proceedings of the 2016 ALTA workshop.

6.1 EOF

The system by team EOF (Khirbat et al., 2016) follows a two-stage approach. First, in the entity endpoint determination stage, the system determines the most likely underlying entities being referred to by each URL. Second, in the entity disambiguation stage, the two endpoints are disambiguated. Entity endpoint determination is achieved by extracting the named entities of the text pointed by the URL using the Stanford NER, and ranking the entities using logistic regression. The top 3 entities are passed to the entity disambiguation stage, together with additional features based on the URLs, anchor texts of the URLs, and the text pointed by the URLs. This information is processed by a tree ensemble classifier.

6.2 NLPCruise

The system by team NLPCruise (Shivashankar et al., 2016) also follows a two-stage approach but in a different manner. The first stage is a filtering step that rules out cases of dissimilar entities. Those URL pairs which pass the filter pass through to the second stage for more sophisticated processing. The filtering step uses the Stanford NER for detecting the named entities of the titles and the URL pairs. The second stage uses an ensemble of 3 classifiers: one based on Bing search results of the named entities, another classifier based on short-text semantic similarity, and a third classifier that uses additional features extracted from the text pointed to by the URL. An interesting aspect of their system is the use of machine translation as a means to compute semantic similarity, by computing the probability that one text translates into the other.

6.3 BCJR

The systen by team BCJR (Yu et al., 2016) uses a statistical classifier that takes as input features from the pair of URLs. The features are based on the word, character and character bigram embeddings of the text pointed by the URLs. The team has also made available an expanded training data set with about 1700 training pairs.

System	Category	Public	Private
EOF	Student	**0.91**	**0.86**
NLP-Cruise	Student	0.86	0.78
LookForward	Student	0.89	0.78
BCJR	Student	0.75	0.69
ZZ	Student	0.81	0.67
(Baseline 1)		0.67	0.66
STEM	Open	0.79	0.64

Table 1: F1 on the public and private test sets.

6.4 Baseline 1

This is a trivial baseline system provided by the organisers of the shared task. This system returned 1 (the URLs are co-referring) for every instance.

7 Results

Table 1 shows the results of the public and the private test sets. The results are sorted by the outcome of the private test set.

Results from the top three systems in the range $[0.78, 0.86]$ are encouraging, suggesting that cross-KB coreference can be performed with good accuracy even for long-tail entities. Overfitting is a particular challenge with the small data set here and we observe changes from -0.05 to -0.15 F1. Some changes affect system ordering between public and private data, indicating that good generalisation is important to success on this task.

8 Conclusions

The 2016 ALTA Shared Task was the 7th of the series of shared tasks organised by ALTA. This year's shared task focused on cross-KB coreference, and the participants were asked to determine whether two URLs were referring to the same entity. Teams used an array of techniques including logistic regression, ensemble classifiers, and training set aggregation.

The training data set was small, with only 200 pairs of URLs. The small training and test sizes might have caused some of the systems to overfit to the public test set, but overall very good results were achieved. The winning team EOF achieved an F1 score of 0.91 in the public test set, and 0.86 in the private test set, while the second and third teams achieved 0.78 in the private test set.

For full details on participating systems, refer to the shared task section of the 2016 ALTA workshop proceedings.

References

Javier Artiles, Julio Gonzalo, and Satoshi Sekine. 2007. The SemEval 2007 WePS Evaluation: Establishing a benchmark for the Web People Search task. In *SemEval*, pages 64–69.

Amit Bagga and Breck Baldwin. 1998. Entity-based cross-document coreferencing using the vector space model. In *COLING-ACL*, pages 79–85.

Andrew Chisholm, Will Radford, and Ben Hachey. 2016. Discovering entity knowledge bases on the web. In *NAACL Workshop on Automated Knowledge Base Construction*, pages 7–11.

Silviu Cucerzan. 2007. Large-scale named entity disambiguation based on Wikipedia data. In *EMNLP-CoNLL*, pages 708–716.

Ivan P Fellegi and Alan B Sunter. 1969. A theory for record linkage. *Journal of the American Statistical Association*, 64(328):1183–1210.

Christian Hachenberg and Thomas Gottron. 2012. Finding good URLs: Aligning entities in knowledge bases with public web document representations. In *ISWC Workshop on Linked Entities*, pages 17–28.

Heng Ji, Ralph Grishman, and Hoa Trang Dang. 2011. Overview of the TAC 2011 knowledge base population track. In *TAC*.

Gitansh Khirbat, Jianzhong Qi, and Rui Zhang. 2016. Disambiguating entities referred by web endpoints using tree ensembles. In *ALTA*.

S. Shivashankar, Yitong Li, and Afshin Rahimi. 2016. ALTA shared task 2016: Filter and match approach to pair-wise web URI linking. In *ALTA*.

Sameer Singh, Amarnag Subramanya, Fernando Pereira, and Andrew McCallum. 2011. Large-scale cross-document coreference using distributed inference and hierarchical models. In *ACL*, pages 793–803.

William E. Winkler. 2006. Overview of record linkage and current research directions. Technical Report Statistics #2006-2, U.S. Bureau of the Census.

Ying Xu, Zhiqiang Gao, Campbell Wilson, Zhizheng Zhang, Man Zhu, and Qiu Ji. 2013. Entity correspondence with second-order markov logic. In Xuemin Lin, Yannis Manolopoulos, Divesh Srivastava, and Guangyan Huang, editors, *WISE*, pages 1–14.

Cheng Yu, Bing Chu, Rohit Ram, James Aichinger, Lizhen Qu, and Hanna Suominen. 2016. Pairwise text classifier for entity disambiguation. In *ALTA*.

Zhicheng Zheng, Xiance Si, Fangtao Li, Edward Y. Chang, and Xiaoyan Zhu. 2012. Entity disambiguation with freebase. In *WI-IAT*, pages 82–89.

Disambiguating Entities Referred by Web Endpoints using Tree Ensembles

Gitansh Khirbat   **Jianzhong Qi**   **Rui Zhang**
Department of Computing and Information Systems
The University of Melbourne
Australia
gkhirbat@student.unimelb.edu.au
{jianzhong.qi, rui.zhang}@unimelb.edu.au

Abstract

This paper describes system details and results of team "EOF" from the University of Melbourne in the shared task of ALTA 2016, which addresses the use of cross document coreference resolution to determine whether two URLs refer to the same underlying entity. In our submission, we develop a two stage system which first identifies the underlying entity for a given URL using entity-level features by ranking the entity mentions present in the crawled text with the help of logistic regression. This is followed by disambiguating entities present in the given pair of URLs using a tree ensemble model to classify if both URLs refer to the same underlying entity. Our system achieved a final F1-score of 86.02% on the private leaderboard[1], which is the best score among all the participating systems.

1 Introduction

The exponential expansion of the World Wide Web has resulted in a large data repository, the majority of which is in the form of unstructured natural language text containing ambiguous name entities. A name entity mention may relate to multiple known entities. For example, the entity mention "New York" may refer to the city of New York or the movie New York which was released in 2009.

Entity linking (EL) is the process of resolving disambiguity between textual entity mentions and the correct entity node in the *knowledge base* (KB). EL systems usually rely on semantic resources like Wikipedia as endpoints for disambiguation (Shen et al., 2015), however,

---

[1]https://inclass.kaggle.com/c/alta-2016-challenge/leaderboard

Chisholm et al. (2016) provide a relaxed definition of a KB as any *uniform resource locator* (URL) which reliably disambiguates linked mentions on the web (Chisholm et al., 2016a). This relaxed definition has motivated the shared task of ALTA 2016 (Chisholm et al., 2016b). The task organizers provided manually selected URL pairs from a heterogenous collection of websites including popular social networking websites like LinkedIn, Twitter, ResearchGate; knowledge bases like Wikipedia, IMDB and news websites like NDTV and Economic Times. The participants are asked to classify whether a given pair of URLs refer to the same underlying entity. For example, in Figure 1, URLs in the pair $< U_{A1}, U_{A2} >$ refer to the same entity "Barack Obama" whereas URLs in the pair $< U_{B1}, U_{B2} >$ refer to two different entities "Donald Trump" and "Ivanka Trump".

```
U_A1 : https://en.wikipedia.org/wiki/Barack_Obama
U_A2 : https://twitter.com/BarackObama

U_B1 : https://twitter.com/readDonaldTrump
U_B2 : https://www.instagram.com/ivankatrump
```

Figure 1: Example of URL pairs

Considerable research has been done in the field of EL using existing KB like DBpedia (Auer et al., 2007), YAGO (Suchanek et al., 2007), Freebase (Bollacker et al., 2008) and KnowItAll (Etzioni et al., 2004). Wikipedia has proven to be a great resource in solving EL tasks (Cucerzan, 2007); (Milne and Witten, 2008) where dictionary-based techniques, contextual features and entity references have been used to train classifiers. Chisholm et al. (2016) study link behaviour and propose a KB discovery method using URL path features by inferring endpoints via logistic regression.

We adopt a two stage approach to solve this problem. First, our system determines the possible underlying entities for a given URL using entity features obtained from the crawled text with the help of logistic regression. Next, entities are disambiguated between the given URL pair to classify if both URLs refer to the same underlying entity. Contextual features in and around the entities are exploited and a tree ensemble model is trained for this task.

The rest of the paper is organized as follows. Section 2 describes the methodology in detail. Section 3 describes the experiments and results. Section 4 discusses the error analysis of the obtained results and Section 5 concludes the paper.

2 Methodology

The goal of ALTA 2016 shared task is to determine if a given pair of URLs refer to the same underlying entity. This is essentially a problem of cross-document coreference resolution. We tackle this task as an EL or *named entity disambiguation* (NED) problem. As compared to the traditional NED problem, where entity mention in the text is disambiguated to the entities present in a KB, the difference in this task lies in disambiguating the entities identified from two given URLs without an existing KB.

We treat this task as a supervised classification problem which involves two sequential subproblems, i.e., entity endpoint determination and entity disambiguation. The complete solution pipeline is show in Figure 2. First, the given URLs are crawled using *Scrapy* (Myers and McGuffee, 2015) to obtain textual content from the webpage. The next steps are described below.

2.1 Entity Endpoint Determination

The first stage of our system is to identify the underlying entity for a given URL. It involves three components as described below.

2.1.1 Preprocessing

The preprocessing module consists of tokenization of a given URL and the page title of the webpage corresponding to that URL. We define regex patterns which split a given URL on forward slash characters and hyphens. Research has shown that the path tokens are good indicators of entity mentions. We leverage the observation made by Chisholm et al. (2016a) that the URLs which contain terms like "profile", "wiki", "name", "people" provide a positive evidence to refer to entity pages, whereas URLs containing terms like "news", "topic" or date patterns like "YYYY/MM/DD" provide a negative evidence.

2.1.2 Named Entity Recognition

The next step is to make use of a *named entity recognition* (NER) system to identify all the entities present in the crawled text. We make use of Stanford's NER system (Finkel et al., 2005) which uses a model trained on MUC6, MUC7 and ACE 2002 datasets to classify words into three categories namely *Location*, *Person* and *Organization*. The details about this NER system is beyond the scope of this paper and can be obtained from Finkel et al. (2005).

2.1.3 Entity Ranking

Entity ranking is the key step in Stage 1. It trains a logistic regression model using the features obtained in Sections 2.1.1 and 2.1.2 to assign a score for each entity identified in the crawled text. We consider four main features:

1. Comparison of entity mention with the text obtained from URL - Hamming distance is measured for a partial and exact match.

2. Comparison of entity mention with the text obtained from webpage title of the given URL - Hamming distance is measured for a partial and exact match.

3. Frequency of occurrence of entity mention - We observe that in most cases, the most frequent entity is the most probably endpoint.

4. Position of entity mention in the crawled text - We observe that in most cases, the most probable endpoint is an entity mention which is located within the first five tokens in the crawled text.

Using these features, we train a logistic regression model which gives us the probability of an entity being a possible webpage endpoint. This probability score is used to shortlist top-3 entity mentions as the most likely endpoints for a given URL. We observe that an entity endpoint is usually characterized by some related entities. This motivates us to retain the top-3 entities which prove to be useful in the next stage.

2.2 Entity Disambiguation

The second stage of our system solves the problem of determining whether a given pair of URLs refer to the same underlying entity. It makes use of the output of Stage 1 and involves two components as described below.

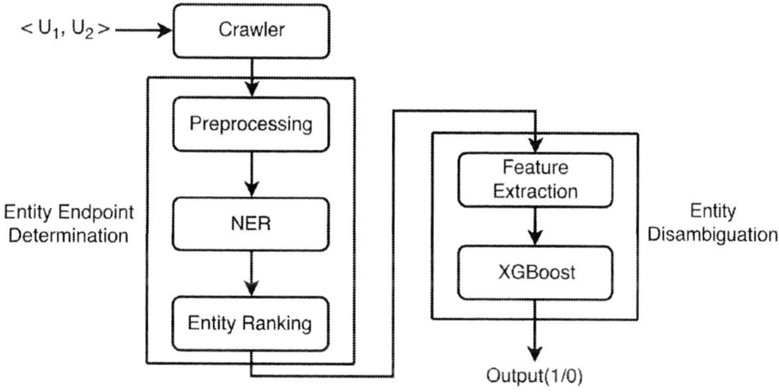

Figure 2: System pipeline

2.2.1 Feature Extraction

This module makes use of contextual features in and around the identified entities. A concept vector is created to represent the semantic content of the crawled text from the URL. This concept vector contains TF-IDF of URL path, page title and top-3 entity mentions obtained from Stage 1 and adds features of bag of words (Guo et al., 2013); (Ratinov et al., 2011) and anchor texts (Kulkarni et al., 2009) as described below.

- Bag of words - TF-IDF summary of the entire crawled text is generated and top-20 words after removal of stopwords are chosen as the representative bag of words.

- Anchor texts - The URLs referred in all the anchor texts are preprocessed according to Section 2.1.1 to obtain the URL endpoint. A vector containing all such endpoints and anchor texts is used to define a TF-IDF vector for the given URL pair.

2.2.2 XGBoost

The features defined in Section 2.2.1 are used to train a supervised tree ensemble classifier called extreme gradient boosting (XGBoost) (Chen and Guestrin, 2016). The intuition behind XGBoost is that since it is not easy to train all the trees at once, an additive strategy is employed to fix what has been learnt which adds one new tree at a time. XG-Boost tackles regularization very carefully, which improves the overall score. Detailed working of XGBoost is beyond the scope of this paper and we refer the readers to Chen et al. (2016) for details.

3 Experiments and Results

The ALTA shared task is to classify whether a given pair of URLs refer to the same underlying entity. We first describe the given dataset briefly, followed by the experimental setup and results.

3.1 Dataset

The shared task organizers provide a corpus of URLs from a heterogenous collection of websites including popular social networking websites, knowledge bases and news websites. The training data consists of these URLs in the form of a pair along with their annotations, i.e., 0 if the URLs in a pair refer to different entities or 1 if they refer to the same entity. In addition to this, information about the webpage title and a small snippet is provided for both URLs. The training and test data consist of 200 pairs of URLs each. Data details are given by Chisholm et al. (2016b).

3.2 Experimental Setup and Results

In the Stage 1 sub-problem of entity endpoint determination, we leverage the output of NER to manually annotate the given 200 URL pairs of training data with the top-3 possible entity endpoints, which become the gold standard annotations for this sub-problem. We split this data equally into training and development datasets. We train a logistic regression model on this training data to learn the regression parameters. Using the learnt parameters, we run the model on development data and obtain a F1-score of 89% in classifying if an identified entity mention is one of the top-3 manually annotated entity endpoints for

Table 1: Results on public and private leaderboards

Features	Precision	Recall	Public F1	Private F1
{URL, Title}	68.63	87.5	76.92	80.85
+{Bag of Words}	80.39	85.42	82.82	83.49
+{Entity Features}	78.43	97.56	86.96	81.82
+{Anchor Texts}	86.27	95.65	90.72	**86.02**

the given URL. This gives us a positive confidence to proceed with combining the training and development datasets (i.e. the given original full training dataset consisting of 200 URL pairs) on which we train the logistic regression model, thus obtaining the final regression parameter values. This regression model is used to calculate the probability score for all the entity mentions in the crawled text obtained from the URL pairs in the given test dataset.

For the Stage 2 sub-problem of entity disambiguation, we split the given training data into training and development datasets to perform 5-fold cross validation using XGBoost tree ensemble method. First, we made use of the TF-IDF feature vector obtained from the given URL and its page title. In the second attempt, we added the bag of words TF-IDF feature vector as described in Section 2.2.1. Next, we added the feature vector containing TF-IDF of the top-3 entity mentions for both URLs. Finally, we added the anchor text feature vector.

The trained model is used for predictions corresponding to the public leaderboard which contains 50% of the total data. Finally, at the end of the competition, the predictions are measured against the remaining 50% of data which corresponds to the private leaderboard. The results obtained by using the aforementioned features is shown in Table 1. Standard precision, recall and F1-score metrics are used to report the prediction results.

4 Discussion

Our system performs well on both public and private leaderboards. Table 1 shows that a collective use of contextual features in and around the entities leads to an increase in the F1-score. In our system, we make use of TF-IDF of top-20 words and a bag of words approach to train the system. As compared to using just the URL and page title features, the bag of words led to an increment of 5.69% F1-score on the public leaderboard. Next, we identify top-3 entity mentions as

the most probable endpoints for a given URL. This gives us a high confidence in disambiguation as most of the URLs are characterized by their top-3 entity mentions. An incorporation of this entity feature has led to an increment of 4.14% F1-score on the public leaderboard. Additionally, it has increased the system recall by a significant 12.14%. Finally, anchor texts prove to be informative features and provide another 3.74% improvement on F1-score. Our system does well in classifying most of the URL pairs as referring to the same underlying entity. However, it does not perform well in certain cases:

- **Lack of identified entities** - There are cases in which the crawled URL text contains just one entity which is usually the name of a person or organization. With no further information about that entity mention, our system fails to leverage the strength of contextual features and is unable to disambiguate the entities, e.g., the URL `www.imdb.com/name/nm5513294` refers to a person named "Johnny Dwyer". There is no more information about that person on this URL. Its corresponding URL in the given pair is a LinkedIn profile and refers to a person named "Johnny Dwyer" who is an <u>author</u> based in <u>New York</u>. The gold annotations indicate that our system scores a false negative on such URLs.

- **Website search results** - Some URLs refer to search results within a website, which provides a listing of all articles containing an entity mention. While we tackle this problem by avoiding the URLs for news websites in a way so as to prune them for terms like "news" and "topic" as described in Section 2.1.1, there are few cases which were missed, e.g., the URL `deadline.com/tag/secrets-lies` refers to all the articles with a tag of secrets-lies. Our system gives a false positive for the disambiguation of this URL with the Twitter URL of the TV show "Secrets and Lies".

- **Dynamic URLs** - There are some dynamic URLs in the given dataset. A dynamic URL changes with time, i.e., either the contents of that URL change over time or the URL becomes void after some time. Since such URLs do not contain any information, our system is not able to disambiguate them to their valid static URL counterparts.

5   Conclusion

Disambiguating entities referred by web endpoints is an important and challenging problem which gives us insights to an important concept of knowledge base discovery and creation. In this paper, we described our system, which ranked the best with an F1-score of 86.02% in the official private leaderboard of the ALTA 2016 shared task. Our solution was based on a supervised classification method using gradient boosted trees which exploited contextual entity-level features.

References

Sören Auer, Christian Bizer, Georgi Kobilarov, Jens Lehmann, Richard Cyganiak, and Zachary Ives. 2007. Dbpedia: A nucleus for a web of open data. In *Proceedings of the 6th International The Semantic Web and 2Nd Asian Conference on Asian Semantic Web Conference*, pages 722–735.

Kurt Bollacker, Colin Evans, Praveen Paritosh, Tim Sturge, and Jamie Taylor. 2008. Freebase: A collaboratively created graph database for structuring human knowledge. In *Proceedings of the 2008 ACM SIGMOD International Conference on Management of Data*, pages 1247–1250.

Andrew Carlson, Justin Betteridge, Richard C. Wang, Estevam R. Hruschka, Jr., and Tom M. Mitchell. 2010. Coupled semi-supervised learning for information extraction. In *Proceedings of the Third ACM International Conference on Web Search and Data Mining*, pages 101–110.

Tianqi Chen and Carlos Guestrin. 2016. Xgboost: A scalable tree boosting system. In *Proceedings of the 22Nd ACM SIGKDD International Conference on Knowledge Discovery and Data Mining*, pages 785–794.

Andrew Chisholm, Hugo Australia, Will Radford, and Ben Hachey. 2016a. Discovering entity knowledge bases on the web. *Proceedings of AKBC*, pages 7–11.

Andrew Chisholm, Ben Hachey, and Diego Molla. 2016b. Overview of the 2016 alta shared task: Cross-kb coreference. In *Proceedings of the Australasian Language Technology Workshop 2016*.

Silviu Cucerzan. 2007. Large-scale named entity disambiguation based on Wikipedia data. In *Proceedings of the 2007 Joint Conference on Empirical Methods in Natural Language Processing and Computational Natural Language Learning*, pages 708–716, June.

Oren Etzioni, Michael Cafarella, Doug Downey, Stanley Kok, Ana-Maria Popescu, Tal Shaked, Stephen Soderland, Daniel S. Weld, and Alexander Yates. 2004. Web-scale information extraction in knowitall: (preliminary results). In *Proceedings of the 13th International Conference on World Wide Web*, pages 100–110.

Jenny Rose Finkel, Trond Grenager, and Christopher Manning. 2005. Incorporating non-local information into information extraction systems by gibbs sampling. In *Proceedings of the 43rd Annual Meeting on Association for Computational Linguistics*, pages 363–370.

Stephen Guo, Ming-Wei Chang, and Emre Kıcıman. 2013. To link or not to link? a study on end-to-end tweet entity linking. In *Proceedings of NAACL-HLT*, pages 1020–1030.

Sayali Kulkarni, Amit Singh, Ganesh Ramakrishnan, and Soumen Chakrabarti. 2009. Collective annotation of wikipedia entities in web text. In *Proceedings of the 15th ACM SIGKDD International Conference on Knowledge Discovery and Data Mining*, pages 457–466.

David Milne and Ian H. Witten. 2008. Learning to link with wikipedia. In *Proceedings of the 17th ACM Conference on Information and Knowledge Management*, pages 509–518.

Daniel Myers and James W. McGuffee. 2015. Choosing scrapy. *J. Comput. Sci. Coll.*, 31(1):83–89, October.

Lev Ratinov, Dan Roth, Doug Downey, and Mike Anderson. 2011. Local and global algorithms for disambiguation to wikipedia. In *Proceedings of the 49th Annual Meeting of the Association for Computational Linguistics: Human Language Technologies - Volume 1*, pages 1375–1384.

Wei Shen, Jianyong Wang, and Jiawei Han. 2015. Entity linking with a knowledge base: Issues, techniques, and solutions. *IEEE Transactions on Knowledge and Data Engineering*, 27(2):443–460, Feb.

Fabian M. Suchanek, Gjergji Kasneci, and Gerhard Weikum. 2007. Yago: A core of semantic knowledge. In *Proceedings of the 16th International Conference on World Wide Web*, pages 697–706.

ALTA Shared-task 2016: Filter and Match Approach to Pair-wise Web URI Linking

S. Shivashankar
Department of CIS,
University of Melbourne
shivashankar@student.unimelb.edu.au

Yitong Li
Department of CIS,
University of Melbourne
yitongl4@student.unimelb.edu.au

Afshin Rahimi
Department of CIS,
University of Melbourne
arahimi@student.unimelb.edu.au

Abstract

This paper describes the method and results of our approach, submitted as team 'NLPCruise' at ALTA shared task 2016. The goal of the shared task is to predict whether two given web Uniform Resource Identifiers (URIs) correspond to the same entity or not. Retrieving the URI content in addition to the dataset provided, we built a two stage filter and match technique that utilises search engine scores, semantic similarity and machine translation features. Our model achieved an $F1$ score of 0.85714 on the public test-set and ranked second finally on the private leaderboard.

1 Introduction

In general, establishing a mapping from entities in a knowledge base to URI end-points is a useful task both to collate information about entities and to disambiguate them. Typically, semantic sources such as Wikipedia, DBPedia are used as end-points. Although they provide a rich context for entities, they do not achieve sufficient recall over different domains and entities. On the other hand, domain-specific sources such as DBLP, IMDb or MusicBrainz cover only a single target domain (e.g. movies, music) well but aren't useful in other domains. To benefit from both general purpose and domain-specific knowledge bases, one could use WebKB (URIs) as end-points. In-order to do that one must infer its existence on the web. For every entity endpoint we discover, we may recover thousands of entity mentions via inlinks. While the effectiveness of inlink-driven entity disambiguation is known for a single KB setting, this can be extended to leverage inlinks across a collection of automatically discovered web KBs (Chisholm et al., 2016). Thus in this task, we classify whether a pair of URIs correspond to the same entity or not.

Similar tasks were addressed in other shared tasks/challenges, such as Web People Search task (WePS [1]), defined as the problem of organizing web search results for a given person name. At a more generic level, TREC relevance feedback track[2] had multiple tasks related to relevance classification for a set of documents given a query, which we can treat as similar problems to ours when formulated as pair-wise binary document classification.

The goal of ALTA shared task 2016 is to determine whether two URLs refer to the same underlying entity or not. For example, `http://www.nytimes.com/topic/person/barack-obama` and `https://twitter.com/BarackObama` refer to the same person, but `https://twitter.com/realDonaldTrump` and `https://www.instagram.com/ivankatrump` refer to different entities.

2 Data preparation

The original data includes URLs of entities which link to the HTML pages, titles of the HTML pages, and snippets or brief descriptions of pages. Titles and snippets were obtained using BING search API, where the input query was the named entity. The top two URLs from BING search are the URL pairs given for classification. Instances containing non-representative web-pages were removed, more details can be found here [3]. In addition to the given data, we automatically fetched the whole HTML page content using *xdotool*[4]. We removed HTML tags and Java scripts to clean the downloaded HTML documents. Now we have two lev-

---

[1] http://nlp.uned.es/weps/weps-3

[2] http://trec.nist.gov/data/relevance.feedback.html

[3] https://inclass.kaggle.com/c/alta-2016-challenge/forums/t/23480/how-was-the-data-obtained

[4] `http://www.semicomplete.com/projects/xdotool/`

S. Shivashankar, Yitong Li and Afshin Rahimi. 2016. Filter and Match Approach to Pair-wise Web URI Linking. In *Proceedings of Australasian Language Technology Association Workshop*, pages 170–174.

els of data: title & snippets at the sentence-level and cleaned HTML text at document-level.

3 Proposed Approach

Our proposed approach is shown in Figure 1. We employ filtering at the first step which includes pattern matching heuristics for both named entity and URL pairs. Pairs of URLs that are not disproved to be the same entities in the filtering step are considered for further analysis. The next step involves three different classification models: (a) based on Bing search results obtained by querying named entity from URL_a and domain name of URL_b and vice versa (b) building a semantic similarity based classifier using short-text (title and/or snippet) (c) using complete HTML content, we compute distributed representation based similarity scores, MT scores, Inverse Document Frequency (IDF) based scores, simple word-count and document length based measures and use them as features in a RandomForest binary classifier.

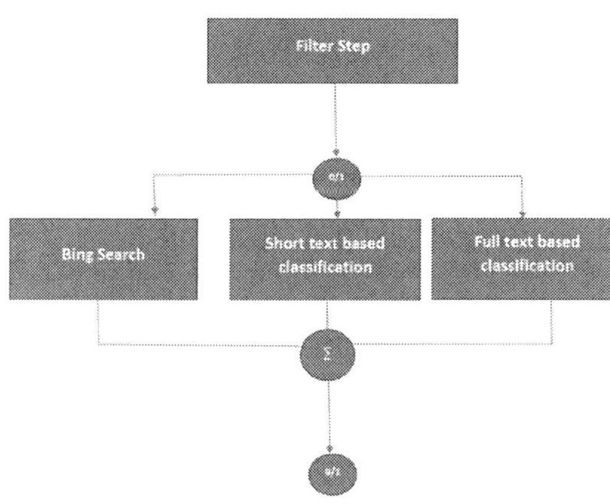

Figure 1: Proposed Approach

3.1 Filtering Step: Named Entity and URL matching

We leverage the title text for getting the named entity by considering words before delimiters such as $'|'$, '-' and extracting the capitalized words from the beginning until any special character. If there are no $'|'$ or '-' then we use Stanford NER tagger to annotate PER, ORG and LOC entities. Then if the names from both the URLs match by a minimum length of 2 and a match score of $\frac{n-1}{n}$, the pair is considered as a 'pass' for further analysis.

For URL match, we consider only pairs from the same domain. We compare path length of URL (number of sub-directories), and match names which can be either of the last two strings (non numeric) after $'/'$. If a URL pair doesn't pass through either of the criteria: named entity or URL matching (if both length and name match fails), then it is disapproved for further processing. Over the test set, we observed that 20% of the records were filtered out (classified as not correspond to the same entities) in this step.

3.2 Bing Search based Classification

3.2.1 Query Construction

We construct queries for Bing Search[5] by using named entities from URL_a and domain name of URL_b. We repeat the same with named entities from URL_b and domain name of URL_a. For instance, for URL pairs `www.imperial.ac.uk/people/f.allen` (URL_a) and `https://www.linkedin.com/in/franklin-allen-0557906` (URL_b), we create queries as "Franklin Allen LinkedIn", "Franklin Allen Brevan Howard Centre at Imperial College London LinkedIn" and "Franklin Allen Finance and Economics LinkedIn". Here, the name "Franklin Allen" is obtained from title & snippet of URL_a. Similarly other context phrases such as *Howard Centre at Imperial College London* and *Finance and Economics* are extracted from URL_a. We combine name and context words from URL_a with domain (in this case LinkedIn) of URL_b for constructing queries. We repeat the same with name and context from URL_b and domain name of URL_a. Named entities are fetched as given in 3.1 - using heuristics (for name) and Stanford NER output (for PER, ORG, LOC). If there are no named entities for querying, we use capitalized chunks of words. For example, "Shark Tank", "America's Most Wanted" and "America Fights Back" are obtained as capitalized chunks from title & snippet of `www.imdb.com/name/nm5507573`, since there were no context words such as ORG, LOC obtained using Stanford NER. Note, for capitalized chunks of text we break the chunks if there are any special characters such as ",",":","!", and so on. Shorter context words are preferred and any common words are removed from longer phrases. Also, for URLs from Twitter, we fetch location information using Twitter API[6].

---

[5]https://datamarket.azure.com/dataset/bing/search
[6]http://twitter4j.org/en/

3.2.2 Match Score Computation

After querying on Bing Search engine with name and context words from URL_a and domain name from URL_b, we check if URL_b is present among top 10 search results (we refer to this as a 'hit'). We repeat similar querying with name and context words from URL_b and domain name from URL_a. We compute $P(match|URL\ Pair)$ as the ratio between number of hits and number of queries ($\frac{number\ of\ hits}{number\ of\ queries}$). We refer to above probability score as P, and $Q = P(mismatch|URLPair) = 1 - P$. If $P = Q$, we consider length of queries to weigh the hits. In the following formulation $length(q)$ is the length of query q (number of words in a query), $HITS(q)$ is a Boolean value that indicates if that query was a hit or not,

$$P(match|URL\ Pair) = \frac{\Sigma_q length(q) \times HITS(q)}{\Sigma_q length(q)}.$$

If there is a tie still, then it is broken by using the prior for a given pair of domains, for instance $P(match|IMDb, LinkedIn)$.

3.3 Short-text similarity

We set a threshold for classification at 50%, assuming the data is balanced, using semantic similarity and MT based similarity scores (after geometric mean). The predictions are combined by complete consensus for class 0 (mismatch) and atleast one vote for class 1 (match). The intuition is that we expect the filtering step would have removed a good number of mismatches in the previous step.

3.3.1 Semantic Similarity

We use combined title & snippet short text to compute the semantic similarity of pairs using Dandelion API [7]. It is claimed to work well for short text. Here the words are mapped to a Wikipedia like knowledge base and similarity is computed using the mapped vectors.

3.3.2 Machine Translation based Similarity

We compute Machine Translation (MT) evaluation metrics between two short texts. If two URLs refer to the same entity, intuitively, the scores should indicate one text being a paraphrase of another. We score the similarity for both snippets using MT evaluation metrics, including BLEU (BiLingual

---

[7]https://dandelion.eu/semantic-text/text-similarity-demo/

Evaluation Understudy) (Papineni et al., 2002), METEOR (Metric for Evaluation of Translation with Explicit ORdering) (Banerjee and Lavie, 2005), TER (Translation Error Rate) (Snover et al., 2006), at token-level. In general, MT evaluation metrics are designed to assess whether the output of a MT system is semantically equivalent to a set of reference translations. MT scores are combined using geometric mean ($combined\ score = \sqrt[3]{BLEU * METEOR * TER}$).

3.4 Document-level similarity

3.4.1 Machine Translation based Similarity

We also compute MT scores between two documents. Similar to short text setup, we calculate BLEU, METEOR and TER metrics and use them together with distributed representations similarity scores (3.4.2 and 3.4.3) and vector space models (3.4.4).

3.4.2 Distributed Similarity (Word2Vec) based Scores

We calculate the document representation by averaging the pre-trained word embeddings, which are generated by Word2Vec. And then, we compute the cosine similarity between document representations for both training and test pairs as the feature.

3.4.3 Job Descriptions Similarity

Intuition behind using job similarity is that we expect it could uncover profession based similarity that can be effective for web KB instances such as LinkedIn, Avvo, IMDb, etc. To find the job similarity of two pieces of text from a pair, we first find the similarity of each piece of text with each of the 1000 job descriptions existing in Occupational Information Network (ONET) (Peterson et al., 2001) resulting in a 1000d vector for each text. Then we use the similarity of the 1000d vectors of the two pieces of text together and use it as a feature for training the classifier. To find the similarity of a piece of text with one of the job descriptions we use the similarity of the average word vectors using Cosine measure.

3.4.4 Similarity Scores with Inverse Document Frequency (IDF)

The cleaned HTML text is still noisy with many web-page items and unimportant context. Aim to reduce the influence of unrelated tokens, we use

---

172

basic idf scores to quantify the importance of tokens (Wu et al., 2008). The inverse document frequency, defined as

$$idf(t, D) = log\frac{N}{|\{d \in D : t \in d\}|}$$

with $N = |D|$ and training corpus D. The idf is a measure of how much information the word provides, that is, whether the term is common or rare across all documents. Considering the web-page tokens could be repeated more times than entity information, we omit the term frequency score in our method.

First, we build a dictionary mapped with idf scores based on English Europarl corpus (Koehn, 2005). Then, empirically we build two kinds of idf features of the documents:

$$f_1 = \Sigma_{t \in (D_A \cap D_B)} idf(t)$$
$$f_2 = |\{d : d \in (D_A \cap D_B), idf(d) \geq idf_m\}|$$

Where, D_A and D_B are documents of entity A and B, idf_m is the mean of all the idf scores in the dictionary. Furthermore, we normalize f_1 and f_2 by the average document length $l = \sqrt{|D_A| \cdot |D_B|}$. Last, we use both normalized and un-normalized features (4 totally) in our method.

3.5 RandomForest Classifier

We build a RandomForest classifier using 16 document level similarity features computed using MT based techniques - 3 types of scores (BLEU, METEOR, TER) for translating both ways (text 'A' to 'B and vice versa), that gives 6 scores totally; distributed word similarity (word2vec) & job similarity based scores - 2 totally; IDF based scores - 4 totally; word count and document length for both URLs using complete HTML text - 4 totally. Since the document level text can be noisy, we consider only high confident (> 0.7) predictions of this model in the next stage for overall prediction.

4 Overall Prediction

The overall prediction is done by combining three classifiers: Bing search, short-text based classification and document level classification. The heuristic used to combine the predictions is given as follows:

- For a given URL pair, if domain specific IDF scores for short-text are high, i.e., it contains common words in all the Title & snippets, for example LinkedIn, then short-text based classification would be unreliable. So we set a threshold empirically using training set, to decide if predictions based on short-text similarity can be used or not.

- Similarly, only confident predictions using RandomForest classifier on document level data are considered reliable.

- With this we consider a URL pair to be 'match' (or 1) if any one of the classifiers predict 'match, and 'not-match' (or 0) if all the classifiers predict 'not-match'. The intuition is that, since we consider a variety of information: short-text, document level information and collaborative information through search engine, we label it as a positive instance, if any of the information/views classifies it as positive, and negative otherwise.

5 Discussion

Combining multiple approaches (lexicon & corpus based) to compute semantic relatedness is an important research topic (Lee et al., 2016). We have employed an approach where the similarity between two pages are obtained by a combination of semantic, machine translation scores (para-phrase) and corpus driven measures such as word2vec. On the test data, we observed the performance of individual models as follows: short-text based semantic similarity (threshold for classification is set at 0.37) gave an F-measure of 0.62, short-text MT features gave a score of 0.53, RandomForest classifier with document level features (distributed similarity, IDF features and MT similarity) gave an F-measure of 0.63. Apart from that, similarity measures based only on distributed models such as averaged word2vec score, job descriptions similarity were not discriminative. Though they are potential directions, it might require more data to re-train the embeddings for this problem. Finally, combined with filtering and Bing Search, we obtained an F-measure of 0.85714 on the public test-set. We believe that this can be more effective if the proposed models are combined together (on a larger dataset) using a stronger ensemble method such as Boosting.

References

Satanjeev Banerjee and Alon Lavie. 2005. Meteor: An automatic metric for mt evaluation with improved correlation with human judgments. In *Proceedings of the acl workshop on intrinsic and extrinsic evaluation measures for machine translation and/or summarization*, volume 29, pages 65–72.

Andrew Chisholm, Will Radford, and Ben Hachey. 2016. Discovering entity knowledge bases on the web. In *Proceedings of the 5th Workshop on Automated Knowledge Base Construction*, pages 7–11.

Philipp Koehn. 2005. Europarl: A parallel corpus for statistical machine translation. In *MT summit*, volume 5, pages 79–86.

Yang-Yin Lee, Hao Ke, Hen-Hsen Huang, and Hsin-Hsi Chen. 2016. Combining word embedding and lexical database for semantic relatedness measurement. In *Proceedings of the 25th International Conference Companion on World Wide Web*, WWW '16 Companion, pages 73–74.

Kishore Papineni, Salim Roukos, Todd Ward, and Wei-Jing Zhu. 2002. Bleu: a method for automatic evaluation of machine translation. In *Proceedings of the 40th annual meeting on association for computational linguistics*, pages 311–318.

Norman G Peterson, Michael D Mumford, Walter C Borman, P Richard Jeanneret, Edwin A Fleishman, Kerry Y Levin, Michael A Campion, Melinda S Mayfield, Frederick P Morgeson, Kenneth Pearlman, et al. 2001. Understanding work using the occupational information network (o* net): Implications for practice and research. *Personnel Psychology*, 54(2):451–492.

Matthew Snover, Bonnie Dorr, Richard Schwartz, Linnea Micciulla, and John Makhoul. 2006. A study of translation edit rate with targeted human annotation. In *Proceedings of association for machine translation in the Americas*, volume 200.

Ho Chung Wu, Robert Wing Pong Luk, Kam Fai Wong, and Kui Lam Kwok. 2008. Interpreting tf-idf term weights as making relevance decisions. *ACM Transactions on Information Systems (TOIS)*, 26(3):13.

Pairwise FastText Classifier for Entity Disambiguation

Cheng Yu[a,b], Bing Chu[b], Rohit Ram[b], James
Aichinger[b], Lizhen Qu[b,c], Hanna Suominen[b,c]
[a] Project Cleopatra, Canberra, Australia
[b] The Australian National University
[c] DATA 61, Australia
cheng@projectcleopatra.com.au
{u5470909,u5568718,u5016706,
Hanna.Suominen}@anu.edu.au
Lizhen.Qu@data61.csiro.au

Abstract

For the *Australasian Language Technology
Association* (ALTA) 2016 Shared Task, we
devised *Pairwise FastText Classifier* (PFC),
an efficient embedding-based text classifier,
and used it for entity disambiguation. Compared with a few baseline algorithms, PFC
achieved a higher F1 score at 0.72 (under the
team name BCJR). To generalise the model,
we also created a method to bootstrap the
training set deterministically without human
labelling and at no financial cost. By releasing
PFC and the dataset augmentation software to
the public[1], we hope to invite more collaboration.

1 Introduction

The goal of the ALTA 2016 Shared Task was to
disambiguate two person or organisation entities
(Chisholm et al., 2016). The real-world motivation for the Task includes gathering information
about potential clients, and law enforcement.

We designed a *Pairwise FastText Classifier*
(PFC) to disambiguate the entities (Chisholm et
al., 2016). The major source of inspiration for
PFC came from *FastText* [2] algorithm which
achieved quick and accurate text classification
(Joulin et al., 2016). We also devised a method to
augment our training examples deterministically,
and released all source code to the public.

The rest of the paper will start with PFC and a
mixture model based on PFC, and proceeds to present our solution to augment the labelled dataset

deterministically. Then we will evaluate PFC's
performance against a few baseline methods, including SVC[3] with hand-crafted text features. Finally, we will discuss ways to improve disambiguation performance using PFC.

2 Pairwise Fast-Text Classifier (PFC)

Our *Pairwise FastText Classifier* is inspired by
the *FastText*. Thus this section starts with a brief
description of *FastText*, and proceeds to demonstrate PFC.

2.1 FastText

FastText maps each vocabulary to a real-valued
vector, with unknown words having a special vocabulary ID. A document can be represented as
the average of all these vectors. Then *FastText*
will train a maximum entropy multi-class classifier on the vectors and the output labels. Fast Text
has been shown to train quickly and achieve prediction performance comparable to Recurrent
Neural Network embedding model for text classification (Joulin et al., 2016).

2.2 PFC

PFC is similar to *FastText* except that PFC takes
two inputs in the form of a list of vocabulary IDs,
because disambiguation requires two URL inputs.
We specify that each of them is passed into the
same embedding matrix. If each entity is represented by a d dimensional vector, then we can
concatenate them, and represent the two entities

---

[1] All source code can be downloaded from:
https://github.com/projectcleopatra/PFC

[2] The original paper of FastText used the typography
fastText
[3] SVC: Support vector classification

Cheng Yu, Bing Chu, Rohit Ram, James Aichinger, Lizhen Qu and Hanna Suominen. 2016. Pairwise FastText Classifier for
Entity Disambiguation. In *Proceedings of Australasian Language Technology Association Workshop*, pages 175−179.

by a 2d dimensional vector. Then we train a max-imum entropy classifier based on the concatenated vector. The diagram of the model is in Figure 1.

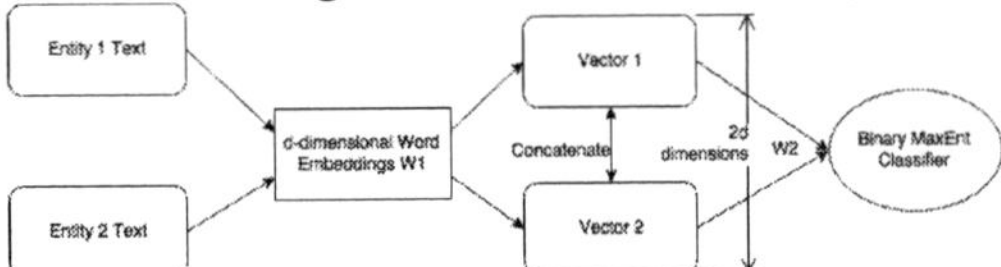

Figure 1: PFC model. W1 and W2 are trainable weights.

2.3 The PFC Mixture Model

The previous section introduces word-embed-ding-based PFC. In order to improve disambigua-tion performance, we built a mixture model based on various PFC sub-models: Besides word-em-bedding-based PFC, we also trained character-embedding-based PFC, which includes one uni-character PFC, and one bi-character PFC. In the following subsections, we will first briefly explain character-embedding-based PFC, and then show the Mixture model.

2.3.1 Character-Embedding-Based PFCs

Character-embedding-based PFC models typi-cally have fewer parameters than word-embed-ding-based PFC, and thus reducing the probability of overfitting.

Uni-character embedding maps each character in the URL and search engine snippet into a 13-dimensional vector, take the average of an input document, concatenate the two documents, and then train a maximum entropy classification on top of the concatenated vectors.

Bi-character embedding model has a moving window of two characters and mapped every such two characters into a 16-dimensional vector.

Our implementation of the character-embed-ding based PFC model includes only lowercase English letters and space. After converting all let-ters to lowercase, other characters are simply skipped and ignored.

2.3.2 Mixing PFC Sub-models

The mixture model has two phases. In phase one, we train each sub-model independently. In phase 2, we train a simple binary classifier based on the probability output of each individual PFC. The di-agram of the PFC mixture model is shown in Fig-ure 2.

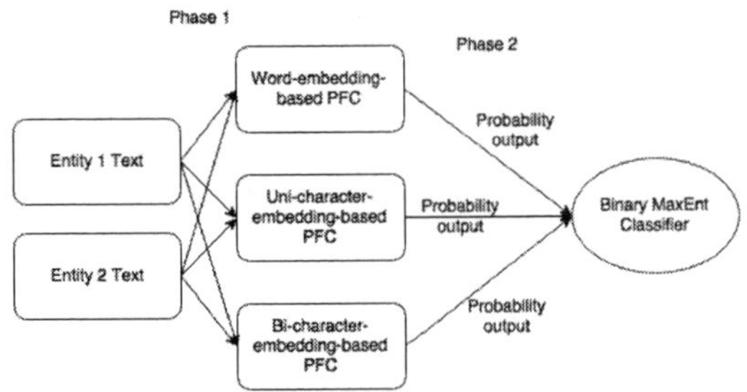

Figure 2: The PFC Mixture Model.

3 Augmenting More Training Examples Deterministically

Embedding-models tend to have a large number of parameters. Our word-embedding matrix has over 3700 rows, and thus it is natural to brain-storm ways to augment the training set to prevent overfitting.

We created a method to harvest additional training examples deterministically without the need for human labelling, and the data can be ac-quired at no additional cost.

3.1 Acquiring Training Examples for the Negative Class[4]

To acquire URL pairs that refer to different peo-ple, we wrote a scraping bot that visits LinkedIn, and grabs hyperlinks in a section called "People that are similar to the person", where LinkedIn recommends professionals that have similar to the current profile that we are browsing. LinkedIn re-stricts the number of profiles we can browse in a given month unless the user is a Premium user, so we upgraded our LinkedIn account for scraping purpose. We used the LinkedIn URLs provided to us in the training samples, and grabbed similar LinkedIn profiles, which ended up with about 850 profiles, with some of the LinkedIn URLs no longer up to date.

3.2 Acquiring Training Examples for the Positive Class

To acquire training examples of different social media profiles that belong to the same person, we used examples from `about.me`. About.me is a platform where people could create a personal page showing their professional portfolios and links to various social media sites. We wrote a scraping bot that visits about.me/discover, where the site showcases their users, and clicks open

---

[4] In the Shared Task, if a pair of URL entities refer to differ-ent persons or organisations, the pair belongs to the negative class. if a pair of URL entities refer to the same persons or organisations, the pair belongs to the positive class.

each user, acquires their social media links, and randomly selects two as a training example. For example, for someone with 5 social media profiles, including Facebook, Twitter, LinkedIn, Pinterest, and Google+, the bot can generate (5, 2) = 10 training examples.

4 Experimental Setup

Using the training data provided by the Organiser and data acquired using the method mentioned in Section 3, we evaluated the performance of our PFC and PFC Mixture against a few baseline models.

4.1 Datasets

The organiser prepared 200 labelled pairs of training samples and 200 unlabelled test samples (Hachey, 2016). All baseline methods and PFC methods are trained using the original 200 URL pairs. The only exception is "PFC with augmented dataset", which uses the method in the previous section to acquire 807 negative class URL pairs, and 891 positive class URL pairs.

4.2 Pre-Processing

Text content for the PFC comes from the search engine snippet file provided by the Organiser and text scraped from the URLs provided by the training examples. Unknown words in the test set are represented by a special symbol.

4.3 Baselines

The reason we choose a few baseline models is that there is no gold-standard baseline model for URL entity disambiguation. Baseline models are explained as followed.

Word-Embedding with Pre-Trained Vectors: The training corpus Google comes from News Articles (Mikolov et al., 2013). For each URL entity, we calculated the mean vector of the search result snippet text by using pre-trained word embedding vectors from Google. Unknown words were ignored. Then we concatenated the vectors and trained a maximum entropy classifier on top of it.

SVC with Hand-Selected Text Features: Our Support Vector Classifier is built on top of hand-selected text features. For each pair of URLs, we manually selected the following text features. Explanation of these features is available in Appendix-A.

LSTM Word-Embedding: We passed each document token sequentially using word embedding into an LSTM layer with 50 LSTM units (Brownlee, 2016) (Goodfellow et al., 2016), concatenated the two output vectors, and trained a maximum entropy classifier on top of it. To reduce overfitting, we added dropout layers with the dropout parameter set to 0.2 (Zaremba, Sutskever, & Vinyals, 2014).

Neural Tensor Network: Inspired by Socher et al., by passing a pair of documents represented in vector form into a tensor, we built a relationship classifier based on the architecture in the paper (Socher et al., 2013). Document vectors are calculated from pre-trained Google embedding word vectors.

5 Results and Discussion

The experimental results from the setup is summarised in the table.

	Method	F1 Public	F1 Private	F1 Total[5]
PFC-based	PFC with Word-Embedding	0.75	0.64	0.69
	PFC Mixture Model	0.74	0.71	0.72
	PFC with augmented dataset	0.65	0.69	0.67
Baseline	Neural tensor network	0.67	0.6	0.64
	SVC using hand-selected features	0.75	0.69	0.72
	LSTM word-embedding	0.51	0.53	0.52

Table 1: Result comparison.

5.1 Issues with Augmented Dataset

Adding more training data seems to hurt the F1 score for the Shared Task. However, if we allow the newly acquired training examples to be part of the validation set, the validation set accuracy could reach 0.92. Due to time constraint, we were only able to acquire about 1700 training examples,

---

[5] F1 total is the simple average of F1 Public (calculated from half of half of the test data) and F1 Private (from the second half of the data)

with approximately equal number in each category. Whether adding more training data can improve disambiguation performance remains to be experimented.

5.2 Improve PFC

The performance of the PFC might improve if we use a similarity scoring function $s(v_1, v_2) = v_1^T \mathcal{D} v_2$, where $\mathcal{D}$ is a diagonal matrix. The binary classifier becomes $y = \sigma(s(v_1, v_2))$, while the original PFC classifier is $y = \sigma(\mathcal{W}^T[v_1, v_2])$. Both $\mathcal{D}$ and $\mathcal{W}$ are learnable weights.

5.3 Compare PFC with Baseline SVC

In our experiments, the PFC mixture model achieves the best performance, comparable to SVC with hand-selected features. Uni-character model by itself tends to under fit because the training data themselves cannot be separated by the model alone. PFC is robust because allows text features to be learnt automatically.

6 Conclusion

We introduced *Pairwise FastText Classifier* to disambiguate URL entities. It uses embedding-based vector representation for text, can be trained quickly, and performs better than most of the alternative baseline models in our experiments. PFC has the potential to generalise towards a wide range of disambiguation tasks. In order to generalise the application of the model, we created a method to deterministically harvest more training examples, which does not require manual labelling. By releasing all of them to the public, we hope for the continual advancement in the field of disambiguation, which could be applied to identity verification, anti-terrorism, and online general knowledge-base creation.

Appendix A

Appendix A includes manually selected text features for the SVC baseline model.

A.1 URL Features

ID	Feature Name	Description
		Below are a list of URL features specific to one URL.
3	isEducation(url_a)	If the first URL contains domain names such as ".ac.uk" or ".edu", then the value is 1. Otherwise 0.
4	isEntertain-ment(url_a)	If the url includes imdb, allmusic, artnet, mtv.com, or band, it returns 1. Otherwise 0.
5	isProfes-sional(url_a)	If the url contains linkedin.com or re-searchgate.com, it returns 1. Otherwise 0.
6	isNonProfitOr-Gov(url_a)	If the url contains ".org" or ".gov", then it returns 1.
7	isSportsStar(url_a)	If the url contains "espn", "ufc.com", or "sports", then the feature is 1. Otherwise 0.
8 - 12	Features for url_b	Analogous to Feature 3 - 7

A.2 Title Features

ID	Feature Name	Description
13	Edit distance of the first part of the title for the two URLs	Due to the differences of length between different titles, only the first part of the titles is preserved for calculating the Levenshtein distance. This feature is chosen because the first part of the title usually contains the first and last name of the person or the name of the company.
14	Cosine distance of the embedded matrices	The vector representation of the text is same as FastText except that the embedding matrix is pre-trained from Google. Any token not trained by Google will be ignored (Weston, Chopra, & Bordes, 2015).

A.3 Snippet Features

This refers to features made from fields "ASnippet" and "BSnippet" of the search result file provided by the Organiser.

ID	Feature Name	Description
15	Word Mover Distance between the nouns and named entities between "ASnippet" and "BSnippet" (Pele & Werman, A linear time histogram metric for improved sift	Using pre-trained Google word-embedding vectors

| 16 | Word Mover Distance between the nouns and named entities between "ASnippet" and "BSnippet" | Using the pretrained Stanford GloVe vectors (Pennington et al., 2014). |

matching, 2008) (Pele & Werman, Fast and robust earth mover's distances, 2009).

Reference

Brownlee, J. (2016, July 26). *Sequence Classification with LSTM Recurrent Neural Networks in Python with Keras.* Retrieved from Machine Learning Mastery: http://machinelearningmastery.com/sequence -classification-lstm-recurrent-neural-networks-python-keras/

Chisholm, A., Hachey, B., & Molla, D. (2016). Overview of the 2016 ALTA Shared Task: Cross-KB Coreference. *Proceedings of the Australasian Language Technology Association Workshop 2016.*

Chisholm, A., Radford, W., & Hachey, B. (2016). Discovering Entity Knowledge Bases on the Web. *Proceedings of the 5th Workshop on Automated Knowledge Base Construction*

Goodfellow, I., Bengio, Y., & Courville, A. (2016). *Deep Learning*, pages 373 - 420.

Hachey, B. (2016). *How was the data obtained? - ALTA 2016.* Retrieved from Kaggle: https://inclass.kaggle.com/c/alta-2016-challenge/forums/t/23480/how-was-the-data-obtained

Joulin, A., Grave, E., Bojanowski, P., & Mikolov, T. (2016). Bag of Tricks for Efficient Text Classification. *arXiv preprint arXiv:1607.01759.*

Jurafsky, D., & Martin, J. H. (2007). *Speech and Language Processing, 3rd edition [Draft].* Chapter 2.

Mikolov, T., Chen, K., Corrado, G., & Dean, J. (2013). Efficient Estimation of Word Representations in Vector Space. *arXiv preprint arXiv:1301.3781.*

Pele, O., & Werman, M. (2008). A linear time histogram metric for improved sift matching. *Computer Vision--ECCV 2008.*

Pele, O., & Werman, M. (2009). Fast and robust earth mover's distances. *2009 IEEE 12th International Conference on Computer Vision.*

Pennington, J., Socher, R., & Manning, C. D. (2014). GloVe: Global Vectors for Word Representation. *Empirical Methods in Natural Language Processing*, pages 1532 – 1543.

Socher, R., Chen, D., Manning, C., & Ng, A. (2013). Completion, Reasoning With Neural Tensor Networks for Knowledge Base. In Advances in Neural Information Processing Systems, 2013a.

Weston, J., Chopra, S., & Bordes, A. (2015). Memory Networks. *arXiv:1410.3916.*

Zaremba, W., Sutskever, I., & Vinyals, O. (2014). Recurrent Neural Network Regularization. *arXiv preprint arXiv:1409.2329.*

Association for Computational Linguistics
209 N. Eighth Street
Stroudsburg, Pennsylvania 18360

ISBN 978-1-5108-3316-6